Management and Neoliberalism

After the financial collapse of 2008 and the bailing out of banks in the US and the UK, the long-term viability of the neoliberal doctrine has come under new scrutiny. The elimination of regulatory control, the financialization of the economy including the growth of increasingly complex financial innovations, and the dominance of a rentier class have all been subject to thorough criticism. Despite the unexpected meltdown of the financial system and the substantial costs for restoring the finance industry, critics contend that the same decision-makers remain in place and few substantial changes to regulatory control have been made.

Even though neoliberal thinking strongly stresses the role of the market and market-based transactions, the organization theory and management literature has been marginally concerned with neoliberalism as a political agenda and economic policy. This book examines the consequences of neoliberalism for management thinking and management practice. Managerial practices in organizations are fundamentally affected by a political agenda emphasizing competition and innovation. Concepts such as *auditing, corporate social responsibility, shareholder value*, and *boundariless careers* are some examples of managerial terms and frameworks that are inextricably entangled with the neoliberal agenda. This book introduces the literature on neoliberalism, its history and controversies, and demonstrates where neoliberal thinking has served to rearticulate managerial practice, including in the areas of corporate governance, human resource management, and regulatory control of organizations.

Alexander Styhre is Chair of Organization Theory and Management in the Department of Business Administration, School of Business, Economics, and Law, at the University of Gothenburg, Sweden. Styhre has published extensively in the field of organization theory. His recent books include *Organizations and the Bioeconomy* (Routledge, 2012) and *Visual Culture in Organizations* (Routledge, 2010). Styhre serves as Editor-in-Chief of the *Scandinavian Journal of Management*.

Routledge Studies in Management, Organizations and Society

This series presents innovative work grounded in new realities, addressing issues crucial to an understanding of the contemporary world. This is the world of organised societies, where boundaries between formal and informal, public and private, local and global organizations have been displaced or have vanished, along with other nineteenth-century dichotomies and oppositions. Management, apart from becoming a specialized profession for a growing number of people, is an everyday activity for most members of modern societies.

Similarly, at the levels of enquiry, culture and technology, and literature and economics, can no longer be conceived as isolated intellectual fields; conventional canons and established mainstreams are contested. **Management, Organizations and Society** addresses these contemporary dynamics of transformation in a manner that transcends disciplinary boundaries, with books that will appeal to researchers, students, and practitioners alike.

15 Gender Equity in Science and Engineering
Advancing Change in Higher Education
Diana Bilimoria and Xiangfen Liang

16 Commitment to Work and Job Satisfaction
Studies of Work Orientations
Edited by Bengt Furåker, Kristina Håkansson and Jan Ch. Karlsson

17 Fair Trade Organizations and Social Enterprise
Social Innovation Through Hybrid Organization Models
Benjamin Huybrechts

18 Organizations and the Bioeconomy
The Management and Commodification of the Life Sciences
Alexander Styhre

19 Managing Corporate Values in Diverse National Cultures
The Challenge of Differences
Philippe d'Iribarne

20 Gossip and Organizations
Kathryn Waddington

21 Leadership as Emotional Labour
Management and the 'Managed Heart'
Edited by Marian Iszatt-White

22 **On Being At Work**
The Social Construction of the Employee
Nancy Harding

23 **Storytelling in Management Practice**
Dynamics and Implications
Stefanie Reissner and Victoria Pagan

24 **Hierarchy and Organisation**
Toward a General Theory of Hierarchical Social Systems
Thomas Diefenbach

25 **Organizing Through Empathy**
Edited by Kathryn Pavlovich and Keiko Krahnke

26 **Managerial Cultures**
A Comparative Historical Analysis
David Hanson

27 **Management and Organization of Temporary Agency Work**
Edited by Bas Koene, Christina Garsten, and Nathalie Galais

28 **Liquid Organization**
Zygmunt Bauman and Organization Theory
Edited by Jerzy Kociatkiewicz and Monika Kostera

29 **Management and Neoliberalism**
Connecting Policies and Practices
Alexander Styhre

Other titles in this series:

Contrasting Involvements
A Study of Management Accounting Practices in Britain and Germany
Thomas Ahrens

Turning Words, Spinning Worlds
Chapters in Organizational Ethnography
Michael Rosen

Breaking Through the Glass Ceiling
Women, Power and Leadership in Agricultural Organizations
Margaret Alston

The Poetic Logic of Administration
Styles and Changes of Style in the Art of Organizing
Kaj Sköldberg

Casting the Other
Maintaining Gender Inequalities in the Workplace
Edited by Barbara Czarniawska and Heather Höpfl

Gender, Identity and the Culture of Organizations
Edited by Iiris Aaltio and Albert J. Mills

Text/Work
Representing Organization and Organizing Representation
Edited by Stephen Linstead

The Social Construction of Management
Texts and Identities
Nancy Harding

Management Theory
A Critical and Reflexive Reading
Nanette Monin

Management and Neoliberalism

Connecting Policies and Practices

Alexander Styhre

NEW YORK AND LONDON

First published 2014
by Routledge
711 Third Avenue, New York, NY 10017

and by Routledge
2 Park Square, Milton Park, Abingdon, Oxon OX14 4RN

First issued in paperback 2018

*Routledge is an imprint of the Taylor & Francis Group,
an informa business*

© 2014 Taylor & Francis

The right of Alexander Styhre to be identified as author of this work has been asserted by him in accordance with sections 77 and 78 of the Copyright, Designs and Patents Act 1988.

All rights reserved. No part of this book may be reprinted or reproduced or utilized in any form or by any electronic, mechanical, or other means, now known or hereafter invented, including photocopying and recording, or in any information storage or retrieval system, without permission in writing from the publishers.

Trademark Notice: Product or corporate names may be trademarks or registered trademarks, and are used only for identification and explanation without intent to infringe.

Library of Congress Cataloging-in-Publication Data
Styhre, Alexander.
  Management and neoliberalism : connecting policies and practices / by Alexander Styhre.
    pages cm. — (Routledge studies in management, organizations and society ; 29)
  Includes bibliographical references and index.
  1. Neoliberalism. 2. Capitalism. 3. Management. 4. Corporate governance. I. Title.
  HB95.S79 2014
  658.001—dc23
  2013046362

ISBN 13: 978-1-138-61727-8 (pbk)
ISBN 13: 978-0-415-73724-1 (hbk)

Typeset in Sabon
by Apex CoVantage, LLC

Contents

Preface ix
Acknowledgements xv
Introduction xvii

PART I
From Mont Pèlerin to the Fall of the Washington Consensus

1 The Concept of Neoliberalism 3

2 Neoliberalism and Financialization: How Markets Are Sites for Capital Circulation and Accumulation 48

PART II
Management Practices in the Neoliberal Era

3 Corporate Governance and the Financialization of the Firm 87

4 Human Resource Management, Leadership, and the Re-Articulation of Professionalism 129

5 Auditing and Accounting in Organizations 156

PART III
After Neoliberalism

6 Neoliberalism and Its Implications for Management Practice 187

Bibliography 213
Index 239

Preface

For me, this is a personal book. I consider myself a liberal in the European sense of the term, as a person that approves entrepreneurialism, free trade, and an enterprising culture characterized by competition. Yet, I believe in the role of the state as what regulates economic activities and counteracts the economic inequality caused by free-market capitalism. The brew of state-financed, university-based research in the fields of science, technology, and governance (including management), and enterprising, competitive capitalism overseen by a professional state administration has proved to be a most successful combination, enabling an unprecedented economic growth and quality of life over the last half a century.

Like so many others growing up in the 1970s and 1980s, I consider myself "second-generation middle class." In a country like Sweden, geographically disfavoured, as it is located up far to the North, acute poverty is only a few generations away. In the mid-nineteenth century, at the height of poverty and despair, more than a million young, healthy, and enterprising Swedes emigrated to settle in the United States, but also to South America in countries like Brazil and Argentina. Having an understanding of this tradition and being fortunate to live in a welfare state that occasionally has been admired and at times been portrayed as some kind of "socialist hell" by neoconservatives and free market protagonists (in my mind, such criticism is uninformed and fails to see that Scandinavian Social Democracy is in essence distributive rather than regulatory), I have developed a firm belief that social security, welfare benefits, and economic transfers to low-income groups is a viable way to build a society that is both competitive, yet secures at least a decent life for less fortunate or competitive members of society. That is, I do think there is such a thing as a society out there. Such belief includes an understanding of the need for government, regulation, and taxes—political activities and actions that are part of what neoliberals and neoconservatives stanchly dismiss as a form of "collectivism" that is a threat to "economic freedom." In the election of the fabled year of 1968, at the height of left-wing political radicalism and counterculture (in hindsight, and seemingly in paradox, a counterculture representing a discovery and celebration of the individualism that eventually became a leitmotif of the neoliberal era), and only a few years before I was born, more than 50% of the Swedish voters gave their vote to the Social Democratic Party, which was at its peak in power and popularity. During the last four decades, Sweden has moved on in many ways, and in February 2013, *The Economist* claimed in an editorial that, "When it comes to choice, Milton Friedman would be more at home in Stockholm than in Washington, DC," testifying to the establishment of neoliberal policy in the Scandinavian and Nordic countries.

As a consequence of this upbringing, and with what I hope is some intellectual capacity to digest various political and economic arguments and theories, I view many of the neoliberal statements and propositions as either based on strong neoconservative ideologies and convictions that I have a problem sharing (e.g., that all people failing to support themselves or otherwise live up to contemporary standards of self-discipline and self-sufficiency are to be morally questioned), or poorly substantiated by evidence and robust data. I do not deny economists and other social scientists the right to formulate daring propositions and conjectures (e.g., the rational choice theories underlying the *homo oeconomicus* model), but sciences that take on the authority to claim they are capable of predicting the future, or at least being able to provide a toolbox that helps "make things work" (i.e., make the economy to run smoothly without bubbles and financial breakdowns), must stay true to such scientific professional ideologies and not compromise their integrity. That is, ideology is always of necessity part of any scientific endeavour—undertaken, after all, by humans limited by our own cognitive capacities and abilities for self-reflexivity—but as soon as ideology overrules empirical evidence, or bars critical self-reflection, claims of scientific objectivity quickly erode.

In many cases, the economic and financial theories that served to justify and legitimize much neoliberal policies have suffered from ideological orthodoxies. Backed by neoliberal and neoconservative funds and foundations, much of the neoliberal doctrines have been commissioned by people with interest in a shared belief in the efficiency of free markets and a mildly regulated capitalism. There are, in other words, economic and political interests underlying what have been advanced as being scientific observations, theories, and theorems based on robust data. I don't deny, for instance, Gary Becker the right to think of obese persons as allowing themselves to put on weight on the basis of rational calculations of the likelihood of the pharmaceutical industry being able to develop an obesity cure (Kahneman, 2011: 412)—no matter how absurd such claims are, Becker has certain academic liberties that need to be defended—but to induce policies and economic political programs on the basis of propositions that serve to inform academic research work without validating their empirical robustness (or even while ignoring data or studies made in other disciplines) is quite another matter. Gary Becker's claim to be able to explain obesity on basis of formal, mathematized neoclassical economic theory and rational choice thinking is indicative of the economics profession's entrenched belief that they possess what Mirowski (2013: 23) refers to as "a Theory of Everything at the End of History," and that they can legitimately apply what they call their economics approach "to everything great and small under the sun." The concern is, however, that the formalist models and operative vocabulary of economic theory are so general and imprecise that they can apply to virtually everything; "choices," "incentives," "decisions," "information," and so forth, are everywhere in human lives, and the tragedy of the declared omnipotence of economic theory is that what claims to explain everything in fact explains nothing at all. "We can of course, by suitable abstraction, be exact about anything. Nothing is inherently immune to measurement," Charles Wright Mills (1959: 73) stated in *The Sociological Imagination*. In other words, individual activities and social relations lending themselves to formal descriptions and calculations do not of necessity imply any theoretical or practical relevance or social value.

Economists get significant amounts of critique from many quarters for constantly expanding their domain of jurisdiction and having a firm belief in their right to and competence in prescribing various remedies for perceived social malfunctioning and concerns. The constant adding of *ad hoc* hypotheses to what Lakatos (1970) referred to as the core of their research program, to secure principally important assumptions from being falsified—commonly centred around the all-too-familiar narrative "the theories are correct but their application is fallible"—ultimately undermines the credibility of the core proposition. No one would believe a medical doctor whose diagnoses and therapies fail time after time, but when it come to the champions of free market capitalism and their theoretical assumptions and beliefs, scientific rigor is curiously marginalized. Such a scholarly project represents a far-driven idealism, based on a firm belief in the value of deductive armchair thinking founded on elementary axioms when explaining the world as we know it (and yes, I am aware of the data crunching that follows, the advanced econometric work done in universities to prove the theorems to be correct). It represents a form of modern-day scholasticism. One may suspect that it is more important to advance the "right ideas" than to prove ideas to be right.

Still, this text, regardless of its collection of criticism of neoliberal theorems and doctrines—conceptual as well as empirical—recognizes that economic theory is important. That is precisely why it is alarming when certain actors believe they are "bigger than the game," that their statements and propositions should be worth more and be truer than other statements and propositions sharing the predicament of not (yet) being substantiated by empirical data. In making such assumptions, social scientists and economists became little more than court astrologers, advising their benefactors on basis of meagre and disputed scientific evidence.

One of Milton Friedman's most well-known *bon mots* is that "there is no such thing as a free lunch": In any economic system, someone has to carry the costs and all the efforts necessary to serve the proverbial meal. At the same time, neoliberal economic theory has over and over suggested that there are in fact free lunches—perhaps for anyone, or at least a majority—if only the government would "back off" and leave self-regulating capitalist markets alone. There is money left on the table, free for anyone to pick up (but most likely absorbed by various market actors, ultimately economic elites) if only markets are de-regulated and competition runs freely. This story is mesmerizing and, in a way, beautiful—the idea that competitive capitalists per se would be capable of solving social problems—but while many political programs and policies have been shaped on the basis of this neoliberal master-narrative over the last three decades, it is today less credible and, quite frankly, increasingly hard to believe. Economic prosperity has been essentially fuelled by debt, and neoliberal policies have, according to research, been capable of producing only limited economic growth and few jobs. In contrast, it has made work life more insecure, increased economic inequality, and undermined democracy as the national state and governments have increasingly taken the role of working in accordance with the interests of economic and political elites articulated through institutions such as the World Bank, the IMF, and the World Trade Organization. The neoliberal project is above all, *in its consequences*—and that must be what is evaluated on the basis of data and empirical studies, rather than on the basis of engaging stories about the possibilities of free-market capitalism—a project serving to restore class inequality and to deconstruct the welfare state, including the taming of labour power. In this view, neoliberal protagonists have been most successful, especially in their ideological homestead, the United States, where today more than 15% of the population is poor by objective measures, trade unionism is marginalized and plays a very limited role in industrial relations, and more than 1% of the population is incarcerated. Such apparent political failures unfortunately seem to bother free-market evangelists little, as they tend to think of all such undesirable outcomes as being either the failure of individuals to compete in the contemporary society (i.e., they violate the ethos of self-reliance in neoliberal ethics), or as being evidence of the need to secure even *further* de-regulation and less state-governance (i.e., they are essentially right but there is a need for more consistency in the implementation of policy). In other words, market-based transactions are given all the merits for economic growth, for example, but failures are mysteriously always emerging from outside of the markets. Nietzsche (1984: 87, §119) remarked that Christianity is a curious religion inasmuch as it rewards its faithful followers only in the life to come, not in this earthly existence, and therefore he predicted a secularization in Western Christian societies, as no religion can afford to postpone its benefits and locate them in a some distant future. Similarly, neoliberal policies operate on basis of a similar "wait-and-see" and "in the future we will all be rewarded for our patience" narrative where free-market economies are expected to soon demonstrate their capacity to solve economic and social problems. Today, fewer people are prone to believe in the virtues of such patience.

Despite this quite sceptical, at times downright critical (especially regarding the idea of the finance industry as the primus motor of competitive capitalism), view of neoliberalism and its limited contribution to society and the economy in this volume, not everything is entirely mistaken in the liberal/neoliberal discussions. To be discussed in greater detail in the final chapter, neoliberalism has opened up a conversation about the role of the state, and factors such as the role of entrepreneurialism in economic growth have been underlined. The concern is that such debates all too early ossified into conservative and moralist positions, in which the project to restore economic inequality, thinly veiled as the abstract objective to install "economic freedom," has overruled all other concerns and discussions. The ambition of this book is first to critically discuss the neoliberal tradition of thinking and its political and economic effects and, second, to examine the surprisingly limitedly explored connection between neoliberal doctrines and management theory and practice. This latter objective is grounded in a frustration over the inability of business school researchers to lift their eyes, see beyond quite narrowly defined domains of jurisdiction, and seek to locate their field of research in a wider social context. In a society in which the market is given a close to divine significance, management of necessity becomes a sacred activity. In other words, the institutional and cultural shifts and changes during the last few decades have certainly played in the hand of business school directors and faculty. It is therefore no wonder that business school training and degrees in, for example, management are today the academic subject attracting the largest number of students in many Organisation for Economic Co-operation and Development (OECD) countries. In the neoliberal era, younger people regard, for good reason, a business school diploma as a safe bet. Some business school disciplines, such as finance, are today capable of attracting mathematically talented students who would have traditionally aimed for careers in the sciences (e.g., physics or engineering), thereby tapping scarce resources from other professional domains. "The best and the brightest from leading universities dreamt not of careers as scientists, in government, or even in corporate management, but rather of careers as Wall Street hedge fund operators," Mizruchi (2010: 127) remarks. The curious thing is that these shifts have been very little reflected upon in the community of business school researchers. This volume therefore aims to connect what are obviously two closely entangled domains, that of neoliberal thinking and that of management literature. I hope this volume will be part of a broader engagement with neoliberalism in business school settings.

Acknowledgements

I would like to thank Terry Clague and Laura Stearns, commissioning editors at Taylor & Francis/Routledge, for handling the original book proposal and the final manuscript. The anonymous reviewers of the book proposal offered good advice on what literature to add to the story. My colleagues at the School of Business, Economics, and Law, University of Gothenburg, have also been helpful over the years in providing new and innovative perspectives on managerial practices and organization. I would also like to thank all my friends who vote for conservative parties for helping me understand how they perceive liberal and Social Democrat solutions to social problems as ineffective and questionable.

Sävedalen, October 2013
Alexander Styhre

Introduction

> Titus Livy as well as all other historians affirm that nothing is more uncertain and inconsistent than the multitude ... I say ... that individual men, and especially princes may be charged with the same defects of which writers accuse the people. For whoever is not controlled by law will commit the same errors as an unbridled multitude.
>
> Niccolo Machiavelli, *Discourse in Livy*

> The principle in orthodoxy: to use the same recipe, administer the same therapy, to resolve the most various types of problems; never to admit complexity and try to reduce it as much as possible, while ignoring that things are always more complicated in reality.
>
> Albert O. Hirschman (1998: 110)

> The classical theorists resemble Euclidians geometers in a non-Euclidean world who, discovering that in experience straight lines apparently often meet, rebuke the lines for not keeping straight—as the only remedy for the unfortunate collisions which are occurring.
>
> John Maynard Keynes (1953: 16)

OF MARKETS AND IDEOLOGY

Aspers (2010:1) defines markets as "a social structure for the exchange of rights in which offers are evaluated and priced, and compete with one another." The history of capitalism, especially in the neoliberal era (beginning at the end of the 1970s), is a history of the expansion of markets, spatially as well as "qualitatively," to include basically all human endeavours and activities. "By 1790 ... 80 percent of all clothing in the United States was made in the home, while a century later 90 percent was made outside the home," Swedberg (2005: 240) writes. Today, basically all sorts of goods, commodities, and services are available on the market, from relatively standardized manufactured consumer goods, such as cars and clothing, to more advanced and professional health care services, such as cosmetic surgery (Blum, 2003) and gestational surrogacy (Pande, 2010). In some cases, the development of markets are prevented by legislation (as in the case of narcotics), opening up "black" or "grey" markets that are either still heavily policed (as in the case of the American "war on drugs" initiative) or, in other cases, for which legislation is becoming more lenient. The latter is often an attempt to curb criminality, to increase the transparency of previously "black-boxed markets," and to—if possible—make the market subject to income taxation (as in the case of prostitution, legal in many European countries and in the American state of Nevada). While the development of markets has undoubtedly lowered transaction costs and contributed to the general prosperity in the late modern period, there are also downside risks to market creation and market expansions, especially in terms of a need to control and monitor opportunistic behaviour and a general tendency to externalize costs, leading to a need to institute practices for, for example, pollution prevention and labour relations. In many ways, the neoliberal doctrine is the theory of the benefits of market expansion. For proponents of neoliberalism, markets are the most effective mechanism for economic transactions, while for critics, such claims are substantiated by empirical evidence in some cases, while in other cases, there is not yet any proof of market creation as beneficial for all stakeholders in the economy. In addition, critics contend that the assumption that markets emerge "naturally" and "effortlessly" and that governments and other regulatory bodies therefore should avoid intervening in market creation processes is, at best, a chimera and, at worst, an ideological proposition articulated to justify individual interests. No matter what position one takes, the concept of neoliberalism and its consequences for economic growth, income distribution, and managerial practices remain contested.

When examining the neoliberal literature, the concept of ideology is a useful analytical construct. However, one needs to keep in mind that ideology here, as Žižek (1994: 7) suggests, "has nothing to do with 'illusion' "—with a "mistaken, distorted representation" of its social conditions. Instead, ideology is highly visible and explicitly articulated, but always brought into the discussion as what is capable of explaining what is visible on the surface. Ideology is therefore abstract while it is manifested in social relations and conditions. For instance, the *efficient market hypothesis*, a key proposition developed in finance theory in the 1970s and 1980s, and the University of Chicago economics department's "perhaps best known product" (Fourcade and Khurana, 2013: 149), justified the de-regulation of financial markets, which paved the way for both an unprecedented expansion of financial markets and the subsequent global finance market collapse in 2008. The efficient market hypothesis is based on a conceptual framework, theoretical assumptions, and other abstract lines of reasoning, but its *practical* manifestations and consequences are unobtrusive, material, and most immediately experienced by the various actors either directly or indirectly suffering from such events. In fact, the ability of ideology to operate "at a distance," while at the same time escape criticism, even in the case of unanticipated failures and breakdown, is the very essence of ideology. Ideology is highly practical in terms of producing immediate material, social, and cultural effects.

One of the key elements of ideology is the development of an operative vocabulary that institutes a certain mode of thinking that survives occasional setbacks and critiques, a way of knowing the world that constitutes an infrastructure that is commonly overlooked or ignored in everyday thinking. Klamperer's (2000) classic study of the transformation and abuse of language and conversation in the Third Reich demonstrates how Germans in the 1930s and 1940s gradually learned to think in new ways, barely noticing how such a shift came along:

> [T]he most powerful influence was exerted neither by individual speeches nor by articles or flyers, posters or flags; it was not achieved by things which one has to absorb by conscious thought or conscious emotions. Instead Nazism permeated the flesh and blood of the people through single words, idiom and sentence structure which were imposed on them [the people] in a million repetitions and taken on board mechanically and unconsciously . . . But language does not simply write and think for me, it also increasingly dictates my feelings and governs my entire spiritual being the more unquestioningly and unconsciously I abandon myself to it. (Klamperer, 2000: 15)

"Language is the landmass that is continuous under our feet and the feet of others and allows us to get to each other's places," Birkerts (1994: 82) says, emphasizing how our language sets the boundaries for our world and enables us to communicate and share ideas and experiences. In the neoliberal period, Duggan (2003) suggests, economic theory, effectively translated into the more neutral, but also more authoritarian, term "economic policy," a powerful blend of the academic discipline of economics and *Realpolitik*, has enjoyed the privilege of providing concepts, analytical terms, and narratives that have constituted this "landmass" and have defined economic conditions, politics, and everyday thinking for more than three decades. In addition, this way of enacting economic and social relations has been surprisingly immune to external criticism because its spokesmen have been remarkably successful in advancing this framework as being a form of neutral, technical expertise separated from ideologies and preferences:

> The most successful ruse of neoliberal dominance in both global and domestic affairs is the definition of economic policy as primarily a matter of neutral, technical expertise. This expertise is then presented as separated from *politics* and *culture*, and not properly subject to specifically political accountability or cultural critique. Opposition to material

inequality is maligned as 'class warfare,' while race, gender or sexual inequalities are dismissed as merely cultural, private, or trivial. (Duggan, 2003: xiv)

George's (2013) study of the shift in the use of concepts and vocabularies in *New York Times* over nine decades is telling of how the neoliberal worldview and terminology have become institutionalized, dividing concepts into mutually exclusive categories: "markets over governments," "competition over cooperation and monopoly," "consumers over citizens," "management over labor," and "growth over progress, justice and equality," in George's (2013) analysis (see also Smith, 2007).

Ideology is thus both a "surface phenomenon" (what is immediately visible and observable) and what operates on the level of social infrastructure (the social institutions, regulatory bodies, language, symbolism, and culture above and beyond everyday life). In the medieval period, the Catholic Church instituted a firm belief in economic venturing as being sinful because it violated the Bible's insistence on human life as an existence of toil and sweat (Wood, 2002; De Roover, 1974; Tawney, 1998). Similarly, more recent ideologies (liberalism, socialism, communism, neoconservatism, libertarianism, etc.) have in their own idiosyncratic ways developed quite sophisticated theories, models, systems of thought, and so forth, advancing certain practices and beliefs while discrediting other competing practices and beliefs. The crux is that once ideologies are established and have produced institutional arrangements and practices, they generate their own momentum, inasmuch as certain actors are encouraged, trained, and disciplined to justify and explain certain "dysfunctions" or perceived shortcomings of the predominant system. When examining, for example, neoliberal doctrines, policies, and practices—a politico-economic regime of thinking that places the market at the very centre of social and economic relations—it is important to pay attention to the abstract reasoning that justifies the practices advocated and implemented while simultaneously examining actual practices and outcome. A politico-economic regime is at the same time ideological and material, being constituted by both the theoretical and symbolic work done to advance and further justify certain practices and the very practices per se. At times, the ideological realm precedes and anticipates the practices and events, while in other cases practices and events need to be explained and justified ex post facto. As this book is written in the 2012–2013 period, there is a significant outflow of publications seeking to explain the 2008 finance market collapse. Much of that literature is referenced and cited in this volume, especially in Chapter Two. Embarrassingly for the economists, financial market analysts, regulatory bodies, and a variety of other professional communities investing their credibility and successfully building careers advocating *laissez-faire* economic doctrines over the last three decades, very few were capable of anticipating and predicting the 2008 events and their devastating consequences for the finance industry. When Queen Elizabeth visited London School of Economics in November

2008, this was precisely what she asked the *bien pensant* economists of this most prestigious school: "If these things were so large, how come everyone missed them?" (cited in Helleiner, 2011: 68). Answers are perhaps given in the totality of literature examining the events.[1]

DEFINING NEOLIBERALISM

The concept of neoliberalism is a complex term in the social science vocabulary, having both a more precise academic meaning at the same time as it has wider connotations in political discourses. Social scientists also warn against defining neoliberalism too narrowly and stress some of the internal tensions and contradictions within the term. "It is impossible to define neoliberalism purely theoretically," Saad-Filho and Johnston (2005: 1) argue. They continue: "Neoliberalism straddles a wide range of social, political and economic phenomena at different levels of complexity." "Neoliberalism cannot be understood as a *singular* set of ideas and policy prescriptions, emanating from one source," Plehwe and Walpen (2006: 2) add. "By neoliberal policy, we do not refer to a coherent policy agenda but to the development of a series of state practices that favour market rather than regulatory or administrative solutions," Tomaskovic-Devey and Lin (2011: 542) say. Wacquant (2009) addresses neoliberalism accordingly:

> Neoliberalism is an elusive and contested notion, a hybrid term awkwardly suspended between the lay idiom of political debates and the technical terminology of social science, which moreover is invoked without clear referent . . . Whether singular or polymorphous, evolutionary or revolutionary the prevalent conception of neoliberalism is essentially economic: it stresses an array of market friendly policies such as labor deregulation, capital mobility, privatization, a monetarist agenda of deflation and financial economy, trade liberalization, interplay competition, and the reduction of taxation and public expenditures. (Wacquant, 2009: 306)

Wacquant (2009: 307) speaks of neoliberalism in terms of the establishment of a "new institutional logic" that includes at least four components: (1) "economic deregulation," (2) "welfare state devolution," (3) "the cultural trope of individual responsibility," and (4) "an expensive, intrusive, and proactive penal apparatus." In a similar manner, Griffin (2009: 9) lists four underlying propositions in neoliberal thinking:

1. A confidence in the market (*marketization*) as the mechanism by which societies should be made to distribute their resources (although market imperfections may hamper distributive patterns, should we remove these the 'allocative efficiency' of the market is restored);[2]

2. A commitment to the use of private finance (in place of public spending) in public projects (*privatization*);
3. *Deregulations*, with the removal of tariff barriers and subsidies ensuring that the market is freed from the potential tyranny of nation-state interventions, thereby granting capital optimal mobility;
4. A commitment to *flexibilization*, which refers the ways in which production is organized in mass consumption society (i.e., dynamically and flexibly). (Griffin, 2009: 9)

In Harvey's (2005a: 145) view, "neoliberalism is in the first instance a theory of political economic practices which proposes that human well-being can best be advanced by the maximization of entrepreneurial freedom within an institutional framework characterized by private property rights, individual liberty, free markets and free trade." In this politico-economic program, the state is given an entirely different role than in the Keynesian post-World War II regime, that is, to secure and support the creation of markets and entrepreneurial possibilities:

> The role of the state is to create and preserve an institutional framework appropriate to such practices. The state has to be concerned, for example, with the quality and integrity of money. It must also set up those military, defense, police and juridical functions required to secure private property rights and to support freely functioning markets. Further, if markets do not exist (in areas such as education, health care, social security or environmental pollution) then they must be created, by state interaction if necessary, but beyond these tasks the state should not venture. (Harvey, 2005a: 145)

Contrary to the belief that neoliberal doctrine downgrades the role of the state, it is in fact actively encouraged to play a key role in a more specific and narrow domain (e.g., in providing a juridical and penal system). Brown strongly emphasizes this new role of the state in the neoliberal project:

> Part of what makes neoliberalism 'neo' is that it depicts free markets, free trade, and entrepreneurial rationality as achieved and normative, as promulgated through law and through social and economic policy—not simply as occurring by dint of nature. Second, neoliberalism casts the political and social spheres as both appropriately dominated by market concerns and as themselves organized by the market rationality. That is, more than simply facilitating the economy, the state must construct and construe itself in market terms, as well as develop policies and promulgate a political culture that figures citizens exhaustively as rational economic actors in every sphere of life . . . Third, neoliberal political rationality produces governance criteria along the same lines, that is, criteria of productivity and profitability, with the consequence that

governance talk increasingly becomes market-speak, businesspeople replace lawyers as the governing class in liberal democracies, and business principles replace juridical principles. (Brown, 2006: 694)

Theoretically speaking, the roots of neoliberalism are quite diverse, and it "amalgamates insight from a range of sources" (Saad-Filho and Johnston, 2005: 2), including Adam Smith, neoclassical economics, the Austrian critique of Keynesianism and Soviet-style socialism, German *Ordoliberalismus*, American Libertarianism, University of Chicago monetarism, and the "supply-side economics" advocated by the Thatcher government and the Reagan Administration. In addition, neoliberalism is closely associated with the neoconservatism movement in both the United States and the United Kingdom and, for its critics, a neocolonialist agenda derived from the ambition to expand market opportunities through what is called the *globalization* of the economy, which involves free trade agreements and the de-regulation of, for example, financial markets. Seen in this light, the neoliberal project is what Wacquant (2009) calls a *transnational policies project* aimed at exporting the neoliberal model overseas:

> Neoliberalism is a *transnational policies project* aiming to remake the nexus of market, state, and citizenship from above. This project is carried by a new global ruling class in the making, composed of the heads and seniors executives of transnational firms, high-ranking politicians, state managers and top officials of multinational organizations (the OECD, WTO, IMF, World Bank, and the European Union), and cultural-technical experts in their employ (chief among them, economists, lawyers, and communication professionals with germane training and mental categories in their different countries). (Wacquant, 2009: 306–307)

In Peck's (2010) view, this heterogeneity and assemblage-like nature of neoliberalism is part of its nature and is an inevitable feature of the neoliberal discourse and its non-discursive practices:

> The ideational, ideological, and institutional moments of neoliberalization have always been mixed up, mutually constituted. 'Finding neoliberalism' is therefore not about locating some essential center from which all else flows; it is about following flows, backflows, and undercurrents across and between these ideational, ideological, and institutional moments, over time and between places. (Peck, 2010: xiii)

Peck (2010) continues:

> Perplexingly, its [neoliberalism's] success as an ideological project reflects its deeply contradictory nature, as a combination of dogmatism

and adaptability, strategic intent and opportunistic exploitation, programmatic vision and tactical smarts, principle and hypocrisy . . . Notwithstanding its trademark antistatist rhetoric, neoliberalism was always concerned—at its philosophical, political, and practical core—with the challenge of first seizing and then retaking the state. (Peck, 2010: 4)

Despite this heterogeneous and fluid nature, making neoliberalism appear only in "impure" form and in "messy hybrids" (Peck, 2010: 7), its many elements are unified by what Peck refers to as its "utopian vision of a free society and free economy." Unfortunately, Peck (2010) argues, this utopia—like any other utopia—is ultimately unrealizable. Neoliberal thinking is therefore coupled with "[t]he endless frustration borne of the inevitable failure to arrive at this elusive destination" (Peck, 2010: 7). At the same time, this frustration nevertheless "[c]onfers a significant degree of forward momentum on the neoliberal project," (Peck, 2010: 7) suggests. In Peck's view, neoliberalism's curse is that it "[c]annot help itself but to be a kind of interventionist project, which confers on the project a certain dynamic directionality, if not a destination." As a consequence, to the extent that neoliberalism has, since the 1970s, been "victorious" in the war of ideas, Peck says, "its victories have always been Pyrrhic and partial ones": "The neoliberal lemmings, in this sense, are always prone to throw themselves (not to mention others) off the cliffs of deregulation," Peck (2010: 79) argues. In Peck's (2010) view, neoliberalism is a tragic, even cursed, utopian project, riddled with internal contradictions and anxieties regarding its inability to fulfil its vision of the "good society," characterized by economic freedom, lack of governmental interventions, and an absence of trade union bargaining to distort market transactions. "[Neoliberalism] represents a series of far-from-perfect attempts to wrestle with the challenges and contradictions of governance in a malmarketized world," Peck (2010: 24) summarizes. This view of neoliberalism is consistent with Miller and Rose's (1990) enactment of the Foucaultian term *governmentality*, composed of two basic elements: (1) *programs*, the totality of theories, vocabularies, and ideologies, and other symbolic resources justifying a specific regime of government, and (2) *technologies*, the "instrumentation" and "operationalization" of programs securing desirable effects and outcomes. Techniques of government include, Miller and Rose (1990: 8) suggest, "techniques of notation, computation and calculation procedures of examination and assessment; the invention of devices such as surveys and presentational forms such as tables; the standardization of systems for training and the inculcation of habits; the inauguration of professional specialisms and vocabularies; building design and architectural forms." The term governmentality does not assume some end-point or final destination but is instead an ongoing, ceaseless pursuit—just like the neoliberal project in Peck's (2010) account. Miller and Rose (1990) say:

> Whilst 'governmentality' is eternally optimistic, government is a congenially failing operation, the world of [governmentality] programmes is

heterogeneous and rivalrous and the solution for one programme tends to be the problem for another. 'Reality' always escapes the theories that inform programmes and the ambitions that underpin them; it is too unruly to be captured by any perfect knowledge. Technologies produce unexpected problems, are utilized for their own ends by those who are supposed to merely operate them, are hampered by underfunding, professional rivalries, and the impossibility of producing technical conditions that would make them work—reliable statistics, efficient communication systems, clear lines of command, properly designed buildings, well framed regulations or whatever. (Miller and Rose, 1990: 10–11)

Neoliberalism as a regime of governmentality shares this ongoing struggle to "make things right." What neoliberalism is capable of accomplishing is, therefore, not so much presenting a vision of "pristine spaces of market rationality and constitutional order" (Peck, 2010: 31), but rather intervening into situations and conditions not exactly characterized by the harmonious market transactions envisioned by free market protagonists.

Centeno and Cohen (2012) identify three complementary perspectives on neoliberalism: (1) as a "technical policy debate regarding the best mode of operating an economy," (2) as an "institutionalized crisis containment strategy involving political choices and power," and (3) as "the rise of a hegemonic ideology or system of thought" (Centeno and Cohen, 2012: 318). As these three views are far from easily kept separate and compartmentalized, theories, ideologies, and empirical observations and data are commonly combined into aggregates that need to be dismantled and discerned in detail. If there is one single unifying theme in the neoliberal doctrine it is, in Centeno and Cohen's (2012: 318) formulation, that "neoliberalism sought to dismantle or suppress extramarket forms of economic coordination." In the following, the economic, political, ideological roots of this firm belief in market transactions will be examined in detail.

HYPERMODERNITY AND THE MORAL ECONOMY OF NEOLIBERALISM

One of the key aspects of neoliberalism and the policies it advances is the emphasis on what Amable (2011: 6) refers to as an ethics of self-reliance as the social norm *par excellence*. Despite all the emphasis on market liberalization and self-regulation and self-organization in the neoliberal tradition (a stance first developed by Adam Smith and eventually re-articulated by Friedrich von Hayek in *The Road to Serfdom* [1944]), there is a perhaps surprisingly strong emphasis on morals in neoliberal thinking. Daston (1995: 4) uses the term *moral economy* to address how the economy—defined quite vaguely (after all, Daston is more concerned about the sciences than with formulating a general economic theory) as "[a]n organized system that displays certain regularities, regularities that are explicable but not always predictable in their details" (see also Sachweh, 2012: 421–422)—is of necessity embedded in certain norms, beliefs, and rules that regulate actual practices. "What I mean by a moral economy is a web of affect-saturated values that stand and function in well-defined relationship to one another. In this usage, 'moral' carries its full complement of eighteenth and nineteenth century resonances: it refers at once to the psychological and to the normative," Daston (1995: 4) explains. As Daston (1995: 6) emphasizes, moral economies always needs to be based more on "self-discipline" rather than "coercion," and consequently one of the key objectives in a neoliberal and market-based society is to institute a belief in, first, the value of *competition* and, second, the moral imperative to execute *self-discipline*. Over the last three decades, it has been repeated time and again in political speeches and in social policy and economic theory that competition and self-discipline is the backbone of economic prosperity. In a way, this message has many theological overtones; in a similar manner, religious teachings make references to abstract objectives ("salvation" and "kingdom come" versus "economic growth" and "prosperity") as what ultimately justifies all this competition and self-discipline. In many cases, as will be shown in the forthcoming chapters of this volume, the fruits of the ordeal are still not always benefitting the working classes; rather, the profits generated are piped into the capital-owning class. What neoliberalism has accomplished above all, empirical studies demonstrate, is not so much economic growth and prosperity as a redistribution of economic wealth. In addition, there are specific cultural aspects of neoliberalism that extend outside of economic analyses that deserve some attention.

Lipovetsky (2005) introduces the term *hypermodernity* to capture the *Zeitgeist* of the neoliberal era dominated by an ethos of competition and self-discipline. While the modern period was famously characterized by Jean-François Lyotard (1984) as the era of "grand narratives" of progress and emancipation, of the hope that human societies once and for all would overcome their own limitations, the present hypermodern period is instead characterized by an "anxiety about the future," gradually replacing what Lipovetsky (2005: 35) calls "the mystique of progress." Competitive capitalism is characterized by what Lipovetsky (2005: 36) refers to as "accelerated obsolescence," where commodities; professional domains of expertise; and other material resources, skills, and competencies that originally appeared to have a stable economic worth or were capable of generating economic value become subject to the Schumpeterian "gale of creative destruction" at a higher pace. These anxieties proliferate in combination with a far-driven and aggressive consumer culture in which "freedom of choice" and the joys of consumption are imperative and produce "[a] paradoxical combination of frivolity and anxiety, euphoria and vulnerability, playfulness and dread," Lipovetsky (2005: 40) suggests. Lipovetsky (2005) explains:

> A whole hedonistic and psychologistic culture has come into being; it incites everyone to satisfy their needs immediately, it stimulates their

clamour for pleasure, idolizes self-fulfilment, and sets the earthy paradise of well-being, comfort and leisure on a pedestal. Consume without delay, travel, enjoy yourself, renounce nothing: the politics of a radiant future have been replaced by consumption as the promise of a euphoric present. (Lipovetsky, 2005: 37)

In this economic regime, which is carried forward by the fear of becoming obsolete or failing to remain productive in the market-based competitive capitalist regime of accumulation, yet actively encourages consumption and the circulation of finance capital more widely—household debt has risen sharply. This rising debt has occurred, for example, in the United States during the neoliberal period, making it fertile soil for the expansion of the neoliberal project (Kelly and Enns, 2010). Since household debt has skyrocketed, both in everyday consumer good consumption and especially in home mortgages, there is little choice other than to continue to expand consumption because it further fuels economic growth. One way to enable economic growth is to open up previously closed markets for private investment—for example, in health care, penal institutions, the armed forces, and other domains that historically have been under the state's jurisdiction. In that way, the neoliberal condition that originally produced the expansion of household and state debt—that is, caused the macroeconomic and financial instabilities (the so-called "bubbles" in, for example, the housing market)—is advanced as the remedy to the very problems it has created. The politico-economic doctrine at this point creates its own momentum in which it is increasingly difficult for analysts, commentators, and policymakers to find a vantage point outside of the system to make a fair and balanced assessment of the situation. Under these conditions, the neoliberal doctrine becomes a dogma part of a moral economy that is not only justifying its proposed policies and practices on the basis of their practical and political consequences but also on the basis of moralist terms. In such situations, concepts such as moral economy may inform a more critical standpoint vis-à-vis the object of study.

In summary, then, neoliberal thinking and its consequences for management practice is not a marginal political *or* economic *or* cultural event, but represents a major shift in the politico-economic regime of regulation in late modern competitive capitalism. It would be unfair to assume that the protagonists of neoliberal policies and theories both supported by and constituting neoliberal doctrines (e.g., agency theory and finance theory) could foresee and anticipate all the consequences of what Harvey (2005b) calls the "neoliberal revolution," but many of the spokespersons and emblematic figures of neoliberalism (such as Margaret Thatcher, Ronald Reagan, Milton Friedman, and Michael Jensen) have been most critical of the post-World War II welfare state capitalism grounded in Keynesian economics, and they actively aimed to shift the role of the state. Only history can tell whether these persons made a lasting contribution the organization of human society, but for the time being the entire neoliberal doctrine is in a state of legitimacy crisis, both liberal (Jones, 2012; Campbell, 2010) and Marxist commentators (Duménil and Lévy, 2011) claim. A substantial literature is discerning the accuracy of assumptions made, scrutinizing the official declarations, and comparing policies enacted to actual outcomes, and when all is said and done, the neoliberal doctrine may have accomplished few things beyond the financialization of the economy, the conspicuous and unprecedented expansion of debt, and the redistribution of capital back to the levels of the pre-1930s depression—but that is, again, what remains to be demonstrated.

PURPOSE AND RESEARCH QUESTIONS

The concept of neoliberalism has played a key role in political and economic regulation since the end of the 1970s. *Neoliberalism* is a complex term that includes a variety of theoretical frameworks and orientations, but the quite substantial literature examining neoliberal thinking emphasizes the central role of the market and market-based transactions in this diverse field of thinking. Neoliberal politics and economic policy have been most influential in changing the state's role and in institutionalizing a set of international organizations, including the WTO, the IMF, and The World Bank, that support (and at times enforce) a neoliberal agenda. Neoliberal politics, and especially its economic agenda, emphasizing de-regulation and economic growth through enabling economic incentives for entrepreneurial activities, have been controversial from the very beginning. Even though neoliberal thinking strongly stresses the role of the market and market-based transactions, the organization theory and management literature has been relatively marginally concerned with neoliberalism as a political agenda and economic policy (Styhre, 2014). This book examines the consequences of neoliberalism for management thinking and management practice. Managerial practices in organizations are fundamentally affected by a political agenda emphasizing competition and innovation. Concepts such as *auditing, corporate social responsibility, shareholder value*, and *boundariless careers* are some examples of managerial terms and frameworks that are inextricably entangled with the neoliberal agenda. Taken together, the neoliberal shift and its influence on both national and international policy-making and regulatory bodies have immediate and very detailed implications for managerial practice. Unfortunately, much management writing has been only marginally concerned with such connections between macro-level policy and meso- and micro-level managerial practices. Sociologists and other social scientists have stressed the "trickle down effects" of neoliberal thinking, but they are not always informed about managerial practices and the management literature. Accounting research is arguably the business school discipline that has been the most articulate in terms of making such connections. This volume is thus making a contribution to the literature on neoliberalism and the management theory corpus by pointing at how the diverse and manifold discourse on neoliberalism is of great importance for understanding changes in managerial practices over the last three decades. The management literature and the practices it advocates do not emerge *ex nihilo*, but are rather based on perceived practical problems in a social world. If social worlds change as they are shaped by new political programs and agendas, so will managerial practice. Therefore, it is important to account for the socio-economic and political changes over the last three decades in the light of managerial practice.

OUTLINE OF THE BOOK

This volume introduces the literature on neoliberalism, its history, and its controversies, and thereafter points at three domains in which neoliberal thinking has served to rearticulate managerial practice. First, in the field of corporate governance, the financialization of the economy, the emergence of academic finance theory and operative models, and macroeconomic changes have shifted the focus from firms as bundles of tangible assets and productive resources to firms as portfolios of financial assets that can be productively invested. Second, the neoliberal emphasis on market-based transactions and an enterprising culture has changed human resource management and served to rearticulate the concept of professionalism. Human resources are increasingly treated as the temporal optimization of skills and competencies, rather than being a fixed or semi-stable stock of co-workers to be trained and further developed in the face of new challenges. In addition, professionalism, a key concept in industry sociology, is transformed into what has been called "expert professionalism," regimes of expertise to be bought and sold in the market place. Third, what has been called the "audit explosion" in the regulatory control of organizations—the increased reliance on control executed from the outside of the organization through so-called auditing firms and the strong emphasis on performance metrics and other forms of quantitative measures—is tied to a re-articulation of the firm as a financial asset whose internal resources need to be monitored and controlled.

NOTES

1. This literature includes, for instance, Jeffrey Friedman and Wladimir Kraus's *Engineering the Financial Crisis* (2012), Neil Barofsky's *Bailout* (2012), Jeff Madrick's *Age of Greed* (2011), Gary B. Gorton's *Slapped by the Invisible Hand* (2010), Joseph E. Stiglitz's *Freefall* (2010a), Andrew Ross Sorkin's *Too Big to Fail* (2009), and Justin Fox's *The Myth of the Rational Market* (2009), in addition to a series of journal papers and reports (e.g., Engelen et al., 2012; Helleiner, 2011; Crotty, 2009).

2. Lazzarato (2009) makes the important remark that for neoliberal thinkers, the market is not just a site for "exchange," as Adam Smith put it. In addition to exchange, for markets to function as "regulatory principles," there is a need for *competition*. But competition is not the result of what Lazzarato (2009: 117) calls the "the 'natural play' of appetites, instincts or behaviours," but is rather "a 'formal play' of inequalities that must be instituted and constantly nourished and maintained." In Lazzarato's view, the neoliberal view of the market qua regulatory principle demands and presupposes inequality because "only inequality has the capacity to sharpen appetites, instincts, and minds, driving individuals to rivalries" (Lazzarato, 2009: 117). Inequality is thus more of a precondition enabling efficient marketization than its effect or outcome.

Part I

From Mont Pèlerin to the Fall of the Washington Consensus

1 The Concept of Neoliberalism

INTRODUCTION

The subject matter of this book is capitalism or, perhaps better, the capitalist society. There have been many ideas over the centuries on how to organize and structure both the economy and the society wherein the economic system is embedded (Appelby, 2010; Ingham, 2008). Socio-economic and political regimes such as feudalism, mercantilism, monopoly capitalism, and so forth have all succeeded one another in the early-modern and modern period (Goody, 2004; Braudel, 1992; Maddison, 1982). There have been a number of different candidate labels for how to describe the contemporary regime of capital accumulation including *knowledge capitalism* (Burton-Jones, 1999), *knowing capitalism* (Thrift, 2005), *investor capitalism* (Useem, 1996), or quite simply *new capitalism* (Sennett, 1998; Gee, Hull, and Lankshear, 1996). In addition, even more provocative terms such as *necrocapitalism* (Banerjee, 2008), underlining the destruction of natural resources and the exploitation of humans and animals, have been proposed. Weber (1999: 48) identifies the following characteristics of capitalism: "Appropriation of the physical means of production by the entrepreneur, freedom of the market, rational technology, rational law, free labor, and finally the commercialization of economic life." While these institutional pillars of the contemporary economy and society are today widely taken for granted—they have become part of our life-world—it is important to remember that capitalism is an advanced form of social organization that cannot make claims to hold any specific rationalities per se, but rather its accomplishment lies precisely in its unique and quite often very delicate balancing of various interests and concerns (Hirschman, 1977). "Capitalism is no sheer rationality: it is a definite form of cultural order, or a cultural order acting in a particular form," Marshall Sahlins (2000: 181) says. Slavoj Žižek (2009), making reference to Alain Badiou, emphasizes that capitalism is of necessity embedded in preexisting cultures and social formations, and therefore there are many varieties of capitalism. In fact, the strength and vitality of capitalism derive from its ability to be bound up with various social relations and to become part of such "infrastructures":

> [C]apitalism is effectively not a civilization of its own, with a specific way of rendering life meaningful. Capitalism is the first socio-economic order which *de-totalizes meaning:* it is not global at the level of meaning (there is no 'global capitalist world view,' no 'capitalist civilization' proper; the fundamental lesson of globalization is precisely that capitalism can accommodate itself to all civilizations, from Christian to Hindu and Buddhist. (Žižek, 2009: 25)

"Capitalism as an historical reality is the contingent product of an institutional framework and positive rule (legal and extra-legal) that constitute its conditions of possibility," Lazzarato (2009: 113) adds. In Thrift's (2005) view, capitalism has become a "set of networks" that is never a "total system" but rather evolves as "a project that is permanently 'under construction.'" Because genuine uncertainty heavily influences capitalist enterprises, the system of capitalism is in a perpetual process of becoming and evolving:

> Capitalism firms may be able to mobilize power and enroll allies but they are as uncertain about the future as we all are because the future unfolds as a virtuality—it is continually creating temporary actualizations out of new questions—not a known quantity, or at least a distinct possibility. So capitalist firms may sit on the bridge of this world, able at their best to steer it in certain directions, but they still cannot know what is around the corner, whether it be an emerging energy crisis, a financial downturn, a set of protests that threaten a brand's image, or something more mundane like a cashflow crisis. This essentially performative notion of capitalism, conceiving of it as a continually renewed set of responses to new drivers, means that I see capitalism, to repeat, as a constantly mutating entity, made up of a field of networks which are only ever partly in its control. No matter how many assets are engaged, it must constantly face the pressure of unexpected events. (Thrift, 2005: 3–4)

Karl Marx's contribution to economic theory and social science, Dumit (2012) suggests, lies in his ambition not to understand the capitalist system so much as the combination of actors and institutional arrangements that make up the capitalist system but through exploring the abstract principle of capital *per se*, the lifeblood of these uncoordinated activities—famously referred to as the *invisible hand* by Adam Smith—and how capital is capable of manifesting itself in various social relations and encouraging various forms of risk-taking and venturing. Seen in this view, Marx almost conceived of a post-humanist view of the capitalist regime of accumulation in stressing the notion of capital as the real master of the economy—not the capital owners or any other human actor. "Capitalism is and always was about capital accumulation, or in a more modern expression: economic growth," Streek (2012: 5) remarks. He continues: "Capitalism, a non-violent, civilized mode of material self-enrichment through market exchange, had to extricate itself from feudalism in an alliance with liberal anti-authoritarianism and with popular movements for democracy" (Streek, 2012: 13). This ability to overcome violent and armed conflicts is perhaps one of the greatest contributions of capitalism. In the late-modern era, capital accumulation is war pursued by other means. In addition to Žižek's (2009) stress on the fluid and ephemeral nature of capitalism and Thrift's (2005) underlining of the genuine uncertainty it has to cope with, Streek (2012: 25) adds that capitalism has a problem with its inability to "create or preserve" the "non-capitalist embedding" which it is dependent on; instead, capitalism tends to "erode or consume" such conditions, which makes capitalism, if unchecked, "a self-destructive social formation."

In these accounts, the capitalist regime of accumulation is dependent on, yet seems to consume, its surrounding society; it is what is fragile and temporal, yet resilient enough to outlive or overtake certain social formations. The concept of neoliberalism, regardless of all its different schools of thought, traditions, and orientations, can be understood as a specific recipe for how to strike a balance between the different elements of the socio-economic system of late-modern capitalism. The issue is just that what is a "balance" in such a setting is a highly disputed matter. The perhaps most significant quality of the neoliberal version of capitalism is the expansion of markets into all domains of human existence, and the accompanying process of privatization of the economic transactions taking place in these markets. "The development of modern capitalism can be viewed as a process of the expansion of markets as mechanisms for the production and allocation of goods and services," says Beckert (2009: 245). For some commentators and policy makers, such marketization has been beneficial for the efficiency of the economy, while for others, it is indicative of the crisis of contemporary capitalism and its inability to provide any alternative to supposedly self-regulating markets. Under all conditions, neoliberal thinking and its insistence on critically examining a long series of assumptions and doctrines that has dominated in the post-World War II period has served as something like "a gale of creative destruction"—with Joseph Schumpeter's much-cited metaphor—for economic theory, policy, and, as it is claimed in this volume, management. "The wave of creative destruction which neoliberalization has visited across the whole landscape of capitalism is unparalleled in the history of capitalism," Harvey (2005a: 156) argues. Neoliberal thinking is not just a matter of theorizing capitalist regimes of accumulation; it is a specific form of governmentality composed of both programs and technologies.

The history of neoliberal thinking is also a quite evocative story of how groups of liberals located in places like Vienna, Freiburg, and eventually Chicago and elsewhere have been able to move from the margin to the centre, from small Alpine villages to the economic advisory boards of the White House. Seen in this view, the neoliberal consolidation on the basis of a series of shared commitments and beliefs is a success story—not the least in terms of academic credentials, as no less than eight members of the Mont Pèlerin Society, a neoliberal interest group funded by Friedrich von Hayek in 1947, have to date been awarded the Nobel Prize in economic sciences. "[In 1977] neo-liberalism was heretical. More than 30 years later, it has become the dominant orthodoxy," Kinderman (2012: 50) reminds us. At the same time, neoliberalism has been advanced by a quite diverse group of advocates, ranging from interwar period German liberals stressing the role of a "strong state" to North-American libertarians and neoconservatives committed to a key objective of fighting the labour movement and the trade unions—and in between, finance theory professors and finance industry actors interested in de-regulating and globalizing financial markets. It is thus close to impossible to pin down one single unified definition of neoliberalism. One may say that neoliberalism as a term is just as fluid and fluxing as the capitalist regime of accumulation itself that it seeks to understand, theorize, and govern.

This volume is an attempt to cover some of the various schools, themes, and disputes bought into discussion under the label of neoliberalism. In addition, the concept of *management*, the actual practice of leading, administrating, and monitoring the market-based activities prescribed by neoliberal theories, will be related to the neoliberal tradition of thinking. In the following pages, a substantial literature, being either affirmative or sceptical regarding the contributions of neoliberal thinking, will be reviewed and discussed. As will be noticed, many of the scholars invoking the term *neoliberalism* tend to use it with negative connotations (Boas and Gans-Morse, 2009), as representing an unconditional commitment to free-market capitalism and a genre of literature turning a blind eye on the negative consequences of such programs in contemporary society. On the other hand, there are several books and journal articles following Kinderman (2012) in perceiving neoliberalism as today being either an "orthodoxy" or being "hegemonic," a claim that can justify the use of literature that takes an explicitly sceptical view on neoliberal statements and claims. Under all conditions, no matter what position vis-à-vis neoliberalism one takes, the story of neoliberalism is an intriguing one, populated by heroes and villains, tragic events and major occurrences, self-declared leaders and counter-movements, closed communities and interest groups and their financiers and sponsors (on this point, see, e.g., Chabrak, 2012), accounts for periods of growth and declines in the global economic system and so forth. No matter what we think about the different versions of neoliberalism, from its "milder forms" in the German Ordoliberal tradition underlying the "German economic miracle" of the 1950s and 1960s (Bonefeld, 2012), to the more radical North-American libertarian versions mingling with neoconservatism, concepts such as marketization, privatization, and, above all, financialization remain important concepts in what in this volume is referred to as the *neoliberal era*, beginning in the end of the 1970s and still dominating—perhaps with a few minor modifications following the spectacular and in many ways embarrassing 2008 finance market collapse. Neoliberalism has moved from the margin to the centre, and today we live in societies determined by its concepts and analytical models.

I. THE ROOTS OF NEOLIBERALISM

Economic Roots of Neoliberalism

The idea of *laissez-faire* politics and the idea of the economy as a self-regulating system—a "natural order"—can be traced to the French physiocrats, led by the physicologist François Quesnay, who developed the first systematic economic theories in the mid-eighteenth century (Harcourt, 2011). The young Scottish moral philosopher Adam Smith read and translated contemporary French economic theory, and his idea of the "invisible hand" of market transactions grounded in self-interest has served as a foundational principle in economic theory since the publication of Smith's *The Wealth of Nations* in 1776. Being highly critical of the mercantilist economy and its emphasis of the *accumulation* of stocks of capital, Smith argued that economic growth and prosperity was, on the contrary, based on the *circulation* of capital and that such circulation was based on free trade and the exploitation of differences in production factor costs and the regional division of labour. In the 1920s and 1930s, a group of economists in Freiburg in Germany, including Wilhelm Röpke and Walter Eucken, published a journal named *Ordo* in which they criticized too-tight state control and regulations of the economy. These economists were referred to as Ordo-liberals (Bonefeld, 2012; Boas and Gans-Morse, 2009; Foucault, 2008). In nearby Austria, what was eventually referred to as the Austrian School of Economics, including economists such as Eugene Bahm-Böwerk, Friedrich von Hayek, Ludwig von Mises, and future Harvard Business School professor Joseph Schumpeter, engaged in a similar critique of state-regulated economies. Friedrich von Hayek, who moved to the London School of Economics in 1950, published his *Road to Serfdom* in 1944, a book that strongly emphasized the self-regulating nature of the economy and warned against too-detailed state control. Hayek's work, especially his *The Constitution of Liberty* (1960), became a significant source of inspiration for the Thatcher government, which initiated a political program aimed at disarming the trade unions and other stakeholders blocking free enterprise.[1] In 1949, Hayek (1949: 117) had announced that the role of the trade unions was "one of the most important of all the questions to which we must give our attention," a primary target for political action because the trade unions were claimed to counteract what Hayek referred to as a "freer economy."[2] Such political action should reduce the powers of the trade unions "in law as well as in fact," Hayek (1949: 117) urged. After more than 30 years, Hayek's call led to action from the highest political level.

The post-World War II period was characterized by economic growth and stability (Appleby, 2010), but the Bretton Woods systems regulating the international financial systems and exchange rates in making a connection between currencies and a gold reserve had its limitations (Eichengreen, 2008). In 1971, President Nixon abandoned the Bretton Woods system. After the decline of Bretton Woods, the financial markets became increasingly virtual, as capital became increasingly disconnected from underlying assets. In the 1970s, the capitalist system began for the first time in decades to become shaky. There were oil crises in 1973 and in 1978, strongly increasing the cost of production, and economic growth declined. "Adjusted for inflation, the S&P 500 dropped even more from 1973 through 1977 than in the five years starting in 1929," Fox (2009: 163) notices. Productivity growth stagnated and the costs for labour increased significantly in the period. Worse still, Keynesian economic theory prescribing state-governed economic intervention in the downturns of the economic cycles that have worked very well during the post-World War II growth years could not explain the new economic phenomenon of *stagflation*, inflation in combination with high unemployment. Mainstream neoclassic economic theory assumed that the presence of unemployment had a chilling effect on compensation claims. However, Mirowski (2005) argues that the widespread explanation for the decline of the hegemonic Keynesian model as its inability to cope with stagflation is somewhat simplistic. In Mirowski's (2005) view, neoliberal thinkers were successfully bringing politics back into economic theory when they questioned some of the basic assumptions in the Keynesian theory:

> They understood that they have to come equipped with theories of politics that were more serious than the Keynesians had. What is one of the standard complaints about Keynesianism? That it looked at the government as if it were totally benevolent and it would engage in fiscal and monetary policy for the good of all, with no thought as to its own persistence and viability. The neoliberals would retort, 'No, no you can't trust them, the government is as self-interested is as any of our other actors.' (Mirowski, 2005: 88)

In this view, neoliberalism was already from the outset politics clad in neoclassical economic theory. "Neoliberalism was a movement to revive pro-market conservatism in the mid-twentieth century when it was at its lowest ebb, in the period just after the Great Depression. It was superimposed on neoclassical economics," (Mirowski, 2005: 86) contends.

Mizruchi and Kimeldorf (2005) describe the new economic situation and how the business community responded to the new challenges by pointing at state regulations and the trade unions as explanatory factors of the economic decline:

> With inflation and unemployment both high, and with profits and stock prices both low, the American business community faced a crisis [in the mid-1970s]. . . . Having seen enough, the business community mounted a counteroffensive that would dramatically remake the country's political and economic landscape. Their response, bankrolled by wealthy individuals and leading corporations, targeted what many conservatives believed was responsible for the decline of the American economy; a lack of productivity, caused in part by a labor movement whose long-standing work rules purportedly impinged on the flexibility of firms; and government regulation that presumably increased the cost of doing business. (Mizruchi and Kimeldorf, 2005: 217)

The idea that the labour movement and the trade unions, representing a conspicuous form of "collectivism" in the eyes of neoliberal intellectuals and policy makers, were responsible for the economic decline in the 1970s is not supported by empirical evidence. Wolff (2003: 451) demonstrates that the net profit in U.S. manufacturing "shows a very similar trend to that of the total economy, first falling from a peak at 32.3% in 1953 to a low point of 8.3% in 1983 and then recovering, in part, to 15.9% in 1997." However, in the 1947–1979 period, real wages grew at the same rate as labour productivity; after 1979, wages rose more slowly than labour productivity. Over the entire period 1947–1997, Wolff (2003: 451) reports, "labour productivity gains outstripped those of mean compensation (a ratio of 2.19 versus 1.96)." Rather than, as suggested by neoliberal intellectuals, that trade unionism leads to inadequate levels of compensation and therefore being an explanatory factor for the recession, there were, Wolff (2003: 496) suggests, "structural changes, particularly in the shift of employment toward labour intensive services," that acted as an "important offset to the tendency of the rate of profit to fall." Wolff (2003: 497) concludes: "If wages increase more slowly [than productivity], we might suspect that the balance in power has shifted towards capital, and conversely . . . one must conclude that economic and political power shifted in favour of capital, beginning in the early 1980s." This claim is supported by studies of the correlation between de-unionization and the growth of economic inequality (e.g., Brady, Baker, and Finnigan, 2013), suggesting that unions have served a key institutional role in competitive capitalism to counteract economic inequality: "From 1973 to 2007 [in the United States], union membership in the private sector declined from 34 to 8 percent for men and from 16 to 6 percent for women. During this time, wage inequality in the private sector increased by over 40 percent" (Western and Rosenfeld, 2011: 543). In practice, this economic inequality has led to a significant increase in American wage-earners who are unable to subsist on their incomes. In comparison to average unemployment figures, a key political performance indicator, the proportion of working poor in the United States is three times that of the unemployed: "The unemployed poor averaged only 3.4 percent of the U.S. population from 1974 to 2004, whereas the working poor averaged 10.4 percent" (Brady, Baker, and Finnigan, 2013: 873). Unions have traditionally served in the role to counteract such economic inequality: "In countries with high unionization, inequality and poverty are lower and wages are higher," Brady, Baker, and Finnigan (2013: 873) write. The political objective of neoliberal intellectuals such as Friedrich von Hayek to strongly reduce the influence of unions, a constitutive element in Thatcher's and Reagan's agendas, proved to be most efficient in changing income distribution.

In 1977, Paul Volcker was named chairman of the Federal Reserve by President Carter, and Volcker initiated a new low-inflation policy, not so much on basis of his beliefs in the monetarist doctrine as on a more general understanding of the need to reduce inflation to secure economic growth and stability. By and large, Volcker is portrayed as a qualified chairman of the Fed with good intellectual capacities and integrity (Jones, 2012). While Nixon had famously declared that "We are all Keynesians now," Carter initiated de-regulation policies and claimed in a State of the Union address, very much in line with his successor Ronald Reagan, that "government could no longer solve people's problems" (cited in Jones, 2012: 254). University of Chicago economists such as Milton Friedman, an ardent critic of state regulation, the welfare state, and minimal wages, had prescribed what was called a monetarist policy, and Friedman and colleagues had served as economic advisors to the Nixon administration. Volcker did not really believe in the monetarist theory (a theory that at the time was poorly substantiated by empirical evidence or even "historical examples," and later on proved to be wrong, Madrick (2011) suggests).[3] Nevertheless, Volcker's period in office is characterized by a persistent inflation-fighting policy.

The last few years of the 1970s were, in Harvey's (2005b) phrase, "revolutionary." In China, the Communist Party Chairman Deng Xiaoping started to de-regulate the strictly state-controlled Chinese economy. In the United Kingdom, Margaret Thatcher was elected Prime Minister, and in the United States, Reagan entered the White House—both determined to advance a neoliberal and neoconservative political agenda. While Thatcher focused on reducing the influence of the trade unions, Reagan endorsed what was called a *supply-side economics policy*, which included substantial tax cuts for the highest income groups and more moderate tax cuts for middle and lower income groups, a policy that was based on what was called the Laffer-curve (after the economist Arthur Laffer), the assumption that tax-cuts in high income groups would "trickle down" the economic system and thereby create jobs and economic growth "further down" in the economy (Quiggin, 2010, Ch. 4); "*Supply side economics* argued that reducing taxes can unleash enormous gains in economic efficiency," Taylor (2011: 222) writes.

Despite such claims, this model was never credible in the eyes of mainstream and more moderate economists:

> There is no evidence to support the notion that the economy is on the bad side of the curve [where increased taxation reduce state income], but supply-siders found it easy to convince themselves and their political masters that the U.S. and U.K. economies (most notably) were there. Hence cutting taxes would get rid of the fiscal deficit and . . . give a big boost to economic growth. (Taylor, 2011: 250–251)

Regardless of the accuracy of such predictions, the Reagan tax reform, especially that of his second term in 1986, was a vehicle for the diffusion of neoliberal policies because policy makers in other developed countries had to respond to the new conditions (Swank, 1998). The long-term effect is that tax policy has experienced structural change, a shift in explicit goals from "redistribution" towards "efficiency" (Swank, 1998: 96). The regressive taxation was also justified by neoconservative arguments and ethics emphasizing self-reliance and the virtues of competition. Madrick (2011) points at the consequences of Reagan's tax cuts, "the largest in the post-World War II era":

> Earners in the middle fifth of Americans would now pay 9.8 percent of their income in payroll taxes, while those in the top 1 percent now paid 1.4 percent of their income in payroll taxes. . . . The rate of actual federal taxes of all kinds on the middle fifth of income earners in America (households) fell only by 0.7 percent between 1979 and 1989, but for the top 10 percent it fell by 3.3 percent, and 8.1 percent for the top 1 percent of earners. (Madrick, 2011: 170–171)

Unfortunately, the economic advisors' theories about what was referred to as "trickle-down economics" did not hold water: "The supply side tax cuts did not generate nearly the rapid growth in tax revenues promised" (Madrick, 2011: 169). One immediate effect was substantial budget deficits. In 1982, Reagan's first fiscal year, the budget deficit was nearly $130 billion. During his two terms in office, Reagan had consistently higher budget deficits than any other post-World War II president. Much of this public spending was allocated to the military defence: "By 1986 the defense budget would be twice 1980's allocation" (Troy, 2009: 63). Reagan had promised his voters "less government" and had famously claimed that "government is not the solution, it is the problem,"[4] but what he delivered was in fact a growing national debt.

Political Roots of Neoliberalism

In addition to economic conditions and policies, neoliberalism needs to be understood as the outcome of a new political agenda in which concepts such as the welfare state and "embedded liberalism" have become fiercely criticized as that which intervenes into the economy and disrupts the "natural order" of the market. "The fear of neoliberal thought is one of excessive state intervention. This anxiety that 'if one governs too much one does not govern at all' precisely encapsulates the indirect style of social control that typifies governmental reason," McNay (2009: 58) writes. While both Great Britain and the United States have historically endorsed liberal politics and free market trade agendas, if for no other reason than because they benefitted the colonial projects of the nineteenth century, in the 1960s and 1970s a new political force was consolidating. In the United States, the critique of Soviet-style plan economies was significant and the fear and hatred of communism as a political system was exploited by aspiring younger conservatives (Mulholland, 2012; Himmelstein, 1992). Ronald Reagan had, for instance, earned a reputation as a patriotic activist fighting "un-American beliefs" (i.e., what was regarded as communism at large) in Hollywood during the McCarthy craze of the 1950s. At the same time, as Talcott Parsons remarked (cited in Himmelstein, 1992: 3), "What the right-wing is fighting, in the shadow of communism, is essentially 'modernity.'" Many neoconservatives were not, after all, regarding the USSR as a major threat to their lifestyle, but were more concerned about the lack of moral fibre and a sense of decline in the nation, especially as the 1950s, "characterized by comfortable conformism" (Mulholland, 2012: 236), ended and brought the social and cultural unrest of the 1960s.

American neoconservatism cannot be treated as a "coherent movement," and "its ideological sources are diverse, and this has given neoconservatism its markedly protean character," High (2009: 476) claims. Himmelstein (1992: 14) names three key elements in neo-conservatism: *economic libertarianism, social traditionalism,* and *militant anti-communism.* Neoliberals, neoconservatives, what Durham (2006) speaks of as paleo-conservatives and paleo-libertarians, and the Christian right are all part of this community, advocating their own interests, not always of necessity being aligned and mutually supportive. For instance, one important distinction can be made between the libertarian and the neoconservative view of the market. The former, represented by, for instance, Milton Friedman, assumed that the market "enforced its own morality." In contrast, High (2009: 480) writes, "neoconservatives were not so sure: if capitalism sells pornography, discourages thrift, and cashes in on counterculture, it cannot produce 'virtue' as well." In addition, for Friedman, Reagan was a "disobedient pupil" when he presented massive budget deficits and thereby violated the "small government" ideal of libertarians, while for the neoconservatives Reagan was a "munificent patron who had tantalized them with power" (High, 2009: 480). By and large, the neoconservatives from the Reagan era onwards allied themselves with big business and helped lift the burden of free market orthodoxies laid on American industry by the neoliberal economists. As leading neoconservative thinkers and pundits working in the industry-funded think-tanks understood that "big business did not want to be told that it had to conform to free-market purity," they served to advance the view that "oligopoly and government subsidy were as American as apple pie" (High, 2009: 485).

McGirr (2001, 2002) traces the neoconservatism movement to the suburban sprawl of Orange County in southern California. After World War II, many veterans who wanted to start over settled in the greater Los Angeles area. Being trained in the American military, they subscribed to a neoconservatist agenda that included harsh anti-communist sentiments, scepticism towards "east-coast liberals," and what they perceived as the ever-expanding role of the federal government. "By the 1970s, liberalism had been discredited in the United States in so many people's eyes, a reflection of the perceived excesses of the 1960s and dissatisfaction with the economic situation," Jones (2012: 102) writes. In McGirr's (2002: 333) account, similar cultures were growing elsewhere in suburban middle-class America, but Orange County can be seen as a "prototype" for the neoconservative expansion—"the first functional form of a new kind of conservative milieu that appeared less distinctively elsewhere." The neoconservative mindset endorsed free-market capitalism, a critical view of the trade unions and the labour movement, which was regarded as a thinly veiled form of communism in the middle of the American continent, a critique of government spending, and secularization and liberalization more generally, allegedly threatening traditional "family values" (on this latter point, see Petchesky, 1981). "[M]ost of the individuals, groups, and organizations labeled conservative in the postwar United States have been supporters of free market capitalism," Gross, Medvetz, and Russell (2011: 328) note. One of the most significant accomplishments of the neoconservative spokespersons and pundits was the ability to re-define the concept of *elites* from being strictly "economic elites" to instead "political and cultural elites," centred in the Northeast, which was more "cosmopolitan than patriotic" and that was, in the neoconservative worldview, "soft on communism, driven to favour ill-fated social engineering schemes, and supportive of pernicious social trends like secularization" (Gross, Medvetz, and Russell, 2011: 334). In pursuing their goals, neoconservatives have been "vigorous, even aggressive, rather than conciliatory," Mulholland (2012: 278) suggests.

In general, neoconservatism favours a traditional way of life and is in that respect highly provincial in its fear of social changes.[5] Needless to say, the 1960s, with all its political turmoil and counterculture—the civil rights movement, the gay and lesbian movement, the pacifist movement, and so forth—were a fertile soil for neoconservatist political agenda. As Blee and Creasap (2010: 274) remark, regardless of the conservatist worldview, the neoconservatist movement has been quite successful in revising its agenda and adopting new enemies that pose a threat to the American way of life: "New enemies were needed to replace those that had become irrelevant to conservatism such as Soviet-era communists. Immigrants, liberals, working women, counterculturists, abortion providers, welfare recipients, secular humanists, feminists, and later, global jihadists and Muslim terrorists became the new target."

In 1964, the arch-conservative Republican Senator Barry Goldwater announced his presidential campaign but failed to get into office. By liberals and mainstream commentators, Goldwater was an "extremist,"[6] but in less than two decades, Ronald Reagan, who had publically endorsed the Goldwater campaign, took office. In 1968, another southern California neoconservative, Richard Nixon, was elected President. However, after close to a decade of economic decline in the 1970s, the Reagan presidency became the political turning point for the neoconservative voters:

> [R]eagan's election in 1980 was a turning point, particularly insofar as his vision for the country offered a more coherent ideology for the deepening assault on labor and the state. In his view, which has since become a foundation of neoliberalism, unions, regulations, or anything else that interfered with the workings of an unfettered market constituted unnecessary impediments to economic growth. By freeing up markets and implementing fiscal and tax policies designed to encourage investment, Americans, in this view, would enjoy a level of personal freedom never before experienced under the shadow of big government. (Mizruchi and Kimeldorf, 2005: 218)

During more than four decades, various foundations and businessmen had been financing neoliberal thinkers to develop and institutionalize their pro–free-market ideas (Jones, 2012: 134), and by the end of the 1970s, it was time to roll out the neoliberal political agenda. In the 1950s and 1960s, these neoliberals were widely regarded as "eccentric right-wingers" (Jones, 2012: 178), but neoliberal ideas "[f]it alongside the anticommunist, traditionalist, religious, and fusionist conservatives in a broad church of rightwing activism that was flying under the radar of mainstream politics for much of the period" (Jones, 2012: 146). The antistatist stance taken by the Chicago economists in the United States resonated with the growing neoconservatism movement and a more general anti-communism attitude—"neoliberal intellectuals, in particular economic and political theorists, felt themselves foot-soldiers in the fight against communism," Jones (2012: 120) says—further increased their credibility in these circles. "In both Britain and the United States, during the 1950s and 1960s, neoliberalism had to find a place within conservative politics," Jones (2012: 136) contends. Decades of neoliberal consolidation had suddenly paid off for its sponsors:

> Reagan and Thatcher both built on the new economic strategies that were in place by the late 1970s with a radical new economic policy philosophy governed by the neoliberal belief in the supremacy of the free market. Many of the most important advisers, government colleagues, and supporters were drawn from the transatlantic neoliberal network. (Jones, 2012: 268)

In summary, one can argue that there are two pillars of the neoliberal project; one based on economic theory and economic writing (explored in greater detail in Chapter Two) and one based on political writings and policy. In many ways, these two pillars are difficult to separate analytically, as certain political beliefs are based on economic arguments (e.g., the detrimental influence of governmental spending) while on the contrary some economic arguments are based on political (or ethical) statements (e.g., the idea of freedom of choice). In many ways, these two literatures share a certain ethical standpoint that will be examined next.

The Ethics of Neoliberalism

The roots of neoliberalism are traced both to economic theory and political ideologies, but these two roots of neoliberalism are unified by an underlying ethos. Amable (2011) identifies two basic tenets of the neoliberal ethos. The first principle is that of the moral worth of "competition," a "supreme principle, which should be placed above political influences," Amable (2011: 5) says. For Hayek (1979: 76), in an almost Hegelian passage, competition is more than just a regulatory principle, but is precisely what secures what Hayek refers to as "rational behavior": "[I]t is . . . in general not rationality which is required to make competition work, but competition, or traditions which allow competition, which will all produce rational behavior." Secondly, Amable (2011: 6) argues, "[t]he ethics of self-reliance is a social norm in the neo-liberal society." In order to uphold the "supreme principle of competition," each actor must enact themselves as enterprising agents capable of providing for themselves and no longer relying on welfare state transfers and other forms of public sector initiatives. "[N]eo-liberalism fosters the ethics of being responsible," Ericson, Barry, and Doyle (2000: 554) argue. In other words, "rational capitalism is . . . the coupling of an individual search for profit and a strict work ethic" (Amable, 2011: 14).

Perhaps no other neoliberal protagonist has played a more central role in justifying this ethos than Milton Friedman. Despite being an economist, Friedman's more "popular writing" in the libertarian vein emphasizes the need for competition and the consequent redefinition of the welfare state. In his bestselling *Capitalism and Freedom*, first published in 1962, Friedman suggests that "economic freedom," understood as the minimization of state intervention into allegedly rational markets, is a social goal that precedes that of political freedom. Says Friedman:

> Economic arrangements play a dual role in the promotion of a free society. On the one hand, freedom in economic arrangements is itself a component of freedom broadly understood, so economic freedom is an end in itself. In the second place, economic freedom is also an indispensable means towards the achievement of political goals. (Friedman ([1962] 2002: 8)

Friedman continues:

> Viewed as a means to the end of political freedom, economic arrangements are important because of their effect on the concentration or dispersion of power. The kind of economic organization that provides economic freedom directly, namely competitive capitalism, also promotes political freedom because it separates economic power from political power and in this way enables the one to offset the other.
> (Friedman ([1962] 2002: 8)

According to Friedman ([1962] 2002: 14–15), the "market organization of economic activity" is characterized by the lack of "coercion." Friedman thus suggests that the market and competition needs to be protected against political interventions because economic freedom is the basis of prosperity in competitive capitalism. As political initiatives—the welfare state at large, that is—undermine economic freedom, self-reliance becomes the supreme principle for agency. In the neoliberal regime, the concept of economic freedom and its accompanying virtue of self-reliance were translated into a political agenda dominated by the endeavour to privatize previously public sector activities. "Privatization . . . was one of the central means of reversing the corrosive and corrupting effects of socialism . . . privatization is at the centre of any programme of reclaiming territory for freedom," Margaret Thatcher writes in her memoirs (cited in Kinderman, 2012: 42). This view of the virtues of privatization was primarily ideological and abstract; the actual privatization of public assets in the United Kingdom in fact resulted in a net transfer of £14 billion from "the taxpaying public to stockholders and other investors," derived from the undervaluation of the public assets (Judt, 2010: 110–111). In addition, the £3 billion in fees to the bankers who handled the transactions must be added to the bill (Judt, 2010: 110–111). Only when offered a deliberately low price did private investors show any interest in owning formerly public assets. Recurrent terms such as "corruption" and "freedom" in the vocabularies of neoliberal intellectuals remain rather imprecise terms.

Mudge (2008: 705) speaks of initiatives such as privatization as being the "ideological core" of neoliberalism, "the elevation of the market—understood as a non-political, machine-like entity—over all other modes of organization." It is noteworthy that Friedman, not being a political scientist or philosopher, does not care to define economic freedom. Mudge (2008: 718) speaks of the "implicit religiosity" of neoliberalism and the "semi-evangelical tone of Milton Friedman's articulation of markets as the source and arbiter of human freedom." For Madrick (2011), however, Friedman's text needs to be understood not so much as an abstract treatise with religious overtones as a quite straightforward critique of welfare state institutions:

> His broader philosophical view that government social programs and regulations, inflationary spending aside, were almost always damaging

interference with the efficient workings of an economy. They undermined opportunity, social justice, and above all personal freedom, he felt. His economic views were indistinguishable from traditional libertarian political philosophies whose overriding concern was personal liberty. He sought to eliminate one social policy after another, including Social Security, unemployment insurance, the minimum wage, and a wide range of regulations governing labor organizing, pharmaceuticals, consumer safety and job safety. Friedman, in effect, provided the intellectual map for a reversal of the progressive evolution of the nation. (Madrick, 2011: 27)

In Madrick's view, Friedman's texts were not exemplary pieces of qualified philosophical writings, riddled as they were by declarative statements and ill-defined terms, and as economic treatises they were ignorant of actual conditions and data. Friedman, Madrick (2011: 27) argues, "insisted he was not ideological" and "adamantly claimed he based his theories on facts," but such claims were greatly "exaggerated": "His policy essays and speeches were well written and often ingenious but overtly simple assertions of free market claims based on straightforward interpretations of Adam Smith, disregarding Smith's many caveats and philosophical and psychological writings. Friedman's social policies as opposed to his work on monetary policy were rarely substantiated by empirical research or even historical examples."[7] In many cases, available data do not reveal any opposition between economic growth and political regulation and taxation as suggested by Friedman. For instance, the American economy and the typical worker's standard of living grew rapidly in the 1950s and 1960s "despite higher taxes, progressively applied, and the growth of government" (Madrick, 2011: 41–42). In addition to having limited interest in supporting his claims with empirical data, Friedman made certain counterintuitive assumptions that served as axial principles in his politico-economic theory—for instance, the assumption that in the market, "no one will take advantage of others"; "[t]he consumer is protected from coercion, wrote Friedman, because here are other sellers; the seller is protected because there are other consumers; and the employer is protected because there is a pool of workers from which to pick" (Madrick, 2011: 41). Friedman's highly influential work was thus in many ways an ideological statement, testifying to his strong libertarian beliefs and his disregard of the welfare state as a form of "collectivism" undermining economic freedom.

The ethos of competition and self-reliance is, Amable (2011: 17) argues, bound up with an elitist position wherein the people are "ignorant and capricious and by no means sovereign." In the neoliberal tradition, there is a strong preference for an elite to govern and establish political institutions, laws, and regulations that no longer put any pressure on elites to protect a "population of losers" (Amable, 2011: 17).[8] In Hayek's *The Road to Serfdom*, a foundational text in the neoliberal mobilization, Hayek defended "intellectual freedom" among the literati because most people, Hayek claimed, "[d]o not have the capacity for 'independent thought'" (cited in Jones, 2012: 66). The ethos of competition and self-reliance and the underlying rational choice models all represent a far-driven individualist worldview and political program where the failure to be successful is a matter of "bad decisions" and "bad investments." For instance, Gary Becker's *human capital theory* regards most choices made in life as investments, and return on investment is explained strictly on basis of personal qualities and capacities for competing.[9] In Becker's world, there are no sources of discrimination, other forms of structural inequality, or other forms of opportunistic behaviour that intervene into rational market transactions. "Neo-liberalism chooses inequality. Within a neo-liberal regime of responsible risk taking all difference, and the inequalities that result from it, is seen as a matter of choice. If one ends up poor, unemployed, and unfulfilled, it is because of poorly thought-out risk decisions" (Ericson, Barry, and Doyle, 2000: 554).

Since welfare state activities are by definition a failure to pursue economic freedom in Friedman's sense of the term, individuals "failing" to compete in the market—i.e., those who make uninformed and mistaken decisions, in Gary Becker's view—become a problem to handle for the state. Since one of the few domains where the state can legitimately play an active role in the neoliberal perspective, besides upholding the free circulation of capital, is to provide penal institutions, there is a conspicuous growth of the incarceration rate in, for example, the United States (discussed in detail below). The neoliberal state thus cannot help its citizens economically and financially because that would violate the ethos of competition and self-reliance, but putting them in prison is consistent with the individualism and elitism of the neoliberal credo.

In summary, neoliberal thinking is not just an economic program or a political agenda; it is articulated as an integrated and unified worldview, placing the free and preferably unregulated circulation of capital in the first room. Competition and self-reliance are the two pillars of the neoliberal ethos, embedded in individualism and elitism that, taken together, enable economic freedom. In the next section, the institutions of the neoliberal program are examined.

II. THE INSTITUTIONS OF NEOLIBERALISM

The International Organization of Neoliberal Institutions: The International Monetary Fund, the World Bank, the World Trade Organization, and the Washington Consensus

As many commentators have made clear, the neoliberal political program that Margaret Thatcher initiated in 1979 was not praised by all conservatives at the time. Thatcher's agenda appeared extreme in its anti-unionism and free-market thinking. For her detractors, Thatcher, even more so than the charming and positive Ronald Reagan, embodies class hatred and ignorance. Like perhaps no other figure in post-World War II politics (Mikhail Gorbachev being another candidate), Thatcher managed to individually represent an entire political program and a seismic shift in economic policy and politics. Political programs that appeared to be innovative and daring in the late 1970s and 1980s gradually became institutionalized, and by the mid-1990s, the so-called Washington consensus was widely endorsed in the industrialized world by governments representing a wide political spectrum. "The U.S. model" included a number of components, such as the "deregulation of financial markets, privatisation, weakening of institutions of social protection, weakening of labour unions and labour market protections, shrinking of government, cutting of top tax rates, opening up of international goods and capital markets, and abandonment of full employment under the guise of the natural rate" (Pulley, 2005: 25).

Prior to neoliberalism being endorsed in the United Kingdom and United States, countries in Latin and South America become workshops for the new economic policies and political agendas. The CIA supported a coup in Chile in 1973 in which the elected president and socialist Salvador Allende was killed and replaced by a right-wing military junta. Under the leadership of General Augusto Pinochet, Chile became a testing ground for monetarist policies and free-market experiments. A number of economists trained at the department of economics at University of Chicago became Pinochet's economic advisors. Before 1973, Massey, Sanchez, and Behrman (2006: 12) argue, Chile had been "[a] relatively stable, middle-class society with a long democratic tradition characterized by respect for private property and the rule of law, essentially preconditions for the successful functioning of markets." In short, the Chilean economy benefitted from a "well-established infrastructure of reliable social, economic, and political institutions" (Massey, Sanchez, and Behrman, 2006: 13). The "Chicago boys" pushed forward an agenda that included privatization, fiscal austerity, and deregulation, all consistent with their University of Chicago training. These new policies led to relatively limited economic growth, but "Chilean poverty rates initially soared and inequality rose markedly before the economy finally stabilized and more balanced growth resumed" (Massey, Sanchez, and Behrman, 2006: 14). That is, the neoliberal experiment did little more than to destroy institutions and increase economic inequality, all under the credo of establishing "economic freedom." "At its crudest," remarks Andy Becket (cited in Mulholland, 2012: 249), "the Chicago programme was class vengeance."

These early neoliberal experiments were therefore not successful in terms of producing economic growth and prosperity. The formula prescribed, consisting of "balanced budgets, reduced taxes, decontrolled interest rates, floating exchange rates, liberalized trade relations, open foreign investments, and privatization" (Massey, Sanchez, and Behrman, 2006: 8), was gradually enacted by international organizations such as the International Monetary

Fund (IMF), the World Bank, and the World Trade Organization (WTO). At the IMF, capital freedom became the operative principle (Chwieroth, 2010). In his study of the IMF, Chwieroth (2010) argues that the assumption that the IMF is one homogeneous organization promoting "a uniform set of policies consistent with a singular interpretation and application of a particular norm" cannot be justified (see also Singer [2007] on the regulation of the international financial system). While the IMF may appear monolithic from the outside, in fact there are "lively and vigorous internal debates" among the economists and advisors working in the organization. Still, Chwieroth (2010) says, there is a tendency that "theory wins over empirical data" because data rarely falsifies theory (the so-called Duhem-Quine thesis frequently observed in the sciences). Chwieroth (2010: 54) explains:

> Economic theories are quite sophisticated, and each school of thought tends to have strong arguments in its favor. Empirical research is also rarely so conclusive that it sweeps aside prevailing beliefs immediately, which may simply indicate skepticism towards available information rather than challenging adaptation and learning . . . If actors have strong priors about goals and weak priors about means to achieve those goals, then failure should lead actors to change means before they change goals. (Chwieroth, 2010: 54)

Due to these mismatches between theory and empirical data, the IMF provides possibilities for what Chwieroth (2010) calls "internal entrepreneurship," the capacity to pursue individual agendas. As a policy-making body, organizations like the IMF "do not possess a single set of interests or a mindset" (Chwieroth, 2010: 58), and therefore individual functionaries and advisors can develop their own projects. Chorev and Babb's (2009) study of the IMF and the WTO suggests that there are some differences between how these two organizations are managed, and whereas the IMF "relies more heavily on technocratic reputation," the WTO depends on "procedural legitimacy" (Chorev and Babb, 2009: 460; see also Conti, 2010). The IMF is an "international *financial institution*" (Chorev and Babb, 2009: 462; emphasis in the original) relatively autonomously pursuing its own goals, but the WTO is a political institution based on negotiations. Regardless of these differences, both organization shifted from "post-war 'embedded liberalism' and became pillars of a global neo-liberal order," Chorev and Babb (2009: 460) say. In practice, WTO has been able to advance what Chorev and Babb (2009: 477) refers to as a "patchwork of universalistic neoliberal principles and particularistic exceptions"; that is, overarching neoliberal goals have been compromised by local demand and needs. The IMF and the World Bank have been persistently criticized for advising and even enforcing neoliberal policies, especially in third world countries and in Latin and South America, that have destabilized economies and have produced more rather than less economic inequality (see, e.g., Davis, 2006). In a quite original perspective, Griffin (2009) argues that the World Bank pursues a masculine, neoliberal agenda based on the principles of rational choice and competition that is poorly aligned with the needs of poor third world countries. Others have argued that the excess of capital derived from high savings in, for example, Japan and the oil producing states led the World Bank to entice third world dictators to take more loans—money that was frequently unproductively invested in armed forces and similar dead-end projects (Graeber, 2011). International debt has also been a standing concern for the organizations monitoring the global economy.

In the 1980s, and especially in the 1990s under the "New Labour" government of Tony Blair and the Democratic presidency of Bill Clinton, the neoliberal agenda was generally endorsed, but more recently the program has lost much of its momentum. "During the past several years, the escalating crisis of neoliberalism has threatened to render both the IMF and the WTO irrelevant . . . Both institutions have simultaneously been subject to severe and repeated criticism—not only from Third World political leaders, but also from world famous economists," Chorev and Babb (2009: 477) write. Massey, Sanchez, and Behrman (2006) stress that the Washington consensus has gradually lost its legitimacy (see also Sheppard and Leitner, 2010): "Despite early optimism, however, the faith in the Washington consensus was shaken during the latter half of the 1990s by a series of financial crises and economic meltdowns, which were often most severe in countries characterized as having adhered steadfastly to the gospel preached from Washington" (Massey, Sanchez, and Behrman, 2006: 10). "In retrospect," Massey, Sanchez, and Behrman (2006: 11) continue, "the Washington consensus was in many ways as much myth as fact at several levels." Much of the economic advice given and/or enforced was untested "by systematic empirical research" and at times it even ran counter to "well-established economic findings." That is, the politico-economic agenda was primarily ideological, rather than based on a technocratic concern with articulating advice on basis of sound empirical evidence. Massey, Sanchez, and Behrman (2006: 11) summarize: "The true believers of the Washington consensus had single-minded faith in laissez-faire liberalism and fervently believed that by removing the yoke of government, 'free markets' would naturally emerge to solve the nation's social and economic problems." The *coup de grace* for the Washington consensus came with the financial collapse of 2008 (discussed in the next chapter), which finally undermined the long-term acclaim of laissez-faire liberalism as the anchor point for the neoliberal politico-economic agenda. At the G20 meeting in the spring of 2009, British Prime Minister Gordon Brown declared the Washington Consensus "to be dead" (Chorev and Babb, 2009: 459).

The Neoliberal State

In much neoliberal writing, the state is conceived of as being that which intervenes into efficient market transactions and, therefore, that which increases transaction costs—and violates the ethos of competitiveness and self-reliance by implementing costly welfare state policies that distort the efficient circulation of capital. One may thus get the impression that the role of the state should be kept at a minimum. That is not necessarily the case, as the state plays a key role in safeguarding and securing the circulation of capital through both enacting policies and through creating markets previously sheltered from competition (in many European welfare states, e.g., in the domain of schooling and health care) and otherwise supports and enforces a laissez-faire politico-economic agenda. Ferdinand Lasalle introduced the German term *Nachtwachterstaat*, the "Nightwatchman state," in a speech in 1862 (Elias, 2009: 8), and for many neoliberal protagonists, this is the ideal role of the state: to primarily finance juridical and penal institutions, such as courts, armed defence, and the police. However, this minimal state proposed by early liberal and neoliberal writers like Friedrich von Hayek has not emerged; instead, as Munck (2005: 63) suggests, "we can say that neoliberalism has transformed the state rather than driven it back." Munck (2005: 63) continues: "The much-vaunted policies of 'deregulation' (removal of state regulatory systems) have, in fact, been creating new forms of regulation with new market-oriented rules and policies to facilitate the development of the 'new' capitalism." For instance, while markets are regarded by neoliberal economists as being "natural orders" emerging without any need for oversight—a principal belief preceding the 2008 finance industry collapse discussed in Chapter Two—the neoliberal state is, in fact, contrary to such a self-organization perspective, investing quite a bit of effort to de-regulate certain domains of the market in order to create new market opportunities. In this new neoliberal state, the traditional political vocabulary, including terms such as *citizenship* and *solidarity*, and service based on taxation to finance "the common good," is gradually replaced by an economistic language of profit, efficiency, and consumption (George, 2013). Citizens that in any way have failed to compete in these newly emerging and, above all, constructed markets were increasingly labelled by conservatives as "welfare moms," "dole-scroungers," or "indigent free riders" (Jones, 2012: 338; see also Wacquant, 2009). The neoliberal state is essentially governed like a corporation that cannot afford to hold any unprofitable products in its portfolio.

Willse's (2010) study of the American housing market shows that the neoliberal doctrines that have been designed to create a housing market in fact create chronic homelessness, rather than solving housing problems. Willse speaks of the de-regulation of the housing market as a "biopolitical programme," a shift from a "social programme" as part of the welfare state assignment to an "economic programme":

> The biopoliticization of homelessness signals and produces the transformation of social programmes into economic programmes, a transformation that is characteristic of what Jacques Donzelot (2008) has described as the transition from the social welfare state to the social

investment state . . . Chronic homelessness programmes are part of neoliberal economies, and thus they enable rather than challenge the very conditions and systems that produce housing insecurity and deprivation. (Willse, 2010: 173)

In the United Kingdom, the Thatcher government aimed to create a deregulated housing market, but what was originally perceived as beneficial for the British working class quickly led to unanticipated consequences:

> Thatcher's programme for the privatization of social housing in Britain appeared as a gift to the lower classes which could now convert from rental to ownership at a relatively low cost, gain control over valuable assets and augment their wealth. But once the transfer was accomplished, housing speculations took over, particularly in prime central locations, eventually bribing or forcing low-income populations out to the periphery in cities such as London, and turning erstwhile working-class housing estates into centres of intense gentrification. (Harvey, 2005a: 155)

In de-regulated housing markets, attractive traditional inner-city working class neighbourhoods quickly become "gentrified"—a fashionable term in the 1990s—and the former residents, unable to pay the higher living costs, are pushed to the margins. Worse still, the supposedly "efficient housing market" bore evidence of "market failure," as housing units with lower profit margins were unattractive investment opportunities for construction companies and real estate developers. As a consequence, in the United States, African Americans are hugely overrepresented in homelessness programs in metropolitan areas. By and large, the neoliberal project to privatize the housing markets opened up attractive investments, but failed to handle housing problems. In Thatcher's Britain, the showcase of neoliberal policies and what was referred to as supply-side economics, "[t]he number of homeless Britons soared by 38 percent between 1984 and 1989 alone" (Jones, 2011: 10).[10]

Another role that the state could legitimately play was in law enforcement. Wacquant (2009) argues that in the neoliberal state, the poor population is handled through three procedures: By "socialization," by "medicalization" (to be discussed below), and by "penalization." Wacquant is concerned about the quick expansion of the third practice in the United States. "Neoliberalism correlates closely with the international diffusion of punitive policies in both the welfare and the criminal domains," Wacquant (2009: 305) argues. Beckett and Western (2001) and Western and Beckett (1999) point at two principal changes in American policy as being the drivers for the escalating incarceration rates in the USA. The first is the "reduction of welfare" during the Reagan era: "Driven by a philosophy of self-reliance and justified by claims of welfare fraud, OBRA [the 1981 Omnibus Budget

Reconciliation Act] removed nearly half a million working families from AFDC [American welfare] rolls between 1981 and 1983 alone," Beckett and Western (2001: 44) report. Without welfare support, many families had their entire economic situation changed almost overnight. Second, the political program announced as the "war on drugs"—for some reason, the metaphor of war is a favourite metaphor in American political rhetoric, and over the years we have also witnessed the declaration of "war on poverty," "war on cancer," and "war on terrorism" by elected Presidents—led to an unprecedented expansion of criminal acts where, for example, petty crime (e.g., carrying marijuana) was increasingly treated as being on par with more severe criminality: "[T]he percentage of state prison inmates convicted of nonviolent drug offenses jumped from 6% in 1979 to nearly 30% in 1994" (Western and Beckett, 1999: 1037). Today, more than 1% of the American population is incarcerated, by far the highest rate in the world. "According to the Bureau of Justice Statistics (BJS), between 1980 and 1996, the number of people imprisoned in the United States grew by 300%, from 500.000 to 1.6 million," Western and Beckett (1999: 1034–1035) write. In the case of the United Kingdom, between 1993 and 2010, England and Wales's prison population "[n]early doubled, from 44,500 to around 85,000" (Jones, 2011: 214). The massive growth of the number of American prison inmates correlates very well with the enactment of neoliberal politico-economic policy:

> After more than fifty years of relative stability in our prison populations, the inmate population skyrocketed nationwide beginning in the early 1970s, rising from fewer than 200,000 persons to more than 1.3 million in 2002 . . . In 2008, the United States reached a new milestone: it incarcerated more than one percent of its adult population—the highest rate in the world, five times the rate in England and twelve times the rate of Japan, and the highest raw number in the world as well. (Harcourt, 2011: 198)

In addition, the new penal state had a strong ethnic bias, inasmuch as the male African American is highly overrepresented: "By 1994, one of every three black males between the ages of 18–34 was under some form of correctional supervision, and the number of Hispanic prisoners has more than quadrupled since 1980" (Beckett and Western, 2001: 43). The incarceration rate may be consistent with the neoliberal ethos of competition and self-reliance and underlying rational choice models (Becker, 1968), but it simultaneously violated the principle of the minimal state. In fact, the American penal system is today a quite costly activity:

> In the early 1990s, $91 billion were spent on courts, police, and prisons, dwarfing the $41 billion spent on unemployment benefits and employment related services . . . By 1996, 1.63 million people were

being detained in American prisons and jails—a threefold increase from 1980 . . . These figures suggest that incarceration generated a sizeable, nonmarket reallocation of labor, overshadowing state intervention through social policy. (Western and Beckett, 1999: 1031)

This is "a world in which a majority of Americans are worried about excessive regulation by the government, yet seemingly turn a blind eye to mass incarceration," Harcourt (2011: 43) remarks. Harcourt (2011: 41–42) continues: "Across the country, state legislatures are far more willing to spend dollars and to intervene in the penal sphere than they are in education or elsewhere, because that is where the government is perceived to have a legitimate and efficient role. That is where the government is, relatively speaking, believed to be competent." The explanation for this seemingly irrational and deeply problematic expansion of the penal state—a state that is not so much "for the people" as it "imprisons people"—is that it is "a *technique for the individualization of the social 'problems'* that the state, as the bureaucratic level of collective will, no longer can or cares to treat at its roots" (Wacquant, 2009: xxii; emphasis in the original). *Ipso facto*, Wacquant (2009: xxii) says, "[t]he prison operates as a juridical garbage disposal into which the human refuse of the market society are thrown." Harcourt (2011: 41) suggests that the expansion of the penal system serves to "naturalize the market": "By obscuring the rules and making the outcomes seem natural and deserved, neoliberal penalty makes it easier for certain market players to reorganize economic exchanges in such a way as to maximize their take, a move that ultimately increases social inequality; and there is strong evidence of sharp increased inequality in the United States since the 1970s." The increased economic inequality of the neoliberal era (to be examined below) tends to produce "[h]eightened punitive repression to maintain social order," Harcourt (2011: 42) says. Such claims are supported by the study of Western and Beckett (1999), which stresses the double effect of incarceration as both what is caused by social inequality (in Gary Becker's definition, criminality emerges as a rational choice when there are no employment opportunities, nor any welfare programs in place) and what is further reinforcing social inequality, as ex-convicts have a problem competing on the labour market. Beckett and Western (2001: 51) found a negative correlation between social welfare and incarceration rates in U.S. states, and conclude that "[i]n 1995, incarceration rates were significantly lower in states with generous systems of social welfare (and vice versa)." The effects of the reduction of social welfare programs were not fully visible until 1995. In addition, the African American population was not overtly discriminated by the juridical-penal system until the mid-1990s:

> The robust model provides evidence of a strong and significant positive effect of the black population on incarceration in 1995 . . . These robust results show that the effect of the African-American population

was positive but small in 1985 and essentially zero in 1975. In short, the association between race and incarceration has also grown substantially larger over the last three decades. (Beckett and Western, 2001: 52)

In addition, Beckett and Western (2001: 52) found differences between party lines in terms of incarceration rates in different states: "We also find that Republican Party representation in state legislature has a significant positive impact on incarceration." Beckett and Western (2001) conclude their study:

> [W]e conclude that the concentration of welfare programs aimed at the poor and the expansion of penal institutions in the 1980s and 1990s reflects the emergence of an alternative mode of governance that is replacing, to varying degrees, the modernist strategy based on rehabilitation and welfarism. Reduced welfare expenditures are not indicative of a shift toward reduced government intervention in social life (as is implied by the claim that welfare reform reflects the rise of 'neoliberalism'), but rather a shift toward a more exclusionary and punitive approach to the regulation of social marginality. (Beckett and Western, 2001: 55)

In summary, the lower unemployment vis-à-vis the European economies reported in the U.S. economic data, used as evidence of the superiority of the neoliberal policy, can in fact be explained by the incarceration rate (Western and Beckett, 1999). Redefining the role of the neoliberal state from a welfare state to a penal state, securing competition, and penalizing the pauper and least competitive groups on the labour market, the state is still spending quite bit of money. Reagan's claim was that "government is not the solution, it is the problem," indicating a goal to reduce the role of government, but, in fact, his administration expanded the military sector and significantly increased budget deficits; similarly, the costs of the penal state are perhaps, as Harcourt (2011) suggests, what is simply overlooked by free market protagonists. Regardless of what explanations various groups would inscribe into the growth of the penal system, if the prison population of the United States could be co-located, it would be the fifth largest city of America, only slightly smaller than Houston, Texas.

Neoliberalism and the Sciences: The Case of Medical Neoliberalism

Medicalization denotes the process wherein diseases, medical disorders, or general medical conditions (e.g., alcoholism) become subject to medical therapies. For students of medicalization (Clarke et al., 2010; Conrad, 2007; DeGrandpre, 2006; Blech, 2006; Fishman, 2004; Healy, 2002), it is problematic when therapies are prescribed in cases in which there is no clear aetiology of the illness or where there is a low degree of what Lakoff (2006) calls *disease specificity* because that may indicate that the therapy is developed and advanced on basis of the financial interests of, for example, the pharmaceutical industry, rather than being justified on the basis of experimental medicine or clinical needs. The concept of medicalization indicates the triumph of finance over medicine; there are several scholars that speak about "medical neoliberalism" (and similar terms) to denote how, for example, the major multinational pharmaceutical industry and emerging industries such as biotechnology are embedded in a neoliberal program aimed at exploiting the financial potential of the life sciences and health care. Cooper (2008) stresses such a connection:

> What neoliberalism seeks to impose is not as much the generalized commodification of daily life—the reduction of the extraeconomic to the demands of exchange value—as its financiation. Its imperative is not so much the measurement of biological time as its incorporation into the nonmeasurable, achronological temporality of financial capital accumulation. (Cooper, 2008: 10)

In addition, Sunder Rajan (2012), explicitly drawing on Karl Marx's analysis of capital, points at the coproduction of life science and neoliberal policy:

> There are uncanny overlaps between the development of life-science epistemologies and the epistemologies of neoliberal economics since the early 1970s . . . This is not a relationship of cause and effect—the life sciences do not change because of neoliberalism, nor is neoliberalism a consequence of the biotechnology revolution. Rather, what one can trace is an emergent epistemic milieu in which both economics/capitalism and the life science/biotechnology are undergoing radical transformation and dealing with apparently similar types of problem-spaces (such as, for instance, the understanding and management of complex systems of risk) at similar moments in time, and often drawing on one another for metaphoric and epistemic sustenance. (Sunder Rajan, 2012: 7)

"[T]he fundamental nature of the market, its value systems and epistemologies, is itself shifting, in what might broadly be considered a 'neoliberal' direction," Sunder Rajan (2012: 7) contends. This shift in "value systems" and "epistemologies" occurs in many places and emerges through different procedures, both in terms of how biological matter, such as tissue, and renewable biological materials, such as blood or sperm, acquire certain economic value,[11] and also in terms of how demands for de-regulation are opening up new domains of the life sciences and the exploitation of biological matter. McAfee (2003), examining the introduction of genetically modified organisms (GMOs), stresses how neoliberal policies operate through what she refers to as "reductionist discursive practices"—that is, a "molecular-genetic reductionism," the reduction of analysis of the feasibility of, for example, new crops to a genetic and molecular level, and "economic reductionism," the idea that it is primarily economic considerations that justify the uses of new GMOs. In the neoliberal regime of thinking, the molecular-genetic image of biological systems fits nicely with a calculative and instrumental worldview, McAfee argues, and consequently she addresses the debate over GMOs as a "neoliberalism on the molecular scale." Also, Pitts-Taylor (2010: 636) makes a connection between neoliberal ideologies and the recent interest for what has been called *brain plasticity* or *neuroplasticity*, the "[c]apacity of the brain to modify itself in response to changes in its functioning or environment" (see also Rose and Abi-Rached, 2013; Abi-Rached and Rose, 2010; Changeux, 2004). Advances in neuroscience research enacting the brain as a ceaselessly adaptable and changing structure invite humans to conceive of themselves "neuronal subjects" (Pitts-Taylor, 2010: 639), subjects capable of executing full control over their own neurological capacities and fitness. The concern is, however, that this neoliberal image of the entrepreneurial self in the position to shape its own future is devoid of power. Pitts-Taylor writes:

> Plasticity is deployed to encourage us to see ourselves as neuronal subjects, and is linked to the continued enhancement of learning, intelligence, and mental performance, and to the avoidance of various risks associated with the brain, including mental underperformance, memory loss, and aging. While endorsing a view of the body/self which resists biological determinism, I find that the popular discourse on plasticity firmly situates the subject in a normative, neoliberal ethic of personal self-care and responsibility linked to modifying the body. (Pitts-Taylor, 2010: 639)

In Pitts-Taylor's view, a neoliberal regime, both encouraging and actively promoting "market-based health care policies" (Pitts-Taylor, 2010: 639), replaces an "an ethic of state care." One of the cornerstones of this new neoliberal regime is the emphasis on "individual responsibility":

> The ideal subject constructed here should see herself in biomedical terms and should relate to her body at the molecular level, taking on a regimen of practices to ensure her neuronal fitness . . . Overall, brain potentiality represents a competitive field in which one's willingness to let go of sameness, to constantly adapt, and to embrace a lifelong regimen of work on the self (and one's children) are the keys to individual success. (Pitts-Taylor, 2010: 644; see also Rose and Abi-Rached, 2013: 47–52)

The other side of the coin of the neoliberal regime and its emphasis on individual responsibilities and the freedom to choose is what John Abraham (2010) refers to as *consumerism* in the field of pharmaceuticals. "[C]onsumerism has an ideological dimension," Abraham (2010: 612) argues, "namely the discursive *appropriation* of the health needs of patients as the demands of consumers in a market." The problem is that when consumerism is the dominant doctrine for, for example, new drug development activities, there will be an increase of so-called "me-too drugs," imitations of therapies that have already proved to have a market and that have been appropriated by the health care sector. In a review of 3,100 new drugs developed, only 10% offered "moderate to significant therapeutic advance," Abraham (2010: 615) says, testifying to the ambition to exploit established therapeutic areas. At the same time, there is evidence of an increased medicalization, the increased consumption of drugs—Abraham (2010: 615) speaks of the "expansion in pharmaceuticalization"—that cannot be explained by what Abraham (2010: 615) calls "a growth in techno-scientific discoveries of therapeutically significant innovations that meet health needs."

One of the consequences of consumerist ideology is that large multinational pharmaceutical companies engage in copying existing commercial products but add very little to preexisting therapies, and another is that medical doctors are partly bypassed as the gatekeepers of medication. Consumer products advertised in the United States, for example, frequently instruct the viewers to "ask their doctors" about a certain therapy, giving unwarranted authority to the consumers. Best's (2012) study of the influence of "organized patient groups" on government spending is indicative of this shift from professional-based health care to a consumerism-based regime. While the U.S. Congress' decisions regarding which research projects to finance has historically been based on testimony by health institutions, in the 1980s and 1990s such practices declined substantially; by 2004, fewer than 7% of witnesses were from health institutions (Best, 2012: 791). Instead, "disease advocates" took their place, making up over 20% of witnesses by the 1990s. These disease advocates were regarded as legitimate actors and spokespersons by the members of the Congress as they "expressed an interest in the distribution of funding to diseases." Using data on 53 diseases over 19 years, Best (2012) found that these new lobbyist groups were very successful in influencing federal research funding. Their first accomplishment is that they managed to establish the data endpoint of mortality as the legitimate and widely accepted metric for assessing the demand for research. Since such metrics were based on official government statistics and "provided a simple and seemingly rational way to compare funding across diseases" (Best, 2012: 789), members of Congress liked and approved this shift in the policy-making procedure:

> In promoting mortality as a metric for commensuration and framing deserving patients as beneficiaries, advocates changed the rules of the competition for medical research funds . . . These cultural changes had concrete effects on the funding distribution, shifting money towards high-mortality diseases and away from stigmatized diseases. (Best, 2012: 795)

In the new regime of federal research funding, arguably embedded in the ethos of self-reliance widely endorsed in the neoliberal era, stigmatized diseases such as liver cancer and lung cancer, related to but not exclusively caused by alcohol consumption and smoking, were on the losing side, as research on these deadly diseases were receiving comparatively less than they should if mortality statistics were the only basis for resource allocation: "Stigmatized diseases received less funding in the new political climate . . . By 2006, lung cancer and liver cancer were receiving about $100 million and $35 million dollars less, respectively, than would have been expected based on how many people they killed" (Best, 2012: 793). In addition, Best found that, with the noteworthy exception of breast cancer, diseases in which women and black people were overrepresented received comparatively less funding than diseases in which white people and men were overrepresented (Best, 2012: 794). Best argues that the disease advocates were successful in asserting that diseases were relevant categories for distributing National Institute of Health (NIH) research funding, and in accomplishing such goals they managed to bypass the historical professional preference for funding transdisciplinary research:

> [A]dvocacy organizations do not create categories in a vacuum, and the move to hold the NIH accountable for funding to diseases reveals an unexpected relationship between advocacy and established disease categories. Patients mobilized around disease definitions and diagnoses provided by healthcare systems . . . They then created political pressure for the NIH to target research funding to these diseases, despite NIH officials' preference for funding research that might cross traditional disease boundaries. (Best, 2012: 794)

In this new regime of consumerism and medical neoliberalism, moving beyond the regime of professional jurisdiction regarding where to allocate research funding, "[a]dvocacy organizations can secure large benefits for their constituents," Best (2012: 794) concludes. In fact, "the most organized patients secured dramatic increases in research funding" (Best, 2012: 780). In the era of lobbying, skilled political advocacy apparently pays off very well.

Another effect of neoliberal, consumerist discourses is that health is redefined as *reduced risk* for a certain illness, leading to health as being an "infinite phenomenon" since for "for every risk you reduce or eliminate, you still have a 100 percent risk of dying from something else" (Dumit, 2012: 49). As a consequence, "the limit to health research is not, then, a realizable healthy body, but a risk-free body, which instigates a virtually infinite process" (Dumit, 2012: 49). If health is what constantly needs to be guarded and protected against the risks of living, health is also matter of consumerist strategies. Besides the consumerist effects, naturally of immediate benefit for major pharmaceutical companies, the new drug development practices of pharmaceutical companies are affected by this new regime of thinking, inasmuch as clinical trials, the very testing of the safety and efficacy of candidate drugs, are modified. In Dumit's (2012) view, clinical trials are not conducted so much to identify new therapies treating new diseases as they are a method to identify biomarkers that "define" the illness and, in turn, justify the therapy. Says Dumit (2012: 74): "Symptoms become commodities not because they are paid for, or even because they involve biomarkers, but because that is the only way to decide on illness." The biomarkers here play a key role in accomplishing disease specificity, a stable set of symptoms that can be associated with certain therapies. In Dumit's view, in the new consumerist era of medicalization, the aggregate of biomarker-diagnosis-therapy is anchored in calculative practices where the size and worth of certain therapeutic areas are calculated:

> [O]nce disease comes to be defined as on a continuum with health, the only meaningful diagnosis is that which indicates treatment. Treatment therefore equates with diagnosis, and the market indicated by a diagnostic threshold is both a measure of profit and the very definition of 'health.' (Dumit, 2012: 68)

As Bartfai and Lees (2006, cited in Dumit, 2012: 66) point out, "[o]f the 400 disease entities identified, only 40 are commercially attractive by today's requirements of return on investment." That means that only every tenth disease is worthy of further attention when applying a calculative mode of thinking. In Dumit's view, drawing on the writings of Marx and his ambition to understand and reveal the operations of capital, it is paradoxical that clinical trials that would be an amazing way to increase the healthiness of the population, instead lead to a situation where we in fact spend considerably *more* time, energy, money, and effort concerned about health (Dumit, 2012: 65).

In order to support such a shift in focus, benefitting the bottom line results of pharmaceutical companies while basically ignoring a number of illnesses that kill hundreds of thousands annually, especially in the poorer countries, the very regulatory frameworks that monitor and oversee new drug development have been modified to comply with such economic interests:

> [N]eoliberalism as a political movement and ideology has redefined the regulatory state to have much greater convergence of interests and goals with the drug industry than previously, particularly regarding acceleration and cost reduction of drug development and regulatory review. (Abraham and Ballinger, 2012: 445)

Examining the specific case of a less time consuming and cheaper alternative to carcinogenicity testing systems, Abraham and Ballinger (2012: 445) suggest that the results and outcomes were influenced by "the commercial interest of the pharmaceutical industry." The gold standard for clinical testing has been robust evidence based on statistical significance—in itself a tricky term (see Ziliac and McCloskey, 2008)—but recently, the regulatory demands have been negotiated by the International Conference on Harmonisation of Technical Requirements for Registration of Pharmaceuticals for Human Use (ICH) so that "standards for drug judgments are not 'technical' in the sense of being divorced from political judgments and social interests" (Abraham and Reed, 2002: 360). In other words, professional standards have been compromised by the commercial interest of the industry. The carcinogenicity testing systems, based on "knock-out mice"—mice whose genome have been modified to short-circuit certain protein translation processes—have provided "satisfying evidence," but as one researcher remarked (cited in Abraham and Ballinger, 2012: 465): "'Experimental evidence shows that [non-genotoxic] cancer is often secondary to some other biological effects' not reducible to genetic make-up." That is, by only examining one type of specimen, a genetically modified laboratory animal, synchronically, one cannot account for all the diachronic and wider effects that the environment has on the type of specimen that are relevant to the study of cancer. Only by studying the laboratory mice over longer periods of time and by applying a wider set of research methods can one understand the aetiology of certain forms of cancer. Abraham and Ballinger summarize:

> [S]hort-term mouse models pose small risks to the commercial interests of pharmaceutical firms, but provided little reassurance that they would not permit patients to be exposed to greater risks than before from undetected carcinogens that find their way to clinical trials or the market. (2012: 468)

The new, less time- and energy-consuming testing procedure, an infrastructural component in the new drug development procedure, thus benefits the pharmaceutical industry's ambition to increase the return on investment, but it essentially fails to ensure that therapies developed on basis of the model take into account the "secondary factors" that may lead to cancer. In Abraham and Ballinger's (2012) argument, neoliberal thinking and its emphasis on competition and the benefits of market-based transactions has managed to penetrate the domain of clinical trials, opening them up for less rigorous and robust research methods. Medical neoliberalism thus operates throughout the entire spectrum, from disciplining patients to think of themselves as consumers and "neurological subjects" to negotiating the "upstream activities" of clinical trials in order to enable new, faster drug development practices. In medical neoliberalism, life and capital are co-produced, as "[l]ife is increasingly appropriated (or at least appropriable) by capital" (Sunder Rajan, 2012: 9; see also Mirowski, 2011, on the "privatization of science" more broadly).

III. THE CONSEQUENCES OF NEOLIBERALISM

Introduction

The neoliberal politico-economic regime has undoubtedly led to a number of deep-seated changes in how Western economies and societies are governed and how the economy is regulated. New institutions have been established, and many ideas of central importance to the welfare state and the "embedded liberalism" of the post-World-War II era through the early 1970s have been fiercely criticized or silently abandoned. Since neoliberal doctrines emphasize economic freedom in order to accomplish the highest possible amount of economic growth, it is quite important to investigate whether the recipes prescribed by neoliberal protagonists have led to economic growth and prosperity that justifies the deconstruction of many welfare state institutions and practices. There are basically two key performance indicators to examine: first, how the income and economic resources are distributed in a population, and second, how big this shared pie is. The former issue is essentially a political matter rooted in taxation and economic transfer systems (e.g., social security programs). The issue of economic growth is a more complex matter, being both based on economic policies and political initiatives, such as the investment in tertiary education, investment in infrastructure, and similar areas that drive economic growth. In the following sections, these two issues will be addressed.

Changes in Income Distribution

Duménil and Lévy (2004) demonstrate that the era of neoliberal governance (1979–) has been a period where economic inequalities have been restored and returned to 1930s levels (see Table 15.6, p. 139; for more recent data, see Zalewski and Whalen, 2010; Quiggin, 2010: 154, Fig. 4.2). The "portion of assets held by the richest one percent of households" has grown significantly since 1980. In the 1980s, the period in which neoliberal policies were widely endorsed, inequality was reduced in one country (Italy), remained the same in eight, and increased in ten countries studied (Duménil and Lévy, 2004: 37). Palma (2009: 841) reports that, in the case of the United States, "in real income terms (i.e., US$ at 2006 values) the average annual income of the bottom 90% actually fell during the 33-years period between the 1973 oil crisis and 2006 (from US$31,300 to US$30,700). Meanwhile, that of the top 1% increased *3.2-fold* (from US$286 thousands to US$1.2 million)." These structural advantages of the top 1% of income earners also seem to have grown over time:

> [D]uring the seven-year period of economic expansion of the Clinton administration the top 1% of income earners captured 45% of the total growth in (pre-tax) income, while during Bush's four-year period of

expansion no less than 73% of total income growth accrued to the top 1%. (Palma, 2009: 842; emphasis in the original)

In the 28-year period between 1978 and 2006, average income for about 20 million American families remained "roughly stagnant," while the average of the top 0.01% increased 8.5 times (Palma, 2009: 842). In the case of the United Kingdom, the other centre of neoliberal policy, a similar tendency is observable: "The top 1% own 38% of total wealth; the top 10% owns 85% of all publically traded stocks," Dore (2008: 1107) reports. In certain professions, return on human capital investment—to use Gary Becker's rational choice theory vocabulary—has been quite favourable:

> A recent British report (Institute of Fiscal Studies) found that the top 0.1% of taxpayer (average income £478,00 = 600,000 Euro), 80% of their income was labour income—as bankers, fund managers, accountants, lawyers, etc. On top of such annual incomes, they had already accumulated enough to get capital incomes four to five times the average annual salary. The accumulation of wealth at the top is increasingly a function of growing inequality of 'labour' incomes rather than inherited money. (Dore, 2008: 1107)

In contrast to these "bankers, fund managers, accountants, and lawyers," traditional blue-collar jobs in manufacturing that were reasonably well paid and relatively secure have been replaced by a growth in service sector jobs that have been less well paid: "According to 2008 figures, half of all service sector workers were on less than £20,000 a year. But the median in manufacturing was £24,343, or nearly a quarter more," Jones (2011: 151) writes. Many jobs, such as female hairdressers—an occupation held by no less than 170,000 women in the United Kingdom today—are paid as little as £12,000 annually. Piketty and Saez (2003) provide a time-series analysis of after-tax income in the United States for the period 1913–1998, and demonstrate that during both world wars, changes in income tax increased and thus served to reduce economic inequality. After 1970, economic inequality began to grow and to return to the levels of the early twentieth century: "In 1915 the top 0.01 percent earned 400 times more than the average; in 1970 the average top 0.01 percent income was 'only' 50 times the average; in 1998 they earned about 250 times the average income" (Piketty and Saez, 2003: 13). Piketty and Saez's (2003) analysis also shows that there are, in fact, large differences between the highest income groups in terms of how they earn their money:

> [I]ndividuals in fractiles P90–95 and P95–99 rely mostly on labor income (capital income is less than 25 percent for these people), while individuals in the top percentile derive most of their income in the form of capital income... This evidence confirms that the very large decrease

of top income observed during the 1914 to 1945 was to a large extent a capital income phenomena. (Piketty and Saez, 2003: 17)

Shifts in income structure in the American economy after 1970 and especially after 1980 cannot, Piketty and Saez (2003: 34) suggest, "be the sole consequence of technical change" for two reasons: First, the increase in income is very high in the highest income earners and a more even distribution of income could have been expected in cases of technological change and/or other changes in production factors. Second, "such a large change in top wage shares has not taken place in most European countries which experienced the same technical change as the United States [did]" (Piketty and Saez, 2003: 34). Instead, it is policy and taxation that makes the difference between the different periods and the different income groups: "Our results suggest that the decline in income tax progressively since the 1980s and the projected repeal of the estate tax might again produce in a few decades levels of wealth concentration similar to those at the beginning of the century," Piketty and Saez (2003: 24) suggest. They continue:

> From 1986 to 1988 the top shares of earners increased sharply, especially at the very top (for example, the top 1 percent share jumps from 7.5 percent to 9.5 percent). This sharp increase was documented by Feenberg and Poterba [1993] and is certainly attributable at least in part to fiscal manipulation following the large top marginal tax rate cuts of the Tax Reform Act of 1986. (Piketty and Saez, 2003: 31)

Thus, with President Reagan in the White House, new policies rewarded the highest income groups. Speaking more broadly about the Organisation for Economic Co-operation and Development (OECD) countries, Epstein and Jayadev (2005: 47) claim they have "[s]ubstantial evidence that the personal income distribution has become more highly skewed in the US and OECD countries in the last several decades." At the same time, Alderson and Nielsen (2002: 1248) report from the study of 16 OECD countries that in 10 of these countries economic inequality grew in the 1967–1992 period. Alderson and Nielsen (2002: 1272) found, contrary to neoliberal pundits' argumentation, "only modest evidence" in support of the idea that "increasing inequality is an inherent feature of postindustrial development." "Clearly," Alderson and Nielsen (2002: 1272) suggest, "the inequality experience of the advanced industrial countries in recent decades has been shaped by more than processes of economic development alone." Kelly and Enns (2010: 856) share this view: "While former treasury secretary Henry Paulson and many other economists have attributed economic inequality to market forces that are beyond the control of government and the political parties . . . the idea that government cannot effectively redress economic inequality simply does not ring true compared to empirical reality" (Kelly and Enns, 2010: 856). More specifically, growing economic inequality in the neoliberal era is better explained by the growing direct investment overseas that accelerates de-industrialization and reduces employment opportunities for lower income groups, "weakening the bargaining position of labor," and a change in distribution from labour to capital (Alderson and Nielsen, 2002: 1261). All these effects are based on policy rather than technological changes or other forms of liberalization of trade.

Several studies emphasize the role of policy as what propels economic inequality. Volscho and Kelly (2012: 693) examine the emergence of what they refer to as the "super-rich" in the American economy and identify key explanatory factors, all related to policy and politics, including "congressional shifts to the Republican Party, diminishing union membership, lower top tax rates, and financial asset bubbles." In Volscho and Kelly's (2012) view, economic inequality is the effect of political decisions, rather than the effects of inevitable economic conditions:

> [I]nequality is in part an outcome of political contestation. A common refrain holds that inequality has risen substantially but is merely the result of natural market forces that are in large part out of our control. By this logic, policy and partisan politics are unimportant players in rising inequality. But the evidence does not support this idea. Both specific policies and the partisan balance of Congress are associated with distributional outcomes. Conservative shifts in policy and Republican strength in Congress are associated with higher levels of inequality. Political outcomes have implications for distributional outcomes. (Volscho and Kelly, 2012: 693)

As Piketty and Saez (2003) emphasize, the highest income groups make higher proportions of their earnings from capital rents, and, consequently, the substantial growth of the finance industry explains part of the growth in income inequality, in addition to lower income tax for the richest:

> Financialization of the economy has also played a significant role in the rise of the top 1 percent. We found that stock and home prices had substantial effects on the super-rich. Because the rich receive substantial income from dividend payouts and capital gains from stock trading, it is not surprising that stock prices appear to have helped concentrate income. Similarly, the wave of mortgage backed securities rooted in mortgages derived from rising home prices appears to have contributed to income concentration. (Volscho and Kelly, 2012: 694)

Hacker and Pierson (2010: 154) address what they call the American "winner-takes-all inequality," and point at "fundamental shifts" in "four core areas" of U.S. policy related to financial markets, corporate governance, industrial relations, and taxation. "That income inequality has grown substantially over the past thirty years is no longer in dispute,"

Hacker and Pierson (2010: 155) say, but they add that "[t]he growing share of national income captured by the richest of Americans is a long-term that does not appear to be related to either the business cycle or the shifting partisan occupation of the White House" (Hacker and Pierson, 2010: 156). Apparently, there are deep-seated substantial changes in American policy and the American economy that drive the growth of economic inequality. Between 1980 and 2003, the Gini index—the generally accepted measure of inequality—of the United States "fell substantially" (i.e., inequality grew) (Hacker and Pierson, 2010: 164), but there were little concern for this in policy-making quarters. "[T]hese striking winner-takes-all outcomes are of surprisingly recent vintage and reflect not only longstanding features of the U.S. politics and public policy, but also of substantial changes in policy that reflect equally substantial changes in the landscape of American politics," Hacker and Pierson (2010: 168) argue. In addition, contrary to the Reagan administration economic advisors' claims, "[f]ew of the benefits of economic growth at the top between 1979 and 2005 trickled down" (Hacker and Pierson, 2010: 157).

In explaining the growth of economic inequality, the new "winner-takes-all-policy," Hacker and Pierson (2010) point at two principal policy changes: the shift in taxation and the reduced bargaining power of unions (and the weakening of the labour movement more broadly). For Hacker and Pierson (2010: 182), "taxes represent perhaps the most viable way in which policy makers influence the distribution of income." Beginning with Reagan taking office, taxation has been modified to benefit the richest:

> The changes of the tax rate for those at the ninetieth percentile, and even the ninety-eighth percentile, have actually been quite modest over the last four decades. By contrast, there has been startlingly large change for those in the top 1 percent. This is mostly because of the declining role of the corporate income tax and the estate tax. *Progressively used to be very pronounced at the very top of the tax code; now it is almost entirely absent.* (Hacker and Pierson, 2010: 183; emphasis in the original)

In addition, the structure of American industrial relations has changed over the last three decades, and union density is significantly lower (Lichtenstein, 2003). The trade unions once organized roughly one-third of the American workforce, but today they represent merely one in ten workers in the private sector (Hacker and Pierson, 2010: 186). Since unions have historically served the role to counteract economic inequality by emphasizing the importance of low income distribution and the role of taxation and economic transfers in avoiding growing economic inequality (Brady, Baker, and Finnigan, 2013), one of the consequences of lowered union density is that "wage inequality is greater in the lower half of the income distribution in the United States than it is in any other affluent democracy" (Hacker and

Pierson, 2010: 186). When the U.S. Congress wanted to lower the estate tax, the biggest organized opposition did not come from the unions or the labour movement, but from a group of billionaires led by William Gates Sr. (Microsoft founder Bill Gates' father), testifying to the marginal role played by the unions in American industrial relations in the neoliberal era (Hacker and Pierson, 2010: 187). Hacker and Pierson (2010) conclude their argument by claiming that growing economic inequality is an effect of policy—not economic conditions or technological and scientific shifts: "Policy—both as what government has done and what, as a result of drift, it has failed to do—has played an absolutely central role in the rise of winner-takes-all economic outcomes ... A winner-takes-all politics accompanied, and helped produce a winner-takes-all economy" (Hacker and Pierson, 2010: 196).

The concern is that inequality is a self-reinforcing phenomenon—that is, groups losing their economic security tend to become more conservative: "[E]conomic inequality may be self-reinforcing, with economic inequality generating political inequalities that prevent the poor from using the democratic process to push for government action that would increase their well-being and reduce economic inequality" (Kelly and Enns, 2010: 855). Kelly and Enns (2010: 857) show, perhaps not entirely surprisingly, that Republican presidents increase inequality in the United States, but also, that policy is "much more likely to shift" when "the rich support a change than when the poor are supportive of a change" (Kelly and Enns, 2010: 857). That is, Congress more easily responds favourably to policies supported by the rich. More surprising, Kelly and Enns (2010: 859) found that "[b]oth the rich and the poor respond to rising inequality by shifting in a conservative direction": "[W]hen inequality rises, the public shows less support for welfare spending," Kelly and Enns (2010: 865) say. In other words, economic inequality leads to political and social inequality—first, because lower income groups have difficulty influencing the policy-making process, and second, because they tend to become more conservative themselves. Inequality becomes self-reinforcing.

The Increase in Debt

In addition to the increased and significant economic inequalities, household debt has risen substantially during the neoliberal period. In the United States, the average household debt was around $40,000 (in constant dollars) in 1980, while in 2010 it was close to $130,000 for every household (Harvey, 2010: 17).[12] "Seventy percent of US economic activity depends on consumerism," Harvey (2010: 107) remarks. In the United Kingdom, similar figures can be reported:

> In 1980 the ratio between debt and income was 45. By 1997 it had doubled, before reaching an astonishing 157.4 on the eve of the credit crunch in 2007. As people's purchasing power slowed, more and more

credit was splashed out on consumer goods. Between 2000 and 2007, consumers spent £55 billion more than their pay packets, courtesy of the plastic in their wallet or hefty bank loans. (Jones, 2011: 158)

The inflow of capital and the expansion of capital markets in the neoliberal era, especially in the United States and the United Kingdom, will be discussed in greater detail in Chapter Two of this volume. Regardless of such a favourable position, the Reagan administration rapidly expanded federal debt. In the period after 1948, there were only three years where budget deficits exceeded 3.0% of average GDP. To finance regressive tax cuts and increase government spending on, for example, armed defence, the Reagan administration had average budget deficits at 5.9% of GDP (Crotty, 2012: 85). When Reagan left office in 1988, the debt-to-GDP ratio had risen from 26% after the Carter presidency to 41%—an increase of almost 61%—and during the presidency of George Bush Sr. it continued to rise to 48.1%, almost double what it had been in 1981. During the Clinton presidency the debt-to-GDP ratio was temporarily lowered, until the tax reform of George W. Bush that, Crotty (2012: 85) says, "haemorrhaged trillions of dollars of government revenue" and was calculated to cost "$5.4 trillion over a decade" (Crotty, 2012: 98). In addition, Bush Jr. started wars in Iraq and Afghanistan that have cost, Crotty (2012: 85) claims, "at least $1.4 trillion to date." Under the Bush Jr. presidency, debt-to-GDP ratio grew from 32.5% to 40.3%. "The oft-heard claim that Republicans are fiscal conservatives is utterly inconsistent with the historical record," Crotty (2012: 89) contends. This federal spending was not benefitting the poor or the middle class, but was used to finance tax cuts for corporations and the highest income groups (Crotty, 2012: 84). In fact, in 2010, "25 of the 100 highest paid US Chief Executive Officers earned more than their companies paid in federal taxes," Crotty (2012: 93) reports. In 2009, when Barack Obama took office and inherited Bush's substantial tax cut programs and two ongoing wars, neither of which could be de-escalated nor stopped at short notice, the federal debt-to-GDP ratio was 53.5%. In 2010, it was 62.5% (Crotty, 2012: 90).

Taken together, neoliberal policies have served to restore economic inequality to 1930s levels and have served to increase the income distribution. As an effect of capital accumulation, household debt and national debt have increased significantly—not in themselves major concerns in periods of economic growth, but more worrisome when the economy slows down.

Declining Economic Growth

Economic freedom (effectively operationalized into competition between actors and agents) and market-based economic transactions are the axial principles of neoliberal economic policy. Much of the critique of the regime of embedded liberalism and the Keynesian economic regime articulated by neoliberal protagonists emphasized the slow or stagnating growth in the

1970s. Growth and economic prosperity prior to 1970 was more or less indisputable, but as the 1970s arrived, the Bretton Woods currency regulation regime collapsed, and oil crises and general social turmoil made the 1970s a dark decade, economically speaking. Cohen and Centeno (2006) examine the effects of neoliberal policies over the three last decades and report a few unexpected findings. First, despite the efforts of the IMF, the World Bank, and especially the World Trade Organization, Cohen and Centeno (2006: 48) only "discern a slight increase in trade over the neoliberal period," a growth in international trade that is more likely to be explained by "exogenous factors": "Given such a slow rate of increase, one might well argue that the shifts have less to do with the widespread liberalism than with exogenous factors, such as advances in telecommunications technology, improvements in transportation infrastructure, or the accumulation by multinational firms" (Cohen and Centeno, 2006: 48). In contrast, Cohen and Centeno (2006: 52) found a "clear evidence" of an increased mobility of "foreign direct investment during the last decades of the twentieth century." That is, neoliberal policies have served to expand the basis for capital investment. In addition, despite the strong argument in favour of deregulated labour markets in neoliberal discourses, Cohen and Centeno (2006: 59) did not find any evidence of a "[s]ubstantial, sustainable reduction in unemployment over the neoliberal period." Perhaps even more surprising, they did not find any reduction of government budgets or a decline in government payments for "distributive programs" (Cohen and Centeno, 2006: 41). By and large, the role of government has remained the same size throughout these years of social change. Still, the ultimate test for the efficacy of the neoliberal programs advocated by economists and policy makers is its ability to accomplish economic growth. That has not been the case, Cohen and Centeno (2006: 53) conclude: "Post-1980 growth has been inferior to growth during the period 1945 to 1975 in most areas of the world, except, of course, for the emerging markets of Asia." Empirical evidence provides no support for the neoliberal model of reducing the influence of trade unions and de-regulating markets, in terms of economic growth and prosperity. Real GDP, adjusted for purchasing power parity, increased by 61.5 percent between 1979 and 2005 in the United States in the EU fifteen (Austria, Belgium, Denmark, Finland, France, Germany, Greece, Ireland, Italy, Luxembourg, the Netherlands, Portugal, Spain, Sweden, and the United Kingdom) (Hacker and Pierson, 2010: 198, note 7). The U.S. economic model did not work better than the EU fifteen average. In addition, there were higher inflation and unemployment in what Gordon (1996: 163, Figure 6.4) refers to as "conflictual economies" (e.g., U.S., U.K., Canada) than in the "cooperative economies" (e.g., Sweden, Japan, and Germany). The frequently made claim in neoliberal and neoconservative circles that the trade unions and the labour movement pursued excessive compensation claims during the 1970s also seems unsupported by empirical evidence, as it overlooked the need for investment to maintain competitive advantages:

Between 1973 and 1989, Japanese manufacturing wages grew 8 times those of the United States, without Japanese industry losing competiveness (Gordon, 1996: 29).

Speaking about the more general case of Thatcherist Britain and the supply-side economics policy Thatcher strongly believed in, Healey (1992) examines the effects on economic growth (see also Vogel, 1996: 65–134). The Thatcherist agenda is well-known, but deserves to be revisited to recall its comprehensive changes: "Over the following eleven years [after 1979], her administration privatized public enterprises, overhauled British tax and social security systems and injected competition back into markets, long ossified by regulations and state control," Healey (1992: 7) writes. Thatcher's accomplishments are indisputable in terms of the radical shift in politics and economic policy: "From being synonymous with socialism, labor union militancy, and the welfare state in the 1970s, Britain had become an international symbol of aggressive, free market capitalism, by the end of the Thatcher era" (Healey, 1992: 9). While Thatcher is commonly held in esteem in neoliberal and neoconservative quarters for this shift in policy, the long-term effect of her regime is more dubious, Healey argues:

> The improvement in productivity growth between 1982–90 was undoubtedly genuine, although it appears to have been as much due to the salutary effect of the savage labor shakeout during the 1979–1982 recession—which saw employment double from 6% to 12%, so breaking the will of unions to resist change—as to the restrictive union legislation passed by the Thatcher government. But these productivity gains have been almost wholly due to the intensification of work effort and the abolition of restrictive labor practices and there is little evidence that companies have underpinned these advances with new investment. (Healey, 1992: 10)

This "intensification of work" is perhaps not so much a matter of economic growth based on free competition and an increase in human capital and the production of new know-how as it is the outcome from the political struggle aimed to reduce the trade unions' power:

> A series of employment acts was introduced, which severely limited the power of organized labor to pursue industrial action and several large unions had their assets 'sequestrated' (ie seized) for failing to comply with the new codes of conduct. Partly as a result of the new legislative environment, union density fell sharply from the peak of 58% reached at the end of the 1970s to 45% by 1990. (Healey, 1992: 9)

In addition to the effects of labour intensification, Britain enjoyed considerable economic benefits of North Sea oil and innovations in information technology in the period (Healey, 1992: 8). Besides these short-term economic wins and the effects of exogenous factors, Healey (1992) is concerned about the long-term competitiveness of the British economy. In Thatcher's Britain there was lower investment in R&D, lower investment in physical capital, and lower human capital investment than in comparative countries such as France, the United States, Germany, and Japan. First, "[t]he proportion of GNP devoted to total R&D is somewhat lower in Britain than in the United States, Germany and Japan" (Healey 1992: 11). Second,

> Investment in physical capital was also disappointingly low in the 1980s. Overall the capital stock in Britain rose by only 2% pa [per annum] in real terms between 1979–88 ... net real investment in banking, finance and business services rattled along at a healthy 8.2% pa, while in manufacturing it stagnated at a mere 1.5% and actually fell by 2% in the transport sector. (Healey, 1992: 11)

Third, and finally, despite the efforts of the Thatcher government to reform industrial training programs, the proportions of manufacturing workers in training fell "sharply during the 1980s"—"from 4.5% in 1979 to 2.1% in 1988 for males and from 2.4% to 1.1% for females" (Healey, 1992: 11). Also in the higher organization tiers, the United Kingdom was disfavoured vis-à-vis comparable countries: In the United Kingdom, 24% of the top managers had a degree. In the United States, 85%; in Japan, 85%; in Germany, 62%; and in France, 65% (Healey, 1992: 11, Table 4, Column 2). Taken together, Healey claims it is reasonable to believe that despite evidence of economic growth in the early 1980s, the Thatcher government and the supply-side economic policy have not been able to produce a situation in which sufficient investment can ensure future growth.[13]

Neoliberal policy has led to a sharp growth in economic inequality; an increased stock of federal, state, and household debt; and to no substantial economic growth or decline in unemployment. In other words, many of the arguments in favour of economic freedom as the motor for economic growth and prosperity have failed to accomplish the outcomes that have been promised. However, what neoliberal policy has accomplished is to restore class power through uneven income distribution, a significant reduction of trade union influence on policy, and (in the case of the United States) a sharp growth of the incarceration rate, on the basis of an ethic of self-reliance in combination with cutting back welfare benefit programs and promoting the war on drugs policy. In other words, more than perhaps anything else, neoliberal policy has emerged as a political agenda serving to advance and secure the interest of a rent-seeking capital-owning class.[14] At the same time, it would be a functionalist explanation to claim that this neoliberal policy has been pursued because "it was useful for capital" (Palma, 2009: 839). Rather than succumbing to conspiracy theories, the neoliberal policy has been pursued by a variety of actors—whereof only very small proportion are likely to have been the libertarian, Chicago-style free-market economists being stereotyped as the representative advocates of a neoliberal agenda—in their own ways conceiving of the neoliberal program as having something to offer them in their own attempts to handle pressing social and economic problems. In other words, neoliberal policy (and its effects) is not to be "unmasked" and brought into the broad daylight as much as it is a set of propositions that needs to be discussed and critically examined.

Concluding Remarks

The great accomplishment of neoliberal thinkers, theorists, and activists has been the ability to organize themselves, beginning in the academy, and gradually advance their positions through aligning them with various interests and groups willing to share their commitment to market freedom and capital accumulation. As economic historian Philip Mirowski (2005) notes in an interview, the neoliberal vocabulary has gradually managed to penetrate and become taken for granted in both economic theory and in political discourses (see also George, 2013; Smith, 2007):

> Q: So neoliberalism prevails?
> A: It seems so. It becomes so natural that people don't even realize that they frame problems in these terms. I know lots of economists who think of themselves as opposed to the Chicago school, or what it used to stand for. Yet I do not think they realize the extent to which their presumptions about what a human being is, what thought is, and what the market consists of have been defined by neoliberal traditions over the past fifty years. (Mirowski, 2005: 93–94)

While many have considered some of the assumptions made in neoclassical economics and in praise of market efficiency in neoliberal rhetoric as being not very credible—or likely to comply with neither common sense nor empirical evidence, some of its underlying axial principles regarding competition, the need for enterprising individuals, and some of the ideas regarding "rational choices" have apparently struck a chord in many various settings and communities. Neoliberalism has consequently been widely embraced across a wide political spectrum, and social democrat and socialist governments and politicians are frequently endorsing neoliberal policies simply because they seem to be the only alternative at hand. In a way, we are all neoliberals now, and the question is how to fine-tune the politico-economic system of the contemporary regime of capital accumulation.

NOTES

1. The fact that Margaret Thatcher was the first female British Prime Minister has naturally acquired significant attention and comments. Thatcher is

also one of very few women featuring in the literature on neoliberalism (the Russian-born author and libertarian cult-figure Ayn Rand and Milton Friedman's wife Rose Friedman, sister to Friedman's colleague Aaron Director, are the two other cases of females found in this corpus.) Since women tend to earn less than men and are to a higher extent working in public sector organizations (e.g., in education and health care), the neoliberalism program proposing tax cuts and a reduction of government spending generally do not benefit women. However, Thatcher was not exactly renowned for her feminist politics. The British author Martin Amis accounts for this absence of solidarity with other women: "She [Thatcher] has never expressed any admiration for the women's movement or shown any concerns for women's rights. Far from it, 'I hate the those strident tones we hear from some of the women's libbers' [Thatcher remarked]. . . . When the Yorkshire Ripper [a serial killer] was at his most active in 1980, Mrs. T. [Thatcher] told the home secretary that she was going to Leeds to take charge of the investigations. This ridiculous proposal was until then her only gesture of female solidarity" (Amis, 2002: 22).

2. This passage from Hayek's later works can be cited at length as it effectively captures the attitude towards labour movements, the fear of what neoliberal and neoconservative intellectuals referred to as *collectivism*, and the accompanying praise of enterprising individualism in the neoliberal era: "What is not generally recognized is that the real exploiters in our present society are not egoistic capitalists or entrepreneurs, and in fact not separated individuals, but organizations which derive their power from the moral support of collective action and the feeling of group loyalty. It is the built-in bias of our existing institutions in favour of organized interests which gives these organizations an artificial preponderance over market forces and which is the main cause of real injustice in our society and of distortion of its economic structure. More real injustice is probably done in the name of group loyalty than from any selfish individual motives" (Hayek, 1979: 96).

3. "Later statistical analysis did not bear out Friedman's claim that inflation was always a monetary matter. The economist Alan Blinder showed that changes in money did not nearly correlate well with rising inflation in the 1970s," Madrick (2011: 48–49) writes.

4. In the U.K., Mrs. Thatcher made similar antistatist declarations, saying she would be "rolling back the frontiers of the state" (cited in Peck, 2010: xv).

5. For instance, studies show that conservative voters have demonstrated a declining trust in the sciences over the 1974–2010 period. "Conservatives' trust in science clearly declined over the period: they begin the period with the highest levels of trust and end with the lowest," Gauchat (2012: 174) reports. Rather than trusting experimental science and systematic inquiry, "[c]onservatives were far more likely to define science as knowledge that should conform to common sense and religious traditions" (Gauchat, 2012: 183). Given the general distrust of "liberal elites" and cosmopolitan worldview (a pillar of all scientific research) among conservative groups, such findings are perhaps not surprising.

6. Statements like, "Extremism in the defense of liberty is no vice," (cited in Troy, 2009: 22) did not help to fashion an appealing public image of Senator Goldwater, but his neoconservatist program was taken over by the rising star Ronald Reagan, trained in showmanship and public communication and less concerned with facts and dull statistics, like so many of his competitors, and more inclined to rely on what Troy (2009: 78) speaks of as "warm fuzzy image-making." Faludi (2000) describes Reagan as the first "postmodern" president, as he was more prone to engage in patriotic storytelling about the

greatness of the American Republic than to discuss the nitty-gritty details of his politics.
7. The work of Adam Smith is one of the favourite references in neoliberal thinking, and his legacy has been, Jones (2012: 115) suggests, "used and abused," not only by Friedman and other neoliberal intellectuals, but also by politicians such as Margaret Thatcher in constructing a neoliberal mythology: "A myth of eternal verities first articulated by Smith, restated by the classical liberal and English politician John Stuart Mill (though only in *On Liberty*), rediscovered and understood by Hayek, and adapted by Friedman, was propagated. The myth was mutually reinforcing. It helped convey an impression of philosophical depth on the part of the politicians, and it flattered the intellectual egos of neoliberal academics, who claimed Smith, making them feel politically important and part of a rich canon" (Jones, 2012: 115). This *Schwärmerei* for Smith was accompanied, Madrick (2011) suggests, by piecemeal and highly selective uses of citations from his texts.
8. One of the major events of the disaster-ridden presidency of George W. Bush was when the hurricane Katrina broke the levees in New Orleans in Louisiana, demonstrating in broad daylight the failure of the both the Federal authorities to cope with the situation and the incompetence and ignorance of the Bush administration, which was only modestly concerned about the event. When Republican politicians and neoliberal think tanks wanted to handle the post-Katrina restoration by transforming the Gulf Region and the already poor city of New Orleans into what Democratic senator John Kerry would call "a vast laboratory for right-wing ideological experiment . . . recycling all [the conservatives'] failed policies and shipping them to Louisiana," the Heritage Foundation, a pro-free market, neoliberal institution, immediately responded that "the root causes of the problems facing the region were those Great Society programs of welfare, housing, education, and job training, which in effect rendered the poor defenseless" (Peck, 2010: 166). In other words, *too much* government spending and initiatives—rather than the more plausible, diametrically opposed interpretation, that *too little* government spending explained the emergent situation—was put forth as a credible explanation of the situation. The Heritage Foundation thus used one of the most spectacular and embarrassing failures of post-World War II American politics to advance their agenda of discrediting the welfare state.
9. Such a rational choice model has also been advanced to explain criminality. "Some persons become 'criminals,'" Becker (1968: 178) proposes, "not because their basic motivation differs from that of other persons, but because their benefits and costs differ." In other words, criminality and the state's responses should be understood not so much as the effect of policy and social welfare spending but as a process strictly regulated by economic functions. Becker suggests: "Whether crime pays is then an implication of the attitudes offenders have toward risk and is not directly related to the efficiency of the police or the amount spent on combatting crime" (Becker, 1968: 179). Based on such calculative practices and modelling of individual choices on basis of rational choice theory, Becker claimed the Nobel Prize in economic sciences (not in "economics," as is at times claimed, as there is no such prize) in 1992.
10. In general, cities and city management (unquestionably a most conspicuous contemporary term) have been influenced by neoliberal thinking. Urban centres have always been sites where capital accumulates and trade is located, and consequently there are strong incentives for what has been called "urban regeneration." While such projects have previously been committed to social concerns, such as providing housing and public transportation systems, today

they are more explicitly committed to the circulation of capital and capital investment. Consequently, "gentrification," "cultural innovation," and "physical up-grading of the urban environment" have all become part of the neoliberal program to strengthen the attractiveness of cities (Harvey, 1989: 9; see also Miles, 2012; Kornberger, 2012; Dovey, 2010; García, 2004; Davis, 1990). Social services and quality of life issues for the inhabitants, especially for lower income groups, have thus been displaced by the ambition to provide consumer attractions and entertainment. Places like Dubai are based on a curious combination of conspicuous luxury for the visitors and forms of modern slavery, as contract workers are shipped to the emirate from Bangladesh, Pakistan, and other areas to work for very low levels of pay and under appalling conditions. Tendencies in place in Europe, North America, Australia, and elsewhere become quite visible and open to inspection in such locations. These "evil neoliberal paradises," "the bright archipelagos of utopian luxury and 'supreme life styles,'" are for Davis and Monk (2007: xvi) little more than "mere parasites on a 'planet of slums.'" Outside of these more extreme cases, fuelled by oil money and the lack of few other natural resources but sun and sand, there is an establishment of the commonplace neoliberal competition between different cities. In order to attract what Richard Florida (2002) speaks of as the "creative class," cities have to be able to offer certain possibilities for creative life styles. "Creatives want edgy cities, not edge cities," as Peck (2010: 166) summarizes Florida's argument. One of the consequences is that it is increasingly popular to rank cities on the basis of their capacity to provide "quality of life" and other favoured "performance metrics." Kornberger and Carter (2010: 334) examine such rating procedures and suggest that, for instance, the so-called Anholt-GfK Roper Nation Brands Index™, a rating list that has managed to entrench a position as one of the city management league tables that city managers pay careful attention to, is primarily concerned about the opinions of certain people regarding the attractiveness of a particular city: "When Anholt says 'people,' he does not mean just anybody—but 'people' who visits a city, buys its products and relocate their business. The 'people' Anholt includes are well-off knowledge workers—the corporate, professional metrosexual glitterati and the members of the creative class—who are able to buy into a certain lifestyle. The working class and those who work several McJobs to stay afloat (not to mention the homeless, jobless, and other marginalized communities) enjoy little representation on the league table. In fact, their cultures are excluded" (Kornberger and Carter, 2010: 334). In the light of such criticism, city management is thus a practice pervaded by the neoliberal concern for capital accumulation and capital circulation. Little else appears to matter.

11. There is a quite extensive literature on how various biological resources and capacities become commodified and subject to economic interest. This literature examines various forms of commodification of, for example, reproductive capacities (Pande, 2010, 2009; Markens, 2007), reproductive materials (Almeling, 2007; Spar, 2006), human tissue (Waldby and Mitchell, 2006; Andrews and Nelkin, 2001), organs (Sharp, 2007, 2003; Cherry, 2005; Lock, 2002), body parts and cadavers (Hoeyer, 2009; Dickenson, 2008; Roach, 2003), services such as the banking of umbilical cord blood (Brown and Kraft, 2006), or even entire populations where clinical trials can be undertaken (Petryna, 2009; Prasad, 2009; Fischer, 2009). In addition, there are studies of how life science concepts such as the genome are subject to enterprising activities (Calvert, 2007; Parry, 2004). For an overview of this literature, see Styhre (2012).

12. Hyman (2011) demonstrates that household debt started to grow substantially during the 1960s when credit cards were aggressively marketed. Credit card loans tripled during the 1970s and the marginal profits on credit cards started to grow. "By the early 1990s, investments in credit cards were twice as profitable as conventional business loans," Hyman (2011: 220) writes.
13. In contrast, Evans and Rauch (1999) demonstrate that there is strong positive correlation between what they refer to as the "Weberianness Scale," measuring the degree of professional government administration in a country (i.e., the degree of state governance in the economy) and economic growth during the 1970–1990 period in 35 developing countries. "There is a strong and significant correlation between score on the Weberianness Scale and total growth of real GDP per capital during the 1970–1990 period ($r = .06$; $p<.001$)" (Evans and Rauch, 1999: 755). Rather than free market de-regulation being the motor of economic growth, "[s]tate bureaucraticies characterized by meritocratic recruitment and predictable, rewarding career ladders are associated with higher growth rates," Evans and Rauch (1999: 760) suggest. In addition, Block and Keller (2009) show that public institutions and public funding, rather than private interests, play an increasingly important role in advancing new innovations, and, as an effect therefrom, economic growth.
14. Jones (2011) provides some evidence of how class increasingly matters in the United Kingdom, at least in terms of making it into the most prestigious university education programs. "In 2002–03, 5.4 per cent of Cambridge and 5.8 per cent of Oxford students came from low participation neighbourhoods. By 2008–09, it had fallen back to 3.7 and 2.7 per cent respectively. Or consider the fact that, in the academic year 2006–07, only forty-five children claiming free school meals [i.e., from poor families] made it to Oxbridge—out of around 6,000 successful applicants" (Jones, 2011: 180). Without access to elite education, certain social classes will fail to be represented in policy-making bodies and decision-making communities, potentially further reinforcing the social and economic inequality. Similar mechanisms are in place in North American elite universities (see, e.g., Washburn, 2005).

2 Neoliberalism and Financialization
How Markets Are Sites for Capital Circulation and Accumulation

INTRODUCTION

"Rational markets can take care of themselves," the chairman of the Federal Reserve, Alan Greenspan (cited in Palma, 2009: 831), has declared at numerous times, thereby subscribing to the so-called efficient market hypothesis[1] advanced by the University of Chicago economists and Eugene F. Fama, more specifically.[2] Greenspan was at times hailed as master of the global capitalist economic system during the 1980s and 1990s, but not everyone was equally impressed (Batra, 2005). For instance, when making assertions regarding the rationality of the markets and justifying the use of new financial innovations, such as derivative instruments, Greenspan occasionally cited Joseph Schumpeter to substantiate his claims and argued that such innovation "represents an acceleration of the process that noted economist Joseph Schumpeter many years ago termed 'creative destruction'" (Alan Greenspan, cited in Leathers and Raines, 2004: 669). Leathers and Raines (2004: 668–669) suggest that Greenspan's interpretation and use of Schumpeter is "seriously flawed," and that Greenspan "stands virtually alone" in insisting that the rapid development of new financial instruments would have been approved by Schumpeter. Instead, Leathers and Raines (2004: 668) argue, "Schumpeter's dislike of financial speculation and 'reckless' banking would lead him to favour greater regulation of financial derivatives to curb their use by banks, other financial institutions and corporations such as Enron." The outcomes from the deregulatory activities firmly grounded in the belief in the efficiency of market-based transactions and control eventually proved to be not very favourable for the American economy. When being interrogated during a Congressional hearing at Capitol Hill, on "the fourth Tuesday of October 2008" and in the face of the 2008 finance market collapse, Greenspan had to admit that he had vastly misunderstood the nature of markets:

> Chairman of the House Committee on Government Oversight and Reform, Henry Waxman (D., CA): 'In other words, you found that your view of the world, your ideology, was not right. It was not working.'

Alan Greenspan, former Federal Reserve Chairman: 'Precisely. That is precisely the reason I was shocked, because I had been going for forty years or more with very considerable evidence that it had been working *exceptionally well.*' (cited in Fox, 2009: xi; emphasis added)

The expression "exceptionally well" is a most idiosyncratic opinion when taken as a general statement regarding the functioning of the financial markets. The period after 1980 has included a series of financial crises and events in which the judgment of finance market actors and regulators have been subjects to severe criticism (Gorton, 2010; Black, 2005). The global financial system appears to be inherently unstable (Engelen et al., 2012), but it still manages to generate substantial incomes for certain groups (Volscho and Kelly, 2012). In that respect, the deregulated financial markets have indeed been successful. Yet, it is hard to see how Greenspan in his official role as the chairman of a regulatory authority could praise such a biased and highly politicized outcome without comprising his integrity. This is how Joseph Stiglitz (2009) regards Greenspan's role in the period leading up to the events that eventually brought Greenspan all the way to Capitol Hill:

> Given the war [in Iraq] and the consequent soaring oil prices given Bush's poorly designed tax cuts, the burden of maintaining economic strength fell on the Fed. The Fed could have exercised its authority as a regulator to do what it could do to direct the resources into more productive uses. Here, the Fed and its chairman [Alan Greenspan] have a double culpability. Not only did they fail in their regulatory role, they became the cheerleaders for the bubble that eventually consumed America. (Stiglitz, 2009: 335)

Jabłecki and Machaj (2009: 393) support this view: "The regulatory authorities remained largely satisfied with the situation until it dissolved beneath their feet." In the aftermath of the 2008 finance market collapse, there has been a persistent critique that economists failed to predict the event, but in a paper published in June 2008, a few months before the bankruptcy of Lehman Brothers that was the spark that started the events, James Crotty, professor in economics at University of Massachusetts at Amherst, published a paper listing a number of worrisome conditions regarding risk-taking and leverage in the finance industry. "Risk taking has been so widespread and leverage has become so high that a systemic crisis is not out of the question," Crotty (2008: 181) warned. Within just a few months, Crotty would be proven to be right. One may suspect that a commentator like Crotty did not share Greenspan's affirmative view of and belief in the efficiency of financial markets, and where, for example, Greenspan saw only minor bumps in the road, others saw entire roads being washed away by excessive risk-taking and leverage.

This chapter will examine in greater detail the perhaps most significant effect of neoliberalism—that of the financialization of the economy.

Financialization denotes the process by which increasingly higher proportions of the accumulated economic value derive from the finance industry, rather than from manufacturing industry, service industry, or any other industry. In addition, the process of financialization denotes the process wherein finance theory, financial measurement methods and procedures of inquiry, and other practices developed in finance industry entrench a key position in determining what counts as economic value and qualified economic performances. In other words, once a financialization process has been initiated, it creates its own momentum, leading to further emphasis on regarding all economic resources in financial terms. As will be demonstrated in this chapter, while much of the finance theory that has justified the relatively unregulated financialization of, for example, the American economy has claimed to rest on empirical evidence, in fact many of the foundational claims are based on ideologies and conceptual propositions that are not substantiated by empirical evidence. To put it differently, advocates of the benefits of unregulated financial markets have confused the map and the territory, and as the map provided a most schematic and at times misleading image of the actual world, finance industry practitioners ended up in the 2008 finance market collapse, leading to one of the most significant socialization processes in American economic history when major financial institutions were bailed out by the federal government. Paul Krugman would refer to this form of Republican-supported state intervention into what was previously seen as "rational, self-regulating markets" as "lemon socialism," where "taxpayers bear the cost if things go wrong, but stockholders and executives get the benefit if things go right" (Paul Krugman, cited in Palma, 2009: 863).[3]

I. FINANCIALIZATION OF THE ECONOMY IN THE NEOLIBERAL ERA

Defining Financialization

"If neoliberalism is a policy and intellectual movement away from state regulation, financialization is perhaps its most fundamental product," Tomaskovic-Devey and Lin (2011: 556) remark, pointing at the central role of financial markets in the neoliberal era. "I define financialization as a pattern of accumulation in which profits accrue primarily through financial channels rather than trade and commodity production," Krippner (2005: 174) writes. Similarly, Dore (2008: 1097–1098) speaks of financialization as "[t]he increasing role of financial motives, financial markets, financial actors and financial institutions in the operation of domestic and operational economies." In Krippner's (2005) view, it is important to distinguish between an *activity-centered view* (e.g., the discussion about "the post-industrial society," the "knowledge economy," etc.) and an *accumulation-centered view* that stresses "where profits are generated in the economy" (Krippner, 2005: 176).

At the same time, Krippner agrees that it is complicated to provide a watertight distinction between the "financial" and "non-financial" sectors of the economy (Krippner, 2005: 179). Speaking in more concrete terms, Krippner identifies at least four meanings of the term *financialization* in the literature: (1) the use of shareholder value corporate governance, (2) the dominance of capital-markets over bank-based finance, (3) the increased power of the *rentier* class, (4) the "explosion of financial trading associated with the proliferation of new financial instruments" (Krippner, 2005: 181). While Krippner recognizes the significance all of these four changes in the economy, in her mind, financialization is a process that both preceded and embodied all these changes. For instance, Krippner (2005: 199) writes, "[w]hile the stock market mania of the 1980s and 1990s is clearly associated with the financialization of the US economy, it would be a mistake to reduce financialization to developments in the stock market." Instead, the very essence of financialization is the gradual shift to increasingly regard all economic resources—all production factors—in financial terms and to assess them through finance theory methodologies. Says Krippner:

> [M]y central empirical claim is that accumulation is now occurring increasingly through financial channels... During the 1980s and 1990s, the ratio of portfolio income to corporate cash flow ranges between approximately three and five times the levels characteristic of the 1950s and 1960s. The ratio of financial to non-financial profit behaves similarly. (2005: 199)

There is ample evidence of the increased growth of the finance sector in the advanced economies. In the European Union, for instance, Deutschmann (2011) says, the FIRE (Finance, Insurance and Real Estates) sector contributes more than any other sector, and this is also true in countries that have managed to maintain a strong manufacturing industry: In EU-27 the FIRE sector amounted to 28.8% of GDP in 2010 (manufacturing industry was 18.5%); in Germany, the FIRE share was at 30.4%, above the EU average, with manufacturing industry at 23.4% (Deutschmann, 2011: 353). In the United States, a similar situation was observed, and an increasing proportion of taxable profits emerged in the finance industry:

> Financial sector profits as a proportion of all profits in the economy grew slowly between 1948 and 1970, dropped across the 1970s, and increased dramatically after 1980... This trend peaked in 2002 when 45 percent of all taxable profits in the private sector were absorbed by finance sector firms. (Tomaskovic-Devey and Lin, 2011: 539–540)

In addition, traditional manufacturing companies such as General Motors and Ford Motor Company reported that their profits derived primarily from its financial operations. In 2004, General Motors reported that 66% of its $1.3 billion quarterly profits came from financial services, and Ford announced that its $1.7 billion in net income mostly derived from financial operations (Lin and Tomaskovic-Devey, 2013: 1293).

These long-term trends were salient in some countries at the forefront of the neoliberal project, such the United States and United Kingdom, but even in relatively small economies, such as that of Iceland, the finance market became larger than the so-called "real economy": "Iceland is no longer a country. It is a hedge fund," one IMF representative said (cited in Peck, 2010: 12). In France in 2008, the three largest banks held assets worth nearly two and a half times French GDP (Blyth, 2013: 6). "The publically traded equity" accounted for 159% of the GDP in the United Kingdom and 150% in the United States, while only 50% in Germany in 2005, Dore (2008: 1106) reports. In periods of economic growth, an oversized finance industry may not be a problem, but as, for example, Iceland and the Icelandic people hosting a finance sector growing larger than the national economy learned the hard way, in periods of economic decline, small economies may face substantial challenges in bailing out collapsing finance institutions. In addition, in the era of financialization, new financial products and instruments, increasingly difficult to value and price, and consequently to regulate and monitor, have been widely used. "The global market for derivatives rose from $41 trillion to $677 trillion in 1997–2007," Callinicos (2009: 74) notices. By and large, as Krippner (2011: 3) remarks, "there is little question that the U.S. economy has experienced a remarkable turn towards financial activities in recent years."

Pertinent questions would then be why the finance industry managed to grow at this speed and to this size and how it could claim an increasingly larger share of national income after 1980. The neoclassical economic theory explanation would naturally be that finance sector productivity soared in this period on the basis of, for example, increased human capital investment (Tomaskovic-Devey and Lin, 2011: 540). Such explanations are typically circular: *productivity* is defined as "value realized in markets," and references to increases in productivity are therefore tautologically true. The most credible explanation is that finance industry actors successfully enrolled various institutions and actors that worked in accordance with their interests. In addition, political and macroeconomic conditions happened to favour the growth of the finance industry. That is, rather than human capital investment explanations, institutional explanations are more likely to shed light on the financialization of the economy in the neoliberal era. In the following sections, these new conditions and coalitions between actors and institutions will be examined.

Macroeconomic Drivers of Financialization

Krippner (2011) makes the most important point: No official or policy maker operating at the end of the 1970s to counteract a stagnating world economy and growing inflation and unemployment could foresee the full scope of the financialization and its long-term effects, which would lead to the events of 2008. Instead, there was a combination of macroeconomic changes, new policies and regulations aimed to handle short-term concerns, and new economic theories and doctrines developed—all contributing to the new regime. However, all these changes must be understood as being anchored in the overarching ambition to enable more efficient circulation of capital and to increase competition through a combination of market de-regulation and state intervention when deemed appropriate.

"In the 1970s," Tomaskovic-Devey and Lin (2011: 542) write, "there was a strong perception of political and economic threat to U.S. capitalism. Following post-WWII prosperity, this was the first postwar crisis for U.S. capitalism . . . The resulting low-growth, high–inflation macro-economy undermined the legitimacy of Keynesian economic solutions." In order to curb inflation, a major economic challenge in the world economy following the oil crises of 1973 and 1978, the fashionable monetarist policy prescribed by Chicago economists such as Milton Friedman was advanced as a key economic policy. Paul Volcker was named chairman of Federal Reserve by President Jimmy Carter. As Ronald Reagan took office in 1981, there was an implicit conflict between Volcker's agenda and the new deficit spending administration. Fortunately, as an effect of the combination of positive trade deficits (in, for example, Japan), high overseas savings, and an overrated U.S. dollar, in the early 1980s the Reagan administration experienced a situation where the ambition to lower the taxes *and* increase public spending could be combined:

> What the Reagan policymakers discovered in the early 1980s, then, was that they lived in a world in which capital was available in a potentially *limitless* supply. Access to global political financial markets would allow the state to defer indefinitely difficult political choices that had confronted previous administrations struggling to allocate scarce capital between competing social priorities. (Krippner, 2011: 101–102)

This money flowing into the U.S. economy "funded deficit and initiated a continuous stream of foreign capital to feed debt-based consumption by consumers, corporations, and the U.S. federal government" in this period (Tomaskovic-Devey and Lin, 2011: 543). The inflow of foreign capital was $85 billion in 1983, $103 billion in 1984, $129 billion in 1985, and "a staggering $221 billion in 1986" (Krippner, 2010: 157); budget deficits in the same period, data from the *1989 Economic Report of the President* shows, amounted to $208 billion in 1983, $185 billion in 1984, $212 billion in 1985, and $221 billion in 1986 (Krippner, 2010: 169). In the period, a "debt-finance consumption boom in the U.S. economy" occurred, Krippner (2011: 104) summarizes.

The Reagan administration, brought into the White House on a "pro-business" and neoconservative agenda, started to deregulate financial markets and to pursue an "anti-union" agenda similar to that of Thatcher's in the U.K. Deregulation in combination with an inflow of capital had two consequences. First, it "encouraged financial investment over physical capital investment" (Tomaskovic-Devey and Lin, 2011: 545; Stockhammer, 2004) as finance market investment generated quick and relatively safe return-on-investment, and second, it led to instabilities in the financial markets: "Because these [deregulation] policies led to increased volatility in interests rates and stock market performance, they also encouraged the creation of new financial instruments to profit from risks, including variable rate mortgages, credit default swaps, and mortgage-based and other derivative securities" (Tomaskovic-Devey and Lin, 2011: 545). Derivative instruments started to play a key role in financial markets. In addition, previously unseen financial operations started to surface. In the 1970s, the growing industrial conglomerates lost much of their stock value. Finance industry actors, equipped with new methods and supported by finance theory, initiated what was to become known as "hostile takeovers" in the 1983–1988 period (Zorn et al., 2005: 273, Figure 13.1). The Celler-Kefauver Act of 1950 had made vertical integration "suspect" (Zorn et al., 2005: 283), but boards of directors and CEOs could still invest profits in unrelated diversification, leading to industrial conglomerates where the integral parts were only loosely coupled. These strategies were justified on the basis of what was called *portfolio theory* and the practices named *portfolio planning* in the 1970s. "By the end of the 1970s, 45% of the Fortune 500 had adopted these portfolio planning techniques" (Zorn et al., 2005: 283). The new generation of finance analysts noticed it was possible to buy these companies, split them up, and sell the parts at a profit. Based on a combination of agency theory (to be discussed in Chapter Three) and what Zorn et al. (2005: 283) refer to as "core competence theory" (see, e.g., Prahalad and Hamel, 1990), these moves played a role in decomposing conglomerates (Nicolai, Schultz, and Thomas, 2010; Davis, Diekmann, and Tinsley, 1994).

This inflow of capital into the American economy and the finance industry continued into the new millennium. The 1997–1998 East Asian financial crisis was clumsily handled by the IMF, and its role was "[w]idely seen in the East Asian region as unhelpful, too intrusive, and overtly influenced by U.S. policy makers' goals" (Helleiner, 2011: 72). The lesson learned was that policy makers in this region sought to "to build a war chest of reserves to defend themselves against volatile capital flows as well as dependence on the IMF" (Helleiner, 2011: 72). In practice, that led to an inflow of savings into the American economy. Export-led economies in advanced, democratic countries such as Germany and Japan were also motivated to avoid developing bank-based finance systems that competed with the American system because they saw the American dominance as a warrant for their positive trade balances (Helleiner, 2011: 72). For instance, the export-based Chinese economy generated a reserve that stood at over $1.5 trillion (of which approximately 70–80% was in dollar-dominated assets) before the 2008 financial crisis (Helleiner, 2011: 72). This inflow of capital into the U.S. economy, similar to that of the Reagan era, helped to "[f]und ballooning fiscal deficits generated by tax cuts and increased defense spending during the Bush administration" (Helleiner, 2011: 82). In addition, as the deregulated and increasingly competitive labour market offered little stability and security, home ownership served as a key means for building personal wealth and was, therefore, popular among Americans; it was a key component of what Davis (2010) refers to as the "ownership society."[4] When the inflow of capital spilled over into a housing-led boom propelled by a variety of finance industry innovations (i.e., all the MBSs, CDOs, etc.), there were many groups that benefitted. In addition, finance theory justified the inflow of capital and assured that markets were capable of rationally pricing assets.

The shift in focus—from thinking of corporations as what was best managed by hired and salaried executives with oversight and understanding of their own business, to finance market focus, where finance market actors determine the value of a firm and choose to "decompose it" if the finance markets value the parts higher than the combination under one unified management—was a major shift in economic thinking:

> During this time, the finance conception of a firm as a bundle of tradable assets replaced nonfinance sector managerial commitments to investment and innovation in specific markets . . . Finance-oriented managers now controlled major corporations, and short-term planning to increase stock prices became a primary managerial focus. (Tomaskovic-Devey and Lin, 2011: 545)

However, this shift in policy and practice was not entirely the product of the inflow of capital and the advancement of finance theory; it was also embedded in new laws and regulations that corporations had to respond to. Zorn (2004) argues that new demands for increased details in financial reporting after 1978 led to the implementation of Chief Financial Officer position in major American corporations (cf. Fligstein, 1987). In a study of 429 "large, public American corporations" between 1963 and 2000, Zorn (2004) found that at the beginning of the observations, "none of the sample firms had a CFO," while in the year 2000, "more than 80 percent did" (Zorn, 2004: 346). As Dobbin and Sutton (1998) argue, organizations tend to respond to regulation through implementing quite substantial changes, since the law does not dictate precisely how they are expected to respond. "Organizations created new offices not because the law dictated that they do so but because the law did not tell them *what* to do" (Dobbin and Sutton, 1998: 470; see also Sutton et al., 1994; Edelman, 1992; Baron, Dobbin, and Jennings, 1986). In general, Dobbin and Sutton (1998: 472) argue, Americans have a problem recognizing the role of law and regulation in shaping organizational practices: "Americans develop collective amnesia about the state's role in shaping private enterprises." As a consequence, Dobbin and Sutton,

1998: 472) suggest, Americans "[s]ubscribe to the theory that firms operate in a Hobbesian economic state of nature, in which behavior depends very much on managerial initiative and markets and very little on political initiative and law." In other words, the implementation of Chief Financial Officers in major corporations was not only a rational and conscious response to new threats of "hostile takeovers," but was also a response to the new demands for providing more detailed financial reporting. However, the presence of finance-theory–trained business school graduates in the board of directors in major corporations inevitably contributed to the shift in policy.

In addition to the institutional and regulatory changes in the period, Aglietta (2000) emphasizes that the demand for capital and loans and the growth of the finance sector also need to be understood on the basis of demographic factors. Drawing on theories of life cycle behaviour over whole populations, which suggest that household financial saving depends on the age structure of the population, Aglietta (2000: 153) claims that beginning in the late 1980s, "the post-war bulge of the baby-boomers had started moving into the mature-worker stratum, swelling the demand for financial assets." Therefore, Aglietta (2000: 154) suggests, "the demographic trend towards ageing supports a long bull market where stock prices deviate from the historically trendless real stock-price index." Today, in an essentially regressive "population pyramid" in many countries of the world (e.g., Italy and Japan), there is an oversupply of pension fund capital, favouring low-risk investment. The growth of the finance industry is therefore to be understood at least partially by demographic conditions and savings behaviour across the life cycle.

The bear market of the 1970s, the portfolio theory strategy of corporations, and the inflow of capital (derived from macroeconomic conditions), in combination with a neoliberal policy de-regulating financial markets, led to an entirely new situation in which CEOs had to be mindful of stock prices to block hostile takeovers. The emerging policies and strategies were ultimately embedded in macroeconomic changes and economic policies, but the new role of economists and finance theory professors contributed to the legitimacy of the new agenda.

The Role of Economic Theory and Finance Theory

In combination with a new neoconservative political agenda in the United States and United Kingdom, determined to fight labour power that was treated as a major impediment of economic growth, and macroeconomic conditions that put the United States in the favourable position as the issuer of bonds *per excellence*, there were intellectual changes occurring in the 1970s that would play a key role for future policies. Until the 1970s, the Keynesian economic policy had served as the bedrock in economies subscribing to embedded liberalism. Writing in the most turbulent times of the 1930s, an age of economic depression and political unrest in, for example,

Germany and Italy, the Cambridge economist John Maynard Keynes formulated the economic framework that would dominate the capitalist economy for many decades. "Keynes provided a breath of fresh air for those optimists who wanted economic and political change. Keynes's ideas seemed to arm politicians and public officials with a workable set of tools with which to deliver the reform of capitalism they desired in the wake of its seeming collapse," Jones (2012: 185) argues. In the 1970s, a decade characterized by oil crises, labour market conflicts, increasing costs, and a bear stock market, in combination with a persistent and systematic critique of Keynesianism as being part of a political program that ruled out governmental spending and interventions, Keynesianism was under siege. There was an acute need for new explanatory political-economic frameworks that could lead the way out of the crisis.

University of Chicago economists, fuelled by a variety of convictions, but in most cases proponents of free-market capitalism and minimal state interventions, gradually took a position to provide a new integrated model of capital circulation. Centeno and Cohen (2012) summarize their contributions to economic theory during the last few decades, all playing a key role in shaping and justifying neoliberal policies, such as de-regulation of markets:

> Substantially, academic economics over the past 50 years has witnessed (in rough order) the victory of monetarism (and thus a focus on interest rates and inflation) and rational expectations (explaining why public economic interventions were useless), and the efficient market hypothesis (which explained why such interventions were useless). (Centeno and Cohen, 2012: 328)

Milton Friedman, a relatively marginal figure in the 1960s and a long-standing critic of the welfare state, became the economic advisor of the Nixon administration. In 1970, Eugene F. Fama advocated what was called the *efficient market hypothesis*, which stated that all available information is always already included in the market price—by implication branding all kinds of regulatory activities as unnecessary and costly state interventions. Says Fama:

> The primary role of the capital market is allocation of ownership of the economy's capital stock. In general terms, the ideal is a market in which prices provide accurate signals for resource allocation: that is, a market in which firms can make production-investment decisions, and investors can choose among the securities that represent ownership of firms' activities under the assumption that security prices at any time 'fully reflect' all available information. A market in which process always 'fully reflect' available information is called efficient. (Fama, 1970: 383)

"In this formulation," Bryan and Rafferty (2013: 132–133) writes, "the economic orthodoxy consolidated a triumvirate of categories: efficiency, fundamental value ["the price that will be revealed when there is full transparency and mobility, when markets are complete and in equilibrium"], and competitive conditions. Combined, they were believed by the economic orthodoxy to verify the competitive markets not only to gravitate to an equilibrium (balance) but to the Pareto optimal allocation." Mizruchi and Brewster (2005) explicate the *efficient market hypothesis*:

> The weak form suggests that prices efficiently reflect all the information contained in the past series of stock prices. It is therefore impossible to earn superior returns simply by looking for patterns in stock prices. The semistrong form suggests that prices reflect all published information. This means it is impossible to make consistently superior returns simply by reading the newspaper, looking at the company's annual accounts, and other public information. For this reason, analysts can do little to help an investor earn superior returns. The strong form of the efficient market hypothesis (the one the most popular in the 1990s) suggests that stock prices effectively incorporate all available information: the consequence of millions of investors competing for the edge is that virtually no source of information remains unexplored. (Mizruchi and Brewster, 2005: 292)

"We shall conclude that, with but a few exceptions, the efficient-markets model stands up well," Fama (1970: 383) ensured.[5] In general, the neoliberal economic theory formulated at University of Chicago would play a decisive role in shaping the financialization of the economy in the neoliberal era:

> Notoriously, it was the Chicago School that innovated the idea that much of politics could be understood as if it were a market process, and therefore amenable to formalization through neoclassical theory. Politicians, it was claimed, were just trying to maximize their own utility, as were voters. Unfortunately, this doctrine implied that the state was merely an inferior means of attaining outcomes that the market could provide better and more efficiently; and that in turn led to another jaundiced assessment of the virtues and benefits of democracy. (Mirowski and van Horn, 2009: 162)

Consonant with his political beliefs, Friedman held that markets work better than government, and some of the Chicago economists started to believe, based on the works of, for example, Fama, "that markets were *perfect*" (Fox, 2009: 94). "Friedman is driven by the idea that whatever the government does is bad," scoffed Franco Modigliani, a key figure in advancing finance theory (cited in Fox, 2009: 94). In the era of political and economic turmoil, the Chicago economists' assurance that rational markets took care of themselves, in combination with the vilification of government, struck a chord among many politicians and policy makers. In short, they offered an elegant, seemingly unified, and relatively simple recipe for economic prosperity. "A theory begins by breaking up a concrete reality and ends by leaving out most of it," Homans (1951: 17) says. Economic theory is frequently based on these premises. Unfortunately, some of the underlying axial principles were unsubstantiated by evidence and many of the implications were not supported by empirical data:

> In fact, the assumptions underlying [economic] models too often stand in stark contrast to the broad set of regularities in human behavioral economics, as well as in experimental economics. The cornerstones of many models in finance and macroeconomics are maintained despite all the contradictory evidence discovered in such research. Much of this literature shows that in experiments, human subjects act in ways that bear little resemblance to how they are assumed to act in rational-expectation models. Real-world people do not exhibit ultra-rationality. Rather, agents display various forms of 'bounded rationality,' using heuristic decision rules and displaying inertia in their reactions to new information. (Colander et al., 2009: 257)

For instance, the efficient market hypothesis, which Rochester/Harvard professor Michael Jensen spoke of as the one proposition having "more solid empirical evidence supporting it" than any other proposition in economics (cited in Fox, 2009: 201), has been falsified in numerous studies:

> Focusing on firms, researchers found that corporate managers consistently made superior profits when they dealt with their own company's stock . . . that small-firm stocks outperform large-firm stocks, even on risk-adjusted basis . . . that firms with high ratios of book value outperformed other firms . . . and that there was no significant association between stock prices and expected dividend payouts . . . Focusing on investors, research in behavioural finance documented that prices reflected certain cognitive biases such as short-term underreaction and long-term overreaction to information. (Mizruchi and Brewster, 2005: 292; see also Hayward and Boeker, 1998; Zuckerman, 1999)

Also from within the quarters of economics, similar criticism was articulated. For instance, Robert Merton questioned why stock markets that have been conceived of as being by definition "efficient" demonstrate such high volatility vis-à-vis other markets:

> If . . . the rationality hypothesis is sustained, then instead of asking the question 'Why are stock prices so much more volatile than (measured) consumption, dividends, and replacement costs?' perhaps general

economists will begin to ask questions like 'Why do (measured) consumption, dividends, and replacements costs exhibit so little volatility when compared with rational stock prices?' (Robert Merton, Nobel Prize in economic sciences laureate, cited in Fox, 2009: 197)

A standing question regarding the new economic theories being articulated and invoked in policy decisions is whether the work conducted by The University of Chicago economists and other economists was in fact influenced by ideology or if their claims were based on solid and indisputable data. Since economists substantially expanded their jurisdictional domain in the neoliberal era, this is not a moot question. Kogut and Macpherson (2011: 1309) argue that an "innovation" (e.g., a new economic policy) is "ideological" when "its advocacy is no longer based on theoretical merits and materiality, but on its claims for conformity to political programs." Studying the implementation of a number of widely endorsed neoliberal policies, including Central Bank Independence, in a number of countries, Kogut and Macpherson (2011: 1315) found a "strong correlation between the presence of American-trained economists in a country and the subsequent adoption of liberal policies." In addition, these new policies were not so much based on empirical evidence as on other convictions, Kogut and Macpherson (2011: 1310) conclude: "[O]ur claim is that economics in particular historical junctures will be inclined towards a set of policy ideas that outstrip the empirical evidence." For Peet (2007: 3), there is little doubt that economic theory is ideological in the sense of being "committed to class and national interest." Peet (2007: 82) continues: "Economics is not an interest-neutral science of society. Economics is a liberal ideology devoted to the bourgeoisie. Modern economic theory, the pride of social science, rests on an empirical base (i.e., a set of generalized facts about the world) that is precarious to the extreme." For others, the power of economics lies in its *performativity*, its ability to create the world it prescribes (Mackenzie, 2006; Mackenzie and Millo, 2003).

Black (2005), who served as a bank regulator during one of the first substantial financial crises of the neoliberal era, that of the Savings and Loans industry in the early 1980s, claims that economic theory is ideological inasmuch as it blocks certain aspects of human behaviour simply because it is excluded from their analytical frameworks. In addition, economists had happily taken on the role of advisors to finance market actors, and in many cases they lacked the integrity needed when things went wrong to admit their mistakes and faulty predictions. We can cite Black (2005) at length:

> Economists know almost nothing about fraud. The dominant law-and-economics theory is that there is no serious control fraud, so it is not worth studying . . . prominent U.S. economists generally believe that regulation is the problem and deregulation is the solution. The deregulation ideology was the initial problem, but the fact that their

policies led to disaster also brought acute embarrassment. They had the normal human wish to avoid taking responsibility for their mistakes. Their embarrassment was particularly acute because they consider themselves the only true social scientists and believe that theory and facts, not ideology, drive their ideas . . . Economists missed the problem because of social class and self-interest. Few economists are prepared to see business people, particularly patrons, as criminals. Many of the top financial economists worked for the control frauds, and the collapse created such embarrassment that that felt compelled to deny that their employers were frauds . . . Economists developed a conventional wisdom about the debacle and have not reexamined it . . . All aspects of the conventional wisdom proved false upon examination. (Black, 2005: 12–13)

Mirowski (2013) takes Black's (2005) critique further and argues that the concept of fraud is theoretically irrelevant in neoclassic economics as the market, with its superior capacity to process information and to price assets rightly, will always sort out these kinds of "information imbalances." Therefore, fraud is not a major issue for economists: "Orthodox economists tend to see nothing wrong with conflict of interest, since they have generally subscribed to the precept that market arrangements are capable in principle of monitoring, restricting, and resolving any such conflicts in the course of normal operation" (Mirowski, 2013: 220). In general, economists are fond of the idea that they are, in a way, physicists unravelling hidden truth and underlying structures that help explain the inner working of economic systems, but in many cases they are active in far messier social realities, in which there are few possibilities for an articulation of immaculate economic laws devoid of human influence and political interests. Milonakis and Fine (2009), two economists, deplore this failure to recognize the social role of economists as being a form of engineering science—a science aimed at "making things work" based on incomplete data and approximations that need to be continually corrected and modified (see, e.g., Downer, 2011)—rather than being a matter of discovering timeless economic laws. "Economics has been marked by an almost exclusive reliance, at least in principle, upon abstract mathematical formalism married to statistical testing or estimation against given evidence, i.e., data," Milonakis and Fine (2009: 5) say. They continue:

> [M]ainstream economics, trapped between perfecting their increasingly esoteric and formalistic models and techniques, no longer show any interest in anything that lies outside their mode of thinking and their field of competence, including the history of their own subject and the methods employed. (Milonakis and Fine, 2009: 9)

To be fair, it is something like a favourite pastime among, for example, sociologists to express their contempt for formalistic economic theories that in many cases overtly ignore or render irrelevant much of the findings from other social science disciplines (Zuckerman, 2004a). The paper penned by Hirsch, Michaels, and Friedman (1987) is one eminent example of a publication in this genre, and they suggest that assumptions made in economic theory are not consistent with empirical observations:

> A series of heuristic assumptions about human nature, taking their existence and preeminence of markets as given, and other related principles such as fixed preferences are assumed and generally unquestioned. The claim that these are all exogenously determined factors lying outside the realm of economics has a certain disingenuous quality. (Hirsch, Michaels, and Friedman, 1987: 318)

As a consequence of the inability of economists to let their discipline and theories be governed by critical self-correction, some of their propositions— at times tautological, Hirsch, Michaels, and Friedman (1987: 328) say— regarding human nature and preferences, resting on the claim of universality, are static and remain incapable of explaining incorporate major social changes. "Economics pays a heavy price for the very simplicity and elegance of their models: empirical ignorance, misunderstandings, and, relatedly, unrealistic and bizarre policy recommendations," Hirsch, Michaels, and Friedman (1987: 320) contend. In a passage in the end of their paper, Hirsch, Michaels, and Friedman (1987: 333) take a somewhat more moderate position, saying that "pure elegance of models leads to sterility; unwillingness to abstract from and go beyond one's data leads to pure narrative."

For Palma (2009: 864), the field's poor track record in predicting the future as well as understanding the past and the present is explained by "[i]ts remarkable success in engineering an academic environment in which it got rid of all forms of critical thinking." Perhaps Palma (2009) is overly critical of the economics discipline, but the failure to predict major events such as the 2008 finance market collapse is embarrassing for a discipline that regards itself as being a science in the Newtonian tradition, based on laws and structures that lend themselves to formalistic modelling and mathematization. "Economics is supposed to be a predictive science, yet many of the key predictions of neoclassical economics can easily be rejected," Stiglitz (2010a: 245) argues. Needless to say, economists come in many versions and with many political convictions and preferences and engage in many fields of economic activity, but the most prestigious schools and communities have been dominated by key figures (Friedman, Fama, Jensen, etc.) that have managed to advance their economic thinking regardless of substantial empirical evidence. If nothing else, the Bank of Sweden's so-called Nobel Prize in the Economic Sciences, inaugurated in 1969, has rewarded economists that have contributed to the advancement of the neoliberal agenda, perhaps most conspicuously in the cases of Friedrich von Hayek, Milton Friedman, and Gary Becker. Undoubtedly, the Bank of Sweden committee has served an important role in justifying and legitimizing neoliberal economic policy since 1969.

II. THE CONSEQUENCES OF FINANCIALIZATION

The Increase of Intangible Economic Value and Intellectual Monopolies

As suggested by Krippner (2011), the financialization of the economy did not happen overnight but was the outcome of a variety of institutional and regulatory changes and theoretical advancements in the face of the faltering economic performance of the 1970s. Many of the regulatory changes, for instance, were not intended to lead to some of the effects they engendered, and, in many cases, the new economic and political landscapes opened up for new initiatives and explanations that had previously been ignored or overlooked.

One long-term effect of financialization and the offshoring and outsourcing of manufacturing industry is that many companies include more intangible assets—that is, there is a lower degree of fixed capital in firms today than in the 1970s and 1980s. Pagano and Rossi (2009: 670) report that the percentage of intangible assets in Standard & Poor's 500 firms was 16.8% in 1975, 32.4% in 1985, and 68.4% in 1995. By 2005, the percentage of intangible assets had grown to 79.7%. That is, by the first decade of the new millennium, roughly four fifths of the value of the 500 biggest firms in the United States derives from intangible assets. Google, one of the truly emblematic corporations of the contemporary era, is perhaps an exemplary case of how economic value is becoming increasingly virtual:

> [A]t the start of 2009 Google was worth approximately $100 billion but had only $5 billion in physical assets and about $18 billion in cash, investments, and receivables (according to balance-sheet information and financial-market data for December 31, 2008; total financial value is the sum of market capitalization and liabilities). The other $77 billion consisted of intangible assets that the market values but which are not directly observable on the balance sheet. Because the literature is not yet well developed, we expect to see more work in this area in the coming years. Various researchers have estimated that the annual investment in these intangibles held by US businesses is at least $1 trillion. (Brynjolfsson and Saunders, 2010: xiii–xiv)

While corporations used to be valued and priced on basis of the physical assets they controlled, today financial analysts and other economic actors need to be trained in assessing the future economic value that can be generated on the basis of such intangible assets.

One of the direct consequences of the increasing importance of intangible assets is that intellectual property rights and what are called "intellectual monopolies" play a more central role in determining the rights to the fruit of the intellectual labour that takes place in corporations. The domain of intellectual property right law is one of the few areas where the neoliberal program actively supports and endorses increased legislation because it is regarded as important for markets to function effectively. This is an example of an issue for which neoliberal thinking proposes a different solution from classical liberalism, which represented, in Mirowski's (2013: 64) formulation, an "[i]ngrained suspicion of power concentrated in joint stock companies and monopoly." As neoliberal thinking enacts market operations as the most efficient way to process information, actors are expected to participate in market negotiations and transactions. Such market activities always of necessity include elements of risk, and since actors are postulated to be risk averse, albeit to a higher or lower degree, laws need to be in place to set the rules for market-based interactions and negotiations. Law here plays a very central role as what can "safeguard everyone's autonomy and appropriate engagement with risk as businesses," Gershon (2011: 540) argues. More specifically, laws are seen as a "a neutral medium," and what offers "a universal means through which anyone can negotiate with anyone" (Gershon, 2011: 541), no matter if you are a large and influential or a small and marginal actor; "law is particularly useful because of its capacity to define entities as equal, or at least commensurate, despite wide disparities in size and internal organization" (Gershon, 2011: 540). In other words, law is a form of social, even communal, regulation of market activities, but as markets and market transactions are deemed so much more efficient than any other comparable mechanism, laws are tolerated and at times even encouraged in the neoliberal framework. Not all commentators are entirely pleased with the increased importance of legislation when it comes to, for instance, intellectual property rights.

Sell (2003) remarks that intellectual property rights have moved from being regarded as a "necessary evil," in essence at odds with free trade. In the neoliberal era, various actors have managed to increasingly frame intellectual property rights as being "pro-free trade," which is a curious change of the scene. Sell (2003) traces the events, procedures, and changes in doctrine that "catapulted" intellectual property rights to the top of the agenda of the United States' trade policy. In her mind, believing that intellectual property rights are "both necessary and important," the balance between "[p]rivate rights and public access has shifted too far in favour of private rights at the expense of the public weal" (Sell, 2003: 28).

One of the concerns about the tendency to erect barriers for innovative thinking is that what is beneficial for the individual corporation and patent-owner may not be socially beneficial or beneficial for the aggregated economic system because the full potential of certain ideas or findings may not be fully exploited. Boldrin and Levine (2004: 328) are most critical of intellectual monopolies: "In fact intellectual property may be damaging for innovation, growth, and overall social welfare; the monopoly profits generated by intellectual property have played, and still play, a much more secondary role than is commonly believed in determining the rate and pace of economic progress." Boldrin and Levine (2004) argue that the reasoning supporting intellectual property rights may appear convincing because it emphasizes the "near-zero marginal costs of reproducing and distributing new ideas" in comparison to the costs of articulating a new idea, but such a line of reasoning overlooks the costs to transfer "productive knowledge." That is, the fear that "without monopoly there will be no output of new ideas" (Boldrin and Levine, 2004: 329) is based on the wrong premises. Pagano and Rossi (2009) speak of intellectual monopolies in terms of "over-propertisation" and point at two effects: First, it negatively affects the "global division of labour" because there are fewer investment opportunities in countries with "lower IP [Intellectual Property] intensity." Second, due to the "negative effects of over-propertisation on the productive utilization of intellectual resources, there has been a progressive reduction of investment opportunities in the most IP-rich country as well, i.e., the USA" (Pagano and Rossi, 2009: 666). In other words, in Pagano and Rossi's (2009: 670) view, "intellectual monopolies" lead to "investment blockage"—fewer opportunities for capital investment—and to a decreased role of "open science" in modern economies. This new regime of intellectual monopolies has been accomplished by a number of institutional and regulatory changes, including a more liberal application of patent law and its expansion of new domains:

> First, since the 1980s in the USA and slightly later in other developed countries, most notably European countries and Japan, patentability has extended to encompass previously excluded technological domains, such as software, business methods, and biological inventions. Second, patenting standards have been considerably relaxed, leading to the shading of the distinction between pure information and practically applicable knowledge. Both these developments have contributed to the 'upstreaming' of patentability, namely the tendency of IP rights to protect knowledge ever closer to the realm of abstract ideas. Third, the institution of the Court of Appeals of the Federal Circuit, in the USA, has considerably strengthened the enforcement of IPRs in the USA. (Pagano and Rossi, 2009: 671–672)

For instance, in the field of the life sciences, originally developed in the "open science tradition" where scientific findings were a common good and collective accomplishment, universities have increasingly taken on the role of protectors of intellectual property rights, even in cases where the research work has been funded by tax money and other forms of public funding. In addition to this shift in attitude, patent law, originally designed to protect engineered objects such as devices and machines, is now applied to biological specimens and pathways, that is, quite intricate biological systems and their interactions with, for example, active molecules that cannot be easily captured by simplistic cause-and-effect descriptions (see, e.g., Carolan, 2010). The long-term consequences of this new, more liberal, policy is what Pagano and Rossi (2009: 673) speak of as "the tragedy of the anticommons," that is, the failure to fully take advantage of previous research work as intellectual monopolies raise the costs for productive exploration of the findings.

In summary, in the era of financialization, an increasing share of corporations derives from intangible resources. These intangible resources include, for instance, patents and other intellectual property rights, but whether these intellectual property rights—beneficial for the owner but a source of increased transaction costs for others—lead to economic growth or innovation is disputed. According to Boldrin and Levine (2004) and Pagano and Rossi (2009), the opposite is the case: Intellectual properties block competition and prevent potentially productive ideas from being further developed, and consequently much public funding in basic research in universities end up as patents that are not brought forward or play only a limited role in *de facto* protecting future incomes.

The Rentier Society Thesis

One of the more intriguing debates derived from the discussion of intellectual monopolies is the question of whether the neoliberal era has actually promoted the competitive capitalist regime cherished by many neoliberal theorists and thinkers, or if the neoliberal agenda has merely advanced a rentier economy in which the richest few per cent of the population have been spared the need to compete in the marketplace because their economic interests are to a higher degree protected by law and regulations. Some scholars have advanced the thesis that rather than establishing a competitive capitalism, neoliberal policies have served to restore monopoly capitalism: "The re-emergence of the rentier—partly due to neoliberal economic policy—has fostered financial at the expense of industrial profits. Consequently, financialization has indicted poor performance in investment, output and growth in developed countries" (Lapavitsas, 2012: 615). Especially in the United States and United Kingdom, motivated by shareholder value ideologies rooted in the agency theory advocated by Michael Jensen and others, investment in, for example, manufacturing generated lower pay-off than investment in the rapidly expanding finance industry, which was fuelled by the inflow of foreign capital and de-regulations based on efficient market convictions. This lower return-on-investment in manufacturing was interpreted by leading economists such as Jensen (1993) as being indicative of an industry in decline, and manufacturing should preferably be off-shored to third world countries so that the labour force in "advanced capitalist countries" could engage in new creative industries. This analysis proved to be wrong; the decline in manufacturing industry in the Western economies was not an effect of the increased competitiveness of these new countries—some in parts of Eastern Europe that were previously excluded from capital investment—but derived from the raise in income that led to a new demand for services (Kollmeyer, 2009; on the growth of service industries, see Hochschild, 2012). It was affluence that made the service industries more productive investments, and investments in these industries made the off-shoring of manufacturing more attractive. In general, in the 1980s, countries with a strong manufacturing tradition, including West Germany and Japan, stood for a significant proportion of economic growth. Meanwhile, in the United States and United Kingdom, the neoliberal and neoconservative governments fought to break the trade unions and labour power, and the manufacturing industry with which the unions were associated was increasingly regarded as being antiquated and declining in the new era. For Deutschmann (2011), the neoliberal era has been characterized by the restoration of the rentier class, living off capital investment rather than on the basis of productive capital investment:

> There is considerable evidence that the mature economies of Western capitalism are faced with a growing general mismatch between rent seeking financial assets on the one hand, and declining real investment opportunities on the other. What lies behind the phenomenon of financialization is the actual transformation of advanced capitalism into a rentier society, where the private asset holder has become dominant over the entrepreneur. From a sociological view, financialization can be characterized as a hegemonic regime of rentiers over entrepreneurs. (Deutschmann, 2011: 382)

In Deutschmann's (2011) view, the 2008 collapse could be partially explained by the capital surplus that needed to be channelled into new investment (Harvey, 2010), and as intellectual monopolies and the capital-investment–intensive manufacturing industry were in a state of being abandoned by the capital owners, there were few options other than introducing new financial instruments: "Confronted with the lack of primary investment opportunities in the real economy, the financial industry invented secondary (and tertiary etc.) investment opportunities in the financial sphere itself" (Deutschmann, 2011: 383). In Deutschmann's view, the tragedy of the financialization of the contemporary economy is that the unfettered circulation of capital crumbled under its own weight; in a way, the proponents of free and unregulated capital accumulation not only won the war, but their success also led to a capital investment problem that eventually led to the collapse of the entire financial system. If capital investment has been discredited as "unproductive use of capital" over a significant period of time because shorter-term investments in financial assets have generated quicker return-on-investment, the unfettered de-regulation of capital circulation tended to become a Midas' touch. When the real economy declines due to the lack of long-term commitment and investment in know-how and expertise, there is little investment opportunity left, other than to feed the money back into the finance markets.

If the rentier economy thesis is substantiated, then there is an inconsistency in the neoliberal ethos, inasmuch as competition is the prescribed condition for the multitude and the backbone of a vital capitalist economy, while the few super-rich are comfortably sheltered from such ordeal. Says Palma:

> Only in capitalism are there continuous pressures from competitive struggles, which led to the need to constantly improve the forces of production. Therefore, as Alice in *Alice in Wonderland*, only in capitalism it is necessary to run just to stay in the same place. However, what has emerged in practice from the neoliberal experiment is a system in which some has been left with all the running, while others have preferred to catch a lift. (Palma, 2009: 860)

The neoliberal state is therefore in a curious way endorsing two institutional logics: competition and self-reliance for the many, and a secure position as the beneficiary of capital rents for the very few. Apparently, the *de facto* effects of neoliberal policy are that any prescribed rule has its exceptions when those exceptions benefit economic and political elites. No other event during the neoliberal era more conspicuously demonstrated such inconsistencies than the 2008 finance industry collapse, in which the staunch and heroic rejection of socialist policies was suddenly displaced by a most affirmative view of state interventions, as the U.S. government bailed out several of the major American finance institutions populated by millionaire salaried knowledge workers previously taking pride in overseeing and disciplining "the dumb, fat, and happy bureaucracies" (Ho, 2009) of American industry. In many ways, in 2008 neoliberal economic policy had its "Berlin Wall moment" (Peck, 2010).

III. THE 2008 COLLAPSE AND THE RESURRECTION OF FINANCIALIZATION

On Knowing in Hindsight

To fully account for what actually happened during the 2007–2008 period, to provide a comprehensive explanation of the events, and to draw conclusions for future policy is beyond the scope of this volume. It is also beyond the scope of my competence, but there is no shame in admitting such intellectual shortcomings as there are several leading economists and Nobel

Prize laureates that have engaged in this story-telling, and in many cases there are alternative stories and competing interpretations to be drawn (see, e.g., Friedman and Kraus, 2012; Stiglitz, 2010a, 2010b). "There subsists a surfeit of books and articles dedicated to covering the crisis. Many people who rushed to read them in 2009–10 have ended up feeling less informed than before they started," Mirowski (2013: 9) writes, and stresses that mainstream neoclassical economists never fully understood why the crisis happened at all. In brief, the events of 2008 remain contested. Still, there is an agreement among moderate commentators that neoliberal propositions and conjectures regarding market efficiency served to influence a culture of de-regulation that eventually ended up in one of the most severe crises of late-modern capitalism. In Jones' (2012: 270) view, "There is little doubt that the elections of Margaret Thatcher and Ronald Reagan reshaped the political and economic landscape." This new regime represented a "fundamental move" to a new political culture dominated by the belief in "the free market," and this new political culture eventually "led to financial disaster in 2007–10," Jones (2012: 270) suggests.

The objective of this section is to point at some of the consequences of the financialization of the economy and the firm belief in market efficiencies among regulators and policymakers, despite ample evidence of frequently occurring financial turmoil throughout modern history (Gorton, 2010). In a way, it is a moral story, pointing at the dangers of what Janis (1982) speaks of as *groupthink:* the failure to transcend justified true beliefs, derived from the idea that a community of decision-makers are either highly qualified to understand and interpret certain situations and events, and/or the belief that this group has a certain moral standing justifying specific actions and policies. Groupthink is the malaise of intellectual and economic elites who believe that they are intellectually superior to other people and groups, which leads to complacency and the lack of ability to listen carefully to conflicting views and gradually undermines their capacity to make informed decisions, regardless of initial cerebral advantages and relevant credentials and qualifications.

Elements of the Model

The New Financial Architecture
One of the key factors to consider when examining the events of 2008 is what Crotty (2009: 564) refers to as the "New Financial Architecture" (NFA), a term that "refers to the integration of modern day financial markets with the era's light government regulation." The NFA includes two basic components: (1) the new financial instruments being invented and traded, and (2) the regulatory-institutional setting that structured and monitored the financial markets. The NFA had its roots in the early 1970s, when the American real estate market was created as an outcome from a series of new policies and legislations. The U.S. political bodies played an active role in

creating a real estate market in which liquid assets could be traded. According to Gotham (2006), these new policies included three consecutive steps. First, congress passed legislation that opened up a market for mortgage-backed securities (MBS) to make the previously illiquid mortgage assets tradable. Second, new policies created a market for commercial mortgage-backed securities (CMBS; see also Fligstein and Goldstein, 2010). Third and finally, new policies served to establish so-called Real Estate Investment Trusts (REIT) that play the role of integrating various real estate market actors participating. "[T]hese three institutional developments represent a series of ad hoc efforts to increase the liquidity of residential and commercial property and attract new sources to finance real estate," Gotham (2006: 233–234) argues. The effects of the new policies were quite substantial: The real estate market grew from $1.2 billion to $8.8 billion during the 1970s and 1990s (Gotham, 2006: 248). The state-controlled home mortgage institutes Fannie Mae and Freddie Mac were the vehicles for the creation of the MBS market. In 1971, the volume of MBS amounted to $2.06 billion worth of securities; by 2001, the real estate securities issued were worth more than $1.2 trillion (Gotham, 2006: 258). Gotham writes:

> By 2001, Fannie Mae controlled more than 42% of all new issues of MBSs. In 2001, both Fannie Mae and Freddie Mac issued more than 73% of all residential MBSs. In short, Freddie Mac's and Fannie Mae's participation in the U.S. mortgage industry and the global market securities shifts the locus of credit risk away from local lenders and provides a conduit for linking home buyers with global finance. Before the expansion of the secondary mortgage market, investment in home mortgages was low because of the lack of standardization and conformity in underwriting, appraisal, and legal documentation of conventional mortgages. In establishing a secondary mortgage market, Freddie Mac and Fannie Mae spearheaded efforts to create uniform mortgage documentation, and each corporation developed underwriting guidelines that private lenders have applied throughout the nation. (Gotham, 2006: 260)

The next step in the liberalization of the real estate market was to make these MBSs tradable, to create the secondary CMBS market. In addition to the increase in the new commercial finance commodity—the CMBS—the state-led transformation of the illiquid mortgage commodity into a liquid asset was to establish real estate investment trusts (REITs) that served the role of a "[f]inancial vehicle that links diverse actors and interests [that] may be geographically distant and, at the same time, disengaged from local settings" (Gotham, 2006: 266). The total number of REITs grew four times between 1972 and 2003, reaching a peak of 226 in 1994. Gotham's (2006: 256) study shows that the state has deliberately created the real estate market by "[r]edefining property rights and establishing rules of exchange within the residual and commercial securities sectors." The increase of foreign investment in the American real estate sector thus coincided with the passage of "extensive liberalization initiatives" (Gotham, 2006: 244). The new policies enabled financial institutions to "[u]nbundle, repackage and pool commercial mortgages into securities that investors can buy in capital markets" (Gotham, 2006: 262). The government-led creation of the real estate market is thus indicative of what Jacobides (2005: 481) speaks of as the "creation of an institutional backbone for exchange," including "information standards" and "norms of collaboration"—a set of rules, standards, and norms without which no market can operate:

> With information sufficiently standardized and coordination simplified, a market can emerge, even if significant problems of opportunism, dependency, and measurement persist. As the market operates, the problems are gradually addressed, and institutional arrangements are made to cope with them; information also becomes increasingly modularized, enabling more value to be divided through the market; the market itself, then, becomes adept at coordinating increasingly complex activities through a feedback loop of the cospecialization and learning process. (Jacobides, 2005: 480)

Markets are thus created, not naturally emerging; they are politicized and subject to regulation and monitoring, rather than being some primordial sites of economic exchanges.

The creation of MBS and CMBS and markets where they could be traded was only the first step of the NFA. One of the main concerns in post hoc accounts of the events has been the use of financial innovations, including so-called *Collateralised Debt Obligations* (CDO). CDO were financial assets constituted by underlying mortgages and ultimately real estates (and most commonly family homes) (see also MacKenzie, 2011; Davis, 2009). CDO served to re-package and re-sell underlying financial assets to further spread the risks over financial markets. According to White (2009), the subprime mortgage loan market and the use of CDO to securitize the underlying loan was the principal driver of the expansion of the finance industry in the period from the late 1990s to mid-2006:[6]

> The U.S. housing market boom, which began in the late 1990s and ran through mid-2006, was fueled, to a substantial extent, by subprime mortgage lending . . . In turn, the securitization of subprime mortgage loans, in collateralized debt obligations (CDOs) and other mortgage-related securities, provided an important incentive for subprime lending, which made such lending a source of profit, rather than of risk, for mortgage originators. (White, 2009: 394)

The concern was that CDO were *new* financial instruments and it was very difficult for the financial institutions to value and price the CDO: "The relation between the value of a CDO and the value of mortgages is complex and nonlinear. Significant changes in the value of underlying mortgages induce large and unpredictable movements in CDO values. Rating agencies and the investment banks that create these securities rely on extremely complicated simulation models to price them. It can take a powerful computer several days to determine the price of a CDO" (Crotty, 2009: 567). In addition, the value of CDO was hard to determine in a historical perspective because there were no historical data series available over time showing, for instance, how the pricing of CDO was affected by economic downturns. Simulations based on assumptions rather than historical data series were used when pricing these new derivative instruments:

> [H]istorical data were hardly available in most cases, which meant that one had to rely on simulations with relatively arbitrary assumptions about correlations between risks and default probabilities. This made the theoretical foundations of these products highly questionable—the equivalent to erecting a building's foundation without knowing the materials of which the foundation was made. (Colander et al., 2009: 253)

In addition to the pricing difficulties and the "illiquidity" of CDOs (Crotty, 2008: 176), "huge quantities" (White, 2009: 394) of these subprime mortgage-backed securities were held off-balance sheet, in so-called "structured investment vehicles." This led to a much higher capitalization and risk in the finance institutions than during previous periods. When the American subprime market became shaky as homeowners could not pay mortgages and had to leave their homes, the CDOs lost most of their value, and by February 2009, "almost half of all the CDOs ever issued had defaulted" (Crotty, 2009: 567). In comparison, the stock market could quite effectively counteract the decline in the housing market and in the financial markets more generally because stocks have a substantial value that was not affected by the events of 2008 in a short-term perspective.

Regulatory Control and Rating Practices
In addition to the new financial assets implemented, the events of 2008 were also caused by the quite light-handed regulatory oversight of the finance industry. What has been regarded as especially cumbersome is the relationship between the rating agencies (the troika of Standard & Poor's, Moody's, and Fitch) and the financial institutions, but the new liberal regulatory policy has also been criticized. This new regulatory policy has had two consequences. First, the annual borrowing by U.S. financial institutions as a per cent of gross domestic product (GDP) increased from 6.9% in 1997 to 12.8% in 2007. Second, the regulatory framework was relaxed during the 1980s: "Deregulation of bank branching (facilitating merger and acquisitions) occurred gradually. The separation of commercial and investment banking enforced by the Glass-Steagall Act was relaxed in 1987, 1989, and

1997, before finally being repealed by the Gramm-Leach-Bliley Act of 1999" (Hacker and Pierson, 2010: 195). In 1984, in 1990, and in 2005 Congress passed laws "[e]xempting certain financial contracts from the standard provisions of the Bankruptcy Code" (Sissoko, 2010: 6). Moreover, in the period 1973 to 2003, the U.S. Securities and Exchange Commission (SEC) limited bank leverage to 12 times the capital held. Under the presidency of George W. Bush, Goldman Sachs chairman Henry Paulson—eventually named Bush's Treasury Secretary—managed to make SEC accept a leverage ratio to 40 times capital, a more than threefold increase in capitalization (and, *ipso facto*, risk-taking) (Crotty, 2009: 574). Such accomplishments all too evidently demonstrate the accuracy of what has been called "the golden rule of Wall Street": "He who has the gold makes the rules" (Peck, 2010: 251).[7]

For Stiglitz (2009: 333), the "the repeal" of the Glass-Steagall Act was deeply problematic because it "transmitted the risk-taking culture of investment banking to commercial banks, which should have acted in a far more prudential manner." To exemplify the effects of increased capitalization, with a leverage of 33 to 1 (as in the case of Bear Sterns, reported by the Securities and Exchange Commission [SEC]), a mere 3.3% drop in the value of assets wipes out the entire value of equity and makes a bank insolvent (Sikka, 2008: 869). Highly leveraged banks were certainly balancing on the edge. In addition to these new, more lenient regulatory policies, many of the banks could side-line the regulations by manipulating their accounting data:

> Commercial banks appeared to be adequately capitalized, but only because they overestimated the value of on-balance-sheet assets while holding a high percentage of their most vulnerable assets hidden off-balance-sheet. In fact, they were excessively leveraged, as the crisis revealed. Many European banks had leverage ratio of 50 or more before the crisis . . . while Citibank and Bank of America's ratios were even higher. (Crotty, 2009: 574)

Another concern was that the rating agencies systematically underrated the risks involved in the financial transactions preceding the events of 2008. The rating agencies are supposed to have an adequate degree of integrity and serve as stabilizing and reliable actors playing a key role in the finance industry. Still, rating agencies gave large investment banks like Lehman Brothers and Merrill Lynch "solid investment grade ratings that allowed them to borrow cheaply" (Crotty, 2009: 566; see also Swedberg, 2010). In addition, in many cases, the financial reporting and accounting procedures proved to be faulty and manipulated. Lehman Brothers, one of the few finance institutions that was not spared by Henry Paulson and the Bush administration, reported that it had a "net worth of some $26 billion shortly before its demise," yet suddenly proved to have "a hole in its balance sheet approaching $200 billion" (Stiglitz, 2010a: 156). Few of these inconsistencies were recognized, and fewer were acted upon by the regulatory bodies, including the Federal

Reserve, whose chairman was fully convinced of the innate rationality of the de-regulated finance market and its past accomplishments. Where in hindsight there were alarming signs all over the industry (Crotty, 2008; Davies and McGoey, 2012), Federal Reserve executives draw different conclusions:

> Then New York Fed Chairman, and current Secretary of the Treasury, Timothy Geithner stated in 2006: 'In the financial system we have today, with less risk concentrated in banks, the probability of systemic financial crises may be lower than in the traditional bank-centered financial systems' . . . In 2006 the IMF proclaimed that the dispersion of credit risks 'has helped to make the banking and overall financial system more resilient.' (Crotty, 2009: 567)[8]

Such resilience proved to hold thin when the effects of the declining subprime housing market spilled over into the finance market and all finance institutions became acutely aware of their excessive risks. What is perhaps even more remarkable was that some of the free market advocates proved to learn very little from the 2008 events, to the chagrin of moderate economists such as Paul Krugman:

> At every stage, Geithner *et al.* have made clear that they still have faith in the people who created the financial crisis—that they believe that all we have is a liquidity crisis that can be undone with a bit of financial engineering, that 'governments do a bad job in running banks' (as opposed, presumably, to the wonderful jobs the private bankers have done), that financial bailouts and guarantees should come with no strings attached. This was bad analysis, bad policy, and terrible politics. (Paul Krugman, cited in Crotty, 2009: 578)

Deep-seated beliefs in the efficient market hypothesis and other neoliberal policies, unsubstantiated by empirical evidence or more or less falsified by events such as those in 2008, still held a grip around policy makers and regulatory bodies.

Bonuses and Compensation
By the end of 2008, many large banks had "[s]een their equity position evaporate to the brink of insolvency and beyond. Only massive government bailouts kept these 'zombie banks' alive" (Crotty, 2009: 574). The Bush administration and finance industry representatives—all warm defenders of free market policies—were facing a substantial educational challenge in convincing the American taxpayers that a significant amount of the GDP (12.7% of GNP in the United States and 9.1% in the United Kingdom, the IMF calculated, cited in Callinicos, 2010: 88; see also Blyth, 2013: 45)[9] should be fed back into an industry that had conspicuously failed to serve its social and economic role and that had awarded itself

handsomely both prior to—in 2006, Wall Street paid out US$62 billion in bonuses (Freeman, 2010: 167)—and during the very crisis. We can cite Crotty at length to get an overview of the generosity that accrued to the finance market actors:

> In 2006, Goldman Sachs' bonus pool totaled $16 billion—an average bonus of $650,0000 very unequally distributed across Goldman's 2,500 employees. Wall Street's top traders received bonuses up to $50 billion that year. In spite of the investment bank disasters of the second half of 2007, which saw Wall Street investment banks lose over $11 billion, the average bonus fell only 4.7%. In 2008 losses skyrocketed causing the five largest independent investment banks to lose their independence: two failed, one was taken over by a conglomerate, and two became bank holding companies to qualify them for bailout money. Yet Wall Street bonuses were over $18 billion—about what they were in the boom year of 2004. (Crotty, 2009: 565)

In 2007, a year before Goldman Sachs was bailed out by tax money, the company's chief executive officer, Lloyd Blankfein, alone "took home $68 million" (Sorkin, 2009: 4). At Merrill Lynch, in the *annus horribilis* of 2008, about 700 employees "received bonuses in excess of $1 million in 2008 from a total bonus pool of $3.6 billion, in spite the fact that the firm lost $27 billion" (Crotty, 2009: 565). Four executives alone were lucky to receive a total of $212 million for this year's performance, while another top 14 executives shared $249 million. Perhaps most surprising, AIG[10] (owned 80% by the U.S. government and which received 180 billion federal dollars to survive the crisis), while losing $40.4 billion in 2008, paid 377 employees a total of $220 million in bonuses, an average of over $500,000 per employee. Seven fortunate employees received more than $2 million each (Crotty, 2009: 565). "The news triggered an explosion of outrage" in Washington, Barofsky (2012: 138) recalls. Later on, in 2013, when the worst crisis had passed, the story of AIG took yet another turn: "As usual, reality outpaced satire when the former CEO of AIG, Hank Greenberg, brought suit against the U.S. government for not bailing out AIG at a sufficient munificent rate" (Mirowski, 2013: 9).

At the same time as these excesses were tolerated by the Bush administration, the sub-prime loan-holders, the homeowners that risked being evicted from their homes, were treated as a source of "moral hazard" because they could theoretically become eligible for financial support if they stopped paying their mortgages:

> "I . . . found it beyond ironic that Treasury [Department] was now emphasizing moral hazard with respect to homeowners. Though some home owners might try to take advantage of the program by intentionally not making mortgage payments in order to qualify—that risk

paled in comparison to that created by Treasury by the way it had rescued the too-big-to-fail banks. Rather than requiring those executives to suffer the consequences of their failures, Treasury had handsomely rewarded those who had failed to do their jobs, saving the banks and making sure that almost all of them kept their jobs and the enormous bonuses they had taken home before the crisis stuck. (Barofsky, 2012: 197)

To allude to Winston Churchill's famous quote, never before was so much owed by so few rich to so many. "The people who are to pay for the mess are not the same who made it," Blyth (2013: 50) states. The American's taxpayers' money was given to an industry that for close to three decades had benefitted greatly from reaping the profits generated in other industries.

Post Hoc Explanations and Calls for Policy Making

Needless to say, a significant literature has been published seeking to explain, justify, or otherwise shed light on the events of 2008. Explanations vary widely from moralist explanations to shifts in institutional settings and regulatory control and there seem to be just as many likely explanations as there are contributors to this literature. Most commentators agree, though, that the professional community of economists and the neoliberal project have suffered a severe loss of prestige and trustworthiness. In addition, there were substantial losses for the American taxpayers and for the homeowners failing to pay their debts and mortgages:

> In the collapse, Americans lost nearly $13 trillion in the value of their homes and fallen stocks. By late 2009, only some $2–3 trillion was recovered in the stock market and none on average in the housing market. Perhaps three million Americans would lose their homes. The unemployment rate rose to more than 10 percent, and when discouraged and involuntary temporary workers are included, the rate was more than 17 percent in 2010. Wages fell and family incomes were below the levels reached more than ten years earlier. (Madrick, 2011: 395)

The events have generally been conceived of as not sheer chance or hard luck, but as determined by many factors, including that of the "greed" of certain groups of actors. Says Madrick (2011: 397): "The crash of 2008 was not a systemic failure. It was a function of the unchecked greed of a handful of individuals, the culmination of forty years of growing power and weakened government. And the same individuals were essentially still in charge." Others have emphasized the inability to institute robust risk-assessment practices: "Market participants (including banks and rating agencies) systematically ignored (or underestimated the importance of) systemic risk," Stiglitz (2010b: 28) proposes. Yet another group of commentators point at a combination of factors ultimately rooted in neoliberal free market ideologies:

> [The 2008 crisis] was the result of a unique combination of an ideology that became toxic, intrinsically rentier powerful special-interest groups, populist politics (led by the most remarkably unimaginative and accommodating political élite for generations), bad economics, and downright incompetence. (Palma, 2009: 831)

In the aftermath of the largest finance market collapse of the new millennium, explanations abound. In a review of all these different candidates for explanations, Friedman and Kraus (2012) reject many of the theses and explanations for the debacle (including the "too big to fail" and the "greed" hypotheses), but point at the lack of regulatory oversight and the firm belief in market prices' ability to contain all available information—an implication from the efficient market hypothesis. Friedman and Kraus (2012: 2) remind us that the credit rating agencies Moody's, Standard and Poor's, and Fitch were all "protected by competition by a Securities and Exchange Commission regulation dating back to 1975." That is, they had enjoyed a comfortable oligopoly (Wallison, 2009). In combination with what Friedman and Kraus (2012) refer to as *price fetishism*, market actors and regulators failed to respond to emerging risks: "[Financial regulators] were ignorant of the legal oligopoly of the 'rating agencies,' and . . . they were blinded by 'economism,' or the belief that markets are, in the default position, perfect, such that market participants are, in effect, omniscient" (Friedman and Kraus, 2012: 2). Friedman and Kraus (2012: 149) continue: "In the case of accounting regulators, the underlying assumption was not that capitalists' *behavior* should be left alone, but rather than market *prices* somehow have the ability to overcome human limitations and accurately predict the future." Davies and McGoey (2012) advocate a similar explanation, pointing at the actors' failure to understand that their economic and financial models were maps that did not perfectly represent the underlying territories:

> [T]oo many financial traders were beginning to mistake their economic models for economic reality, allowing tidy representations of risk to stand in the way of messy situations of uncertainty . . . The agents of knowledge and the objects of knowledge are both active participants in an integrated system of calculation, which eventually reaches such a level of complexity that neither *prices nor models* can be trusted any longer. (Davies and McGoey, 2012: 73)

"[T]here *were* significant warning signals of impending crisis, signs which were actively ignored or concealed by a range of parties," Davies and McGoey (2012: 66) contend. Other commentators argue that it is important not to strictly consider the events of 2008 as an effect of cognitive limitations, groupthink, and the failure to recognize and respond to systematic risks, but to recall the ideologies and attitudes among finance industry actors—examining the bonus and compensation schemes put to use would perhaps serve as a reminder—during the first years of the new millennium. Say Centeno and Cohen (2012: 331): "It is important to recall the hubris with which the market was proposed as the institutionalized solution to practically every human problem. In this Panglossian view, the market could resolve all conflicts and provide optimal distribution without external regulation." Underlying and preceding the events of 2008 was substantial academic work to advance markets as what are by definition infallible. Such beliefs would eventually couch ideas about what Friedman and Kraus (2012) would call "price fetishism": "The market's first great victory was in the academy. The principles underlying neoliberalism first established their monopoly in the field of economics and from there engaged in an imperial conquest (or delegitimation) of other fields," Centeno and Cohen (2012: 328) claim.

No matter what explanation one favours—the risk ignorance explanation, the incompetence explanation, the de-regulation explanation, the ideology bias explanation, and so forth—the events of 2008 had both short-term and long-term consequences. First of all, the Bush administration's Troubled Assets Relief Program (TARP), implemented during the dour fall of 2008 (see Barofsky, 2012), was an eminent example of what Paul Krugman would refer to as "lemon socialism," in which competition is prescribed for the poor and socialism and economic security are granted the rich (and the incompetent, one may add in this case). TARP was, Barofsky (2012) writes, "by Wall Street for Wall Street." There is a great deal of irony in the fact that a free-market–minded Republican President ended his terms by implementing one of the greatest socialization processes in post-World War II American history when the financial institutions were bailed out by the federal government, and even more so with a former Goldman Sachs' executive at the helm. "The bailout of the financial system, no matter how important it was to preserve the world financial system, saved a set of firms that had, since 1980, increasingly been accumulating the economic surplus of the entire economy," Tomaskovic-Devey and Lin (2011: 554) remark. They continue:

> Somebody, of course, always pays the rent. In this case, it seems to have been the rest of the U.S. economy: nonfinancial firms paid increasing proportions of their income to the finance sector, and households' wages were restricted by their employees' declining market power and their increased payments of fees and interest to a financial sector ever more clever at extracting income from other actors in the economy. (Tomaskovic-Devey and Lin, 2011: 556)

In addition to these gargantuan inconsistencies in policy—mostly derived from pure necessity—the events of 2008 wielded destructive effects on many *bien pensant* experts and commentators: "The near-collapse of US financial markets and the negative repercussions of other countries reliant on US financial or trade markets have severely damaged the United States' international reputation as an example of advanced, sound policy making. Certainly no one is speaking seriously anymore about a perpetual American global empire," Centeno and Cohen (2012: 327) dryly remark. While "international reputation" may be priceless, on the home front, there were many people, especially the poor, who were hit hard, having more to worry about than the prestige of the United States: "Nearly nine million jobs were lost as a result of the financial crisis along with 3.5 million homes, accompanied by a loss of $7 trillion in housing wealth. The poor have suffered the most, with the poverty rate increasing from 12.5 percent to 15.1 since 2007" (Barofsky, 2012: 226). The state's role has been to save finance industry actors and institutions at any costs, and the price paid is the austerity that has been called for in certain quarters (Palley, 2012), demanding the state cut its welfare benefits:

> 'We have spent too much' those at the top say, rather blithely ignoring the fact that 'spending' was the cost of saving their assets with the public purse. Meanwhile, those at the bottom are being told to 'tighten their belts' by people who are earning massively larger pants and who show little interest in contributing to the cleanup. (Blyth, 2013: 15)

At the same time, *plus ça change,* but still the same conditions remain: "Despite the talk of the end of capitalism as we knew it around 2008, the economic rule of the game remained essentially the same" (Centeno and Cohen, 2012: 322). Barofsky (2012) notices that the 2008 events in fact only marginally affected the dominance of the finance industry.

> The top banks are now 23 percent larger than they were before the crisis. They now hold more than $8.5 trillion in assets, the equivalent of 56 percent of our country's [the USA] annual output, up from 43 percent just five years ago. The risk in our banking system is remarkably concentrated in these banks, which now controls 52 percent of all industry assets, up from 17 percent four decades ago. (Barofsky, 2012: 229)

As the IMF once announced, the financial system indeed demonstrated a significant resilience.

Summary and Conclusion

Needless to say, there have been a variety of explanations for the 2008 finance market collapse. One can choose to point at incompetence, greed, misjudged policy, or sheer chance as elements holding explanatory value when examining the derailment, and no matter what explanation one favours, the outcomes are indisputably not entirely flattering for many of the key actors, especially those building entire careers on boldly condemning government and state interventions, only to eventually, when there were no alternatives left, take a more benign view of such activities (e.g., the case of the TARP program and the finance industry bail out). One of the most interesting theses from an academic point of view is to what extent the scientific program (in Lakatos's [1970] sense of the term) of finance theory is capable of living up to what Mirowski (2005: 80) speaks of as the scientific ideal in economics—as being "[a]n abstract, amoral, neutral science like physics." Such a role model is in a way justifiable, even admirable, but it becomes problematic when one thinks one can live up to high ambitions when, in fact, there is little substance behind such claims. It is more likely that the finance theory that propelled the development of advanced financial services, assets, and interactions should be, as suggested by Mackenzie (2006: 245), more adequately regarded as a form of *bricolage*: "To develop a 'good' finance-theory model required extensive, imaginative bricolage or tinkering . . . it also required deployment of the theorist's crucial skill: the capacity to find 'good abstractions'" Such a model of economic theory and finance theory has, however, little to do with what Richard Rorty (1980, 1991) refers to as a foundationalist epistemology; it is based on performativity and pragmatism—the ability to provide tools that work and get the job done. Mackenzie (2006) stresses this pragmatic epistemology of finance theory and its ability to provide various tools and *aide-memoires* that support financial traders in their day-to-day work (see, e.g., Pollock and D'Adderio, 2012; Pryke, 2010; Callon, Millo, and Muniesa, 2007; Beunza and Stark, 2004; Beunza, Hardie, and Mackenzie, 2006):

> Part of the significance of the performativity of economics arises from the fact that individual human beings tend to have quite limited powers of memory, information-processes, and calculation. Those limitations explain the centrality—especially in complex markets—of simplifying concepts (e.g., 'implied volatility') and of material means of calculation . . . The concepts and material means are therefore constitutive of economic action. (Mackenzie, 2006: 265)

In establishing these algorithms, tools, and other "market devices" serving to actively constitute the finance market, finance theory also contributes with what Mackenzie (2006: 250) speaks of as linguistic innovations—a way of speaking about the market, its volatility, its various classes of financial assets and their calculated risks (measured and referred to as the "beta" of stocks), and so forth: "The theory offers a way of talking about markets, especially about markets whose complexity might otherwise be baffling." This performative view of finance theory as a form of toolbox and as an operative vocabulary is something entirely different from viewing economics and finance theory as representing the ideal of a Newtonian science, revealing natural laws, such as the movement of astral bodies, beyond the influence of human interests and concerns. With Mackenzie's (2006) handy metaphor, economic theory and finance theory are not so much a *camera* capturing the "fact of the matter" as they are an *engine* driving the economy. As William James (1975: 100; later rearticulated by Carruthers and Babb, 1996: 1556) once remarked regarding the functioning of a monetary system, it is ultimately based on the firm *belief* in the legitimacy and robustness of such a system: "Our thoughts and beliefs 'pass' so long as nothing challenges them, just as bank-notes pass so long as nobody refuses them." The same goes for the pragmatist finance-theory-as-engine model: As long as all actors believe it works and gets the job done, it continues to serve its purpose, but as soon as it ceases to serve this role, there are suddenly possibilities for discerning fallacies and faulty assumptions, at times quite surprising, in the model. Perhaps this is one of the key insights from 2008: that economic theory and finance theory are not a Newtonian science capable of making predictions. Instead, such theoretical frameworks are always bound up and co-aligned with other human interests and concerns, making economic theory and finance theory resources that can be used more or less effectively to accomplish certain goals.

NOTES

1. For instance, in 2002, Greenspan made the following statement: "As the market for credit default swaps expands and deepens, the collective knowledge held by market participants is exactly reflected in the prices of these derivative instruments . . . [which] embody all relevant market prices of the financial instruments issued by potential borrowers" (Alan Greenspan, cited in Freeman, 2010: 166).
2. On October 14, 2013, it was announced that Eugene F. Fama shared the Bank of Sweden's Nobel Memorial Prize in Economic Sciences with Robert Shiller and Lars Peter Hansen. Few of the commentators mentioned the efficient market hypothesis; rather, they stressed Fama's empirical work in the field of finance theory.
3. "In a supreme irony, 'socializing' the banking system is acceptable when it serves to save capitalism. Socialism is bad—except when it serves to stabilize capitalism," Žižek (2009: 13) remarks, pointing at the most pragmatic and contingent attitude towards state intervention among free-market acolytes. Neoliberalism transformed the "political and economic system into one characterized by socialism for the rich and capitalism for the rest," Palma (2009: 862) contends.
4. Lin and Tomaskovic-Devey (2013: 1306) demonstrate that there is an inverse statistical relationship between financialization and economic equality: "A 1% increase in the reliance on financial income is associated with between a 0.9% and a 3.7% decrease in labor's share in the long run" (Lin and Tomaskovic-Devey, 2013: 1306). "[F]inancialization of the U.S. economy at its core is a system of redistribution that privileges a limited set of actors," Lin and Tomaskovic-Devey (2013: 1310) summarize. Not only does financialization transfer income to the finance sector, but it also, Lin and Tomaskovic-Devey

(2013: 1310) argue, "restructured the social relations and the income dynamics in the nonfinance sector." Increased investment in financial assets "decouples" the generation of surplus from production and therefore strengthens the owners' and elite workers' negotiating power against other workers. This in turn leads to "[a] structural and cultural exclusion of the general workforce from revenue-generating and compensation-setting processes" (Lin and Tomaskovic-Devey, 2013: 1310). The de-unionization of the labour force that has been observed in, for example, the United States since the 1970s is thus closely related to the financialization of the economy; de-unionization, in turn, some studies suggest, further accelerates economic inequality, as unions serve to institute norms and maintain mechanisms for negotiations that counteract economic inequality (Western and Rosenfeld, 2011).
5. In contrast, Whitley (1986) suggests that the efficient market hypothesis "[s]ays remarkably little about market valuation practices or their accuracy." Instead, it "simply specified the conditions under which equilibrium occurs in terms of expected returns reflecting available information." In addition, Whitley (1986: 176) continues, as such models of "ideal worlds" fail to specify under what conditions they are applicable to actual "economic situations," the "numerous so called 'tests' of the EMH are essentially irrelevant," or, on the contrary, the outcome of empirical research can be ignored as being "irrelevant," or as being indicative of econometric methodology problems. In this view, efficient market hypothesis is disconnected from actual, practical problems; it is an form of what Ernst Mach referred to as a *Gedankenexperiment*—a "thought experiment."
6. Poon's (2009) analysis of the expansion of the subprime lending market emphasizes a shift from a screening method based on a risk-averse *risk minimizing* strategy, to a "statistical lending" method based on a *risk management* strategy that embraces risk (Poon, 2009: 667; see also Rona-Tas and Hiss, 2010). Therefore, in Poon's view, the "recent explosion of secondary subprime financial activity" is not so much the effect of "the motivations and psychologies" of the finance market actors as it is derived from a "development of technical apparatuses that have supported the practical activities of a new cadre of financial agents" (Poon, 2009: 655). In other words, new calculative practices, treating risk as an opportunity, not as an obstacle, served to expand the subprime mortgage market, which in turn could be securitized into so-called Residential Mortgage Backed Securities (RMBS).
7. This new financial architecture includes lobbyists paid to work in accordance with the interests of major finance institutions. The role of these lobbyists is not marginal in creating the new finance industry regulatory framework. For instance, the Former Securities and Exchange Commission chief Arthur Levitt (cited in Hacker and Pierson, 2010: 187) accounts for the forceful and quite aggressive lobbyism during his years in Washington: "During my seven and a half years in Washington . . . nothing astonished me more than witnessing the powerful special interest groups in full swing when they thought a proposed rule or a piece of legislation might hurt them, giving nary a thought to how the proposal might help the investing public . . . Individual investors, with no organized labor or trade association to represent their view in Washington, never knew what hit them."
8. Barofsky's (2012) first-hand account of TARP, serving as the Inspector General and appointed by the Bush Administration, does not paint a very flattering picture of Timothy Geithner. Instead, Geithner is arrogant, incompetent, and dodging all kinds of criticism regarding the use of tax money to rescue the global financial system.

9. Sikka (2009) suggests that the total costs for the U.S. government were in fact substantially higher: "The U.S. government has closed 22 banks including Lehman Brothers, Washington Mutual, and Indymac. It has rescued Freddie Mac, Fannie Mae, Bear Stearns and created a bailout fund of $700 billion to purchase stakes in troubled banks . . . Altogether the US government has committed nearly $8.5 trillion, around 60% of its gross domestic production, to arrest the collapse of its financial system" (Sikka, 2009: 869).
10. Over the 2000–2005 period, AIG [American International Group] paid US$1.6 billion in fines for misreporting its books, but despite such a relaxed attitude towards formal accounting procedures, the corporation was "still viewed as one of the great financial institutions in the world," Freeman (2010: 168) writes.

Part II
Management Practices in the Neoliberal Era

3 Corporate Governance and the Financialization of the Firm

INTRODUCTION

As we saw in Part I of this volume, neoliberalism is an elusive and amorphous term, an aggregate of quite heterogeneous elements and intellectual trajectories that share a commitment to free market transactions as being more efficient than various forms of centrally planned and governed economic activities. However, as opposed to the common sense view that proponents of neoliberal policies advocate a "nightwatcher state" where the state only executes a minimal role, in the neoliberal era the state is instead assigned a key role in securing the free circulation of capital. That is, proponents of neoliberal policy are not conceiving of the state as its enemy but as its ally (see, e.g., Hacker and Pierson, 2010). For instance, Ronald Reagan boldly announced that government was not the "solution" to, but instead the "problem" in a series of economic and social malaises, only to quickly become the President creating the largest budget deficits in the post-World War II period. Populist declarations and the *Realpolitik* do not always go hand in hand in contemporary politics. In this section of this volume, the relationship between overarching neoliberal agendas and policies and the practice of management will be examined. The part includes three chapters addressing, in turn, corporate governance, human resource management practices, and auditing. The relationship between the neoliberal theory and policy and the concepts of management is long-standing and complex—deeply intertwined at their very roots. When the first business schools were started in the latter half of the nineteenth century and the first decades of the twentieth century, they were part of a series of professional schools being developed within the university system. In the first decades of the nineteenth century, following the Napoleon wars, the *écoles polytechniques* were developed in France, and they aimed at providing the state-of-the-art engineering competence needed in the Republic to catch up with, for example, the economically successful British empire. In addition, medical schools were developed in close association with the hospitals in the major French cities—at a secure distance from the medieval universities (e.g., Sorbonne) maintaining an arch-conservative medieval or even ancient understanding of medicine, quite different from the program of experimental medicine advanced by proponents of experimental medicine, such as Xavier Bichat and Claude Bernard. In addition to these French innovations, the German states—most noteworthy Prussia—started to actively modernize the Italian medieval university and actively promote collaborations between scientists and the emerging German industry (in, e.g., the chemical industry; Lenoir, 1994). The Wharton Business School at the University of Pennsylvania was founded in 1881 and can be seen as the first major American innovation in the university system. Intended to train the new professional class of managers, a new category of workers who, practically speaking, were non-existent prior to the civil war (Chandler, 1977), the idea of the professional manager was modelled on that of the engineer or lawyer, a professional actor equipped with a combination of theoretical training and practical tools and methods needed to excel in the trade (Fourcade and Khurana, 2013). It is noteworthy that the first contributors to management practice and management literature were, in fact, engineers advancing and advocating concepts such as systematic management and scientific management (Guillén, 1994). Business school graduates, quickly growing in number in the decades following 1881 (Khurana, 2007), managed to catch up with the engineers by the 1930s; the period of engineer-driven management thinking came to an end as what Shenhav (1999) refers to as the "progressive period" (1880–1930) ran out of steam. Business schools were designed to equip future managers and business functionaries with a set of tools and skills, and it was not until the early 1960s that business schools were increasingly criticized for failing to pursue more scholarly ambitions—to become a science based on systematic inquiry and scientific methods (Whitley, 1986; Kieser and Leiner, 2009; Corley and Gioia, 2011). From the early 1960s, business schools have gradually shifted their focus to comply with the demand for scientific rigor, and consequently there have been discussions about the "practical relevance" of the increasingly esoteric models and theories formulated in business schools (Lorsch, 2009; Bennis and O'Toole, 2005; Starkey and Madan, 2001). For critics such as Khurana (2007), the business school as institution is more or less a failed project, inasmuch as it is riddled by ambiguities regarding its social role, and the ambition to institute managers as a professional category has since long been abandoned (Pfeffer, 2011). On the other hand, in most advanced countries, enrolling in a business school program and earning a diploma has been a safe and highly rewarding human capital investment—a ticket to a relatively convenient middle class career and life. In many advanced countries, degrees from business schools are the most popular choice of undergraduate and graduate students, and business administration and management studies are the most prominent academic disciplines in terms of student enrolment.

Neoliberal policy and the neoliberal agenda prescribe market-based transactions, and the very term *management* is inextricably bound up with market-based activities. Public sector organizations have historically been associated with terms such as *administration* or, more recently, the terms including the marker *public*, as in *new public management*. One may actually quip that "neoliberalism is the theory and management the practice." In a famous passage, Jorge Luis Borges asserts that the reader can be sure that the Bible has its origin the Middle East precisely because there are no camels featured in its books, an observation that Borges explains on the basis of the Bible's authors' familiarity with this species, granting them no particular significance. For Borges, what is "present in its absence" can be taken as evidence of origin. By analogy, the very term *neoliberalism* is conspicuously absent in management writing (Styhre, 2014), arguably because an overarching political-analytical framework emphasizing market-based transactions and thereby implying the need for professional—or at least skilled—management practice does not deserve any critical reflection. What is more curious, though, is that self-declared critics of managerial practices and ideologies—that is, the quite diverse community of so-called critical management studies scholars, otherwise keen on pointing out underlying assumptions and ideologies in managerial texts and practices—have more or less failed to address the significance of neoliberalism. However, it is beyond the scope of this book to engage in this kind of self-reflexive practice. Instead, this chapter will address one of the most significant changes in management practice during the last three decades: the shift from traditional management thinking, taking into account the interests of a variety of constituents, to shareholder value based corporate governance, anchored in and justified by agency theory (Dobbin and Jung, 2010). This radical re-enactment of the role and assignment of managers arguably represents a most decisive shift in management practice—Fourcade and Khurana (2013: 151) speak about a "managerial revolution in reverse"—directly related to the financialization of the economy in the neoliberal era.

I. FROM MANAGERIAL CAPITALISM TO FINANCE MARKET CONTROL

Corporate Governance

Corporate governance is the theory of how organizations, and primarily private firms, should be governed in order to accomplish their goals and objectives (Davis, 2005). That is, on the basis of what legal, financial, and industrial relations resources and policies should the firm be controlled and managed? A quite extensive literature (see, e.g., Gourevitch and Shinn, 2005; Fligstein and Choo, 2005; Pagano and Belloc, 2009) points at the differences between different societies, cultures, and regions that reflect national political, social, and cultural trajectories. Fligstein and Choo (2005) list three elements of these "systems of corporate governance": First, *company law* "[d]efines the legal vehicles by which property rights are organized" (Fligstein and Choo, 2005: 63). Second, *financial market regulation* refers to how firms "obtain capital for their operations" (Fligstein and Choo, 2005: 63) and in defining these regulatory frameworks, relations between firms, banks, other financial institutions, and debt markets are specified. Third and finally, *labour law and industrial relations* define how labour contracts will operate in a specific society (Fligstein and Choo, 2005: 63). As there are different versions of corporate governance, a significant amount of effort has been dedicated to the identification of a "one best way" to handle the combination of legal rights, the supply of finance, and industrial relations, and there are a number of alternatives that have their own strength and weaknesses. Free-market–minded economists tend to assume that the American model, strongly emphasizing finance market orientation and the need to secure rents for shareholders, is more effective than the so-called German model that to a higher extent relies on state intervention. However, Fligstein and Choo (2005) argue that there is an increasing agreement among corporate governance scholars that there is "no best way," but a variety of systems that reflect idiosyncratic regional histories and preferences.

In the following, the specific agency theory model of corporate governance, stressing shareholder value as a key goal for any private corporation, will be examined. It will be demonstrated how corporate law is treated as what is important in securing low so-called agency costs and an adequate return on investment for the shareholders. In addition, this version of corporate governance strongly disregards the industrial relations element because trade unions and other forms of organized labour intervene into the overarching objective of the firm, which is to maximize rents for the shareholders.

Agency Theory and the Problem of the Separation of Ownership and Management

As the idea of professional managers was not developed until the post-American Civil War years, when larger corporations such as the North American railroad companies were developed (Perrow, 2002; Yates, 1989), ownership and management was essentially executed by the same person— the owner of the corporation. As long as companies remained relatively small and not too geographically dispersed, owners could effectively oversee their operations in order to assure that their investments were used in their best interests. With the emergence of the larger corporations, such as the divisionalized form developed by, for example, General Motors in the 1920s, ownership and control was gradually separated in time and space. This new demand for professional managers working on behalf of the owners constituted a new set of analytical problems for economists and lawmakers. In 1934, Berle and Means published the seminal work *The Modern Corporation & Private Property*, dealing with the consequences of the separation between ownership and management. Berle and Means suggested that *the principal* (the owner, the "residual claimant" who "contract[s] for the rights to net cash flow," in Fama and Jensen's [1983: 302] technical vocabulary) and *the agent* (the manager, e.g., the CEO or other salaried managers) formulate a contract regulating their mutual responsibilities. Berle and Means' ([1934] 1991) seminal work paved the way for what would be referred to as "the market for corporate control" (e.g., Manne, 1965) and the more specific theory of agency theory. In agency theory, the firm is enacted as a bundle of contracts between the principal(s) and the agents. While the contract is supposed to serve as the legal and psychological bond between the principal and the agent, there is still—which is somewhat ironic given the name of the theory—a mistrust of the agent built into agency theory (Perrow, 1986; Shapiro, 2005). Says Mizruchi (2004: 586): "Agency theory is in many respects a critique of managerialism. Its proponents acknowledge the difficulties that emerge with the dispersal of stockholding and the rise of management, but they want to address them within the framework of more conventional economic theory." As Eisenhardt (1989: 64) points out in her review of the literature, "agency theory reminds us that much of organizational life, whether we like it or not, is based on self-interest." In the following, the concept of agency theory will be examined in greater detail.

The Emergence of Finance Theory View and Shareholder Value Ideologies

While the access to financial capital has always played a key role in all capitalist economies, beginning perhaps with the Italian city-states of Venice and Genua (Arrighi, 2010), the interest in finance was surprisingly low in the era of capitalist expansion of the twentieth century. "Between the 1920s and the 1970s, financial control more or less disappeared from writings about business and the economy. Managerialism became the dominant theory of business control from the 1930s through the 1960s," Stearns (2006: 48) writes. As a consequence, business school training in finance theory and financial matters was quite unsophisticated for a long period of time: "Until the middle of the 20th century, money management was a craft-based vocation that did not rely on rigorous theories, analytical tools and techniques," Lounsbury and Crumley (2007: 999) argue (see also Whitley, 1986). Finance was regarded as a respectable but somewhat dull professional domain of expertise and it certainly did not include any speculative elements.

The American post-World War II economy was characterized by an accumulation of capital derived from savings. Gross savings increased from approximately $30 billion a year in 1945 to $150 billion a year in 1964 ($51 billion to $160 billion in constant 1967 dollars), Stearns (2006: 56) reports. As a consequence, between 1949 and 1965, capital available for investment increased by 258% or "from $511 billion to £1,827 billion ($715 billion to $1,937 billion in constant 1967 dollars)" (Stearns, 2006: 59). In the period beginning in the 1950s, finance theory, a branch of economics, was developed in business schools and in economics department. The new generation of finance professors started to develop their own theories regarding, for example, market efficiency, and they developed an analytical framework that would revolutionize the finance industry and finance work—for instance, the Capital Asset Pricing Model (CAPM), the bedrock of elementary finance theory and financial trading.

After the economically and politically shaky years of the 1970s, the new Reagan administration found itself in a situation in which foreign capital flooded into the American economy, further contributing to the stock of capital available for investment. The oversupply of capital made investment in financial operations relatively cheap, which in turn led to a wave of so-called hostile takeovers, a new phenomenon in the American economy. Equipped with capital funds and new finance theory models, a new generation of financial knowledge workers thus strongly shaped how the concept of management and the role of executives were re-enacted in the neoliberal era. Dobbin and Zorn (2005) explain the procedure:

> Hostile takeover firms dramatically reshaped large corporations in the late 1970s and the early 1980s by dismantling diversified conglomerates and selling off the parts, demonstrating that diversified firms had low stock prices that did them a disservice to their shareholders . . . In a short period of time, they gave a bad name to diversification and focused corporate attention on stock price, because they only took over firms that were undervalued and that could be sold off, piece by piece, at a profit. (Dobbin and Zorn, 2005: 185)

The relatively undervalued conglomerates that had been developed during the 1970s were thus sold off piece by piece. Executives all of a sudden found themselves in a situation in which the stock price had to be carefully attended to because neglecting the valuation of their firms by financial markets could lead to a hostile takeover bids that "left the CEO jobless" (Dobbin and Zorn, 2005: 187). As a consequence, stock prices became of necessity a key executive priority because capital was in over-supply, the bear market on the stock exchange undervalued major corporations, and a new class of finance industry actors played a more active role. While the era of hostile takeovers was relatively short, limited to a few years in the mid-1980s, this new emphasis on stock prices and what eventually would be referred to as shareholder value policies would be more long-lasting. "The conventional wisdom ca. 1980 was that if an investor did not like the way a firm was managed, she could vote with her feet, moving her money elsewhere. Institutional investors came to believe that it made more sense to reform management than to sell off stock," Dobbin and Zorn (2005: 188) write. That is, rather than to have to engage in what was referred to as "hostile takeover," strongly disliked by liberal media and the wider public—Oliver Stone's *Wall Street* (1987) was an early popular culture account of the new financial class and their questionable morals and alleged greed; Tom Wolfe's novel *The Bonfire of the Vanities* (1987), another example—it would have been more advantageous for capital owners if managers acted in accordance with their interests:

> Institutional investors were vocal advocates for replacing the old executive compensation system, which amounted to pay-for-size because the highest salaries typically went to managers of the largest corporations, with pay-for-performance via stock options. They sometimes cited agency theory in economics. (Dobbin and Zorn, 2005: 189)

The finance industry actors thus managed to first force executives and boards of directors to pay attention to stock prices under the threat of hostile takeovers; thereafter, these executives either complied with the interest of capital owners or were simply displaced by the new generation of managers trained in finance theory and committed to the objective of shareholder enrichment. As a consequence, they strongly contributed to the de-institutionalization and abandonment of the conglomerate corporate form (Davis, Diekmann, and Tinsley, 1994). A key aspect of this shift in top management objectives was that the change was not initiated by the traditional capital owning classes and strata—what Mizruchi (2010) refers to as the "American corporate elite"—but by a new category of knowledge workers: professional finance traders. One of the key accomplishments of this new class of professional finance traders was to institutionalize the new shareholder value regime by making a wider set of actors believe that privileging the shareholders over all other organizational constituencies was beneficial for all of the economy (Dobbin and Zorn, 2005: 187). In accomplishing this objective, agency theory and the work done to advance it as a credible analytical framework were of decisive importance. Macroeconomic conditions arguably strongly affected the new situation, leading to the re-enactment of the executive's role in corporations as the guardian of shareholder interests, but these conditions were also accompanied by more theoretical and ideological changes.

Agency Theory: Advocating Finance-Marked Management Control

Finance Theory Developed and Put to Use

A key concern is to understand how a relatively abstract theoretical model could be translated into managerial practice that, in turn, led to radical changes in how capital accumulates and economic compensations are acquired. Lazonick and O'Sullivan (2000) argue that agency theory (Jensen and Meckling, 1976; Alchian and Demsetz, 1972; Williamson, 1975, 1979; Fama, 1980) was the underlying theoretical construct justifying the quite comprehensive changes in corporate governance from the end of the 1970s:

> Given the entrenchment of incumbent corporate managers and the relatively poor performance of their companies in the 1970s, agency

theorists argued that there was a need for a takeover market that, functioning as a market for corporate control, could discipline managers whose companies performed poorly. The rate of return on corporate stock was their measure of superior performance, and the maximization of shareholder value became their creed. (Lazonick and O'Sullivan, 2000: 16)

One path of investigation is to examine how one of the foremost proponents and advocates of both agency theory and financialization, Michael C. Jensen, is articulating a theoretical framework that justifies the shift from traditional managerial practices to the more recent financialization of the economy and the firm, conceiving of the corporation as a bundle of financial resources that can be invested more or less effectively. Dobbin and Zorn (2005: 187) point at Jensen's work as being of central importance to the advancement of agency theory and shareholder value policies:

Jensen . . . legitimized takeover activity as a mechanism for ousting poorly performing chief executives and giving control of the firms to those better suited to run them. In the end, takeover specialists convinced the world that what they did for a living, far from threatening the corporation, was efficient. That it was in the interest of shareholders. (Dobbin and Zorn, 2005: 187)

Jensen's advocacy of agency theory can be regarded as the effect of wider social, political, and economic changes in the 1970s and 1980s (Bratton and Wachter, 2010). At the same time, Jensen is a prominent economic theorist and one of the most renowned proponents of agency theory and the corporate governance practices derived from its propositions. Jensen's work, examined below, is, in other words, not only to be treated as an articulation of opportune and timely ideas conceiving of "old school managerialism" as being inefficient and outmoded, but also as what has served to enact new managerial roles in major corporations, from a position where the interests of a number of constituents influence decision-making to a situation where primarily the interests of shareholders matters. In many ways, Jensen's presidential address at the American Finance Association in Anaheim, California, in January 1993, published in *Journal of Finance* the same year and discussed below, is an exemplary text in its advocacy of an agency theory perspective on corporate governance.

Components of Agency Theory
In 1976, Jensen and Meckling published a paper that would become a seminal contribution to agency theory in which they conceived of the firm as a "nexus of contracts." The nature of the firm is not so much, as proposed by Ronald Coase ([1937] 1991) and transaction costs theorists such as Oliver Williamson (1975, 1979), a site where transaction costs are minimized

through a combination of skilled management and the contracting of external suppliers, as it is a *legal* construct based on agreements between what agency theorists speak of as principals and agents (Moe, 1984). Based on a combination of corporate law and economic theory, agency theory renders the principal (in most cases, the owners, e.g., shareholders) a key position in understanding and explaining the functioning of corporations. "An organization is the nexus of contracts, written and unwritten, among owners of factors of production and customers," Fama and Jensen (1983: 302) state. At the same time, it is the principals, or what Fama and Jensen in their technical vocabulary refer to as the *residual claimants*, the shareholders (in the case of listed companies)—"those who contract for the rights to net cash flow" (Fama and Jensen, 1983: 302)—who are given a privileged position in this totality of contracts formulated. For agency theorists, a major concern is what is referred to as *agency costs,* which in turn are derived from the risks (actual as well as potential) of *opportunistic behavior.* Say Fama and Jensen (1983):

> Agency problems arise because contracts are not costlessly written and enforced. Agency costs include the costs of structuring, monitoring, and bonding a set of contracts among agents with conflicting interests. Agency costs also include the value of output lost because the costs of full enforcement of contracts exceed the benefits. (Fama and Jensen, 1983: 304)

This is the core of the agency theory argument and its scepticism towards traditional managerial practice: that there are "conflicting interests" between not only labour and capital, as theorized and studied by, for example, Marxist economic theory, but also between capital owners and salaried managers and executives. Historically, social theorists and economists have assumed that both capital owners and professional managers, especially those recruited to executive positions, share a basic commitment to capital accumulation. Such assumptions cannot be justified offhand, agency theorists claim. On the contrary, there is ample evidence, they hold, that managers are primarily concerned with securing their own positions, an attitude that leads to agency costs and that justifies a set of activities prescribed by agency theory. Fama and Jensen (1983: 304) state this point:

> Control of agency problems in the decision process is important when the decision managers who initiate and implement important decisions are not the major residual claimants and therefore do not bear a major share of the wealth effects of their decisions. Without effective control procedures, such decisions managers are more likely to take actions that deviate from the interest of residual claimants. (Fama and Jensen, 1983: 304)

They continue: "Without separation of decision management from decision control, residual claimants have *little protection against opportunistic actions of decision agents*, and this lowers the value of unrestricted residual claims" (Fama and Jensen, 1983: 304–305; emphasis added). This overtly negative attitude towards professional salaried managers is a shared thread throughout Jensen's work. In a paper published in 1986, Jensen introduces the term *free cash flow theory* to theorize the troubled relationship between owners and managers:

> Free cash flow is cash in excess of that required to fund all projects that have positive net present values when discounted at the relevant cost of capital. Conflicts of interest between shareholders and managers over payout policies are especially severe when the organization generates substantial free cash flow. The problem is how to motivate managers to disgorge the cash rather than investing it at below the cost of capital or wasting it on organizational inefficiencies. (Jensen, 1986: 323)

Again, there is always the risk, Jensen (1986: 328) warns, that managers "[w]ith unused borrowing power and large free cash flows," if not being monitored and disciplined by the shareholder, will undertake "low-benefit or even value-destroying mergers." "No longer can we assume managers automatically act (in opposition to their own best interests) to maximize firm value," Jensen (1993: 868) writes elsewhere. Much social and economic theory has assumed that capital owners represent a privileged social stratum with good access to resources that can secure their social position and economic interests (see, e.g., Volscho and Kelly, 2012; Hacker and Pierson, 2010). In Fama and Jensen's (1983) and Jensen's (1986) view, very much the opposite is in fact the case. Capital owners are in the hands of decision makers who are not necessarily sharing a commitment to their interest to maximize the return-on-investment. That agency theory is an attractive theory for capital owners is beyond doubt, capable as it is of explaining, for example, failed investments not so much on basis of macroeconomic conditions, immature markets, or sheer luck, but on basis of the insidious negligence of the residual claimants' interests among managers. The trick of agency theorists is how they manage to make the specific interests of the capital owners become a widely shared commitment to capital accumulation and circulation in the wider community. In accomplishing such objectives, the quite recently formulated hypothesis on efficient markets, first articulated by Eugene Fama and fully subscribed to by Michael Jensen, has served as an Euclidian axiom for the extended agency theory framework.

Jensen's Argument in Favour of the Social Benefits of Agency Theory

Writing in the early 1990s, Jensen compares the 1980s with the 1890s as two decades characterized by quick economic growth in the American economy. The merger boom of the 1890s, consolidating capital into larger units, led to an annual growth total factor productivity that was almost "[s]ix times higher than that which had occurred for most of the nineteenth century" (Jensen, 1993: 834). Comparably, in the 1980s, Jensen (1993: 832) suggests, when "the capital markets helped eliminate excess capacity through leveraged acquisitions, stock buybacks, hostile takeovers, leveraged buyouts, and divisional sales," a similar growth in total factor productivity could be observed:

> Total factor productivity growth in the manufacturing sector more than doubled after 1981 from 1.4 percent per year in the period 1950 to 1981 to 3.3 percent in the period 1981 to 1990. Nominal unit labor costs stopped their 17-year rise, and real unit labor costs declined by 25 percent. These lower labor costs came not from reduced wages or employment but from increased productivity: Nominal and real hourly compensation increased by a total of 4.2 and 0.3 percent per year respectively over the 1981 to 1989 period. (Jensen, 1993: 836)[1]

In addition, during the 1980s, the "real value of public firms' equity more than doubled from $1.4 to $3 trillion" (Jensen, 1993: 837). Jensen strongly questions the critique of the alleged "greed" of financial actors and deplores the wide-ranging call for protectionist initiatives in, for example, the manufacturing industry. Instead, Jensen advances finance-based control of corporations as the *only* effective corporate governance regime (Dobbin and Jung, 2010: 42). Hostile takeovers should therefore not be seen as a "form of disruptive speculation, but as a restraint on managerial malfeasance."[2] In his presidential address, Jensen is primarily concerned about exits from markets, the liquidation of resources in the face of insurmountable competition in certain industries, and he carefully advances a series of arguments for why financial analysts are in a better position to evaluate how economic resources should avoid being "wasted"—that is, unproductively invested in industries in decline. Jensen here stresses the inertia and myopic view of both CEO and board members:

> Firms often do not have good information on their own costs, much less the costs of their competitors; it is therefore sometimes unclear to managers that they are the high-cost firm which should exit the industry. Even when managers do acknowledge the requirement for exits, it is often difficult for them to accept and initiate the shutdown decision. For the managers who must implement these decisions, shutting plants or liquidating the firms causes personal pain, creates uncertainty, and interrupts or sidetracks careers. Rather than confronting the pain, managers generally resist such actions as long as they have the cash flow to subsidize the losing operations. (Jensen, 1993: 848)

According to Jensen (1993), there are "four control forces" influencing the corporation: (1) capital markets, (2) the legal/political/regulatory system,

(3) the product and factor markets, and (4) an "internal control system headed by boards of directors" (Jensen, 1993: 850). The legal/political/regulatory system is, Jensen (1993: 850) states, "far too blunt an instrument to handle the problems of wasteful managerial behavior effectively," and products and factor markets are "too slow" to effectively regulate the uses of capital as they are determined by long-term contracts and other juridical agreements. In addition, there is, Jensen (1993: 850) continues, "substantial data" that support the proposition that "the internal control systems of publicly held corporations have generally failed to cause managers to maximize efficiency and value." What remains is capital market-based control: "The capital markets [is] an effective mechanism for motivating change, renewal, and exit," Jensen (1993: 852) asserts. To further justify this proposition, Jensen presents a series of statements. First, "by nature," Jensen (1993: 852) says, "organizations abhor control systems, and ineffective governance is a major part of the problem with internal control mechanisms. They seldom respond in the absence of a crisis." Second, the day-to-day work of corporate boards is also ineffective, in Jensen's (1993: 863) view: "Board culture is an important component of board failure. The great emphasis on politeness and courtesy at the expense of truth and frankness in boardrooms is both the symptom and cause of failure in the system." The CEO is capable of controlling the flow of information to board members and setting the agenda for the meetings, and this autocratic control leads to, Jensen (1993: 864) says, a lower firm performance. All these declarations regarding the alleged work procedures in executive tiers in organizations leave the agency theorist with few alternatives other than to fully endorse capital market-based corporate governance: "The evidence from LBOs, leveraged restructurings, takeovers, and venture capital firms has demonstrated dramatically that leverage, payout policy, and ownership structure (that is, who owns the firm's securities) do in fact affect organizational efficiency, cash flow, and therefore, value," Jensen (1993: 868) summarizes.

In a more recent paper, Jensen (2002) has modified his views somewhat and introduces the quite pompous term *enlightened value maximization*, but his basic view that corporations should maximize market value of the firm for the benefit of the shareholder remains and so does his ignorance regarding the role of professional managers in the capitalist economy. In the 2002 paper, Jensen criticizes stakeholder theory (Keay, 2011; Hillman and Kiem, 2001; Key, 1999) for advocating that corporations should pay attention to the interests of a variety of constituencies. For Jensen, stakeholder theory is "fundamentally flawed" as it "violates" what Jensen's call the "proposition that any organization must have a single-values objective as a precursor to purposeful or rational behavior" (Jensen, 2002: 237). That is, the very idea that corporations should have more than one objective is dismissed by Jensen as a preposterous proposition: "[F]irms that adopt stakeholder theory will be handicapped in the competition for survival because, as a basis for action, stakeholders politicize the corporation, and leaves its managers empowered to exercise their own preferences in spending the firm's resources" (Jensen, 2002: 237). Later on, Jensen's persistent disregard for managers and their competence surfaces again:

> With no criteria for performance, managers cannot be evaluated in any principled way. Therefore, stakeholder theory plays into the hands of self-interested managers allowing them to pursue their own interests at the expense of society and the firm's financial claimants. It allows managers and directors to invest their favorite projects that destroy firm-value whatever they are (the environment, art, cities, medical research) without having to justify the value destruction. (Jensen, 2002: 242)

That Jensen's agency theory itself strongly politicizes the corporations, as it makes claims that corporate law is insignificant and impotent in handling agency costs and the possibility of managerial opportunistic behaviour, does not prevent him from accusing others of politicizing the corporation. Because "multiple objectives is no objective" in Jensen's (2002: 238) view, he proposes that "maximizing the total market value of the firm" would be "one objective function that will resolve the tradeoff problem among multiple constituencies" (Jensen, 2002: 239). For Jensen, financial market control in the form of maximized shareholder value is the solution to all forms of agency costs and efficiency problems.

Critical Responses to Agency Theory

Social and Political Explanation for Corporate Governance Regimes

Agency theory, as advocated by Michael Jensen, has been subject to quite extensive criticism from both social scientists and legal scholars. These two bodies of literature will be reviewed briefly. Agency theory assumes that managers "behave badly" and boards of directors avoid their "fiduciary responsibilities," and therefore financial markets serve to "provide a final check on managerial opportunism" (Fligstein and Choo, 2005: 65). As a consequence, assuming that finance markets are effective in executing managerial control, for agency theorists, "[h]istory, culture, and politics are irrelevant for the issue of how to get the right (i.e., efficient) mix of investments made in a particular economy," Fligstein and Choo (2005: 66) propose. For agency theorists, societies that pursue goals "other than shareholder wealth through their corporate governance structures," or that "ignore the problem of agency costs entirely" are doomed to underperformance because their capital stock will be inefficiently allocated in the economy. In addition, when withholding "free cash flow," they are potentially starving emerging industries while upholding stagnant sectors of the economy and failing to provide capital investment for the entrepreneurial class that propels the economic development in capitalist regimes of accumulation (Fligstein and Choo, 2005: 66). This is a compelling narrative, but it is resting on the wrong assumptions and is inconsistent with empirical data, Fligstein and Choo (2005) suggest, speaking of "the empirical failure of agency theory." First, there is an economic theory fallacy underlying agency theory, inasmuch as it is assumed that systems of corporate governance are aiming at creating the most "efficient solution" to corporate governance problems. That may be the case in a Panglossian best-of-all-possible-worlds scenario, but in actual settings, systems of corporate governance "[r]esult from political and historical processes rather than from efficient solutions to the functional needs of the owners of capital who seek to maximize profits for themselves" (Fligstein and Choo, 2005: 66). "[S]everal major features of American corporations are more parsimoniously explained as outcomes of political struggles than as adaptations designed to serve the best interests of shareholders," Davis and Thompson (1994: 146) say. For instance, Roy (1997) demonstrates that American corporations evolved from within governmental projects aimed at serving public interest, and consequently what Roy refers to as *efficiency theory*, which assumes that "private enterprises, disciplined by an unforgiving market, are inherently more efficient than government decision making" (Roy, 1997: 75), overlooks or ignores historical data. Rather than being based on some enacted "efficiency criteria," the corporate form was developed on basis of practical interests:

> [The] most private of our economic structures, the large business corporation, arose as a quasi-government agency. Some of its particular features, such as limited liability, perpetual life, and parcellized ownership, were established not so much because they were efficient but to compensate for the inefficient tasks corporations were assigned, like building canals, turnpikes, and bridges, where markets would not support them . . . The corporation was after all a delegation of sovereign powers to serve the public interest, thus the corporation did not grow by an evolutionary process by which an organizational form was perfected to its maximum efficiency. (Roy, 1997: 76)

Second, there is ample evidence that many societies have experienced comparable economic growth without converging towards the American form of corporate governance, and such evidence suggests that there is no single best way, but many ways to organize and structure economic activities (Fligstein and Choo, 2005: 66–67). Third, such evidence suggests, at least in the case of developed countries, that economic growth is more likely to come about because there are stable and predictable political institutions overseeing and monitoring the economy rather than because of the application of a specific corporate governance model benefitting a single category of constituencies (Fligstein and Choo, 2005: 67). That is, a stable government that does not seek excessive rents itself (e.g., in the form of payoffs, bribes, and extortion, all making business investment more complicated to predict), that helps resolve the issue of "class struggle," that allows private actors to accumulate wealth protected by property rights, and that more generally provides public order, seems to be a vital recipe for economic growth (Fligstein and Choo, 2005: 67–68). Fligstein and Choo agree with Jensen (1993) that one of the central problems of economic development and growth in any country is how to match people who have money with people in demand for financing their economic ventures (Fligstein and Choo, 2005: 74). Fligstein and Choo (2005) say that the corporate governance literature shows that "well-developed financial institutions" capable of supplying capital to entrepreneurs is an important element of an effective corporate governance model. Agency theory suggests that shareholders claiming rents from their investments are in the position to serve this role, but the unprecedented expansion of the finance market and finance industry and the decline in investment in production resources suggests that these rent-seeking capital owners have not been overtly concerned about supplying capital to insecure entrepreneurial ventures in, for example, the life sciences. In summary, based on these faulty assumptions and limited support from empirical evidence, the agency theory model for corporate governance is not capable of accomplishing much more than enriching the shareholders. Whether that pursuit is beneficial for the wider society and economy remains to be determined, but there is little evidence of such outcomes: In the neoliberal era, economic inequality increases at the same time that economic growth is lower and unemployment is higher.

Managerial Practices and Shareholder Value Polices
Agency theorists, Perrow (1986: 11) says, build theoretical models "almost always without empirical data." In the following, the empirical significance of agency theory will be examined by drawing on available studies. Based on the outcome from the shareholder value regime implemented in the neoliberal era—data that Jensen of course could not access in 1976, 1983, 1993, and 2002 (the years of his publications cited above)—Dobbin and Zorn (2005: 196) argue that agency theory's solution to the problem of "agency costs" led to new forms of opportunistic behaviour (to be discussed shortly) that were just as socially and economically undesirable as previous behaviour, resulting in, for example, amorphous conglomerates:

> If paying CEOs a fixed salary and a small bonus every year failed to resolve the agency problem inherent to hiring managers to run companies they do not own, the use of stock options and other 'long term incentives,' did not resolve the problem either. It has changed the specifics of the problem. Executives focus irrationally on managing earnings, rather than on new corporate conquests. (Dobbin and Zorn, 2005: 196)

That is, when executives are encouraged to target stock prices and enrich shareholders in the short-term perspective, they have few incentives to make investments and make commitments to long-term projects that would secure the firm's survival over time. Instead, they are compensated for taking excessive risks but never penalized for failing:

> The new compensation system encouraged executives to take risks, but because the system was implemented to reward executives for increasing stock prices in the near term, but not to punish them for declines, it encouraged reckless risk-taking. Knowing they could only win, executives could afford to do deals that offered huge potential for profits and losses alike, knowing that for them, there was only an upside. (Dobbin and Jung, 2010: 37)

In the following sections, the empirical accuracy of agency theory will be examined, as a number of different components of the agency theory model of corporate governance have been subject to empirical research work.

Board of directors' size. In the agency theory framework and enactment of the firm, the board of directors serves a key function in enabling the shareholders' interests to be represented in the firm. That is, "effective boards will be largely comprised of independent, outside directors" (Dalton et al., 1999: 679; see also Dalton et al., 2001; Davis and Robbins, 2005). That is, the representation of shareholder interests in the board should, agency theory predicts, positively affect performance. However, based on data comprising 20,620 American firms, Dalton et al. (1999) found no correlation between board of directors' size and firm performance, providing no evidence in support of the agency theory view of the central role of the board of directors. Davis and Robbins's (2005) study of 647, 691 (twice), and 822 firms (over the years 1982, 1986, 1990, and 1994) provides a similar weak correlation between board composition and performance, suggesting that while firms that out-perform their industry "are somewhat better able to recruit CEOs and central directors," there is still is "no evidence that boards composed of these individuals enhance subsequent performance" (Davis and Robbins, 2005: 291). Therefore, Davis and Robbins (2005) conclude, "board composition appears to be an effect of performance, not a cause." In other words, rather than supporting the instrumental view of the board of directors proposed by agency theory, Davis and Robbins's (2005: 290) study support the "traditional managerialist view" that sees directors as "ornaments on the corporate Christmas tree"—"decorative objects chosen by the CEO to burnish the firm's image for the outside world (particularly the financial markets that evaluate them) while interfering as little as possible in the operations of the corporation." Davis and Robbins (2005) summarize their study:

> For better or worse, boards are social institutions first, by positioning the firm in a larger network that influences what information it gets and what kind of normative pressures it is susceptible to. The influence of network position on governance practice is indisputable, but its impact on quality per se is subtle at best. (Davis and Robbins, 2005: 310)

Board of directors' composition. Agency theory suggests that independent boards of directors—that is, directors representing shareholder interest—are capable of reducing agency costs by stressing the importance of the creation of shareholder value (i.e., the performance of the firm). This assumption is not supported by empirical evidence. Bhagat and Black (2002: 236) reference four American studies, plus studies conducted in Australia, Singapore, and the United Kingdom, showing that there is no substantial effect on performance on independent boards of directors. On the contrary, four studies demonstrate that companies governed by independent boards perform worse than companies having a majority of the directors recruited internally. Based on a sample of 934 firms in 1991 and 205 randomly sampled boards in 1988, Bhagat and Black (2002) provide similar evidence that there is no correlation between independent boards of directors and firm performance: "We find a reasonably strong *inverse* correlation between firm performance in the recent past and board independence. However, there is no evidence that greater board independence leads to improved firm performance. If anything, there are hints that greater board independence may impair firm performance" (Bhagat and Black, 2002: 263). In addition to the studies of the boards of directors' correlation with performance, several studies examine the relationship between CEO practices, the board of directors, external agents such as finance market analysts, and the valuation of the stock (the ultimate measurement of economic performance and financial vigour in the agency theory framework). These studies by and large present a much more complex view of corporate governance than the schematic view of the relationship between principal and agents in agency theory advanced to justify shareholder value policies. This literature can be separated into at least three different bodies of work.

CEO and board of directors' relations. The weak correlation between board composition and performance can be explained by many factors and conditions in the CEO and board of directors' joint work. Westphal and Bednar's empirical study (2005) suggests that directors succumb to what they refer to as "pluralistic ignorance," a situation "[i]n which virtually all members of a group privately reject group norms, [practices, or policies, or have concerns about them] but believe that virtually all other group members accept them" (Westphal and Bednar, 2005: 264). Westphal and Bednar (2005: 286–287), suggest that "directors often hesitate to express their concerns about the viability of corporate strategy in board meetings, not because they lack independence from management but because they systematically underestimate the extent to which fellow directors share their concerns." That is, there are human factors and group dynamics at play that influence the work of the board of directors. In contrast to the agency theory model, prescribing the presence of independent board members, Westphal and Bednar (2005: 286) suggest that pluralistic ignorance is "significantly reduced" when there are "friendship ties" and "demographic homogeneity" in the board of directors—that is, there is a relatively low degree of diversity in the board. Bovie et al. (2011) suggest, based on empirical data, that the CEO's identification with the firm, rather than the presence of an independent board of directors, reduces agency costs and opportunistic behaviour. Second, Westphal and Bednar (2008: 62) found that presence of institutional investors in the board directors make CEOs engage in "persuasion and ingratiation tactics" in order to deter these representatives from using their ownership power to counteract the CEOs' interests. Various "interpersonal behaviors" on part of the CEO are, Westphal and Bednar (2008: 52) suggest, "generally effective" in avoiding board reforms that are thought to "[r]educe CEOs' discretion over strategy and policy outcomes." That is, CEOs are capable of handling institutional investors that attempt to reduce their executive discretion. "Our theory and supportive findings suggests that CEOs' interpersonal influence behavior provides an alternative source of influence in manager-shareholder relationships," Westphal and Bednar (2008: 63) conclude. Westphal and Graebner (2010: 35) report a study of how CEOs are capable of counteracting negative analyst appraisals in the form of "less optimistic earnings forecasts and less positive stock recommendations," by signalling an increased board independence to external constituents, but still not actually increasing the boards' "tendency to control management." That is, CEOs are capable of "engaging in communications" that frame board behaviour "[i]n terms of central normative prescription of the agency logic of governance, while making visible changes in board composition that *appear* to lend credence to their claims, but that are decoupled from actual board behavior" (Westphal and Graebner, 2010: 35). In Westphal and Graebner's view (2010: 36), such activities are a form of "impression management" that enable the CEO to respond to negative analyst appraisals in order to avoid downward stock prices, while still maintaining the control over decision-making procedures.

External reciprocal relations and stock market recommendations. Westphal and Clement (2008: 887–888) argue that CEOs are not only capable of influencing the market communication but also actively engaging in "social exchanges" with finance market analysts external to the firm to "neutralize the effects of negative or controversial information about their firms on analyst stock recommendation." Finance market analysts gain access to top executives, helping them to make better market recommendations, and the analysts reciprocate such "executive favor rendering" by maintaining favourable stock recommendations for the focal firm (Westphal and Clement, 2008: 888). In the cases in which analysts did downgrade their stock recommendations, they were punished by reduced personal access to top executives; "[a]nalysts who were aware of another analyst's loss of favor or access to executives after downgrading a focal firm were less likely to subsequently downgrade the firm in response to the disclosure of relatively low earnings or a diversifying acquisition," Westphal and Clement (2008: 889) suggest. These *reciprocal gift relations* (see, e.g., Cheal, 1988) based on "executive favor rendering" and analysts' leniency regarding the assessment

Corporate Governance and Financialization 105

of new negative information regarding firm performance pose a threat to effective and transparent market information reporting, and ultimately, Westphal and Clement (2008) argue, the allocation of resources may be negatively affected as certain investment opportunities appear to be more attractive than what can be substantiated by objective facts and moderate professional assessment:

> Security analysts, by issuing negative recommendations in response to poor firm performance or strategic actions that appear to serve management interest at the expense of shareholders, can direct capital and other resources away from underperforming firms and self-interested managers towards more productive users . . . An implication of our findings is that microsocial factors in manager-analyst relationships, by reducing the objectivity of security analysts' stock recommendation, may ultimately compromise corporate control and financial market efficiency. (Westphal and Clement, 2008: 890)

The role of stock repurchasing programs. Westphal and Zajac (2001) demonstrate that stock repurchasing programs (discussed in more detail below), a method for influencing the value of the stock which, in turn (in many cases), is part of the performance metrics on which CEOs can make claims of compensation, are capable of being "decoupled" from the formal policies that prohibit such practices. Since stock purchasing programs are always at risk of being a moral hazard, such interventions are regulated by policies, but Westphal and Zajac (2001) claim that CEOs and executives are capable of bypassing such policies (for an alternative view, see Zuckerman, 2004a). In a number of studies, CEOs, formally being controlled by financial markets, investors, and capital owners, are in fact capable of navigating in what Anteby (2008) calls a "moral grey zone" wherein what agency theorists refer to as opportunistic behaviour is still part of the accumulated agency costs. Clark (2009) stresses this failure of finance markets to eliminate such behaviour:

> The hegemony of agency theory is unable to countenance the possibility of owner-investor interests may generate inefficiency. A reliance on share options and the promotion of share prices may generate a bigger share of value-added remunerations, but what is empirically less clear is that this may not be the same as an increase in value added activities. (Clark, 2009: 783–784)

For other commentators, it is the belief in the efficiency of finance markets per se that needs to be subject to critical scrutiny. In this view, entrepreneurial capitalism, shaped by the creative destructive effects of novel ideas that can be capitalized, is at risk of being undermined by the short-term interests of an all-too-dominant rentier class. Froud et al. (2000) argue that the shareholder value regime, derived from the agency theory argument, is based on a fallacy, a faulty assumption that stock prices represent an indisputable underlying economic value:

> The promise of SV rests on a fallacy of composition and a paradox of levels of the classic kind Keynes criticized in the General Economy, when discussing how wage cuts might benefit one or a few firms but would not work as an economy-wide principle of action for all firms (except under extreme and unrealistic conditions). The homiletic examples in the consultancy literature obscure the central point that management actions and corporate positions that work to deliver shareholder value for some firms will not work for all. Corporate successes within one sector are in some cases achieved at the expense of failures elsewhere; and in more cases, the management actions or performance of successful firms rest on special case advantages which cannot be copied or will not produce equally large benefits for all who imitate. (Froud et al., 2000: 108)

By the end of the day, agency theory remains theoretically simplistic and unsubstantiated by empirical evidence. Still, agency theory has been remarkably successful in advancing the shareholders' right to the residual cash flow at the expense of all other constituents.

The Role of Corporate Law

In addition to the social and economic theory critique of agency theory, corporate law scholars have much to say in responding to claims made by agency theorists. Bratton and Wachter (2010), law school professors, argue that Jensen's argument fails to take into account how corporate law is written and enforced, carefully considering agency costs and the risks of opportunism. At the same time, legislation assumes, *contra* Jensen, that appointed managers are "better positioned" to oversee the operations than shareholders:

> Corporate law always performed a balancing act with management discretion and shareholder power. The balance, however, has always privileged the directors and their appointed managers in business policymaking because they are better informed than the shareholders and thus better positioned to take responsibility for both monitoring and managing the firms and its externalities. (Bratton and Wachter, 2010: 659)

In addition, Bratton and Wachter (2010: 660) argue that "the shareholder proponents" tend to depict agency costs as "a static, historical constant," while in fact there is ample evidence of finance reporting being both more closely monitored and more effective in communicating economic performance and economic assets held by corporations:

> Some studies show that market prices have become better informed over the past century. The information gaps between those inside and outside of the corporation has narrowed due in part to stricter mandatory disclosure requirements and in part to more liquid markets and larger sector of information intermediaries. (Bratton and Wachter, 2010: 668)

Bratton and Wachter (2010: 676) summarize Jensen's (1993) argument:

> [Agency theory] holds that managers will systematically fail to maximize value in predictable ways. They will favor conservative, low-leverage capital structures, misinvest excess cash in suboptimal projects, fail to reduce excess operating costs, and resist premium sales of control. All these missed opportunities amount to agency costs that could be reduced if the law provided for greater shareholder input. (Bratton and Wachter, 2010: 676)

First of all, Bratton and Wachter (2010: 675) strongly question the proposition that "the [traditional] corporate governance systems leave big money on the table"—a central assumption in Jensen's argument, that economic resources can be more effectively invested elsewhere if released in the form of dividends—and argue that it is both "counterintuitive" and unsubstantiated by empirical evidence. Furthermore, based on empirical evidence, Bratton and Wachter (2010: 659) undermine all arguments in favour of the view that shareholders are "[b]etter positioned to take responsibility for both monitoring and managing the firm and its externalities" on basis of alleged market efficiencies:

> We have seen that strong-form efficiency would support a nearly unassailable case for shareholder empowerment. But financial markets are not strong-form efficient. Information asymmetries are real. Empirical studies confirm this point beyond doubt, showing that managers who trade in the corporation's shares earn abnormally high returns. (Bratton and Wachter, 2010: 696)

On the contrary, the emphasis on what Bratton and Wachter (2010) refer to as "shareholder empowerment" leads to what Ireland (2010) speaks of as "the institutionalization of irresponsibility" as shareholders "[e]njoy income rights without needing to worry about how the dividends are generated" (Ireland, 2010: 845). For instance, as managers and the board of directors are increasingly compensated on basis of the value of the share, repurchasing of shares to manipulate the market price increased eighteen-fold from

1987 to the peak year of 2007 in terms of the annual dollar amount spent on repurchases (Bratton and Wachter, 2010: 686). Contrary to Jensen's argument, Ireland (2010) argues that the corporate legal form was more of a "[p]roduct of the growing political power and needs of *rentier* investors" (Ireland, 2010: 838). That is, from the very outset, the "residual claimants" have been favoured by corporate law. Agency theory is therefore, in Ireland's view, yet another attempt to further advance the interests of a group already enjoying quite substantial rights and privileges:

> At present, corporate shareholders (including parent companies) enjoy the best possible of all possible legal worlds. On the one hand they are, for some purposes, treated as 'completely separate' from the companies in which they hold shares and draw dividends, in that they are not personally responsible for the latter's debt or liabilities (or behaviour). On the other hand the companies in which they hold shares must be run exclusively in their interests: for these purposes the interests of 'the company' (formally a separate entity) are synonymous with those of the shareholders. (Ireland, 2010: 848)

Jensen and other agency theorists, equipped with the efficient market hypothesis, suggest that shareholder value policies reduce agency costs, increase the efficiency in capital allocation (transferring capital from stagnant to emerging industries and markets), and force corporations to maximize their performance. In contrast, legal scholars see few of these claims substantiated by empirical evidence or observe activities that have been predicted by agency theorists. Ireland (2010), for instance, records few of the social and economic benefits referred to by Jensen:

> By the early 1990s, the principle of shareholder primacy had been restored with a vengeance. Corporate managers today are much more accountable than they were—to the *rentier* shareholders with whom they are now much more closely entwined. Hence the relentless pursuit of 'shareholder value' by whatever means and whatever human, social and environmental costs. The consequences have been only too clear: a massive increase in speculative financial exchanges, regular financial crises, numerous corporate scandals, falling growth rates, a reduction in the rates of productivity growth and soaring executive remuneration. (Ireland, 2010: 852)

Faced with evidence that does not really comply with theoretical propositions and predictions made, it is tempting to claim that actors in fact failed to act in accordance with the prescribed theoretical framework. Stock buybacks, corporate crime (as in the much-debated case of Enron), and soaring executive compensations are, for instance, well documented evidence that suggests that opportunistic behaviour has not been eliminated from corporations in the neoliberal and shareholder value-based regime of corporate governance. For Jensen and other proponents of agency theory-based solutions to agency problems, the theory appeared to be able to handle problems facing corporations in the 1970s and 1980s, but more recent data show that their hopes for a fully transparent principal-agent relationship was complicated to fulfil.

Naturalist Fallacies in Agency Theory
A fourth critique of agency theory is concerned not so much with its poor support by empirical evidence and its inability to practically handle agency costs and opportunism (to be discussed shortly below) but the epistemological fallacy that agency theory fails to recognize. Donaldson (2012) discusses the so-called "naturalist fallacy" generally credited to the Scottish philosopher David Hume, suggesting that "[n]ormative prescriptions—that is, action guiding propositions—cannot be reduced without remainder to factual propositions" (Donaldson, 2012: 260). That is, there is an epistemological leap from an "is" to an "ought to" that demands a recognition of political and social interests. Donaldson (2012: 260) exemplifies: "An imperative such as 'Shut the door' does not state any fact about the door. And a statement of fact such as 'The door is locked' cannot be used to tell someone to do something." Much economic theory regularly succumbs to the naturalist fallacy inasmuch as their spokesmen argue that they are in the position to present positive accounts of economic conditions, but they also assume that policy recommendations can be unproblematically derived from the propositions presented. Hence the fallacy, the idea that one can describe the world—make a factual proposition—and advance "normative prescriptions" in the same statement. In the case of agency theory, the collapsing of factual propositions (regardless of their accuracy) and normative prescriptions undermines its value, as it fails to signal to the reader which category of proposition a statement belongs to. "[A]gency theorists' accounts presume straightforwardly that principals have a justified claim or entitlement to their property and that agents are justified—have authority—to act on behalf of the best interests of their principals," Donaldson (2012: 263) argues. In addition, "agency theory neglects to consider what general obligations, moral or otherwise, principals might have either to their agents or to other groups inside or outside the firm" (Donaldson, 2012: 264). As a consequence, the "the normative implications of agency theory" are "hidden behind the veil of presumed positivism and, in some instances, behind misleading uses of normative language" (Donaldson, 2012: 264). That is, Donaldson suggests that agency theory aims for too much, that it wants both to describe the world and prescribe actions that can accomplish certain enacted goals, but when confusing the two objectives, agency theory and practices derived therefrom accomplish neither. As a consequence, Donaldson (2012: 266) argues, agency theory not only fails to "guide corporations" more generally, but it also fails to "include some prescriptive support

for corporate cooperations," which in turn may negatively influence the "integrity of the broader economic system." Jensen's (2002, 1993, 1986) writing on agency theory represents a literary tradition in which highly contestable propositions are presented, often accompanied by limited empirical evidence (Jensen [1986], for instance, offers a few sweeping formulations about the oil industry in the 1980s to substantiate his thesis), and thereafter normative prescriptions follow. The positive proposition that there is a risk for opportunistic behaviour among executives (an axiom of agency theory) is not of necessity followed by the argument that only shareholder value can provide a final check on managers. This is a *non sequitur* argument based on the naturalist fallacy; in between factual propositions and normative prescriptions lie beliefs, norms, and preferences that are, by definition, outside of the scientific domain of expertise. One may either describe worlds or you prescribe normative action in such worlds, but the two activities need to be kept apart, especially in scientific communities that enjoy a significant degree of authority.

In Summary

At the very heart of the agency theory argument are the assumptions that (1) managers act opportunistically, and (2) the finance market can execute a disciplinary check on these managers. Davis and Stout (1992) found in their quantitative study that neither of these two claims was supported by evidence; it was the most successful companies—the best managed firms—that were targeted for takeovers, and "[n]either having a bank executive on the board nor control of a significant block of stock by a bank affected this risk [of takeover]" (Davis and Stout, 1992: 626). In addition, companies having a CEO with a finance background "significantly increased the risk of becoming a takeover target," a finding that suggests that finance CEOs, contrary to agency theory claims, "rather than being particularly skilled at running the firm to serve shareholder interests, were carriers of a conception of control that no longer met their own standards of keeping their share price up" (Davis and Stout, 1992: 627). David and Stout (1992: 626) summarize their findings: "[T]hese results conform to the notion of takeover disciplines poorly performing management only to the extent that one has faith in the efficacy of capital markets in evaluating management and one believes that lower debt is a sign of poor management." Rather than being some kind of superior rationality inherent to financial markets winning over managerial capitalism, the takeover market was constructed on the basis of the access to capital and de-regulation. As a consequence, agency theory fails to enact and substantiate a credible and model of the firm:

> [A]gency theory fares rather poorly as an empirical theory, despite its imposing status as normative theory . . . Agency theorists seriously misconstrue the extent to which boards can be seen as vigilant monitors looking out for their shareholder principals—if anything, boards'

interest are much more closely tied to those of managers . . . Without takeovers and vigilant boards, the foundations of agency theory as an empirical theory is weak, as the null to modest effects reported here attest. Thus agency theory, as it stands, does not provide a credible alternative theory of organizations. (Davis and Stout, 1992: 627)

In Kogut and Macpherson's (2011) terminology, the ideological assumptions of agency theory—that finance markets are capable of effectively allocating capital by executing control over managers—overrules empirical evidence. Unfortunately, even unsubstantiated theories can produce substantial effects if policy makers, managers, and others believe that such theories provide accurate views of particular situations, or if they guide their activities.

II. CONSEQUENCES OF AGENCY THEORY AND SHAREHOLDER VALUE IDEOLOGIES

Shareholder Value and the Redistribution of Corporate Capital

The basic idea in shareholder value regimes is that the shareholder should get as high a return on investment as possible, and thereafter it is the shareholders themselves who should make the decision regarding where to invest their capital—that is, in industries they believe are capable of generating future economic value. Executives and managers should, therefore, not absorb and hide excess capital and make use of it themselves to benefit their own interests. In order to maximize profits, finance industry representatives and institutional investors encouraged corporate CEOs to "[a]dopt the aspects of agency theory they preferred, focusing on short-term stock market value goals and tying executive compensation to stock prices" (Tomaskovic-Devey and Lin, 2011: 546). Gradually, CEOs being trained in engineering schools or in marketing were succeeded by business school graduates trained in finance theory, sharing the commitment to the new idea of shareholder value maximization as the primary goal of the corporation, a corporate governance policy that mirrored University of Chicago economist Milton Friedman's emphasis on the generation of profits for owners as being the firm's only legitimate objective. Lazonick and O'Sullivan (2000: 17) summarize this new policy or commitment to shareholder interests as a shift from "retain and reinvest" in the regime of traditional corporate governance to a "downsize and distribute" in the new finance market-based regime (Clark, 2009: 782). Lazonick and O'Sullivan (2000: 16) continue:

> Given the entrenchment of incumbent corporate managers and the relatively poor performance of their companies in the 1970s, agency theorists argued that there was a need for a takeover market that,

functioning as a market for corporate control, could discipline managers whose companies performed poorly. The rate of return on corporate stock was their measure of superior performance, and the maximization of shareholder value became their creed. (Lazonick and O'Sullivan, 2000: 16)

Empirical studies demonstrate that shareholder value corporate governance failed to accomplish its central goal: to create profits (Fligstein and Shin, 2007: 401). The value generated was someone else's loss, namely the blue-collar worker community losing job opportunities in the 1980s and 1990s. In the 1980s, one-third of the 500 largest American manufacturing companies disappeared (Mizruchi, 2010: 132). The consequences were significant: "Between 1980 and 1985, the US trade deficit increased by 309 percent—from $36.3 to $148.5 billion" (Sell, 2003). The Reagan administration and its advisors were, however, only modestly concerned about the trade deficits, as the American economy now attracted foreign investment to the burgeoning finance industry.

By the end of the day, the financial industry's gain was not derived from higher human capital investments and a more effective allocation of capital; it came at the loss of the blue-collar jobs. Fligstein and Shin (2007: 420) summarize:

> Maximizing shareholder value and minimizing the importance of employees is a not-so-veiled way to increase profits by reducing the power of workers. Our results show that the efforts to make more profits were focused on using mergers, layoffs, and computer technologies to reorganize and remove unionized labor forces. The data suggests that workers were certainly being treated less like stakeholders and more like factors of production. (Fligstein and Shin, 2007: 420)

Expressed differently, the shareholders' gain came at the wage earners' loss, not because of increased effectiveness in managerial decision-making, in corporate governance, or in finance market-based managerial control.

Loss of Capital Investment

The loss of blue-collar worker jobs and traditional manufacturing industry has been frequently understood and explained as being an inevitable shift in the global economy through which the advanced democratic economies are increasingly engaging in more advanced science and technology-based endeavours, while dirty, repetitive, and low-skilled jobs are shipped off to poorer and less developed countries. However, the determinist tone of such explanations needs to be contested. In fact, countries with high economic growth in the 1980s, the first neoliberal decade, such as West Germany, Japan, and Sweden, all had a strong and competitive manufacturing industry. But capital investment, education and training, and political support are vital elements in keeping all industries competitive. Tomaskovic-Devey and Lin (2011: 553) suggest that the emergence of a finance industry and its ability to generate quick return on investment undermined the willingness to engage in long-term industrial activities:

> The finance sector's share of national income likely came at the expense of other actors in the economy. In a neoclassical economic model, one might be tempted to claim that financialization, because it may increase efficient allocation of capital, may also increase economic activity overall, thereby rising all actors' income. However, Stockhammer (2004) and Orhangazi (2008) find that financialization actually reduced nonfinancial firms' capital investment in new productive assets and increased the share of their cash flow diverted to the finance sector as increased profits. (Tomaskovic-Devey and Lin, 2011: 553)

Rather than being bound to disappear and today being some kind of embarrassing remnant of a glorious past (see, e.g., Ho, 2009) the American manufacturing industry was left in decline by the capital owning class, as there were low-hanging fruit elsewhere that could be picked at low cost. That the finance industry actors are concerned to secure their own interests is perhaps not entirely surprising, but politicians, who historically had to pay attention to work opportunities and the interests of blue-collar communities, were also increasingly attracted by neoliberal *laissez-faire* explanations for declining industries, giving them the opportunity to do nothing to counteract declining industries, under the banner of market efficiency. Naturally, changing macroeconomic conditions, including the fall of the Iron Curtain in Europe, opening up new, previously enclosed markets and production facilities, and advancement in human resources and increased political stability in, for example, the Asian and Southeast Asian economies, increased the global competition, but in the era of rapidly expanding financial markets, manufacturing industry appeared a less attractive investment. The capital piped into and generated in the finance industry was not of necessity transferred to new and emerging industries (biotechnology, life science, etc.) but was instead brought back into the finance industry, leading to increasingly complex finance product innovations. The finance industry showed little interest in emerging industries, and in most cases the state had to provide venture capital and capital investment in for example, the biotechnology and life science-based industries (Niosi, 2011; Lazonick and Tulum, 2011; Toole, 2011; Sternitzke, 2010), again demonstrating that capital markets may in fact be efficient when transaction costs are low, but such a condition requires minimal risks and short-term perspectives, and therefore "market failure" become an endemic condition rather than a marginal, anomalous situation. The capital owners benefitting greatly from the new shareholder value regime and the financialization of the economy did not, as Michael

Jensen had predicted, heroically transfer their capital gains to emerging and promising industries, but demonstrated preferences for further moderate risk rents. In the neoliberal era, the risks involved in supporting emerging industries are carried by the state.

In industry, the capacity to innovate can be examined as a function of the amount of slack in the organization. The amount of slack—organizational resources in excess to the minimum needed to accomplish existing operations—has been proven to be positively correlated with innovative capacities in number of studies. More specifically, several studies propose an "inverted U-curve" wherein too little slack inhibits innovation and too much slack also hinders innovation (Nohria and Gulati, 1996; Love and Nohria, 2005; Herold, Jayaraman, and Narayanaswamy, 2006). That is, there needs to be a reasonable amount of slack in innovative companies. Since downsizing has been the favourite remedy for increasing shareholder value, the relationship between downsizing and innovative capacities is interesting to examine. Mellahi and Wilkinson (2010: 497) examined this relationship and found a modified "inverted U-curve" relationship: "[L]ow downsizing—5–8 percent—had a very marginal positive effect on innovation. However, large downsizing had a significant negative impact on innovation output. Therefore the relationship between level of downsizing and innovation two years post-downsizing is more of an inverted '√' than a 'U'-shaped relationship":

> Our analysis of the association between downsizing and innovation over time reveals that excessive downsizing has a significant effect on innovation, but this impact is temporary. Specifically, the results show that there is a critical period—two years after downsizing—during which small downsizing has a positive, albeit very weak, impact on innovation, and large downsizing has its greatest negative impact on innovation. (Mellahi and Wilkinson, 2010: 501)

However, substantial downsizing of the corporation more fundamentally affects the innovative capacities:

> Allocation of resources to innovation activities decreases, starving innovation projects of required resources; human resources slack depletes, resulting in a reduction in risk taking and experimentation with innovative ideas; established innovation processes break up, which in turn disturbs innovation activities; and employment relations deteriorate, creating an environment that is not conducive to innovation. (Mellahi and Wilkinson, 2010: 501)

Richtnér and Åhlström (2006) criticize studies of organizational slack for examining accounting and innovativeness—that is, they grant too much importance to formal financial reporting and underrate how, for instance,

R&D projects are managed in the day-to-day work. Consequently, they define slack on the project level as "the possibility to deviate both from agreed upon deadlines and from original project specifications" (Richtnér and Åhlström, 2006: 429). Richtnér and Åhlström (2006: 436) found, by and large consistent with previous research, that "a lack of organizational slack in terms of project deliverables seems to reduce the possibilities for a focus on tacit knowledge, which hampers the ability to create knowledge and ultimately innovation." Tacit knowledge is of vital importance for innovative capacities and is negatively affected by the loss of slack resources—that is, the loss of possibilities to deviate from specified projects' goals—and therefore serendipities and other forms of emergent knowledge cannot be fully exploited. By and large, downsizing beyond a certain critical point is therefore detrimental to innovation.

The Growing Proportions of Executive Compensation

As an effect of the shareholder value regime, American corporations have dedicated more of their available resources to CEO and board member economic compensation. "The modification of the system of compensation for managers constitutes a central aspect of the financialization process," Widmer (2011: 694) says. Quantitative studies demonstrate that CEO and corporate board member compensation soared during the 1990s and the first decade of the new millennium (Lord and Siato, 2010; DiPrete et al., 2010; Bebchuk and Grinstein, 2005; Bebchuk and Fried, 2004). Especially in the 1990s, CEO compensation grew substantially:

> One study that examined CEO pay levels at publically held corporations found that CEO pay jumped 535 percent in the 1990s, dwarfing the 297 percent rise in the S&P [Standard & Poor's] 500, a 116 percent rise in corporate profits, and a 32 percent increase in average worker pay (not adjusted for inflation) . . . If the minimum wage had risen as fast as CEO pay, it would now be $24.13 an hour instead of $5.15, which is less, in real dollars, than it was in 1970. (Khurana, 2002: 191)

"The median levels of total real annual CEO compensation more than doubled from $1.18M in 1994 to $2.80M in 2007 (in real 1994 dollars)," Lord and Saito (2010: 43) report. Also DiPrete, Eirich, and Pittinsky (2010: 1687) account for the substantial changes in executive compensation: "Adjusted for inflation, the median salary/bonus increased from 1993 through 2006 by 40%, whereas the mean increased 58%. Adjusted for inflation, the median total compensation went from $1.6 million to $3.2 million, a 106% increase, whereas the mean increased by 116%." As a consequence, the "CEO to average full-time U.S. worker" pay ratio monitored by AFL-CIO has changed over the neoliberal period, from 42:1 in 1980 to 107:1 in 1990, and to the record-high 525:1 in 2000. By 2008, the pay ratio went down somewhat to 319:1 (Lazonick, 2010: 699). In 2008, a CEO thus earned the total compensation of 319 American workers, on average. In the United Kingdom, a similar trend has been observed: "At the turn of the millennium, top bosses took home forty-seven times the average worker's wage. By 2008, they were earning ninety-four times more" (Jones, 2011: 163). More importantly, this redistribution of organizational resources is not attributable to larger size, performance, or any other measures (Bebchuk and Grinstein, 2005: 286), but represents a shift in corporate governance policy. Studying executive compensation in Standard & Poor's 500 companies in the period 1993–2003, Bebchuk and Grinstein (2005: 287) found weak explanations for the new executive compensation schemes. "[C]hanges in size and performance can explain only 66 per cent of the total 166 increase, or about 40 per cent of the total increase, with 60 percent of the total increase remaining unexplained." Based on this data, Bebchuk and Grinstein (2005: 289) conclude that "[t]he relationship between pay and firm attributes has changed substantially during the period under consideration." Erturk et al. (2004: 709) make the same point in more straightforward terms: "[T]he 1990s was a significant decade because it established a new cultural norm of mega pay for averagely competent senior managers in the UK and US."

Agency theorists such as Michael Jensen argue that the "[d]esign of the managerial pay package is probably the most potent tool available to the stakeholders to align the interest of the managers with their own" (Lord and Saito, 2010: 40), but if compensation is not based on size, performance, or any other formal measures, what are CEOs compensated for? Brockman, Chang, and Rennie (2007), studying 229 public layoff announcements, show that the total CEO pay increased by 22.8% in firms laying off personnel. "Our research suggests that CEOs are rewarded for making decisions that increase shareholder value primarily through increases in stock-based compensation, the ultimate value of which depends on future performance," Brockman, Chang, and Rennie (2007: 101) conclude. They continue: "[The] CEOs who make layoff decisions are rewarded with higher compensation levels that persist" (Brockman, Chang, and Rennie, 2007: 117). In other words, when corporations downsized to create value for their shareholders, executives and CEOs were paid generously for the reduction of labour:

> The reigning wisdom on Wall Street held that reducing wage rents for workers would help boost shareholder value after a decade of falling profits during the 1970s and early 1980s. Shedding unionized labor was likely an ulterior motive behind much restructuring, particularly in manufacturing industries. (Goldstein, 2012: 272)

As a consequence, Goldstein (2012: 271) argues, "downsizing" in the neoliberal era of financialization had different connotations and rationales than in previous periods: "Firms' attempts to streamline in accordance with shareholder value ideology differed from traditional job reductions because they did not reflect the adaptation to shifting economic circumstances so much as adaptation to an institutional environment that prescribed downsize-and-distribute as a normative orientation of corporate activity." Paired with policies aimed at reducing labour power and the role of the unions in both the United States and United Kingdom, blue-collar workers had to fight a two-front war with both Wall Street and their new cadre of shareholder value-minded executives, and with the new neoliberal political coalitions.

The period after 1980, the neoliberal era, brought a new policy for executive compensation. "Golden parachutes, golden handcuffs, and the whole panoply of mechanisms for lavishly rewarding CEOs without regard to performance—all of which were unheard of before the age of investor capitalism—became standard features of CEO pay packages," Khurana (2002: 191) suggests. *Hochkapitalismus* is no longer dominated by the old school generation of empire builders reproducing "old capital"; in the era of financialization, new values and beliefs were established and justified by the new finance theory, prescribing that activities such as hostile takeovers and downsizing were not only permitted but were in fact *morally justifiable* as such operations served to invigorate stagnating economies. "[T]he restructuring of U.S. companies in accordance with shareholder value ideologies augured the end of postwar managerialism," Goldstein (2012: 273) declares. Unfortunately, claims made by theorists such as Michael Jensen that executive compensation based on finance market performance would demonstrate higher degrees of rational decision-making have not been supported by empirical evidence. Instead, rather than solving agency problems, the shareholder value regime and its accompanying executive compensation schemes have led to new concerns regarding the efficiency of corporate governance. For instance, why do shareholders overcompensate executives in the more recent period in relationship to previous periods? Stiglitz (2010a) speaks of poor corporate governance practices as one explanatory factor:

> American corporations (and those in many other countries) are only nominally run by the shareholders. In practice, to a very large extent, they are run by and for the benefit of management. In many corporations where ownership is widely diversified among disparate shareholders, management effectively appoints most of the board, and it naturally appoints people who are likely to serve their interests most effectively. The board decides on the pay of management, and the 'company' provides good rewards for its board members. It's a cozy relationship. (Stiglitz, 2010a: 154)

The new category of agency problems and the strong emphasis on CEOs' roles opened up what may be referred to as "the fallacy of CEO importance": the belief that the CEO is singlehandedly accountable for firm performance—even in cases where macroeconomic conditions and policy beyond the influence of the CEO play a key role. Erturk et al. (2004) offer one illustration:

> Right at the end of the 1990s, just before the collapse of the Tyco share price and his personal disgrace, Denis Kozlowski, the Tyco CEO publicly defended his 1999 pay by claiming 'while I gained $139 million (in stock options), I created £37 billion in wealth for our shareholders' (*Business Week*, 17 April 2000). Through the canting language of value creation, CEOs like Kozlowski took the credit for increasing shareholder wealth, which were mainly the result of general share price movements driven by rhetoric and middle class savings patterns. (Erturk et al., 2004: 687)

Agency theory was developed to address the relationship between principals and agents and with the intention of reducing agency costs. The advocacy of this theoretical framework cannot be said to be successful in terms of either reducing agency costs or avoiding opportunistic behaviour. Much of the explosion of CEO and executive compensation remains to be explained. The most conspicuous outcome from this new policy, intended or not, has been the downsizing of corporations, the decrease of union influence, and the enriching of the wealthiest strata.

The Slimming of "Fat, Dumb, Happy Bureaucracies" (While Expanding Executive Tiers)

Under the new shareholder value regime, CEOs and corporate boards downsized their operations, with a particular emphasis on reducing the labour force in an attempt to increase the return on equity that would benefit the shareholders (Lazonick and O'Sullivan, 2000: 18). In blue-collar worker communities, the effects were quite substantial:

> Hundreds of thousands of previously stable and well-paid blue-collar jobs that were lost in the recession of 1980–2 were never subsequently restored. Between 1979 and 1983, the number of people employed in the economy as a whole increased by 377,000 or 0.4 percent, while employment in durable goods manufacturing—which supplied most of the well-paid and stable blue-collar jobs—declined by 2,023,000, or by 15.9 per cent. (Lazonick and O'Sullivan, 2000: 18–19)

In Thatcher's Britain, the other leading neoliberal state, the Prime Minister declared "Every man a capitalist!" (Jones, 2011: 62). Still, blue-collar job losses were substantial, and while there were five million in poverty in 1979, by 1992, the number had grown to close to fourteen million (Jones, 2011: 62). In the United States, during a period of an unprecedented inflow of foreign investment, poverty rates grew from 11.7 percent in 1979 to

15.1 percent by 1993 (Gordon, 1996: 100). The downsizing of corporations increasing the shareholder value did not come without costs for other stakeholders.

On the other hand, somewhat surprisingly, given agency theory's strong emphasis on the informed use of the shareholders' resources, the number of managers and the costs for their services have *grown* rather than been *reduced* in the last few decades (Gordon, 1996). "The proportion of managerial employees in the U.S. private sector rose steadily from the mid-1980s through the early 2000s by several different metrics," Goldstein (2012: 269) reports. He continues: "The share of total business income devoted to managerial salaries actually rose from 16 to 23 percent between 1984 and 2001." The growth of managerial ranks in U.S. corporations is a surprising outcome, given the strong emphasis on shareholder value creation through downsizing. Apparently, the managerial class has managed to interpret the shareholder value objective in ways that they have benefitted from: "Ample evidence suggests that top executives learned to rechannel the anti-managerial thrust of shareholder value pressures in self-enriching ways . . . in part because executives' own compensation became tied to their ability to cut labor costs" (Goldstein, 2012: 269). The outcome has been—potentially most unexpected by the agency theorists prescribing finance discipline as a remedy for opportunistic behaviour—a massive growth in size and costs of "managerial and supervisory apparatus of private U.S. corporations" (Gordon, 1996: 34). Rather than being "lean and mean"—disciplined and effective—American corporations became "fat and mean" (Gordon, 1996), carrying the burden of a growing and generously compensated executive class while employing fewer blue-collar and white-collar workers actually producing economic value. Goldstein (2012: 277) concludes: "By favoring sticks over carrots, this low-road employment logic breeds managerial control strategies that demand extensive monitoring, thereby boosting the ranks of managers . . . In other words, strategies nominally oriented toward making firm lean and streamlined had the effect of making them fatter at the top" (Goldstein, 2012: 277).

More Sticks Than Carrots: The Role of Wall Street

Ethnographic studies of the finance industry, the work conducted by financial traders and analysts, are providing some insight into the communities determining what counts as economic worth and a qualified performance in the new corporate governance regime (Lépinay, 2011; Zaloom, 2006; Roth, 2006; Abolafia, 2001; Hertz, 1998; McDowell, 1997). Karen Ho's (2009) ethnography of Wall Street investment banking is of particular interest because Ho, herself a Princeton graduate—Wall Street's recruitment base *par préférence*—and a former Wall Street banker, provides a glimpse of the worldview of the financial traders and investment bankers. Ho (2009) strongly stresses the conspicuous elite culture of Wall Street, the massive amount of work time laid down during the first few years in the industry, the astronomical economic compensations earned, and the fickleness of the Wall Street labour market that leads to occasional short-term layoffs during downturns in the economy—and, as an effect from these cultural traits, the gradual distancing of this community from the wider society and the life led by millions of Americans. In fact, Coser's (1974: 4) concept of *greedy institutions* provides a nice *double entendre* as Wall Street investment banks "[s]eek exclusive and undivided loyalty" and put demands on their employees that are "omnivorous," in Coser's phrasing.

Jensen's (1993) disregard of managerialist capitalism in many industries is widely institutionalized on Wall Street. Ho (2009) writes:

> [One informant talked] about the struggle between the owners of capital versus managers, where managers had squandered the fruits of capital by sharing them with other constituents. He spoke passionately about the poor stewardship and excess of managers and how it was Wall Street investment bankers who realigned managers to their true purpose of increasing shareholder value . . . Wall Street's shareholder value perspective is that employment is thought to be outside the concern of public corporations. Job loss was certainly a sad event, but beyond the responsibility of corporate America. (Ho, 2009: 128)

With what they basically conceived of as incompetent, overtly nostalgic, and slow decision-makers in the executive positions in the corporations, the Wall Street bankers saw no alternative than to serve to release capital—just as prescribed by Jensen (1993)—for more effective investments elsewhere. The favourite metaphors were to speak of traditional industry as being "dumb" and "fat," thus capturing two vices in the neoliberal culture obsessed with competitiveness and self-reliance (Amable, 2011: 5–6):

> 'If you look at the old days,' Stan Clark [one of Ho's interviewees] told me, 'all the companies were basically fat, dumb, and stupid. [T]hey did not change. They were making [enough] money. The [managers] didn't care. Now, you have Wall Street with all their shareholders . . . You can't just be dumb, fat, and happy . . . You have to change. Shareholders are looking at. . . . your excess expenses . . . Back in the old days, wide town employment was big a thing. They didn't even hardly lay off. Nowadays, they have to lay off because shareholders say, "Look, you have all this excess overhead . . . You have to cut out the fat. We want a lean, mean operation." So . . . Wall Street is definitely making a much more efficient corporate America.' (Ho, 2009: 130–131)

Ho's (2009) interlocutors tend to portray the shareholder as an abused, essentially powerless, and almost subaltern figure in contemporary capitalism, exposed to the whims of self-interested and indulgent CEOs and top management teams who have little oversight and understanding of their own operations and industries. This bizarre narrative of the shareholder as a victim, popular in neoconservative and neoliberal quarters where elitism is counterintuitively not defined as being in the position to control economic resources but of being part of an culturally and ideologically influential class—that is, "liberal East-coast intellectuals" (Gross, Medvetz, and Russell, 2011: 334), counteracts the conventional images of the capitalist class as being self-sufficient and powerful, advanced historically by, for instance, the labour movement. Contrary to the narrative of suffering capital owners, Ireland (2010) argues that the historical development of the "corporate legal form," the joint stock company, during the nineteenth century primarily served to advance the interests of rentier investors, and today they take advantage of a most favourable position:

> At present, corporate shareholders (including parent companies) enjoy the best possible of all possible legal worlds. On the one hand they are, for some purposes, treated as 'completely separate' from the companies in which they hold shares and draw dividends, in that they are not personally responsible for the latter's debt or liabilities (or behaviour). On the other hand the companies in which they hold shares must be run exclusively in their interests: for these purposes the interests of 'the company' (formally a separate entity) are synonymous with those of the shareholders. (Ireland, 2010: 848)

Agency theorists thus criticize traditional managerialism at its core, as being in opposition to the free circulation of capital. Such a view has gradually penetrated decision-making communities on, for example, Wall Street.

Stock Repurchases

One of the most puzzling finance market phenomena for protagonists of the efficient market hypothesis is the growth of firm stock repurchases—firms buying their own stocks on the market—in the era of financialization. Economists have advanced a number of hypotheses for how to explain repurchases including *the excess capital hypothesis,* suggesting that firms want to reinvest excess capital, *the undervaluation hypothesis,* suggesting that firms wants to signal their dissatisfaction with the market's valuation of the stock, *the optimal leverage ratio hypothesis,* proposing that firms want to achieve a better balance between equity and stock value, *the management incentives hypothesis,* saying that managers holding stock options or being compensated on basis of stock market valuation may have incentives to increase stock prices, and, finally, *the takeover deterrence hypothesis,* emphasizing that firms want to increase stock market valuation to reduce the risks of a hostile takeover (Dittmar, 2000: 333–336). All these rationales for intervening into the stock market are not mutually exclusive, and all of them can hold explanatory value when studying actual board decisions. No matter

122 Management in the Neoliberal Era

what rationale is invoked, "repurchasing stock, like paying dividends, is one method to distribute excess capital to shareholders" (Dittmar, 2000: 333).

There is an undisputed growth of repurchasing activity in the neoliberal period, the era of financialization. "It was not until the early 1980s that U.S. corporations began adopting share repurchase programs in large numbers," Grullon and Ikenberry (2000: 31) remark; "[t]otal corporate payouts in share repurchase programs during the period 1972–1983 amounted to less than 4.5% of total earnings. Over the period 1984 to 1998, this same ratio exceeded 25%" (Grullon and Ikenberry, 2000: 34). In 1998, for the first time in history, U.S. corporations "[d]istributed more cash to investors through share repurchases than through cash dividends," Grullon and Ikenberry (2000: 31) report. Bratton and Wachter (2010: 686) provide more recent statistics: "In 1987, repurchases amounted to 1.6% of average market capitalization, and total payout amounted to 3.8%; in 2007, repurchases mounted to 4.6%, and total payout amounted to 6.3%. The dollar amount of annual repurchases increased eighteen-fold from 1987 to the peak year of 2007."

Prior to the 1980s, stock repurchase was regarded as a somewhat odd form of corporate governance, but in 1982, the Securities and Exchange Commission (SEC) adopted Rule 10b-18, reducing the "ambiguities" regarding stock repurchases (Grullon and Ikenberry, 2000: 34). As a consequence, there is strong evidence of a shift from dividends to repurchases to distribute capital to shareholders: "[T]he average dividend payout-ratio [in the U.S.] fell from 22.3% in 1974 to 13.8% in 1998, while the average purchase payout ratio increased from 3.7% to 13.6% during the same period" (Grullon and Ikenberry, 2000: 34). As Grullon and Ikenberry (2000) notice, the widespread use of stock options in executive compensation packages may be one explanatory factor when it comes to this *de facto* shift in policy:

> [T]he increased use of executive stock options is a major factor in the general increase in purchase activity in the 1990s . . . managers intent on maximizing the value of their options might be tempted to eliminate dividends entirely—and we rarely see companies take such an extreme step. Nevertheless if the corporation is compelled to pay out capital to shareholders for whatever reason, managers who are heavily compensated through options may feel more inclined to choose a share repurchase over a cash dividend. (Grullon and Ikenberry, 2000: 34)

"Preserving the stock price may be of particular interest when management holds stock options," Dittmar (2000: 335) notices. Empirical evidence suggests that many announcements of stock repurchasing programs are never actualized, but the principal reason is that such announcements have a signalling function in which the corporation's executives and board of directors make clear that they believe the market undervalues the stock. As finance market analysts correct their assessments, there is no need for buying back the stocks. "The most common reason cited by corporate executives and stock analysts is that stock repurchases boost reported earnings per share," Grullon and Ikenberry (2000: 48) say. Dittmar's (2000: 333) study of 1977 through 1996 also shows that "firms repurchase stock to take advantage of potential undervaluation throughout the sample period." Still, the concern remains: Why were the supposedly efficient markets increasingly misvaluing stock after 1982?[3] Dittmar (2000: 333) thinks that her result is "somewhat surprising," since it is primarily large firms that are "the dominant repurchasers," and since this category of firms are carefully monitored and rated, they are "less likely to be misvalued." In other words, either finance markets are not as efficient as suggested by the efficient market hypothesis, or executives and board of directors want to increase the market value of shares because it benefits them in one way or another. Neither Grullon and Ikenberry (2000) nor Dittmar (2000) provide an answer to this question, but Grullon and Ikenberry (2000: 46) notice that repurchasing programs offer "managers a valuable, and relatively inexpensive, option to repurchase stock," suggesting that such finance market interventions are primarily benefitting two constituencies—the shareholders and the executives being rewarded on the basis of their ability to create shareholder value.

In the agency theory prescription, only by implementing far-driven finance market corporate governance practices would managers (agents) be disciplined to act in accordance with the interests of the shareholders (principals). In hindsight, such claims, critics contend, are not supported by empirical evidence, as stock repurchasing programs possibly direct resources away from productive uses. "Corporate executives argue that they conduct stock buybacks because the shares of the companies they manage are undervalued," Lazonick (2010: 696) writes. There are reasons to believe that stock repurchasing programs have been used to increase the value of the stock—i.e., to enrich shareholders—to the point where firms no longer hold enough equity to support themselves in the event of economic downturns and recession. That is, executives and boards of directors have been too eager to distribute the economic value generated to the shareholders because they have themselves been compensated on the basis of their ability to create shareholder value. For instance, of the corporations that were part of the much-debated Troubled Assets Relief Program (TARP) bailout initiated by the Bush administration (Sorkin, 2009), Citigroup had launched stock buyback programs in the 2000–2007 period at the total cost of 41.8 billion US dollars, followed by Goldman Sachs (30.1 billion US dollars), Wells Fargo (21.2 billion US dollars), Merrill Lynch (21.0 billion US dollars), Morgan Stanley (19.1 billion US dollars), American Express (17.6 billion US dollars), and U.S. Bancorp (12.3 billion US dollars) (Lazonick, 2010: 696). "Allocated differently, the trillions spent on buybacks in the past decades could have helped stabilize the economy," Lazonick (2010: 696) proposes. In the decade 2001–2010, Standard & Poor's 500 companies expended $3 trillion on buybacks, quadrupling from approximately $300 million per company in 2003 to over $1.2 billion per company in 2007. During the financial crisis of 2008 and 2009, the activity declined sharply, but in 2011 and 2012 stock buybacks averaged at ~$800 among Standard & Poor's 500 companies (Lazonick and Mazzucato, 2013: 1114). Such stock repurchases—accumulated internal capital reinvested to boost the stock prices of supposedly "undervalued" stocks—are very likely to have benefitted the executives of these corporations in terms of more generous compensation, arguably based on their "performance" (Lazonick and Mazzucato, 2013: 1115). "As bonuses and options for managers were largely coupled to share prices they would benefit from rising share prices too," Deutschmann (2011: 358) notes. In other words, shareholder value ideologies did not, *pace* Jensen (1993), manage to curb opportunistic behaviour in executive quarters, but as the opportunistic behaviour primarily benefitted shareholders, the repurchasing programs are consistent with the overarching objective sanctioned by agency theory—that is, to "maximize the value of the firm" regardless of the additional economic risks not being carried by the shareholders. That is, the maximization of market value of the firm externalized the costs for a too-high leverage, a principal argument in what has been called the "too-big-to-fail" explanation of the 2008 finance market collapse (Sorkin, 2009). One group was able to claim the "residual free cash flow," while another group (in, this case, American taxpayers) carried the risks and ultimately had to pay for the rescue efforts. Agency theory, in brief, justified and legitimized a series of economic transactions benefitting rentier shareholders:

> By the early 1990s, the principle of shareholder primacy had been restored with a vengeance. Corporate managers today are much more accountable than they were—to the *rentier* shareholders with whom they are now much more closely entwined. Hence the relentless pursuit of 'shareholder value' by whatever means and whatever human, social and environmental costs. The consequences have been only too clear: a massive increase in speculative financial exchanges, regular financial crises, numerous corporate scandals, falling growth rates, a reduction in the rates of productivity growth and soaring executive remuneration. (Ireland, 2010: 852)

Agency theorists make claim that shareholder empowerment increases efficiency of capital investment, but what it has practically accomplished is a massive redistribution of wealth to the shareholders at the expense of other constituencies.

New Neoliberal Policies to Regulate Corporations

As we have seen above, the agency theory remedy to reduce agency costs has led to soaring executive compensations that cannot be explained on the basis of available official data, the reduction of blue-collar work and a decline of American manufacturing industry, and excessive opportunistic behaviour as stock buyback schemes have been launched. Facing such widespread managerial behaviour and a few examples of full-scale corporate crime (consider, e.g., the paradigmatic case of Enron; see, e.g., Ailon, 2012), new policy has been developed to compensate for the fallible agency theory-based management system. After the Enron scandal, the U.S. Congress enacted the Sarbanes-Oxley Act (SOX) in 2002. For critics such as Soederberg (2008: 659), SOX, despite the political ambition articulated when it was announced, is little more than a continuation of "the prevalent policy and ideological orientation of neoliberalism." In Soederberg's view (2008: 666), the neoliberal policy has by and large failed to produce "sustained growth in terms of rising productivity rates, higher standards of living, job security and overall economic stability." On the contrary, there is in the U.S. "alarming levels of corporate, consumer, and public debt, as well as the increasing frequency and depth of the underlying crisis" (Soederberg, 2008: 666). These failures are explained by Soederberg on the basis of the firm belief in the efficiency of markets. As a consequence of these "ideological lock-ins," rather than implementing "state-led regulations aimed at protecting society from the irrational behaviour of market forces" (Soederberg, 2008: 666), SOX is essentially an attempt to handle market inconsistencies and failures by implementing "more market-based solutions." Arnold (2009) exemplifies how SOX failed to handle the problem of regulatory control on the basis of market-based solutions, leading to substantial risks carried by "off-balance sheet vehicles" never being fully communicated to market actors:

> Although the US Sarbanes-Oxley Act of 2002 and similar independence rules in other jurisdictions prohibit accounting firms from selling certain types of consulting services to their own audit clients, the consultancy arms of the major firms continue to thrive. Tax consulting and some other types of advisory work can still be done for audit clients, and services to non-audit clients are not proscribed. As a result, a small group of accounting firms continues to operate simultaneously as both auditors and advisors for the banking industry. As auditors, they play a quasi-regulatory role as a watchdog, responsible for assuring third parties that the financial statements present a true and fair picture of the banks' financial condition. As financial advisors, it appears that the same firms may have assisted the financial services industry in designing the structured investment vehicles that enabled them to move operations off the industry's balance sheet, effectively ensuring that the banking industry's financial statement did not reflect the full extent of risk and leverage within the financial system. (Arnold, 2009: 807)

Practically speaking, SOX—or any other policy enacted after 2002 for that matter—"[d]id little to stem the tide of financial innovations that ultimately helped fuel the boom and eventual market collapse in 2008," Centeno and Cohen (2012: 321) argue. More moderate commentators such as Coates (2007: 92) point at the difference between formal policy documents and their practical application—"Sarbanes-Oxley is actually implemented through rules and enforcement strategies set by administrative officials"—and suggests that even five years "after its passage," Sarbanes-Oxley remains a "work in progress." That is, SOX was not a quick fix to handle the opportunistic behaviour bringing down neoliberal protagonists' once-darling companies such as Enron.

In other cases, it is not so much legislation and policy as "mimetic" and "normative isomorphism" (DiMaggio and Powell, 1983) that influence corporate governance. One example is the recent interest in what has been referred to as Corporate Social Responsibilities (CSR), the idea that a corporation should demonstrate an awareness of how they influence human well-being, equality, and the environment. While CSR policies in many cases are hailed as evidence of an increased interest in the corporation as a social actor, for more sceptical commentators such as Kinderman (2012) and Marens (2013), the new CSR polices are closely related to the neoliberal regime. "Social responsibilities" were first recognized and accepted by corporations and business leaders when other forms of corporate oversight and regulation were essentially minimized; "neo-liberalism provided a fertile environment for CSR's mergence and growth" (Kinderman (2012: 33). "What unites CSR and neo-liberalism is an emphasis on the absence of burdensome constraints on business activity," Kinderman (2012: 50) concludes. The neoliberal era has stressed the importance of economic freedom, and this project has been operationalized not so much as the elimination of the state and government as a re-formation of the state's role as what secure capital freedom and capital circulation and as a key partner to industry. That democratically elected governments—right wing, liberal, and socialist, both in North America and in Europe—have enacted and supported policy that has increased inequality, raised the levels of debt, and de-constructed manufacturing industry in parts of the world by means of some allegedly mysterious inevitable force of economic progress is indicative of the pervasive force of "creative destruction" in neoliberal thinking (Harvey, 2005b). Speaking in terms of management practice, there are several implications from the shift in focus from traditional managerialism, rooted in the production of economic value, to the new managerialism derived from financialization and its accompanying theories, including efficient market hypothesis, agency theory, and shareholder value theories. In the neoliberal era, the very concept of management has been strongly rearticulated and now has different connotations than it did a few decades ago.

Summary and Conclusions

As we have seen, the agency theory solution to perceived agency costs, that of finance market control of managers at risk of engaging in opportunistic behaviour, did not manage to handle the control problems derived from the separation between ownership and execution. Much of its prescribed solutions merely produced new forms of agency costs, and the residual free cash released to the shareholders has not been invested in growth industries, but rather has been reinvested in the finance markets. For Dobbin and Jung (2010: 32), agency theory has been so widely recognized and applied that it has "colored the air we breathe," and therefore it is also part of the explanation for the 2008 finance market collapse; it was a theory that "brought down the economy" (Dobbin and Jung, 2010: 31). As Krippner (2011: 7) remarks, one of the key questions posed in the shareholder value literature is how "shareholder value became the privileged metric for assessing corporate success (or failures) in the 1980s and 1990s." According to Erturk et al. (2004: 680), the literature on corporate governance (i.e., agency theory) is "both uninformative and naïve because it fails to consider the political, economic, and social context around governance." In addition, Erturk et al. (2004: 687) say, it is "ironic" that agency theory that was "always theoretically incredible and already empirically discredited" started to become a "huge success in the 1990s." In Erturk et al.'s (2004: 687) view, what agency theory offers is a "narrative" that is compelling not because it appears to be "theoretically rigorous or empirically plausible" but because it can "[c]reate an intelligible world through strong, simple assumptions about what is wrong and the appropriate solutions" (Erturk et al., 2004). Michael C. Jensen's storytelling about the centrality the shareholder/manager agency problem was rooted in the classic work of Berle and Means ([1934] 1991), but was also shaped by the more recent belief in finance market actors' ability to wisely allocate the free cash flow based on the efficient market hypothesis. Combining these two arguments with Jensen's hostile view of corporate leaders and decision-makers as being unfit to make the best decisions for their corporations and the economy at large ("waste" is a frequently occurring term in Jensen's articles), created an argument that, to date, is Jensen's principal claim to fame. As Erturk et al. (2004) persuasively argue, Jensen's story is not so much embedded in a theoretical framework supported by empirical evidence as it is an attempt to discredit previous corporate governance practices in order to benefit one specific group: the owners of the corporations. Jensen's writings on agency theory thus constitute an important element in the neoliberal program, attempting to restore interwar economic relations.

NOTES

1. This affirmative view of, for example, hostile takeovers is represented by other finance theorists. For instance, Rappaport (1990, cited in Franks and Mayer, 1996) argues that such financial operations constitute "the most effective check on management autonomy ever devised." Grossman and Hart (1980, cited in Franks and Mayer, 1996) claim that "the threat of raids encourages

good management." Such claims based on deductive reasoning and wishful thinking is not necessarily rooted in sound empirical evidence. Studying hostile takeovers in the United Kingdom and "[u]sing a number of different benchmarks," Franks and Mayer (1996: 164) found "little evidence that hostile takeovers are motivated by poor performance prior to bids." The U.K. firms were simply not mismanaged or in any other way performing poorly.

2. Jensen's claim that LBOs and "corporate restructurings" in the mid-1980s had anything to do with self-interested or incompetent managers or with "market efficiency" is highly questionable. Davis and Stout (1992) suggest that firms most likely to be taken over in the LBO wave of the 1980s were the ones "most successful by the standard of organization theory." As Stearns and Allan (1996) demonstrate, the wave of LBOs were caused by three factors that had little to do with managerial practice and corporate governance: (1) the inflow of capital through foreign funds, Savings and Loan Associations, and mutual funds, (2) the de-regulation of financial markets and the more lenient interpretation of antitrust law during the Reagan Presidency, and (3) the financial invention of junk bonds, accounting for more than 35 per cent of total public bond offerings in the 1983 to 1989 period (calculated at $160 billion). Innovative actors in the finance industry, such as Jerome Kohlberg, Henry Kravis, George Roberts, and Michael Milken, could thus take advantage of macroeconomic conditions, monetary policy, and political de-regulation during the mid-1980s. When George H.W. Bush took office, his administration started to "clean up the excesses tolerated by Reagan's permissive regulators" (Stearns and Allan, 1996: 712).

3. More generally speaking, according to the efficient market hypothesis, the very term "market misvaluation" is an oxymoron.

4 Human Resource Management, Leadership, and the Re-Articulation of Professionalism

INTRODUCTION

As we saw in the previous chapter, agency theory problematized the relationship between owners (principals) and the managers hired to take care of the day-to-day management of the activities in the corporation. In this view, there is a new concern regarding the relationship between social actors that have previously been treated as if they essentially share a commitment to enterprising activities and capital accumulation. Needless to say, the relationships between employees and managers and employees and owners have demonstrated a more complicated history, characterized by periods of stable industrial relations, with occasional eruptions of conflicts and controversies leading to the need to reach new agreements. For instance, the major strike at General Motors in 1937 was one such historical event (Fine, 1969), and prior to that the militant anti-unionist car industry pioneer Henry Ford had hired his own militia to fight the trade unions and to keep them away from his plants. Ford was described as an "industrial fascist" and the "Mussolini of Detroit" by the *New York Times* (Beynon, 1975: 28), testifying to the social costs and political conflicts between labour and capital owners in this period. Many historians have accounted for conflicts and controversies between labour and capital owners in the modern period:

> [P]olice and national guards grew in size during this period [1870–1900] as a response to labour troubles, with their growth often subsidized or directed by business groups . . . Between the years 1870 and 1900, half of the National Guard deployments involved labour disputes . . . and during the strike wave of 1920–1924 that percentage soared to 90%. (Marens, 2012: 65)

In fact, the work conducted by the Human Relations School under the directorship of Elton Mayo at Harvard University in the interwar period (see, e.g., Mayo, 1946; Roethlisberger and Dickson, 1943) was initiated by the ambition to handle deteriorating industrial relations in the United States (O'Conner, 1999; Bendix and Fisher, 1949). The Rockefeller Foundation was one of the sponsors and financiers. In the neoliberal era, reducing the bargaining power of the trade unions was a highly prioritized political objective in the neoconservative political agendas of both Thatcher and Reagan. In addition, the corporate governance of private industry and the public sector has changed (as discussed in Chapter Three and Chapter Five in this volume), and so have the industrial relations. The neoliberal credo, putting competition and self-reliance in the first room, has not only influenced policy and underlying economic theory and doctrines guiding policy-making over the last few decades, but it has also been brought into the corporations. Today, not only unskilled labour is increasingly exposed to performance assessment procedures and other forms of monitoring and control; those who, in the sociology literature, are referred to as professionals, worker elites capable of claiming discretionary jurisdiction on the basis of entrenched skills and credentials, are also subject to such managerial control. In addition, in the neoliberal era, working life has been characterized by more flexible employment arrangements, more insecure and temporal contracts, the insistence on regarding one's own "employability" as a strategic and tactic concern, and an exposure to much more detailed scrutiny of workplace performance. While these characteristics differ substantially across industries, regions, professions, and occupational groups, there is a shared commitment to managerial and leadership-based solutions to perceived problems derived from market-based economic activities. In many ways, *management* is the primary operationalization of the neoliberal market credo, the principal set of activities securing market efficiency. This chapter will explore some of the implications of the shift from public sector solutions to market failure, privatization, and marketization and how managerial activities have been given a prominent role in fulfilling quite abstract theorems and axiomatic principles.

I. THE NEW NEOLIBERAL WORLD OF WORK

Neoliberal Agency

In the neoliberal doctrine, anchored in classical liberal thinking, people own their bodies and their capacities to labour, and therefore they have the indisputable right to the fruits of their labour (Gershon, 2011: 539). In order to generate incomes from this capacity to labour, they need to sell their labour in the market. These few elementary axioms of the neoliberal credo enact agency as what includes the capacity to act self-reflexively on the basis of a generalized "market rationality":

> A neoliberal perspective presumes that every social analyst on the ground should ideally use market rationality to interpret their social relationships and social strategies. This concept of agency requires a

reflexive stance in which people are subjects to themselves—a collection of processes to be managed. (Gershon, 2011: 539)

In a way, the neoliberal market expects agency to be performed like a managerial or entrepreneurial process wherein both competencies and relations are treated as assets to be exploited for the individual's benefit. Unfortunately, such a separation of agency and division of the subject into a bundle of capacities and relations is complicated to maintain for the individual, and consequently the self become fragmented and porous, ultimately grounded in little more than a series of market transactions:

> The fragmentation of the neoliberal self begins when the agent is brought face to face with the realization that she is not just an employee or student, but also simultaneously a product to be sold, a walking advertisement, a manger of her résumé, a biographer of her rationales, and an entrepreneur of her possibilities. She has to somehow manage to be simultaneously subject, object, and spectator. (Mirowski, 2013: 108)

In addition, in the neoliberal doctrine, the market, the superior and spontaneously ordered information processor, always of necessity includes risk, and therefore the agent needs to recognize and engage with risk to be able to prosper. "According to the neoliberal perspective, to prosper, one must engage with risk. All neoliberal social strategies center on this. Managing risk frames how neoliberal agents are oriented toward the future," Gershon (2011: 540) writes. Risk, originally a calculative term, is here given an ontological status as what is always already in place and what we as enterprising agents must be able to live with; it is the gravity of the neoliberal cosmos. The concept of freedom, held in esteem by neoliberal intellectuals but essentially defined in negative terms (Mirowski, 2013: 107) as the absence of collectivist solutions to economic and social issues intervening with one's own market-based agency, is therefore defined in terms of its relationship to risk:

> Instead of equating freedom with choice, it might be more apt to say that neoliberalism equates freedom with the ability to act on one's own calculations. Freedom of this kind is inevitably unstable, especially since, in capitalism, calculating to one's advantage is too frequently also calculating to someone else's disadvantage. (Gershon, 2011: 540)

The combination of the fragmented self, the demand for an entrepreneurial way of life, and the presence of risk renders neoliberal agency as what is precarious and always needs to be maintained. As a consequence, in the neoliberal world of work, there are few spots where one can avoid competition and the exposure to enterprising cultures; it is a world, as Hochschild (2012) shows, where the market is everywhere (see e.g., Cushen, 2013; Alvehus and Spicer, 2012; Faulconbridge and Muzio, 2009).

This neoliberal agency is by no means an abstract construct separated from practices, but is directly translated into managerial activities. Swan and Fox (2009) examine how what they refer to as *self-flexibility* (related to the concept of flexibility in work life discussed below), the ability to enact oneself as a malleable and adaptable person who willingly responds to the new demands in work life, is being emphasized in management training programs. In such training, based on what Swan and Fox (2009) call "the pedagogics of flexibility," the "ability to change" is postulated as a generic human trait, while at the same time, "any attempt to stall, critique or block change is often coded by trainers as 'being in denial,' or 'resistance'—seen as psychological states of 'irrationality' which can mostly be overcome" (Swan and Fox, 2009: S152). In addition, the ability to receive feedback is treated as a highly important quality, and it is important to not get "defensive," to question the comments received or otherwise fail to see the possibilities for productive change in the remarks. Third, self-flexibility training frequently includes activities in which the participants should take risks. As risk-taking is praised as a principal virtue in the neoliberal era, the individual is encouraged to endure risky situations to enable the organization on the aggregated level to take risks. A lower rate of risk-aversion is understood as being important for self-flexibility and is consonant with the neoliberal principles of competition and risk-taking; abstract principles regarding, for example, the nature of the market, are thus translated into individual practices accompanied by norms regarding attitudes and beliefs that need to be fostered.

Precarious Work in Flexible Times

One of the most widespread terms in the neoliberal era has been that of *flexibility*. Beginning in the end of the 1970s, when the American manufacturing industry became aware of the increased competition from Japan, American executives and production experts found that the Japanese had developed new systems of production, including team-based work organization; new logistics systems, such as the just-in-time logistics and *kanban* systems, cutting down on inventory; and more flexible and "fool-proof" assembly line technologies. In combination with an egalitarian culture and a specific regime of corporate governance based on stable industrial relation and so-called "life-long employment" and ownership in *keiretsus*, industrial groups, the Japanese industry constituted a competing model. In 1984, Michael Piore and Charles Sabel, two MIT-based researchers, published *The Second Industrial Divide*, a treatise that put forth the idea that a production system characterized by what they referred to as "flexible specialization" would be the solution to declining competitive advantage in the American manufacturing industry. Flexible specialization denoted a production system that was flexible enough to produce relatively small batches at low cost, and being able to produce short series, the manufacturing industry would be able to increase its competitiveness. Throughout the 1980s and well into the 1990s, these two themes were discussed in the business literature—in the genres of the "Japanese challenge" (Vogel, 1979; Pascale and Athos, 1981; Cusumano, 1985) and the "flexibilization" of industry (Jessop, 1991; Pollert, 1991; Blyton and Morris, 1991; Smith, 1989)—and eventually one of the reactions was a yet another genre that sought to restore the reputation of American industry, perhaps best represented by the emblematic popular management book of the 1980s, Tom Peters and Robert Waterman's best-selling *In Search of Excellence*.

The master idea of this discourse, that industry needs to be more flexible in responding to market changes and shorter production cycles and shorter life spans of products and platforms, was appealing for actors who had a firm belief in market-based transactions. In addition to technological flexibility, it was suggested that industry should also encourage more a flexible labour force and a more flexible financial situation in which corporations should not accumulate and handle their own capital, but rather acquire it from financial markets. In the neoliberal era, labour relations, in particular, have been rendered more flexible, making working life and employment positions more insecure (Sennett, 1998). Kalleberg (2009: 2) here speaks of the substantial growth of what he refers to as "precarious work," employment that is "[u]ncertain, unpredictable, and risky from the point of view of the worker" in the contemporary neoliberal era. This category of work is today widespread in the global economy. In addition, many of jobs are not paid very well: "The International Labour Organization (2006: 1) estimates that 'in 2005, 84 percent of workers in South Asia, 58 percent in South-East Asia, 47 percent in East Asia . . . did not earn enough to lift themselves and their families above the US$2 a day per person poverty line'" (Kalleberg, 2009: 15). Studies show that in the democratic and advanced economies in, for example, the northwestern part of the world, entry-level jobs (so-called "low-autonomy jobs") that used to be decently paid are today increasingly being paid "bottom-level wages" (Vidal, 2013: 597). Vidal (2013) distinguishes between Fordism and post-Fordism as "two institutional regimes of competition," and suggests that the latter "[r]efers to an institutional regime of competition characterized by highly intense, internationalized competition generating a growing core of service firms and a dominant logic of externalized employee relations, emphasizing lean organizational structures and market-mediated employment, where the latter includes market-determined wages, deunionization and increased competitive pressures on employee performance" (Vidal, 2013: 605). In this post-Fordist institutional regime of competition, Vidal (2013: 605), argues, there is a substantial structural demand for "low-autonomy work"—a category that constitutes over one-third of all jobs—but it is no longer able to "provide decent living standards of the workers that fill these positions." These jobs are indeed "precarious."

In the West, having a long history of industrial relations, the new regime of flexible labour contracts has led to a number of new relations and standards for labour contracting. For instance, the use of temporary workers ("temps" or agency workers), labour employed by another corporation and hired on short-term contracts by a contracting firm, have become more widespread (Hardy and Walker, 2003; Garsten, 1999; Pialoux and Beaud, 1999). Garsten (2002) suggests that this new category of temporal workers need to think of themselves as being a *homo mercaris*, a "market man," always being available for work opportunities and ready to negotiate temporal work opportunities: "Market man is taught to think in terms of financial transactions, value him- or herself as a product of the market, and to take the idea of enterprise as a mode of action. Moreover, he or she is flexible, autonomous, self-reliant and disciplined" (Garsten, 2002: 247). Very much in contrast to what Whyte (1956: 3) spoke of as the "organization man," the white-collar worker that not only *works* for the organizations but that essentially *belongs to it*, the "market man" needs to ceaselessly develop his or her skills in promoting him or herself and to be able to accept new assignments. "The salesman's world has now become everybody's world, and, in some part, everybody has become a salesman. The enlarged market has become at once more impersonal and more intimate. . . . The market now reaches into every institution and every relation," Charles Wright Mills (1951: 161) wrote in the early 1950s in *White Collars*, his classic account of the suburban American middle class in the post-World War II period. More than six decades later, these words appear almost prophetic. The market man is a modern-day industrial nomad wandering between short-term employment contracts.

In this "new world of work" (Beck, 2000), there are relatively fewer secure, long-term positions and, consequently, the career pattern shifts in nature from being an essentially hierarchical or vertical advancement within an internal labour market in a major corporation to a more horizontal career pattern where individuals move back and forth within organizational networks (Roper, Ganesh, and Inkson, 2010; McKinlay, 2002; Lichtenstein, Bergmann, and Mendenhall, 2002; Adamson, Doherty, and Viney, 1998). In these new career patterns, terms such as *employability* (Cremin, 2010: 133) play a key role, as it denotes the totality of skills, experience, reputation, and cultural and symbolic capital acquired by an enterprising individual over time and that either enables or inhibits lasting employment opportunities. The neoliberal ethos of competition and self-reliance is effectively operationalized into the term *employability*. For the "organization man" type of market actor, the failure to become employed would be an embarrassing and most tragic outcome, but today's "market men and women" seem to be aware of the influence of macroeconomic conditions and policies beyond their influence and are therefore not regarding periods of unemployment as a personal failure, but as a characteristic of the new labour market regime (Lane, 2010). Studies show that this insecurity in labour relations is compensated for by higher economic compensation (Morris and Farrell, 2007).

In addition to flexibility, the term *downsizing* has been one of the most widespread managerial terms in the neoliberal era. When shareholder value programs were implemented in, for example, the United States, the easiest way to cut costs and increase profits that in turn directly benefitted the "residual claimants," the shareholders, was to cut down on labour costs and make fewer employees work harder (Brockman, Chang, and Rennie, 2007; Lazonick and O'Sullivan, 2000). In comparison to more uncertain investment in, for example, R&D or other strategic decisions (e.g., to target new markets or segments of markets), cutting down on labour costs was a convenient tactic to increase profit and shareholder dividends. By the end of the 1980s and in the early 1990s, there was consequently an emerging literature on the decline of middle management positions in major corporations. For some scholars, middle managers were bound to disappear as they contributed little, while for others their decline was a more tragic event, indicative of an era reaching its end. Floyd and Woolridge (1994) can be said to represent the former stance, allowing themselves to rant about middle managers as some kind of "prehistoric creatures": "Are middle managers becoming the dinosaurs of the business world? They once dominated the corporate landscape with salaries and perks that were the envy (and career goal) of every MBA. Now, like prehistoric reptiles, these behemoths of bureaucracy appear likely to succumb to a hostile environment" (Floyd and Woolridge, 1994: 47). In contrast, Dopson and Stewart (1990) are more inclined to deplore the lack of respect and understanding for the role of middle managers in corporations:

> Few people have anything encouraging to say about middle management... most people portray the middle manager as a frustrated, disillusioned individual caught in the middle of a hierarchy impotent and with no real hope of career progression. The work is dreary, the careers are frustrating and information technology, some writers argue, will make the role yet more routine, uninteresting and unimportant. (Dopson and Stewart, 1990: 3)

In a more recent study of middle managers in the United States, the United Kingdom, and Japan, Hassard, Morris, and McCann (2012) found that middle managers are still around in major corporations and that they today can take advantage of—or "are exposed to," depending on what view one takes—the globalization of the world economy and corporations:

> [Changes] to the structure and composition of managerial roles in large organizations have typically *led to career stagnation for middle managers*... Second, in attempting to become progressively 'leaner' and 'flatter,' large corporations have also *reduced the traditional career entitlements of middle managers*, a trend that reflects a culture of job insecurity... And third, the above changes to managerial careers and

organizational forms *are increasingly international phenomena*. (Hassard, Morris, and McCann, 2012; emphases in the original)

The middle manager was declared to be an endangered species in the new regime of flexibility and downsizing, but apparently this category of white-collar workers—the principal recruitment basis for Whyte's organization men—seem to have survived (albeit at a smaller number) three decades of neoliberal policy.

Winning the Pay Game

It is frequently remarked that the new flexible labour market is more insecure and characterized by short-term contracts and a project-based organization, but that this insecurity is overall compensated for financially, leaving the responsibility to the individual to save up resources for shorter periods of unemployment. If nothing else, there are certain elite worker categories that come out as "winners" in the new structural changes in the neoliberal era (Lin and Tomaskovic-Devey, 2013: 1289; Dore, 2008). Liu and Grusky's (2013: 1332) study of wage inequality in the American economy between 1972 and 2008 demonstrates that this group of "elite workers" is relatively limited in its scope of competencies, being primarily premiered on the basis of its ability to engage in analytical and critical thinking, including deductive and inductive reasoning. In general, there is a growth of interest in artistic and creative work, testifying to what Inglehart (1997) and Inglehart and Norris (2009) refer to as "postmaterialist values" in society, and during the last decades the proportion of informants that want such "interesting work" has increased from 43.7% in 1989, to 51.0% in 1990, and to 56.8% in 2006 (Liu and Grusky, 2013: 1338). The oversupply of, for example, artists and "creatives" leads to a downward pressure on the wages in this category, a so-called income penalty (see, e.g., Menger, 1999: 553). Liu and Grusky (2013) also found, perhaps somewhat surprisingly, that technical skills (e.g., in engineering and scientific methods) are not always well compensated, but instead it is "analytical skills" more specifically that are rewarded: "[A] standard deviation of analytical skill raised wages by 10.4% in 1980 and 17.5% in 2010, an increase in payout that is far in excess of that observed for any of the other workplace skills" (Liu and Grusky, 2013: 1338).

Based on these findings, Liu and Grusky (2013) criticize the literature on the "third industrial revolution" (and similar concepts labelling the movement from the manufacturing-based economy of the interwar period and the 1950s and 1960s to the contemporary "knowledge economy") for overrating the role of technological change (most importantly the computerization and digitalization of information) and for failing to recognize the central role of cognitive skills—and analytical skills in particular—in combination with social skills. Liu and Grusky (2013) suggest that the "real driving force" of the changes in the economy is not what they refer to as "skill-based technical change," but "skill-based institutional change." In Liu and Grusky's (2013) view, changes in institutions create new demands for skills. For instance, in the neoliberal era, characterized by pervasive institutional changes, including new policies and regulatory frameworks, "[t]he growing demand for analytical labor reflects the accelerating 'creative destruction' of modern capitalism and the associated premium on innovation, problem solving, and rapid response to changing market conditions" (Liu and Grusky, 2013: 1368–1369). In this "new world of work," not all technical skills are well compensated, but the winners are workers with analytical and critical skills. The level of compensation is thus a quite complex empirical question and not all workers receive a compensation closely correlating with their human capital investment. Being able to relate individual skills and competencies with more widespread institutional changes seems to be a recipe for coming out well in the pay game.

Dwyer (2013) suggests that the increased polarization in compensation derives from a structural change in the labour market, the development of what she refers to as the "care economy." The care economy is based on relatively low-paid "care work," primarily conducted by women and minorities in the United States, labour that "[c]ontributes to the well-being or development of other people that is often face-to-face and requires skills in interactions and communication" (Dwyer, 2013: 391). Kristal (2013: 362), on the other hand, emphasizes what she refers to as "class-based technological change," more wide-ranging technological changes that have benefitted various social classes and income groups to different degrees. In addition, the decline of the unionization of the workforce also makes its mark on the compensation. Analytically speaking, Kristal (2013) separates wages and salaries and financial profits, capital generated through the owning of financial assets such as shares. Kristal (2013: 363) notices that according to national accounts data, wages and salaries "[a]ccount for only about half of the total income generated in the economy." Reporting data from the 1969–2007 period, Kristal (2013: 378) found that the computerization of industry and administration, beginning in the 1980s, has "benefited capitalists' profit more than educated workers' compensation"—that is, the efficiency gains accomplished through the technological shift of computerization have not led to higher wages and salaries, but instead, as prescribed by advocates of finance market corporate governance practices, the surplus has been channelled to the finance markets. This effect of financialization represents a major shift in industrial relations policy in the United States:

> From 1948 to 1973, the hourly compensation of a typical U.S. worker grew in tandem with productivity, indicating a relatively equal share social distribution of the fruits of economic growth and productivity gains. The state of inequality dramatically shifted in the past three decades. Although productivity grew 80.4 percent between 1972 and

2011, expanding total income, average hourly compensation, which includes the pay to CEOs, increased only 39.2 percent and—even more strikingly, the median worker's hourly compensation grew just by 10.7 percent. (Kristal, 2013: 383)

The principal explanation for this new policy derives from the weakening bargaining power of American workers, Kristal (2013: 377) argues: "I consistently found a positive relation between indicators for workers' relative bargaining power (mainly unionization) and labor's share, and a negative relation between computer technologies and labor's share, channeled through the decline of unionization." In brief, computerization reduced the employees' compensation, while a greater degree of unionization increased the compensation. The sharp decline in unionization and the marginalization of the unions more broadly as a legitimate actor in industry and society have led to "the erosion of rank-and-file workers' bargaining power," which in turn leads to "the decline in labor's share" (Kristal, 2013: 378). Technological shifts have led to increased efficiency, but the economic performance of industry has not benefitted salaried workers as much as it has rewarded shareholders and other finance market actors. In addition, de-unionization has weakened the economic compensation of employees.

Temporary Work, Agency Work, and Contingent Labour in the Neoliberal Era

The new generation of CEOs and boards of directors have favoured downsizing as the quickest way to boost stock prices and, consequently, their own economic compensation for their work. The immediate effect from this corporate governance practice, in addition to direct job losses, was that fewer blue-collar and white-collar jobs have remained secure and stable over time (Gregg and Wadsworth, 1995). The neoliberal doctrine advanced by the Chicago economists stressed the importance of reducing the influence of the labour movement and the trade unions. In contrast, they were less worried about monopolies and oligopolies being a standing concern in American policy-making since the nineteenth century and the enactment of anti-trust laws: "Chicago economists presented a benign picture of monopolies and a hostile picture of labour and trade unions, which they argued were a much more serious threat to the successful operation of the free market than vertically integrated corporations" (Jones, 2012: 93). Over the period from the 1960s, there has been a steady growth of forms of flexible employment, including forms of temporary work, agency work, short-term contracts, freelance contracting, and so forth. Between the early 1960s and 1982, the number of Temporary Help Services (THS), companies providing staff on short-term contract basis, grew from about 800 to 5,000 in the United States. In 2005, there were nearly 40,000 THSs (Smith and Neuwirth, 2009: 57). In the United Kingdom between 1997 and 2005, temporary work in public administration and education grew by 82% (Hoque and Kirkpatrick, 2008: 331). In many cases, agency work has de facto become more or less "permanent work"—Smith and Neuwirth (2009: 56) speak of the oxymoron "permatemps"; in 2005, "35% of temporary agency workers held a single temp job for more than a year compared to 24% in 1995" (Smith and Neuwirth, 2009: 56–57).

For the employer, agency work has a variety of benefits, including flexibility, the possibility for bypassing trade union bargaining, and externalizing the costs for the recruitment and "quality assurance" of labour. For agency workers, the THSs (to use Smith and Neuwirth's [2009] term, from among many competing concepts; see also Bergström, 2003) provide opportunities for finding work that they otherwise may have failed to identify. However, these new flexibilities of the labour market are not a naturally occurring phenomenon, but instead there is "strong evidence" that the "[s]udden growth in agency working is primarily (if not exclusively) supply led" (Hoque and Kirkpatrick, 2008: 335). That is, flexible labour markets have been developed on the basis of the supply of services, rather than being derived from an acute need for such labour relations on the part of industry and public sector organizations. As will be discussed shortly, labour market reform may have increased the possibilities for employers to regulate their labour needs at a lower costs, but it has accomplished little in terms of reducing levels of unemployment in OECD countries.

Smith and Neuwirth's (2009: 58) research on agency work questions what they regard as the widespread and overtly negative belief that THSs are "machines that eat and spit out workers, treating them as if they were disposable, even interchangeable commodities." Instead, Smith and Neuwirth (2009) suggest that THSs are professional service firms that have created a "set of practices" that "buffer their workers from the most insecure and exploitative aspects of temporary employment" (Smith and Neuwirth, 2009: 58). For instance, in the case of arrogant and poorly behaving managers in the contracting firms, the THS officers take action to avoid allowing the conflicts to escalate (Smith and Neuwirth, 2009: 66–68). Such practices indicate that the agency workers are treated with respect by the THSs and that they not only serve the interests of employers but also certain labour market groups.

MacPhail and Bowles's (2008) study of the effects of a neoliberal market de-regulation reform in British Columbia, Canada, is of particular interest when seeking to understand the consequences of "employer-friendly" reforms derived from neoliberal doctrines regarding market efficiency. The reform primarily targeted public sector organizations and aimed at creating new possibilities for hiring agency workers on a short-term basis. "The policy changes . . . were widespread and were aimed at deregulating the labour market, introducing greater flexibility, and shifting the balance of power between employers and employees, in favour of the former," MacPhail and Bowles (2008: 559) explain. MacPhail and Bowles (2008) had access to labour market data before and after the reform and could therefore measure its immediate consequences. In 2004, the incidence of temporary work in the province was 11.7% for women and 9.4% for men (MacPhail and Bowles, 2008: 553), and if one adds permanent part-time workers to these figures, it would be more accurately measured to 13.6% for men and 30.7% for women. That is, almost one-third of all women in British Columbia work on basis of temporal work contracts. There is apparently a significant gender difference in the data, leaving women (if it is assumed that temporary work is unfavourable vis-à-vis long-term contract) with the shortest straw. These figures demonstrate that the neoliberal reform contributed to the growth of temporary work as British Columbia, taking a lead in labour market reform among the Canadian provinces, "rapidly moved from being below-average to an above-average employer of temporary workers" (MacPhail and Bowles, 2008: 555). More specifically, MacPhail and Bowles (2008: 557) calculate that the labour market reform increased the likelihood of being temporary employed with 14% for men and with 17.4% for women. MacPhail and Bowles (2008) summarize their findings:

> We conclude that the shift in neoliberal policies in BC [British Columbia, Canada] led to significant increases in the likelihood of workers finding themselves in temporal employment . . . we also find that the likelihood of being a temporary worker in BC in the post-policy period increases relative to all other provinces [in Canada] over the same period. Taken together, these results indicate that government policy is a key determinant of the level of temporary work. As such, the level of temporary work should be seen as a policy-sensitive variable rather than as something exclusively determined by 'exogenous' forces such as the globalization and technological change. (MacPhail and Bowles, 2008: 546)

In other words, in the case of British Columbia, Canada, neoliberal labour-market reforms lead to a higher incidence of temporary work. The question is whether such reforms are able to reduce unemployment, as frequently and persistently claimed by neoliberal thinkers and pundits? In the next section, this question will be addressed.

The Effectiveness of Labour Market De-Regulation

As pointed out by Jones (2012) and many others, the neoliberal doctrine regards trade unions and the labour movement as a major threat to the "economic freedom" held in esteem—the observant reader notices that the working masses are implicitly treated as those who are never intended to be included in such liberties—and consequently there has been a standing demand for labour market reform (practically speaking, a de-differentiation of industrial relations as the unions are expected to "take a step back").

Glyn, Howell, and Schmitt (2006) examine publically available OECD labour market data in the period of 1980 to 1999, and report a series of findings that by and large disqualifies the neoliberal conjectures regarding the relationship between labour market reform and unemployment. First, Glyn, Howell, and Schmitt (2006: 9) found no statistically significant correlation between "standard institutional measures" (i.e., "employment-unfriendly" labour market institutions) and employment, indicating that the presence of trade unions do not in any way negatively affect the levels of unemployment in the OECD countries. Secondly, Glyn, Howell, and Schmitt (2006: 10) did not find any correlation between unemployment benefits and unemployment rates. This is an important result because the neoliberal narrative enacts such economic benefits as being fundamentally detrimental not only to the functioning of the economy at large and but also to individual morals and willingness to work. Such simplistic relations between benefits and aggregated unemployment cannot be supported by empirical data: "Despite the widely accepted view that unemployment benefit generosity lies at the heart of the unemployment problem, there is in fact no association between the standard measure of unemployment benefit generosity and unemployment over the 1980–1999 period," Glyn, Howell, and Schmitt (2006: 10) summarize. Third, Glyn, Howell, and Schmitt (2006: 11) argue that collective bargaining is "commonly blamed for the labor market rigidities presumed to be the root of high European unemployment," but when tested against the OECD data, there is "no statistically meaningful association" between "union density" and unemployment (Glyn, Howell, and Schmitt, 2006: 11). These findings serve as the basis for Glyn, Howell, and Schmitt's (2006: 12) concluding remarks:

> [D]espite the ubiquitous reference by economists, policymakers, and media pundits to the employment-unfriendly effects of employment protection law, unemployment benefits, and labor unions, the fact is that the best (OECD-produced) measures of these institutions show little or no association with the cross-country pattern of unemployment. (Glyn, Howell, and Schmitt, 2006: 12)

"[C]hanges in structural employment across the major OECD member countries in the 1990s are not systematically associated with the extent of labor market reform," Glyn, Howell, and Schmitt (2006: 14) conclude. The data set naturally include large regional and national variation, but the analysis underlines that the neoliberal hostility towards trade unions, collective bargaining, and other instituted practices in industrial relations are couched in ideological beliefs rather than being supported by robust data. Glyn, Howell, and Schmitt (2006: 8) thus suggest that "[i]deological attacks" on the welfare state, labour unions, and other "protective labor market institutions" cannot be justified on basis of empirical data. On the contrary, what Glyn, Howell, and Schmitt (2006) refer to as "the overwhelming dominance of the orthodox rigidity view" needs to be carefully scrutinized and become subject to critical assessment. Unfortunately, Glyn, Howell, and Schmitt (2006: 21) see few tendencies for these labour marker reform protagonists to abandon their beliefs because empirical evidence seems to play only a secondary role in advancing the agenda. "[P]roponents of labor market deregulation have not produced robust evidence of systematic positive effects of their proposed reforms on cross-country employment performance, through this result has evidently not dimmed the confidence with which such reforms are promoted," Glyn, Howell, and Schmitt (2006: 21) argue.

In Peck and Theodore's (2000: 120) comment paper on what has been called "welfare-to-work policies" being used in the United Kingdom and United States under Prime Minister Tony Blair's government and the Clinton administration respectively, it is remarked that the prevailing explanations for the causes of poverty and unemployment have been primarily formulated in terms of individual shortcomings and "supply-side terms," including problems of "'welfare dependency,' low motivation and inadequate employability" in the Anglo-American workforce. However, macroeconomic factors and the "demand-side" also play a key role in providing employment (Peck and Theodore, 2000: 129), and a study published in the United States in 1997 demonstrates the relatively marginal influence of welfare benefits in labour market economics:

> Two findings stand out [in the report]. The first is that caseload reductions were overwhelmingly attributable to business-cycle effects rather than to the influence of welfare-to-work policies. The second is that in Wisconsin and Oregon, two states that have diligently pursued 'work first' programmes and have witnessed some the greatest percentage declines in welfare caseloads, 'a substantial fraction of caseload reduction ... would have occurred without welfare reform.' (Peck and Theodore, 2000: 126)

In other words, the individual-centred explanation for unemployment is based on the fallacy of reductionism, arguably again couched in the comfortable ideological belief that markets by definition never fail, and consequently, *ex hypothesis*, any failure of labour markets is to be sought either in the inability of individual actors to take good measures—in Gary Becker's terms, to make adequate human capital investments generating future rents—to ensure their attractiveness on the labour market, or the detrimental intervention of government and other industrial relations organizations allegedly serving to disrupt and distort the functioning of the labour market. In many cases, combinations of the two explanations can be professed by neoliberal thinkers and pundits:

> In transferring yet more of the costs and risks associated with contingent employment onto workers themselves workfare may be performing

a basic regulatory function, in mobilizing a job-ready supply of workers for the very bottom of the labour market. It represents, in this sense, a neoliberal (yet highly interventionist) supply-side response to the demand-side problems of contingent work and labour market insecurity. (Peck and Theodore, 2000: 135)

Gregg and Wadsworth's (1995) study of the U.K. labour market in the 1975–1993 period also stresses the demand side when coping with unemployment; a downward spiral of pay and security is not a long-term solution to the unemployment problems:

> If families dependent on benefits find it hard to take part-time, low-paid, and insecure jobs . . . then this will inevitably generate the observed simultaneous increases in the number of families dependent on welfare support and those with two or more earners. Current patterns of job creation are becoming less and less helpful in reducing the unemployment count. Long-term poverty among families systematically disenfranchised in term of regular access to earned incomes is the ultimate consequence of these developments. (Gregg and Wadsworth, 1995: 89)

In the cases of Glyn, Howell, and Schmitt's (2006), Peck and Theodore's (2000), and Gregg and Wadsworth's (1995) studies, neoliberal orthodoxies are thoroughly challenged. Speaking more generally about corporate governance and what "version" of corporate governance (e.g., the Anglo-American, the German, the Japanese model, etc.) promotes economic growth, Fligstein and Choo (2005: 75–76) suggest that "[t]here is little evidence that labor laws that provide more extensive worker rights and welfare provisions inhibit economic growth." The neoliberal hostility towards labour movement and trade unions may be justified on basis of their ability to counteract the conspicuous economic and political interests of all the sponsors and financiers of the neoliberal transatlantic network (Jones, 2012; Peck, 2010; Bockman and Eyal, 2002) and the academics and ideologues that they pay to advance their agenda, but it cannot warrant the oft-repeated claims that, for example, trade unions and welfare provisions inhibit labour market efficiency and economic growth.

While welfare-to-work and other policies aiming at de-regulating the labour market discussed above primarily affect blue-collar worker jobs, there is also evidence of professional groups being affected by neoliberal thinking. In the next section, the concept of professionalism and professions will be examined. The professions as "worker elites" have historically enjoyed certain privileges and abilities to uphold domains of discrete jurisdiction, but in the contemporary era, such privileges can no longer be assumed, as there are other stakeholders showing interest in controlling and monitoring professional work.

I. STUDIES OF MANAGERIALISM AND PROFESSIONALISM

Expert Professionalism

All societies have a need for organizing their intellectual capital and expert know-how. In Western societies, the monasteries and other forms of cathedral schools served as the model for the Italian invention of the university in the medieval period. In addition, in the less abstract and more mundane activities in the field of technological development and mercantile practices, the guilds served the role of protecting the interests of both the community of professional or occupational groups and individual members. The medieval guild served a number of roles in the medieval period, not the least as a provider of credit and short-term loans to its members (Epstein, 1998: 685. However, during industrialization, the role of guilds was gradually changed and ultimately abolished, beginning in Prussia in the first decades of the nineteenth century, and in 1864 in Sweden and in Denmark in 1849 and 1857 (Hobsbawm, 1975: 36; see also Krause, 1996; Mudambi and Swift, 2009). Brint (1994: 26) traces the history of the professions, beginning in the early modern era in the medieval period. In the "transition period" of the seventeenth century there was a crystallization of two branches of professionalism: the "service occupations" (e.g., legal practices and law) and the "scientific and scholarly occupations" (including medicine and other science-based forms of knowing).

Historically, the professions have enjoyed a great deal of prestige in society. the professionals were relatively few and were recruited from economically favoured classes—every now and then a talented farmer boy or someone with a more modest occupational background managed to enter the professions and make careers, but such accomplishments were quite exceptional—and served as the "knowledge workers" of the medieval, early modern, and modern periods (Le Goff, [1985] 1993). The town physician, a lawyer with a local practice, perhaps the school teacher at the higher level, members of the clergy, and few more made up this community of professionals in the bourgeoisie society. The professional middle class community also played a role in the social, political, and administrative life, holding many positions as policy makers. Professional groups advanced new ideas and enacted policies regarding, for instance, social work in the local community. This professionalism model, based on the bourgeoisie rather than the aristocracy (with England as a possible exception) worked quite fine for centuries and was essentially part of the modernization of society and its institutions. However, beginning in the 1960s, this social trustee professionalism (Brint, 1994) was increasingly attacked for its inability to align itself with the new demands for professional services. Instead, what Brint (1994) calls *expert professionalism*, professional expertise being valued, priced, and exchanged in emerging markets for professional services, gradually replaced the regime of social trustee professionalism. Brint points at some of the consequences of this shift:

> The shift from social trustee professionalism to expert professionalism has led to a splintering of the professional stratum in relation to the market value of different forms of 'expert knowledge.' There is the real possibility in this split for the eventual consolidation of the professional stratum into a more exclusive status category, since 'formal knowledge' implies gradations in the value, efficacy, and validity of different forms of knowledge . . . In this process of splitting, the technical and moral aspirations of professionalism have tended to separate and to become associated, respectively, with the 'core' and the 'periphery' of the stratum. (Brint, 1994: 11)

One of the key consequences of expert professionalism was that the professions were increasingly subject to managerial governance—that is, they lost some of their autonomy as an independent category between the state and the market. In the neoliberal era, much research has been committed to the study of how the two governance regimes of professionalism and managerialism have been co-aligned and mutually adjusted to one another.

Managerialism and Leaderism

As was discussed in Chapter Three, not all theories developed in the neoliberal tradition have been entirely positive regarding management as a regime of governance. Agency theory, for instance, explicitly distrusts executives and their tendency to act in accordance with their own rather than in the shareholders' interests. On the other hand, market transactions are always by definition more efficient in the neoliberal tradition of thinking, and management is the practice of organizing, monitoring, and regulating market transactions. There are, in other words, somewhat mixed emotions about management and managerialism; it is both what promises to handle some of the inefficiencies identified by neoliberal theorists, and also what of necessity includes human beings that are poorly equipped to live up to the quite stern demands for self-discipline enacted in neoliberal thinking. Managerialism is a term that is primarily used in the literature in a critical manner, as what represents an overtly optimistic view of what managerial practices are capable of accomplishing. In this setting, it is intended to denote a regime of governance that relies on professional salaried and otherwise economically compensated managers that work in accordance with the board of directors' strategies and tactics.

"Managerialism is a mode of thought and action based on a desire to control, enhance efficiency, normalize and suppress conflict and promote the universalization of sectional managerial interests," Kuhn (2009: 685–686) says. For Deetz (1992: 222), managerialism is a "discursive genre," a way to conceptualize, discuss and denote certain activities and practices in industry and in public sector organizations. This discursive genre begins, Deetz (1992) says, with "[a]n imaginary identification where the corporation and management become a unitary identity." This identity includes four key elements: "Its central motif is control; its primary mode of reasoning is cognitive-instrumental; its favored expressive modality is money; and its favored site of reproduction is the *formal* organization" (Deetz, 1992: 222–223). Grey (1996) suggests that managerialism as a regime of governance includes the four following elements:

- The assault on trade unionism heralding the 'end of industrial relations' and, significantly, the advent of human resource management;
- The elaboration of 'new techniques' of management, including total quality management (TQM) and business process re-engineering;
- The 'managerialization' of the public sector with attendant debates, especially in relations to healthcare;
- More intangibly, the tendency to lionize 'management' (both in the sense of managers and managerial techniques) as the solution to all types of social and economic ills. (Grey, 1996: 592)

In Leicht and Fennell's (2001) view, various managerial programs have sought to gain control over the professions over the course of the modern and late-modern era. Such managerial programs include *entrepreneurialism* in the period of 1860–1910, *scientific management* in 1910–1940, *human relations* in 1940–1970, *human resource management* in 1970–1990, and, most recently, *neoentrepreneurialism* beginning around 1990 (see also Barley and Kunda, 1992). All these managerial programs have in their own idiosyncratic ways aimed at controlling unruly professional workers, to discipline them to act in accordance with organizational policies and strategies rather than as prescribed by professional ideologies, yet trying to encourage and reinforce the commitment to their work and their role in the organization and society more broadly. Managerialism and managerial practice have to strike a delicate balance between the regulation and control of professionalism and an effective exploitation of its merits—the qualified and economically valued expertise. In many cases, such dual objectives are combined in the combination of ideological and technocratic control (Rennstam, 2012; Fleming and Sturdy, 2011; Sewell, 2005; Kärreman and Alvesson, 2004; Robertson and Swan, 2003; Doolin, 2002): "Professionals operating under managerialism are . . . subject to both the normative control of the profession and the bureaucratic control of the corporate enterprise, leading to both a continual self-surveillance and a narrow technical rationality," Kuhn (2009: 685–686) suggests. For instance, one of the most widespread approaches to professional control is to standardize activities and procedures, that is, to de-contextualize and formalize professional skills: "Under attack, the legitimacy of personal expertise that typifies disciplinary erodes, and the expert community is focused to transfer their legitimacy to independently verifiable rules and procedures. When a profession becomes vulnerable, merit shifts from character to method," Timmermans (2008: 170) says.

Another term closely related to, or better still, sprung from the managerialist discourse is the literature on what has been quite recently branded as *leaderism* (O'Reilly, Dermot, and Reed, 2011), a term that denotes the strong belief in leaders' ability to influence and determine and monitor organizational action. The history of leadership writing and studies stretches back to the ancient period where, for example, Xenophon spoke of *oikonomikos* as a form of leadership. Xenophon stressed the virtues of *sophrosyne*, self-control, balanced measures, and *epimeleia*, order and carefulness of operations. In political history and in military history, leaders like Caesar, Nestor, Darius, Lord Wellington, and Napoleon have all been praised and discussed on basis of their leadership skills. The modern study of leadership is commonly associated with Chester Barnard's monograph *The Functions of the Executive* (1938), the institutional theory work of Philip Selznick (1957), or the more freestanding contribution to a new field of study by Frederick Fiedler (1968). In Selznick's view, leadership is embedded in institutional settings and therefore "leadership is not equivalent to office-holding or legal prestige or an authority or decision making" (Selznick, 1957: 24). Instead, "understanding leadership requires understanding of a broader social process." Selznick suggests. For Fiedler (1968), generally credited with coining the term *situated leadership*, the emphasis on leadership as being not the execution of a set of standardized activities but as what effectively takes into account local conditions and specific needs and demands, leadership is defined accordingly: "The individual in the group given the task of directing and coordinating task-relevant group activities or who, in the absence of a designated leader, carries the primary responsibility for performing these functions in the group" (Fielder, 1968: 8).

Since leadership is one of the most difficult activities in organization, and also one of the most complex issues to study empirically, there has been a massive growth of leadership studies and management training and consulting services offered on the market (see, e.g., Costas and Taheri, 2012; Bell and Taylor, 2004). Chester Barnard was critical of this leadership training industry already by the 1940s (Barnard, 1948: 81, cited in Pye, 2005: 32), claiming that "leadership has been the subject of an extraordinary amount of dogmatically stated nonsense." Despite such early and persistent criticism, leadership training and development continue to be a lucrative branch in the management consulting industry.

In the neoliberal era, what Bryman (1992) has referred to as the "new leadership literature" has stressed the importance of charisma (Conger and Kanungo, 1987; Ball and Carter, 2002; Flynn and Staw, 2003), the ability to lead and inspire creative people (Mumford et al., 2002; Pirola-Merlo, 2002; Basadur, 2004; Shalley and Gilson, 2004), the capacity to create meaningful identities for themselves and co-workers (Carroll and Levy, 2010; Pye, 2005), and more generally of engaging in what is called *transformational leadership* (e.g., Shin and Zhou, 2003), the continuous development of the organization and its competitiveness. For critics of this leadership discourse, the new leadership literature accomplishes little more than portraying everyday leadership as an extraordinary activity (Alvesson and Sveningsson, 2003), presenting leadership as a form of reification of social relations (in Lukács' [1971] Marxist vocabulary; Gemmill and Oakley, 1992), or succumbing to the fallacy of misplaced concreteness (in Alfred North Whitehead's phrasing), assuming that leadership work can be understood as discrete and clearly confined activities that lend themselves to detailed scrutiny in the form of isolated events (Wood, 2005). By and large, the leadership literature and the interests in leadership training and development services seem to grow at an unprecedented rate, making the term *leaderism* a highly relevant analytical term when examining the contemporary obsession with leadership as the solution to all kinds of organizational shortcomings and problems (see, e.g., Khurana, 2002).

When Professional Ideologies Encounter Managerialism: Enterprising Professionals

The Company of One

One interesting tendency directly caused by the flexibilization of major corporations and industries is the growth of temporally employed professional workers. Barley and Kunda (2004) examine how Silicon Valley computer industry cluster knowledge workers are capable of pursuing careers on the basis of short-term contracts. In this account, professional workers are quite satisfied with being able to plan their own time and determine for themselves when they want to have periods of less work to be able to "spend time with the family" or "go to the beach." Lane's (2010) ethnography of the same category of professional computer industry workers in Dallas, Texas—"the Silicon Prairie"—tells a somewhat different story of how these professionals being laid off during periods of economic slowdown were more or less forced to become "a company of one" to be able to provide for their families. Such outcomes were not indicative of their failure to entrench a stable position in the labour market, but were on the contrary seen as evidence of their enterprising capacities:

> As they [computer industry professionals] saw it, the losers were those outmoded men and women who failed to cast off the dependent mindset of the 'organization man,' who foolishly looked to paternalistic employers to provide them with job security and financial stability. In contrast, these workers saw themselves as 'companies of one,' entrepreneurial agents engaged in the constant labor of defining, improving and marketing 'the brand called you.' (Lane, 2010: 9)

Lane found that this category of workers had fully embraced and enacted images of themselves as a *homo mercaris*, including a rejection of virtues widely acclaimed in previous regimes of capitalist accumulation:

> Much of career management's distinctiveness stems from its explicit rejection of previous ways of thinking about loyalty, security, and the social contract of employment, particularly those espoused by the organization men of the postwar era and the meritocratic individualists of the 1980s. Organization men followed the Calvinist tradition of seeing hard work and self-sacrifice as the key to occupational success. Today's white collar workers argue that being a loyal employee, or even a talented employee, is not enough to guarantee success in today's hyper-competitive economy. (Lane, 2010: 47)

In the neoliberal era, "loyalty" and "security" become as antiquated as Victorian ideas about "honour" or "glory," perhaps once able to capture the imagination of humans, but today lingering only as somewhat curious ideas, perhaps even worthy of ridicule or scorn. Lane (2010) made firsthand observations of how interviewees and industry representatives operationalized the neoliberal ethos of competition and self-reliance into effective practices and routines. "To give my employees job security would be to disempower them and to relieve them of the responsibility that they need to feel their own success," one corporate executive claimed (cited by Lane, 2012: 51), sounding almost like some *faux* Jean-Paul Sartre claiming that humans are condemned to live under the burden of freedom and all the existential anxiety such freedom would entail. In some industries with low transaction costs and relatively little fixed capital, such as the computer industry, there are good opportunities for such enterprising professional market men and women to thrive, especially in clusters such as in the San Francisco Bay Area. In other industries, demanding more capital and the co-localization of intellectual capital and know-how, as in the case of the pharmaceutical industry, there is less evidence of such enterprising "companies of one." In such industries, a few major corporations, still enjoying a significant cash-flow derived from historical accomplishments in producing blockbuster drugs, control substantial capital. In addition, many small and medium-sized firms, often grown from successful academic research projects, are the sites where new and innovative research work is conducted. Once these smaller firms are able to present clinical data supporting the demands for efficacy and safety in new therapies, drugs, or medical devices, major corporations show an interest in acquiring these companies to be able to add the new therapies to their product portfolio. In such an industry structure, there is less circulation between firms but the flexibility lies instead in the network-based structure of the industry where major corporations increasingly externalize their R&D costs and live off their historical accomplishments (Whittington, Owen-Smith, and Powell, 2009; Powell et al., 2005; Owen-Smith and Powell, 2004). Under all conditions, the professional categories of life scientists tend to increasingly pursue their careers in more insecure settings (Block and Keller, 2009)—small and medium-sized firms depending on venture capital investment—and are working under conditions where they have to prove their worth by providing clinical evidence of the efficacy and safety of therapies. Taken together, not even professional workers, historically enjoying a privileged position in society, are secured from the ups and downs of the world economy. Past accomplishments and historical records can be invoked to justify privileges no longer. In the neoliberal world of work, you are, as they say in the show business, "no better than your last hit."

Professional and Managerialist Ideologies

One of the key terms for examining and understanding professions is *professional ideology*. "A professional ideology consists of a set of norms, manifested both in explicit ethical codes enforced by professional associations and internalized preferences, often developed during professional training," Nordenflycht (2010: 163) writes. The literature on professionalism (e.g., Larson, 1977; Strauss et al., 1964; Bucher and Strauss, 1961) has emphasized the professional ideologies as the negotiated order that structures and regulates a professional domain of work. At times, these professional ideologies are universally shared in a professional community, while in other cases, as in the study of psychiatry by Strauss et al. (1964), there are complementary, at times competing, professional ideologies existing in parallel. Many studies of professionalism and professional communities examine how, for instance, managerialist initiatives and professional ideologies and practices are either clashing or coexisting. In the following, a few case studies of how managerialist initiatives, operationalized as a variety of practices, methods, procedures, techniques, and technologies will be examined.

Leslie (2010) studied the case of how managerialist ideas about the need for quality assurance (QA) technologies have penetrated the domain of forensic biology. Technicians and biologists working in forensic biology laboratories experience the uses of QA technologies quite differently. For the technicians, working to assist the biologists in their laboratory work, the procedure is "precise, quantified, [and] objective," while for biologists, it represent the gaze of their peers. Still, the QA technologies denote ambiguous qualities, inasmuch as they are both a "[t]echnology of trust and mistrust" (Leslie, 2010: 299). On the one hand, QA is a major "source of credibility," as it supports the evidence presented in court because QA is generally held to be based on an auditing process that creates objective data. On the other hand, it is a technology that is part of a "managerialist control structure":

> The accepted consequence of QA is the institutionalization of mistrust in the form of managerial oversight. As previously noted by a technician,

the drudgery of audit forms is something that everyone knows is important. To be mistrusted is simply a part of the work. (Leslie, 2010: 299)

Institutionally speaking, the use of the QA technology serves the role to bridge the gap between the science and law, the laboratory and the court as it imposes an authoritative view of the activities in the laboratory. The concern is, however, as will be discussed in greater detail in the fifth chapter of this volume, that there is a certain *performativity* in auditing and quality assurance technologies because they do not primarily mirror underlying activities, but actively construct them: "[T]he problem with audits is that it can become a system that describes itself—it creates a kind of virtual reality . . . by *only* taking into account those kinds of activities that it seeks to assess," Parry and Gere (2006: 154), examining organ donation systems, argue. In other words, using Merton's (1957) concepts of *manifest* and *latent functions*, the quality assurance system is a managerialist initiative that has the manifest role of supporting the technicians and the biologists to present their forensic data in court by complementing their professional work with an audit activity, but the latent function is that the professional community is increasingly monitored and distrusted.

Another case where manifest and latent functions are at play is in the field of what Berman (2012) calls the *market university* (see also Nussbaum, 2010; Washburn, 2005; Bok, 2002), the university populated by *entrepreneurial professors* (Lam, 2007) engaging in *academic entrepreneurship* (Stuart and Ding, 2006), increasingly an important component of what has been called *academic capitalism* (Ylijoki, 2005). In Lorenz's (2012) quite harsh critique of the academic entrepreneurship literature, he identifies three genres of "Orwellian newspeak" in the university setting. The first one is what Lorenz refers to as *Qualityspeak*, the ceaseless discussions about the importance of quality in research and teaching, not infrequently operationalized as the ability to entrench a certain position in various rankings and league tables produced by accredited auditing organizations. In the qualityspeak genre, academic performance is strictly understood as what is recognized by others, preferably on an international market and in international evaluations. Second, Lorenz (2012) identifies the genre of *Valorizationspeak*, the emphasis on the economic value of education and the possibilities for capitalizing on investment in basic and applied research, especially in disciplines such as medicine, life science, and engineering, but also increasingly in other domains, such as the humanities and the social sciences. In many cases, patents and other registered intellectual property rights are treated as evidence of the economic value of the underlying findings being patented. Third and finally, Lorenz (2012) points at what he calls *Topspeak* or *Excellencespeak*, the tendency to compare any university or institution of tertiary education as being comparable with e.g., North American elite universities. This discourse, perhaps surprisingly, tends to conceal rather than highlight the different economic, cultural, and institutional settings wherein the most heterogeneous category of universities are operating. A small community college in Idaho, Stanford University, a German state university, or a French École Polytechnique are consequently all part of the same competition over resources and "talent," and naturally it is places like Stanford that come out as the winner in all kinds of comparisons. In other words, the topspeak and excellencespeak genres are ways of enacting the university system that leave professional academic researchers in a perpetual stage of anxiety over their inability to live up to the "high expectations" of their sponsors and financiers. Sauder and Espeland's (2009) study of the implications from the ranking of American law schools is instructive of how such "genres of excellence" are not very helpful in actually advancing the quality of the teaching, but rather leads to a situation in which increasingly more resources are spent on making the school *appear* more qualified, regardless of actual changes. The concern here is the very calculative practice and use of a ranking as being a "zero-sum technology" wherein one school's success "[c]omes at the expense of others and small differences matter" (Sauder and Espeland, 2009: 73). As Kornberger and Carter (2010) point out, in addition to the zero-sum logic of the ranking, many ranking lists and league tables (Kornberger and Carter, 2010, examine the listing of cities and their attractiveness) are commercial services that are being developed by corporations and agencies, and consequently, there need to be some movements up and down to maintain interest in the rankings. If all university ranking lists have the same top ten universities year after year, interest in the ranks would wane. "I only look at the movements," Søren Kierkegaard once announced, and the same goes for ranking lists and league tables. When one university or city either rises or falls on the list, that can attract some attention and some information on how to accomplish a more attractive organization can be acquired. As a consequence, in the world where rankings and league tables become part of the calculative rationality, there is ongoing work—at least among aspiring universities and city managers and city brand consultants—to assure that positions are not lost. Unfortunately, these activities consume resources that could have been used elsewhere.

Another case where managerialist initiatives serve to marginalize professional ideologies and norms are the uses of calculative practices that are widely embraced in managerialist programs. Samuel, Dirsmith and McElroy (2005) present a fine example of how certain calculative practices are increasingly taken for granted in health care organizations and how these calculations institute a vocabulary enacting patients as being primarily economic agents. First, engineers and eventually economists elaborated concepts in "health economics" in order to be able to calculate cost-benefit ratios. Over time, these calculative practices have, Samuel, Dirsmith, and McElroy (2005: 251) suggest, "[c]hanged the perception of the doctor-patient relationship into one between self-interested producers and consumers who trade in a commodity called 'care.'" In this new vocabulary, embedded in calculative practices derived outside of the field of medicine, doctors become "providers" and patients become "consumers." Worse still, in this implicitly market-based calculative practice, "[i]ll-healthed people is no longer viewed as a social problem but increasingly as a 'budget-deficit problem'" (Samuel, Dirsmith, and McElroy, 2005: 270). The concern here is not so much that health care organizations are working in a world where they have to pay attention to costs and incomes, but that what was originally developed to be an aid in calculating health benefits is increasingly becoming the principal framework to enact the patient and the therapies provided. Expressed more to the point, the calculative practices of first engineers and thereafter economists and health care accountants are gradually displacing professional vocabularies and professional ideologies.

Yet another case of how professional expertise has a problem living up to market-based demands for efficiency is the field of architecture. Brown et al. (2010: 529) suggest that there has always been a tension between the "creative ethos" of architects and the construction processes in which small profit margins are quite often the case. While the architect used to be a key player in the domain of the built environment and city planning, today architects have been pushed back to what Brown et al. (2010: 529) call the interstices of "a quintessentially pre-bureaucratic form," and what is generally assumed to be a post-bureaucratic and post-modern organization of the creative industries. Internal professional disputes regarding "architectural knowledge" have not supported the market position of the community of architects, and today the field is characterized by, Brown et al. (2010: 529) suggest, "relatively weak authority over clients and contractors, combined with increased competition." As Brown et al. (2010: 540) notice, the term "creative industry" is an oxymoron, inasmuch as the expressions "to be creative" and "to be industrious" carry different connotations and imply different practices. Instead, in the study of the prestigious EA architecture bureau (a pseudonym), Brown et al. (2010: 534) found that "being creative" did not at all mean to be free to act at will, but on the contrary, to act in accordance with the relatively narrow domain of activities that the fully socialized EA architects regarded as their unique domain of expertise. In addition, being creative in this setting involved being subject to admonitions and correction. Creative work is above all disciplinary work—work that is disciplined in every sense of the term (see, e.g., Daston, 2008: 102). The gradual loss of actual creative work and the insistence on regarding architecture as a creative domain creates a sense of marginalization and discontent in the community of architects (Cohen et al., 2005). Some architects can enact the role of being businesswomen or businessmen or public servants, part of the construction of the material world, but the image of the creative architect turning sketches and full-scale models into actual constructions is an appealing and persistent enactment of a member of the profession. In the case of architects, it is hard to claim that there are immediate managerial initiatives that have served to marginalize the community of architects. Instead, they are both the benefactors of the increased wealth in the neoliberal era and to some extent losing out when short-sighted market solutions to the built environment have come to dominate over timeless aesthetic values. For a handful of "starchitects" such as Frank O. Gehry and Norman Foster, the neoliberal era has offered great opportunities for producing spectacular signature buildings in the major metropolitan areas of the world. For the vast majority of architects, everyday life unfolds as project-based contracts where aesthetic concerns are clearly down-prioritized. A commitment to long-lasting qualitative buildings has been displaced by a shareholder value oriented construction industry that uses architects as early design and planning phase resources that otherwise only limitedly influence the ongoing work.

In summary, the professions and their insistence on serving not only their employer but also wider social interests—the "generalized public," for instance—have been challenged by various forms of managerial initiatives and practices. While professionalism is commonly defined as the successful attempt to erect entry-barriers and to create discretionary jurisdiction (in short, to create "intellectual monopolies"), professionalism is inherently opposed to the free competition cherished in the neoliberal tradition of thinking. Neoliberal and neoconservative theory, policy, and worldviews are thoroughly committed to the reduction of labour power. While professionals arguably represent a specific form of labour, the tendency of the profession to restrict competition in order to control and monitor the inflow of professional actors is fundamentally in opposition to the neoliberal credo. Many studies demonstrate that professional communities have been able to resist, bypass, or overcome various managerial initiatives, but there is also evidence of professional strongholds such as universities increasingly being managed like corporations, with chancellors and rectors recruited from industry and state administration rather than from the ranks of the professors, and board members recruited from industry—and having at times limited understanding of the academic day-to-day work, but nevertheless insisting on implementing performance metrics similar to those of industry. Whether there is a future for the professions, and especially the sub-category of the social trustee professionals, or if a managerial regime of governance will take its place, remains to be explored.

Summary and Conclusion

In the neoliberal era, semi-skilled and skilled manual work has been downsized, outsourced, and offshored, and many jobs today belong to the category of contingent labour, offered by temporal help service companies or as temporal contracts. Neoliberal thinkers and pundits have prescribed liberal and flexible market reforms as remedies to endemic unemployment rates, but studies demonstrate that such reforms accomplish little to push down unemployment figures. Instead, such reforms tend to make working life more insecure and lower the pay for large communities of blue-collar workers. In the case of white-collar professional work, there have been attempts to reduce the discretionary jurisdiction of professional communities by imposing various managerial procedures and technologies. For instance, to be discussed in the next chapter, forms of auditing and performance measurement have been widespread in the neoliberal era. In general, the social trustee professionalism that has served as an important autonomous force in constituting the modern welfare state has been under pressure to become increasingly market-based, as in the case of expert professionalism. By and large, professionalism is in opposition to the demands for transparency and the liquidity favoured in market-making, and consequently professionalism has been targeted as what is principally opposed to market-based transactions. In addition, in the neoliberal era, labour movements and trade unionism have been treated as a threat to "economic freedom"; consequently, leading political figures, think-tanks, and advisors that have rolled out the neoliberal agenda have dedicated significant efforts to discrediting labour movements. Taken together, the neoliberal era brought industrial relations, new human resource management practices, and new forms of managerial control over unruly professional communities.

5 Auditing and Accounting in Organizations

INTRODUCTION

One of the principal effects of the agency theory perspective on the firm was that traditional managerialist capitalism—the managerialist capitalism of Alfred Sloan and his generation—was made suspicious. The decline of economic performance in the 1970s was not just explained on the basis of macroeconomic conditions and the favourite neoconservative explanation, that of the labour unions' claims of economic compensation undermining the competitiveness of industry, but also in terms of managers taking advantage of inconsistencies in the principal-agency contracts that enabled them to "enrich themselves" at the expense of the shareholders. In the finance market solution to "excessive" agency costs proposed by agency theorists, managers were separated from the capital owners. Historically, at least in a Chandlerian management history perspective, capital owners and managers essentially belonged to the same class and shared a commitment to the circulation and reproduction of capital. For agency theorists, such an assumption was a mistake: Capital owners have all reasons in the world to distrust professional managers and their ambition to primarily secure their own interests at the expense of, for example, the shareholders. In order to curb such "opportunistic behaviour," finance market control was called for. In addition to this ideological shift in perspective—not even the graduates of business schools and other business-oriented tertiary education graduates populating the boardrooms and executive offices could be trusted any longer—the development of more narrowly defined finance-reporting and accounting procedures led to a better transparency vis-à-vis external stakeholders, for example, finance traders. As a consequence, another major institutional shift in the neoliberal era was that firms were increasingly audited, and *ipso facto* managed, from the outside by so-called auditing organizations. What could be more effective for principals than having professional auditing organizations monitoring the processes and performance of the organizations wherein they had economic interests?

This chapter will examine the so-called audit society and its relationship to the neoliberal creed. Essentially bound up with the financialization and its demand for transparency, auditing has also been a standard procedure in the neoliberal state apparatus where public organizations such as schools, hospitals, and universities are increasingly monitored and thus managed on the basis of principles and objectives defined from the outside. Being a most complex social phenomenon, auditing practices do therefore have many consequences and effects—some manifest and some latent (i.e., unanticipated), in Merton's (1957) vocabulary—whereof the de-professionalization of certain categories of knowledge workers is perhaps one of the most significant. Auditing is ultimately based on what philosophers, historians, and sociologists have referred to as a *calculative reason*, the belief in the possibility of and ambition to lay bare underlying assets and resources through the capacity to calculate the efficiency of the operations engaging these resources. In other words, the roots of the audit society are to be found within the professional domain of accounting. A substantial part of this chapter will therefore address the epistemological, political, and cultural elements of the audit society and to point at the connections between neoliberalism and auditing as a managerial practice. Needless to say, calculative reason and accounting are historical processes that demonstrate their own trajectories, but the ambition to capture the world in figures, ratios, and graphs—beginning in the domain of accounting but eventually appropriated by scientific communities during the so-called scientific revolution in the seventeenth century—fits well with the neoliberal ethos of competition and self-reliance and strong orientation towards financialization of the economy.

I. THE AUDIT EXPLOSION IN THE NEOLIBERAL ERA

The Concept of Auditing

Contemporary executives and managers need to respond to shareholders' demands for transparency. In the audit society, the concept of transparency is operationalized as "auditability," that is, the capacity to render any organizational activity, asset, or resource subject to an auditing gaze. Power (1996) explains the term:

> Auditability is not just a natural property of economic transactions, not simply a function of the quality of evidence which exists in the environment within which auditing operates. Rather, auditing actively constructs the legitimacy of its own knowledge base and seeks to create the environment in which this knowledge base will be successful. (Power, 1996: 291)

Power (1996: 302) adds, drawing on neo-institutional theory (e.g., Meyer and Rowan, 1977), that while the auditing of the firm may have low *technical* benefits for the organizations (i.e., the auditing does little to handle practical and political internal problems) it may still give *institutional* benefits.

Such institutional benefits include legitimacy and a perceived willingness to render internal processes and resources transparent to outside stakeholders. The crux is, unfortunately, that while auditors and auditing firms make claims to take "a-view-from-nowhere" position—that is, pursue a disinterested and neutral perspective on the object of the audit—auditing always represents certain interests, beliefs, and ideologies.

> Accountants, as auditors, have cemented their status and privileges on basis of claims that their expertise enables them to mediate uncertainty and construct independent, objective, true, and fair accounts of corporate affairs. This expertise, it is claimed, enables markets, investors, employees, citizens, and the state to limit and manage risks. Such claims, however, are precarious as measures of revenues, costs, assets, liabilities, and profits are contested technically as well as politically and also because capitalist economies are inherently prone to crises . . . The claims of expertise are frequently punctuated by unexpected corporate collapses, frauds, and failures. (Sikka, 2009: 868)

Therefore, in its consequences, auditing procedures strongly influence the managerial system of the organization—that is, audits rest on *performativity*: "Far from being a by-product of management systems structures, 'auditability' becomes, in the absence of specific standards of performance, their constitutive ideal" (Power, 1996: 302). "Verifiability" and "auditability" are consequently "less properties of things in themselves" and more of a function of the "institutional credibility of experts," Power (1996: 305) suggests. Consequently, Power (1997: 28) speaks about "the deep epistemological obscurity of auditing." Based on these concerns, Power (1997) stresses, just like Sikka (2009), that auditing may in fact counteract what it seeks to accomplish—transparency in order to be able to anticipate and handle risks—by giving too much authority to these "rituals of verification":

> [T]he audit explosion reflects a distinctive response to the need to process risk. Auditing threatens to become a cosmetic practice which hides real risks and replaces it with the financial risk faced by auditors themselves. Where the audit process is defensively legalized there is a risk of relying too heavily on an industry of empty comfort certificates. The audit society is society that endangers itself because it invests too heavily in the shallow rituals of verification at the expense of other forms of organizational intelligence. In providing a lens for regulatory thought and action, audits threaten to become a form of learned ignorance. (Power, 1997: 123)

Consistent with Power's (1996) argument, in their study of the ranking of business schools, Free, Salterio, and Shearer (2009: 120) identified "a loose coupling" between the level of "programmatic appeal" and the level of "audit practice":

> Where organizations do not have clear measures of productivity which relate their inputs to their outputs, the audit efficiency and effectiveness is in fact a process of defining and operationalizing measures of performance for the audited entity. That is, the efficiency and effectiveness of organizations are not so much verified as constructed around the audit process itself. (Free, Salterio, and Shearer, 2009: 138)

"[Audit cultures] attempt to devise numeric performance measures. In doing so, they all to a greater or lesser degree distort the phenomena they purport to measure," Kipnis (2008: 281) argues, pointing at the performative and distortive effects of auditing. In addition, Kipnis (2008: 281) suggests, concepts such as "information" and "data" are used to underline the neutrality and precision of the audit because such terms are supposed to be understood as having the capacity to embody seemingly objective facts. Still, such conceptual frameworks serve to conceal that audits rarely are based on a more detailed understanding of underlying activities and processes: "To make the auditing efficient, easily accessible, and seemingly reliable, information is required. Information that almost always must be numeric and based on samples or brief inspections rather than exhaustive investigations" (Kipnis, 2008: 281). Free, Salterio, and Shearer's (2009) study of the ranking of business schools presents the same conclusion, that the underlying data used to construct the rankings remain by and large opaque for the outsider:

> What emerges . . . from the field data is a view of auditing as a collection of negotiated and highly adapted pragmatic routines which may add credibility to the rankings, but in a way that cannot be easily communicated to users. Audit procedures, like the statistical underpinnings of the rankings themselves, are opaque enough that very few users outside of the *FT* [Financial Times] can figure out how they work, yet clear enough to convey legitimacy. (Free, Salterio, and Shearer, 2009: 137)

" 'Let the facts speak for themselves' is perhaps the arch-statement of ideology—the point of being, precisely, that facts 'never speak for themselves' but are always *made to speak* for themselves by a network of discursive devices," Žižek (1994: 11) remarks. The very idea of auditing as the production of facts remains of central importance for its success and widespread use. In other words, auditing is not so much anchored in timeless and disinterested universal principles as it is rooted in forms of expertise and knowledge claims that are mostly concealed from the wider public, but still based on "a peculiar mixture of internal (epistemic) and external (institutional) validity in which the 'how' and the 'who' of that expertise are deeply interrelated" (Power, 1996: 307). The ability of the underlying organization subject to auditing to act in accordance with such regimes of validity is frequently referred to as the ability to demonstrate "rational action." The problem is, however, that there are no such universally agreed upon standards for rational action, but, instead, as Lave (1988: 178)—addressing cognitive research—remarks, " '[r]ationality' seems better described as a cultural resource invoked in the fashioning of action than as the quintessential template for rational cognitive processing." The consequence of this belief in auditing experts' prerogative to define the nature and qualities of rational action is that the entire auditing procedure is embedded in social agreements regarding the qualities of skilled and efficient management and how organizational effectiveness can be measured. Says Power:

> [C]oncepts of evidence, observation, experiment, testability and replication are far from being stable elements which can be utilized to explicate audit practice. They are themselves the product of processes which mark out the, often competitive, jurisdictions of knowledge-producing communities. Making things auditable is a constant and precarious project of a system of knowledge which must reproduce itself and sustain its institutional role from a diverse assemblage of routines, practices and economic constraints. (1996: 312)

Like many accounting scholars, Power (1996) thus rejects the idea that auditing or any other form of accounting is capable of mirroring underlying organizational assets within the confines of a realist epistemology. Instead, auditing and accounting are enacted as the performative acts of inscribing certain qualities into organizations on the basis of agreements between professional actors. For instance, Hines (1988: 258) stresses this performative role of accounting: "[F]inancial accounts of an organization do not merely describe or communicate information about an organization, but they also play a part in the construction of the organization, by defining the boundaries." Similarly, Dambrin and Robson (2011: 447) suggest that performance measurement is the "associations" between "technologies, inscriptions, human actors, and calculations" and therefore accounting scholars should once and for all abandon the debate regarding what are the "best measures 'here' for objects 'out there.' " That is, accounting practices are inevitably assemblages of heterogeneous entities, practices, and interests. When such heterogeneous entities, practices, and interests are stabilized and become "black boxes" that are legitimate and widely taken for granted, accounting and auditing serve their role. The experts having the jurisdictional authority over such assemblages of practices and resources are oftentimes unwilling to have these assemblages scrutinized because any constructivist account of auditing and similar practices risks the discretionary jurisdiction of the experts. Still, accounting researchers examine the practices and knowledge claims of such experts and seek to identify how certain claims of transparency reproducing the authority of the experts are secured: As many accounting scholars emphasize time and again, the discretionary jurisdiction of, for example, auditors demand the complicity of other stakeholders. Says Preda (2009: 676): "[C]alculation remains the interaction-based achievement and can be best understood as a relational and situational activity."

In the audit society, several assumptions are made regarding the nature of calculation, inscription, and rationality—assumptions that at times are subject to critical reflection or are directly contested. In the following, some of these underlying ideologies and beliefs will be examined.

Auditing and Neoliberalism

Since neoliberalism is a term that cannot be understood as what denotes a single unified set of ideas, ideologies, and worldviews, it is complicated to make a straightforward argument regarding the relationship between neoliberalism and the practice of auditing. However, neoliberalism in the form of the privileging of market activities over any other form of governance, in combination with the agency theory solution to agency costs (proposing shareholder value and finance market control of executives and managers in organizations), opens up the growth of auditing, accreditation, and other forms of control executed by third party actors operating as an intermediary between the principal and the agent. Still, auditing is just as much grounded in Western epistemologies favouring transparency, calculative practices, seemingly objective measures and performance indicators as widely recognized virtues of good governance. For instance, Kipnis (2008) argues that auditing has been actively promoted in in the Chinese communist economic system, and similar arguments have been advanced by Mennicken (2010) in the case of the Soviet Union. The demand for auditing apparently cuts through ideological and economic systems, and the practices are widely perceived as being beneficial for authorities, policy makers, and officials in various settings. Kipnis (2008) is critical of the view that auditing is a recent, primarily Anglo-American invention in corporate governance and points at the emphasis on the virtues of "self-discipline and self-cultivation"—undoubtedly constitutive elements of audit cultures—in the writings of Confucius, Mao Zedong, and Mahatma Gandhi, as well as of "neoliberal thinkers" (Kipnis, 2008: 283). In Kipnis's view, a notion of self-discipline precedes the neoliberal tradition of thinking, and, Kipnis (2008: 283) suggests, "[i]s better seen as corresponding to the rise of compulsory schooling in all industrial societies than the specific ideology of neoliberalism." Kipnis continues:

> [A]lthough calculability has become central to a diverse range of governing practices over the past century, this centrality correlates with industrialization, the increasing universality numeracy in addition to literacy, and the ongoing growth in the volume and distance of trade,

and, thus, of the gulf between producers and end users. Any form of large-scale society with a division of labor requires means of calculating how the fruits of labor should be divided. (Kipnis, 2008: 283)

In other words, in Kipnis's account, auditing is more closely associated with what Max Weber speaks of as the rationalization and de-traditionalization of society than with a neoliberal credo. Kipnis (2008: 286) speaks more generally about *scientism* and its "abuse of scientific reasoning" as one of the principal drivers for audit cultures. However, the audit procedure is inevitably based on distrust, inasmuch as that is the "raison d'être for constructing the audit" (Kipnis, 2008: 283); distrust is also likely to be "exacerbated in the audit process." Frequently, this distrust, Kipnis (2008: 283) argues, "[m]anifests itself as a disconnection between the expressed motives of some participants and their actual motives as well as between verbal and written depictions of behavior and actual practice." Kipnis (2008) examines the case of communist China, being very concerned about implementing detailed auditing procedures in the economic and administrative spheres, as an example of how auditing is not inherently an Anglo-American and Western phenomenon. A similar view is taken by Mennicken (2010), pointing at a similar application in the Soviet Union planned economy:

Party officials, academics and other actors involved in the political governance of the Soviet State portrayed financial inspection as an important instrument to facilitate the realization of socialism . . . State financial inspections were an integral part of Soviet governmentality rooted in ideals of central planning, surveillance, command and control and social equality. (Mennicken, 2010: 339)

In summary, Kipnis (2008: 286) argues persuasively that audits are spread around the world for a "a variety of reasons," including "[i]ndustrialization, the rising prevalence of numeracy, and, most importantly, the imagined (but not usually actual) benefits that governing agents believe can be derived from measuring the performance of those who are governed." In other words, neoliberalism and auditing have two distinct trajectories, but the general distrust of both public sector administrators and private sector executives and managers, and the general belief in market-based activities, is a fertile soil for an expansion of auditing practices.

A second question, as suggested by Sikka (2009), is whether auditing is a neutral and disinterested procedure that serves to mirror underlying economic conditions, or if there are elements of performativity in auditing activities, i.e., that auditing *constructs* rather than *reflects* organizations. Arnold (2005) advocates an "institutional model of globalization" that postulates that markets are actively constructed, instead of a "market model of globalization" that suggests that industry merely responds to the process of globalization. "The transnational accounting industry, working with and through states and international economic institutions, has worked proactively to create a global market for accounting and auditing services," Arnold (2005: 302) says. The institutional model is, Arnold (2005) claims, more capable of explaining the emergence of a global market inasmuch as it assumes *agency* as a key component in its explanatory model. Such agencies include "states, corporate forms of capital (transnational corporations and industry lobbies), and international economic institutions (such as the WTO, IMF, OECD, and the World Bank)" (Arnold, 2005: 302), and their joint activities "culminate in the creation of global markets." In other words, international economic institutions (i.e., the WTO, etc.) are actively taking part in expanding the markets for capital investment.

Neu et al. (2006) provide an interesting example of how the World Bank is actively framing social policy in economic terms in its auditing and reporting. Using the term *informing technologies*, Neu et al. (2006) suggest that these technologies and procedures first serve "[t]o *inform* one party (in a typically asymmetrical) accountability relationship, about the status and action of the second party, the one being held accountable," and second, that "[t]hese technologies *inform* the practices of governance, and both enable and restrict it" (Neu et al., 2006: 636). As a consequence, these informing technologies, Neu et al. (2006: 636) argue, are "[d]istinctive in how they make the objects of governance knowable in terms of accounting/financial expertises." Neu et al. (2006: 640) stress that the World Bank is a "complex organization with competing objectives and interests," but still its accounting and auditing systems are thoroughly influenced by a distinctively economic and financial vocabulary; this is also the case in the education programs in Colombia studied by Neu et al. (2006). "Terms such as 'value-added' and 'rates of return' were common across all of the lending agreements," Neu et al. (2006: 644) report. The informing technologies developed and effectively put to use was thus couched in neoclassical economic theory terminology, wherein "children are first postulated as economic units, as wage earners" (Neu et al., 2006: 645). More specifically, Chicago economist Gary Becker's *human capital theory*, developed in the 1960s, assumed that investment in education increases the individual's human capital and future employment earnings, and it informed the practice to calculate the Net Present Value (NPV) of education investment. Such standardized calculative practices and inscriptions "[m]ake it possible for bank officials to compare the expected returns from one particular project in other sites, thereby re-presenting the projects in a form amenable to political deliberation and debate" (Neu et al., 2006: 646). In other words, rather than anchoring the evaluation in an education science and schooling discourse, the World Bank imposed calculative practices that derive more or less directly from economic theory embedded in rational choice theory: "Education projects must be framed in economic cost/benefit terms," Neu et al. (2006: 651) say. They conclude:

> [T]he financial management system envisioned by the [World] Bank refers to the collection of corporate management control practices. Accounting controls, internal reporting systems, monitoring systems

and variance analysis represents 'ready-made' solutions to the problem of control. They are borrowed from other fields (i.e., the field of westernized business practices) and implanted into the field of education under the rubric 'best practices.' (Neu et al., 2006: 648)

The *informing technologies* that the World Bank used to monitor and assess its education program in Colombia was, Neu et al. (2006: 653) claim, the "operationalization of discipline," a way to regulate on the basis of economic and financial benefits derived from a Beckerian rational choice theory of the individual's benefits from education and schooling. Economic theory and neoliberal doctrines thus strongly influenced and shaped the World Bank's auditing and accounting procedures. Ellwood and Newberry (2007) present another study of how neoliberal doctrines and assumptions penetrate auditing and accounting practices. Studying accounting practices in public sector organizations in the United Kingdom and New Zealand, they found that "the manner in which accrual accounting has been developed in the public sector has the effect of privileging decisions, which advance the privatization aspect of the neo-liberal agenda" (Ellwood and Newberry, 2007: 566). While neoliberal thinking is not wholly determining contemporary auditing and accounting practices, in many cases the economic theory and financial theory has advanced performance measures and other calculative practices that have gradually penetrated auditing and accounting practice.

II. THE EPISTEMOLOGY OF NUMERACY, METRICS AND AUDITING

The Ideal of Transparency

In the era of neoliberal thinking, transparency, the ability to visually inspect and asses underlying activities and resources, is a highly praised quality. Much effort and thinking have been committed to the solution to the problem of "acting at distance" (Robson, 1992: 700). Roberts (2009) addresses what he refers to as the "virtue of transparency." First of all, Roberts (2009: 957–958) says, "we seem to believe in transparency and with every failure of governance, we have been prone to invest in yet further transparency as the assumed remedy of all failures." In many cases (e.g., the 2008 finance industry collapse), the lack of transparency has been brought forward as an explanation for failures and malfunctions, but for Roberts (2009: 958) such arguments are based on the fallacy of "the ideal of complete transparency." Drawing on the works of anthropologist Marilyn Strathern (2000), Roberts (2009: 963) suggests that transparency "[i]nvolves processes of abstraction and de-contextualization that merely conceal the real workings of the institutions." That is, transparency implies a "[s]ort of masking of the complexity of organizational reality and its reduction to a few simple indicators." Complex and inherently fluid and confusing social realities, open for numerous and at times conflicting interpretations, are thus concealed by what are advanced as "objective measures." Roberts (2009: 968) thus warns that there is no "perfect transparency" or undisputed objective measurement of underlying social and economic activities, but instead both scholars and practitioners must have more realistic expectations on what, for example, auditing procedures are capable of accomplishing. For Roberts (2009), the pursuit to accomplish full transparency, part of what John Dewey ([1929] 1988) referred to as the "quest for certainty," is like the cat chasing its own tail; it is the gradual expansion of a self-organizing and autopoetic system (Luhmann, 1995) that still can never overcome its own boundaries. McKernan (2007), drawing on the work of the analytical philosopher Donald Davidson, reaches a similar conclusion from an entirely different starting point:

> The real grounds for the possibility of objectivity in accounting . . . are surely unlikely to be widely recognized until we stop taking seriously talk about 'correspondence' and 'true representations' and free ourselves of the illusion of objectivity-as-accurate-representation. (McKernan, 2007: 167)

"We cannot talk about *absolute objectivity* in accounting or in any other field," McKernan, (2007: 167) suggests. If accounting scholars seem to agree on the idea that accounting is a social practice based on heterogeneous resources and professional beliefs and norms, why is it the case that auditing, ultimately based on calculative practices and accounting procedures, has been almost universally acclaimed in the neoliberal era regardless of its performative force—its ability to influence what it is supposed to objectively account for—and other unanticipated consequences? One explanation may be found in the success of the quantitative sciences, originally taking economic and mercantile activities as its role model but eventually serving as a normative model for many other social activities in the modern society, and their ability to exploit what Carruthers and Espeland (1991) speak of as "uncertainty absorption" and the "rhetoric of numbers."

Transparency as Liquidity

Auditing has two principal objectives: first, to execute a form of control from the outside so that organizational members act in accordance with prescribed schemes and routines; second, to secure that the organization can be assessed by external stakeholders—most importantly, financial traders. This second objective implies that organizations need to be treated as bundles of financial assets (i.e., to qualify as investment opportunities, they need to become *liquid*; Carruthers and Stinchcombe, 1999). In order to trade assets, especially assets that are held for shorter periods of time and that are held primarily for the purpose of making a profit, assets need to be standardized and made comparable across time and space. Therefore, various market actors and regulatory bodies serve to create liquidity in such markets. "Liquidity, like efficiency, is considered one of the great virtues of perfectly competitive markets. It is associated with free and laissez-faire markets, and hence with the absence of an intrusive institutional or regulatory apparatus," Carruthers and Stinchcombe (1999: 353) say. The latter statement deserves some attention. In markets trading standardized goods and with low transaction costs, "free market" may exists for certain periods, but in many cases, markets and assets are far messier than that, and therefore an "institutional or regulatory apparatus" is of central importance when creating markets. These institutions' capacities to create "homogeneous commodities that buyers and sellers can understand" (Carruthers and Stinchcombe, 1999: 354) lower the transaction costs and create the possibilities for exchange. If they fail to accomplish these conditions, various forms of market inefficiencies emerge:

> Knowledge about an asset has to be socially established in such a way that many buyers and sellers in a market believe the same things about it. If they did not, then market prices would be unstable, bid and ask prices would diverge markedly, the entrepreneurial use of information would create insiders with secret information, or delay for appraisal of value would slow the market. (Carruthers and Stinchcombe, 1999: 354)

This does not mean, however, that the liquidity of the underlying assets is once and for all secured. Instead, the knowledge used to create liquidity is never "absolute" or "complete" (Carruthers and Stinchcombe, 1999: 357). For instance, in bond trading, insider trading is not prohibited because it would destroy perfect knowledge of the bond market but because it exploits the *inequality* in knowledge, giving certain traders an advantage that in turn would bias the market prices. Therefore, contrary to the assumptions of the efficient market hypothesis, liquidity is not the starting point and a "naturally given" condition, but is a social accomplishment of what Carruthers and Stinchcombe (1999) refers to as "market makers":

> Liquidity does not emerge on its own, nor does it flow out of a kind of economic 'state of nature,' characterized by the absence of interventions or regulations. Rather, its developments depend on specific institutional features and organizational activities. By 'market makers,' we mean an individual or (more usually) an organization that takes an illiquid asset and turns it into a more liquid one. (Carruthers and Stinchcombe, 1999: 358)

Different assets and different markets demonstrate higher degrees of liquidity than others. For instance, the market for raw materials is based on standardized qualities and market prices that are negotiated hour by hour based on supply and demand (for instance, the market for Brent oil, traded in the standardized unit of barrels). In contrast, the market for modern art—some of which is sold for the first time in the market and therefore has no historical price that can serve as a guideline for the price-setting—is characterized by a great need for strategic work of influential market makers, such as curators, gallery owners, and art critics before the prices of certain art objects can stabilize (Velthuis, 2011, 2003). Carruthers and Stinchcombe (1999: 378) clarify this point:

> Liquidity depends on 'know-ability.' An asset with transparent economic value, whose features can be credibly communicated to a large enough audience, will enjoy greater liquidity. Such an asset can be 'taken for granted.' This type of social transparency depends, in many situations, on prior organizational work to simplify, stratify, homogenize, and standardized the asset. Minting work creates social knowledge about exchangeable things, built on a foundation of commitments, certifications, guarantees, endorsements, and other risk-reducing and epistemologically simplifying mechanisms. Solid organizational commitments help to produce liquidity. (Carruthers and Stinchcombe, 1999: 378)

Individuals having a firm belief in free markets tend to blame government rules, regulations, and institutions for "interfering" into supposedly "natural" market processes, thereby, they claim, raising the transaction costs in the market. Such a view tends to ignore the elaborate "institutional investments, market rules, and sometimes government regulations" (Carruthers and Stinchcome, 1999: 379) that constitute liquidity and therefore precede and/or accompany the market activities and market transactions. As Carruthers and Stinchcome (1999: 379) contend, "there is nothing 'natural' about [markets]." If transaction costs are low and if markets operate smoothly, it is not because the market per se embodies certain rationalities, but because a variety of heterogeneous actors have been able to agree on how to value and price certain assets and because such agreements, accompanied by institutional arrangements and practices, can last over periods of time.

Commensuration

One of the most important processes in rendering assets liquid is the process of *commensuration*. Espeland and Stevens (1998: 314) speak of commensuration as the "the transformation of different qualities into a common metric." That is, what is inherently heterogeneous—e.g., different Picasso canvases or different used cars, each having its own qualities and deficiencies—are given an economic value—a price—that can be used to assess what Picasso painting or used car an actor wants to buy. Commensuration is thus at the very heart of everyday economic behaviour, and on an everyday basis consumers have to make decisions on the basis of incomplete information, ranging from what sandwich to buy for lunch—chicken or tuna?—to what insurance company to select. Espeland and Sauder (2007: 16) point at the cognitive complexity of the procedure:

> [C]ommensuration works mainly by transforming cognition; it changes the locus and form of attention, both creating and obscuring relations among entities. Commensuration is characterized by the transformation of qualities into quantities that share a metric, a process that is fundamental to measurement. (Espeland and Sauder, 2007: 16)

As the cognitive processes where information is collected, structured, integrated, and evaluated, commensuration is, Espeland and Stevens (1998: 317) say, "fundamentally relative." Commensuration unfolds as a practice where attributes or relations are compared in order to reveal value in the comparison, and when a decision is made, value is derived from "the trade-offs made among the different aspects of a choice" (Espeland and Stevens, 1998: 317). The process of commensuration is thus to be understood as an "abstracting" and "reducing" of information to be able to make a decision on what asset or product that is preferred over other alternatives. A key element of commensuration is therefore to "absorb" uncertainty (Espeland and Stevens, 1998: 317), to eliminate certain alternatives and to make choices predictable and in a way manageable. "Commensuration always is a process, often one that requires considerable social and intellectual investments. Before objects can be made commensurate they must be classified in ways that make them comparable," Espeland and Stevens (2009: 408) say.

Commensuration is of necessity part of the everyday experience in advanced capitalist societies characterized by a significant supply of goods and services, and it is in essence a cognitive process where preferences, previous experiences, and the calculation of alternative costs are brought together in what at times are quite unproblematic decisions while in other cases significant amounts of work is needed. The concern is that there are *market makers* intervening in the process, trying to support consumers and market actors in making such decisions. Such activities are not always mirroring underlying actual conditions, which in turn may make consumers underrate the costs or the qualities of their choice. "Commensuration makes the world more predictable, but at what cost?" Espeland and Stevens (1998: 319) ask, pointing at, for instance, the tendency to assess all resources on basis of a monetary metric.

One of the costs of commensuration is that market makers' activities may induce what Sauder and Espeland (2009) call *reactivity*, tactic and strategic actions to respond to and counteract certain commensuration activities. "Measures elicit responses from people who intervene in the objects they measure," Espeland and Sauder (2009: 2) suggest. Sauder and Espeland (2009) examined the case of ranking of law schools in the United States, and found that law school representatives (e.g., chancellors and boards of directors) do not passively observe how they are ranked vis-à-vis their competitors but instead actively work to influence and improve their rankings. Sauder and Espeland explain the nature of ranking:

> Rankings create a single norm for excellence in legal education and then evaluate each school based on how well it measures up to this standard. Ranking pressures become internalized and change behavior by imposing a metric of comparison that obscures the different purposes law schools serve. (2009: 73)

In addition, ranking is a "zero-sum technology" wherein one school's success comes at the expense of another and where small differences matter (Sauder and Espeland, 2009: 73). This means that law schools that actually perform *better* than in the previous year may nevertheless fall in ranking because there are other schools making even more improvement. The reactivity induced by the ranking system thus tends to have what Merton (1957) refers to as *latent functions*—it produces effects that were not anticipated or even desirable:

> [These] properties transform rankings into a zero-sum affair that encourages meticulous scrutiny, distrust, innovation in gaming techniques [i.e., how to manipulate the system], and pressure for conformity. . . . Despite vigorous critique from academics, ranking methodology seems transparent, rigorous, and reproducible, especially to nonexperts. Audiences imagine that the meaning of numbers is universal, interpretable, to any numerate person. The characteristics of external audiences also shape school's response to rankings. (Sauder and Espeland, 2009: 79)

The case of law school rankings is thus pointing at some of the difficulties involved in imposing quantification and metrics on what is inherently qualitative. Quantification and metrics have many merits in terms of enhancing "predictability, coordination, and impersonality" (Sauder and Espeland, 2007: 4), but the reactivity to, for example, rankings "blurs the line between objects and measurement," which in turn "threatens the validity of our measures" (Sauder and Espeland, 2007: 17). In other words, the ranking enables commensuration, but the metrics used to create the hierarchical order of law schools have less validity as actors tactically and strategically influence the process. Rankings are therefore, not constructed from some neutral vantage point outside of the social system of law schools, as they are claimed to be, but instead become a constitutive element of the social system, a reference point for law school development in managerial quarters and with many other stakeholders. Expressed differently, ranking lists rest on performativity, their ability to construct a social reality rather than just mirror it. As a number of empirical studies of valuation and commensuration discussed below demonstrate, these effects strongly influence any auditing activity.

Calculative Practices

Based on the mutually constitutive processes of liquidity and commensuration, both of central importance in the audit society of the neoliberal period, it is possible to articulate a more theoretical and conceptual framework regarding the role of what accounting scholars and students of finance industry call *calculative practices*. Calculative practices, Miller (2001: 379) suggests, should be understood as a "technology of governance": "[m]echanisms through which programs of government are articulated and made operable." As, for instance, accounting is capable of shaping social and economic relations, such calculative practices must be unearthed and given a proper analysis. Vollmer, Mennicken and Preda (2009: 625) point at three qualities of calculative practices: (1) they "shape, and are shaped by, the social, organizational and institutional setting in which they operate"; (2) they "actively create, rather than merely reflect, economic realities"; and, (3) they should be seen as "a socially and technically embedded activity" (Vollmer, Mennicken and Preda, 2009: 628). In the calculative practices of accounting, diverse and complex processes and heterogeneous assets and resources are translated into "single financial figure[s]" (Miller, 2001: 381; original emphasis omitted). The concern for accounting researchers is that these "financial figures" tend to become reified, taken for granted and sheltered from critical accounts as their origin and underlying epistemological status tend to be overlooked:

> Once the use of financial numbers is embedded in institutionalized and gradually self-supporting superstructures of models, technologies, and standards, numbers become social resources through the self-referential significance they achieve within these systems. Credit ratings, earnings projections, or share prices turn into resources by being put to work as signs within institutionalized systems of circulation in which they trigger near-mechanical specified activities. (Vollmer, 2007: 579)

As Lampland (2010: 383) remarks, "numbers are instruments, not simply transparent signs," and this is precisely what Vollmer (2007) wants to call attention to by pointing at the complex "couplings" of figures, actors, and institutions that create the possibilities for calculative practices:

> It is not the superficial neutrality of arithmetic, but the special coupling of sign utilization to the ordering of ongoing activity which makes the use of numbers such an unique form of social activity . . . While the use of writing is associated with gradual a long-term transformation

of culture and societies . . . *the utilization of numbers is associated with immediate transformations of social situations.* By adding a frame of activity that can be strategically entered and left by participants, it affects the balance of resources and opportunities in social situations in a way that which, on a systematic level, is still little understood. (Vollmer, 2007: 597. Emphasis in the original)

Again, "the numbers" and the calculative practices they enable have a performative capacity that tend to be overlooked as these systems of calculation and inscription enable various social benefits, including the liquidity and commensuration of vital importance for effectively working markets. "Where subjectivity and intuition once reigned, the calculative practices of accounting were to impose objectivity and neutrality," Miller (2001: 388) writes. Vollmer (2007: 593) wants to further extend the role of numbers, suggesting that they not only have a *denotative* role as what expressed underlying processes, assets, and conditions, but also have an *expressive* role: "In being mobilized differentially in segregated settings of regulatory drama, participants make use of numbers not only as means of information or calculation, but of expression, negotiation and communication per se." Espeland and Stevens (2008) share this interest in understanding how numbers, figures, and arithmetic serve a wider and more comprehensive role in society than is generally understood, and a good starting point is not to take too much for granted: "We suggest that the work and conventions used to make numbers, and their meaning and consequences, should never be presumed" (Espeland and Stevens, 2008: 406). Still, the "authority of numbers" ultimately derives from their capacity for handling perceived problems (e.g., how to establish markets for goods). Espeland and Stevens (2008) point at a number of such qualities:

> The authority of numbers may be vested in (1) our sense of their accuracy or validity as representations of some part of the world . . . (2) in their usefulness in solving problems. . . . (3) in how they accumulate and link users who have investments in the numbers . . . or (4) in their long and evolving associations with rationality and objectivity . . . it often is some combination of these phenomenon that makes particular numbers compelling. (Espeland and Stevens, 2008: 417)

Regardless of all the benefits from the use of advanced arithmetic and accounting, at the end of the day, the question regarding the authority of numbers, and especially numbers that express financial worth, in the contemporary society needs to be addressed. "[Q]uantification facilitates a peculiar modern ontology, in which the real easily becomes coextensive with what is measureable," Espeland and Stevens (2008: 432) contend, stressing a tendency in the neoliberal era to render all human accomplishments and natural resources a matter of financial worth, thereby undermining a more balanced and socially embedded use of accounting and other forms of liquidity and commensuration.

The preference for metrics and calculability is not an idiosyncratic trait of neoliberal doctrines, but the strong position of neoclassical economic theory and its specific branch of finance theory, relying on formalist mathematical modelling and abstract numerical representations, have served to promote a calculative worldview and epistemic knowledge that further reinforce such a view. The neoliberal era has been a period where auditing practices have been legitimized and established, and thereafter they have been increasingly advanced as a regulatory service on the market for management control. In the next section, the consequences of this preference for auditing will be examined.

III. STUDIES OF RATING AND AUDITING

Valuation and Commensuration in Finance Markets

Widening the scope to not only include auditing, but calculative practices more broadly, one can draw on a quite substantial social science literature pointing at various forms of calculative practices in organizations. In the following, a series of studies of various calculative practices will be referenced in order to demonstrate that such uses of figures, ratios, and arithmetic are always socially embedded and accomplished in order to handle specific perceived problems and inconsistencies. Consonant with the remark of Hirsch, Michaels, and Friedman (1987: 323) that sociologists do not "take rationality for granted" but rather advance rationalization (in a Weberian tradition) as a field of research *per se*, the studies referenced below point at the social embedding and the accomplishments of various actors. Efficient market hypothesis protagonists merely assume the outcomes of these efforts, and accomplishments are always already in place out of sheer necessity. Opening up the black box of market making reveals another, more complex story, not always fully conducive with the "parsimony" of neoclassical economic theory.

To start with, several studies of calculative practices in the finance industry reveal conditions that are poorly explained on basis of the efficient market hypothesis. Hayward and Boeker (1998) show in their study of securities analysts that these financial traders rate their own bank's clients' securities higher than other companies' securities. Hayward and Boeker (1998: 16) explain: "Analysts' ratings, like other forms of professional advice, are based on highly ambiguous, uncertain, and limited information. While analysts may act rationally, such rationality is bounded by their limited time, localized search for information, and political and social constraints." That is, their calculative practices do not strictly draw on market information and market prices, but include other sources, and their familiarity with certain companies makes them rate their securities higher. Similarly, Zuckerman (1999) examines the role of classification systems used in the finance industry and suggests that the inherent ambiguities in the process of classification leads to a systematic underrating of stocks that are not fitting into the predefined classificatory scheme. Says Zuckerman (1999):

> For a product to compete in any market, it must be viewed by the relevant buying public as a player in the product categories in which it seeks to compete . . . [s]uccess or failure at gaining such recognition has a significant impact on a firm's fate in financial markets. All other things equal, firms that cultivate an egocentric network of reviews to securities analyst that reflects its industrial participation are more highly valued than those that do not. (Zuckerman, 1999: 1429)

In other words, financial traders and other market makers work hard to reduce ambiguities in order to render stocks and other financial assets liquid, i.e., to reduce the transaction costs, but they do so under the influence of what March (1994: 178–179, cited in Zuckerman, 1999: 1409) speaks of as the "opacity of future events." They simply do not know what the future will look like, and financial traders operate under the influence of what Zuckerman (2004b) speaks of as the "principle of self-recursion"—that is, it is not the actual, substantial value per se of the asset that generates future rents, but rather the ability to anticipate how *other* financial traders evaluate the future rents of the financial asset that determine the decision whether to buy or not to buy an asset. "If financial returns are based on buying at a low price and selling high, and if prices are determined by the prevailing valuation, market participants should rationally focus their energies on anticipating trends in conventional opinion rather than on trying to determine the objective value of assets," Zuckerman (2012: 234) argues. Zuckerman's principle of self-recursion is thus illustrative of what Luhmann (2000) refers to as *second-order observations,* where an observer is not so much interested in, for example, the price of assets per se as in the *accumulated changes* in prices over time and across larger populations. In situations where the principle of self-recursion dominates in a market, all new information matters because other financial traders may extract useful information that, in turn, may affect the valuing of specific financial assets. Zuckerman (2004b: 417) has "clearly demonstrated" that "the arrival of public information—even when highly standardized and anticipated well in advance—occasions dramatic increases in market activity," testifying to the inability of market prices to fully apprehend all information needed by financial traders to make their decisions. Taken together, Zuckerman's research shows that financial markets are not detached or separated from social interests and social influences, but rather the valuation and commensuration are determined by the presence of "interpreters and prognosticators" supporting the constitution and reproduction of financial markets:

> Armies of interpreters and prognosticators are present on Wall Street because they fill an important social purpose: they help investors make

sense of the dizzying array of possible investments. No such investment has a clear value, and the struggle to anticipate future prices never ends. (Zuckerman, 1999: 1431)

Fleischer's (2009) study of so-called *market intermediaries* in financial markets—"market makers" in Carruthers and Stinchcombe's (1999) vocabulary—investigates the rating of financial assets. Similar to Zuckerman's (1999) finance traders, market intermediaries both institute and make use of classificatory schemes to rate various assets. "Anecdotal evidence," Fleischer (2009: 555) proposes, suggests that these classification schemes are "not based on meaningful differences," that is, they do not effectively serve to enable liquidity and lower transaction costs, but are rather used to secure the interests of the market intermediaries themselves. Fleischer (2009) explains:

> Ambiguous classification schemes in which the categories used are not significantly different from each other, are problematic for markets precisely because the categories do not differentiate products based on their attributes. Market participants using ambiguous classification schemes believe they are making decisions based on attributes of the products within the categories but, instead, are making decisions based on the choices of the market intermediary. (Fleischer, 2009: 555)

Since market intermediaries are supposed to serve a disinterested and regulatory role, their integrity must not be questioned, and therefore "a rating system must strike a careful balance among the interests of the rating organization, the producers of classified products, and the audience of the system" (Fleischer, 2009: 558). If the market intermediary fails to strike this balance between such interests, its authority and legitimacy is undermined. One such strategy in this is the use of "ambiguous classification schemes" that blur boundaries among objects rather than distinguishing them (Fleischer, 2009: 556). The market intermediary is able to "protect its own interest" by downplaying potential criticism of the market actors (Fleischer, 2009: 556). In her study, Fleischer (2009: 571) found that "rather than using distinct classification schemes," market intermediaries "can act through the use of heavily overlapping sets of categories, increasing the ambiguity of the classification scheme." Such ambiguities enable market intermediaries to eat the cake and have it too: they can appear as a credible and trustworthy advisor at the same time as the "overlapping categories" absorb some of the uncertainty that always prevails in markets operating under the predicament of the "opacity of future events." "Although market intermediaries are typically considered impartial facilitators of exchange, they are also self-interested actors who can influence the structure of the information they share in subtle, but substantive ways," Fleischer (2009: 573) concludes.

To summarize, financial markets demonstrate no more and no less "inherent rationality" than other markets operating under uncertainty and ambiguities. Various market actors are primarily concerned with their own performance and long-term survival, and consequently they make use of any data, information, and other resources that would help them make qualified decisions. By and large, all these studies falsify the efficient market hypothesis and its assumption that market prices are effective in capturing substantial information of relevance for the valuing and commensuration of a financial asset. Since these are findings of relevance for the work of market intermediaries/market makers such as credit rating agencies, we can turn to this specific form of auditing to see how these key regulatory bodies, enjoying an oligopoly situation in the United States since the 1970s (Freidman and Kraus, 2012), are coping with these issues.

The Role of Credit Rating Agencies

As key market intermediaries in the era of financialization, credit rating agencies (CRAs) are quite curious institutions in the contemporary capitalist regime (for an overview, see Partnoy, 1999; Frost, 2007; White, 2010). Rom (2009: 641) speaks of CRAs as being "odd beasts" inasmuch as they are "private firms with public purposes"—hence the term "credit rating *agencies*, not credit rating *firms*"—governed on the same principles as any other corporation. Regardless of their juridical form, CRAs are widely recognized and their power and influence is almost taken for granted and rarely subject to systematic criticism: "Rating agencies fit into a specific capitalist knowledge structure. Market participants view rating agencies as endogenous (rather than exogenous) to global finance. Rating agencies are therefore seen by market participants as legitimate rather than imposed entities," Sinclair (2005: 60) argues. The role of these CRAs is to assess the debt instruments, such as bonds and other securities issued by firms or governments, and to assign "credit ratings" to these instruments on basis of the perceived likelihood that the debt will be repaid by the issuing organization (Rom, 2009: 640). Needless to say, such a role needs to be executed with a great degree of professional expertise and skill and with the highest rate of integrity. In addition, the CRAs needs to be trusted or else their role as market intermediaries and market makers fails and the transaction costs of markets increase substantially. However, the studies reported by Sinclair (2005) and Rom (2009) demonstrate that CRAs valuation and commensuration practices are not immune to social interests and politics. This does not mean that CRAs are incompetent or fail to accomplish what they are expected to do, but simply that credit rating is a domain of professional expertise having problems living up to the ideal of full transparency and lack of ambiguity that certain actors project onto their activities. "Rating is not the technical activity it is thought popularly to be. Instead, it is highly indeterminate, qualitative, and judgment laden. Rating is, first and foremost, about creating an interpretation of the world and about routine production of practical judgment based on interpretations," Sinclair (2005: 61) argues. Rom (2009: 641) shares this view and claims that "rating credit is inherently subjective and reflects professional judgment. Substantial amounts of quantitative data are used, but interpreting these data involves considered opinion." As a consequence, there is evidence of CRA analysts failing to objectively assess and rate financial assets. Vaaler and McNamara (2004: 689) studied the work of rating agencies in the 1997–1998 period and found that agency ratings "[d]eviate considerably and negatively from objective decision-making criteria, with rivalry effects figuring most importantly in explanations of this deviation." Vaaler and McNamara (2004: 689) continue: "The interaction of industry turbulence and positioning apparently distorts decision making by these experts at the very moment when, arguably, their views command greater attention and merit greater fidelity to disinterested objectivity." Like all professional communities relying on systematic analysis of empirical data, there is a need for long-term series collected under the condition of relative stability to be able to predict how financial assets may be valued by the market in the future and under different conditions. The quick and unprecedented expansion of the financial markets and the finance industry and its new product innovations, therefore, posed new challenges for the CRA analysis. Rom (2009) stresses the influence of these changes:

> The mortgage markets grew enormously during the first years of the twenty-first century. Fueled by cheap credit, relaxed lending standards, novel loans, and strong appreciation in home values, increasing numbers of 'subprime' borrowers obtained home mortgages. These mortgages were, in turn, sold by their lenders to investment banks, which 'bundled' them into increasingly exotic securities that were bought by investors hungry for higher returns. Investors were confident of the quality of these securities because the credit rating agencies (CRAs) typically put their seal of approval on them, indicating that the securities were 'investment grade.' (Rom, 2009: 640)

New financial assets such as Residential Mortgage-Backed Securities (RMBSs) and Collateralized Debt Obligations (CDOs) were developed in the 1980s to both counteract increased instabilities of the financial market and to absorb the capital accumulated in the finance industry when profits generated in industry were fed back into the finance market in the form of dividends and stock buyback programs. Between 2002 and 2007, Rom (2009: 647) reports, RMBS revenue "[g]rew by an *average* of more than 100 percent annually; CDO revenues more than *tripled* annually." In addition, in the United States, policy and finance industry interests opened up a subprime housing mortgage market wherein a new category of homeowners, traditionally excluded from that market because of low incomes, were given loans. These loans were designed to allow for a few years without the demands for paying the mortgage, and eventually many of these homeowners failed to repay their loans and were evicted. As a consequence, the rate of subprime delinquencies and foreclosure of the loans tripled between 2005 and 2007, rising to 16 percent; by 2007, "1.5 million homes were entered into foreclosure—50 percent more than the previous year. By May 2008, about one-fourth of subprime mortgage loans were delinquent or in foreclosure," Rom (2009: 644) reports. The question is, for Rom, (2009) why the CRAs failed to pay attention to these fallible financial services playing a key role in the 2008 events. "The tsunami of downgrades devastated the credit markets and the CRAs' credibility," Rom (2009: 644) notes, emphasizing how the CRAs suffered from their own failure to serve their role. Rom's explanation for the collective failure to rate the likelihood of subprime loan-takers inability to repay their debts correctly focuses on the combination of ignorance and the lack of previous data: "With the rise of the subprime market, it appears that the CRAs became much more ignorant, in several ways. First, the raters had little knowledge about the historical performance of subprime loans—indeed, there was relatively little history to guide them" (Rom, 2009: 646).

Another explanation (also endorsed by Freidman and Kraus, 2012) is that the CRAs were poorly regulated, an effect of political interests in turn anchored in economic theory. There was "no one watching the watchers" in the neoliberal era of financialization: "[T]he CRAs were loosely regulated, if at all, throughout the period that the subprime mess was growing" (Rom, 2009: 649). So, by the end of the day, Rom (2009) says, the whole credit rating debacle boils down to the question whether CRAs acted "naively or willfully ignorant?": "If the former is true, the CRAs simply did not understand the risks they were assessing; this speaks ill of the CRAs' competence. If the latter is true, the CRAs lacked integrity" (Rom, 2009: 647).

In Sinclair's (2005) view, the principal concern is that governments and other policy-making bodies failed to recognize what these CRA professionals were actually capable of accomplishing. However, based on ideological beliefs and wishful thinking, the very concept of "judgment," of central importance in professional work (Styhre, 2013), is not fully understood. Judgments are, Sinclair (2005: 74) suggests, based on "diachronic-constructivist accounts"—interpretations conducted on basis of incomplete and socially embedded data—but free market orthodoxies portray these professional communities as being capable of producing "synchronic-rationalist accounts" similar to the predictions made in the sciences. In Sinclair's view, the activities of CRAs are fundamentally informed by political interests and also reflect ideologies that poorly fit into the synchronic-rationalist accounts called for:

> Rating agencies and rating process provide a means for transmitting policy and managerial orthodoxy to widely scattered governments and corporations. In this sense, the agencies are nominally private makers of

global public policy. They are agents of convergence who, along other institutions, try to enforce 'best practice' or 'transparency' around the globe. The most significant effect of rating agencies is not, therefore, their view of budget deficits or some other specific policy but their influence on how issuers assess problems in general. This adjustment of mental schemata is the most consequential impact of their work. (Sinclair, 2005: 71)

For instance, critics claim, American CRAs tend to project an American perception on what happens outside of the United States, thereby failing to understand the institutional and political structures and traditions wherein economic activities are embedded. Moody's and S&P, a Frankfurt banker (cited in Sinclair, 2005: 133) suggested, "[d]isplay a colonial attitude and often fail to take into account the special characteristics in European accounting, disclosure and management practice." Such criticism cannot be treated as general complaints by disgruntled market actors if the civic role of CRAs is to be maintained over time. Sinclair (2005: 117) thus suggests that the CRAs are not serving their role as neutral and disinterested market intermediaries, but rather they "have considerable influence over investment and are able to promote neoliberal policy initiatives." Sinclair (2005: 117) continues by drawing on the instructive cases of how the two cities of Detroit and Philadelphia, both facing severe economic problems, were encouraged to implement neoliberal solutions that exacerbated rather than handled the problems: "The variables the agencies deploy in assessing cities are not socially neutral. They reflect a process of judgment that tends to produce socially partial policy on the bond issuer's part, other things being equal."

Explaining Poor Credit Rating Practices

Sikka (2009: 871) says that what he refers to as *traditionalists* have "often claimed" that external audits "add credibility to financial statements," but the difficulty with this hypothesis is that the present regime of auditing has accomplished little in counteracting the 2008 financial crisis. Sikka (2009) argues that rather than being the solution to a problem in terms of being a free-standing and credible actor, audit firms are too closely bound up with and dependent on their client firms to be able to make trustworthy audits; "auditors may be reluctant to qualify bank accounts for fear of creating panic or jeopardizing their liability position," Sikka (2009: 871) claims. Second, auditors have claimed that the financial crisis "unfolded suddenly," and that they were "ill-prepared to make judgment about the likely financial distress" (Sikka, 2009: 871), but as there have been financial crises in various parts of the global capitalist system on a regular basis over the last decades—Sikka (2009) refers to banking crises in Latin America, Sweden, Norway, and Japan—such excuses are not satisfying. Third, Sikka (2009) argues along a similar line of reasoning as Rom (2009) that auditors have failed to serve their role in the financial and capitalist economic system and that they have demonstrated a lack of integrity:

> The audit firms are capitalist enterprises and are dependent upon companies and their directors for income. The fee dependency impairs claims of independence and has the capacity to silence auditors . . . it poses fundamental questions about the private sector model of auditing which expects one set of capitalist entrepreneurs (auditors) to regulate another set of capitalist entrepreneurs (company directors). (Sikka, 2009: 872)

In summary, Sikka (2009) is not impressed by the explanations of the failure of auditors to fulfil their role and mandate, pointing at the systemic failure to let financial markets regulated by capitalist interests look after themselves: "Auditing firms have shown increasing willingness to violate laws, regulations and assist their clients to publish flattering financial statements . . . Arguably, a steady stream of auditory liability concessions have also eroded economic incentives to deliver good audits" (Sikka, 2009: 872). In Clark and Newell's institutional theory analysis, what they refer to as Professional Service Raters [PSRs] have engaged in what Clark and Newell (2013) call *complicit decoupling*, a decoupling between the formal role of the raters and the actual rating practices, which has not harmed the legitimacy of the PSRs. Under normal conditions, such a decoupling is harmful for an organization because it undermines its legitimacy and poses a threat to its long-term survival. In contrast, in the case of the complicit decoupling, Clark and Newell (2013: 20) argue, it is "[n]ot in the interest of the multiple players in a vast interconnected field to fully repair the practices—too many are benefitting too handsomely." Clark and Newell (2013: 23) thus suggest that the PSRs were not serving their "generally accepted policing role," but rather "they morphed over time into engaging in tacit collusion with the corporate issuers they rate so that the ratings have become gradually decoupled." This opened up for "[i]nter-organizational collusions that led to complicit decoupling and, ultimately, the misleading of mainstream investors" (Clark and Newell, 2013: 23). Both the rating agencies and the companies being rated benefitted from what formally appeared as legitimate market-based control of the finance market, but that de facto collapsed the line of demarcation between raters and the companies being rated.

Agency rating is an activity of central importance for the functioning of the finance industry and the financial markets supplying capital to what at times is referred to as "the real economy." Evidence demonstrates that credit rating agencies have failed to serve as disinterested and neutral market intermediaries, and some alarming cases (e.g., the top rating of Lehman Brothers' financial assets only days before its bankruptcy) have consumed much of the credibility of the credit rating agencies. On the other hand, the whole idea that credit rating agencies would be able to serve this "know-it-all" role in society, operating in markets riddled by skewed and biased information, was perhaps based on the fallacy of the ideal of full transparency in the first place. Auditing and other forms of accounting being based on mathematization, visual inspection, and neutral observation easily underrate the influence of what Herbert Simon (1957) speaks of as bounded rationality, the inescapable fact that all auditing occurs in a social setting and that humans draw on beliefs and preferences when data is ambiguous, confusing, or in short supply. As a consequence, the idea that auditing is capable of mirroring underlying, objectively true, and factual conditions needs to be critically reassessed. Auditing such as credit rating is a professional domain of expertise and always of necessity includes judgment, and judgment is based on a combination of formal training, previous experience, personal and collective norms and beliefs, and perceived and enacted objectives. Judgment is, in other words, a socially embedded practice.

Inside the Organization: Performance-Reward Systems

Auditing and other forms of rating and assessment located in markets (e.g., finance markets or modern art markets) are not the only complicated analytical procedures. In addition, such analyses inside of organizations demonstrate certain inconsistencies and the influence of human behaviour and cognitive limitations. For agency theorists, this may be easier to tolerate and explain than the comparative inconsistencies in the market because organizations are by definition—an organization is conceptualized as "a nexus of contacts," which in turn are associated with agency costs—riddled by inefficiencies and the costs of monitoring unruly executives and managers. Inefficient and skewed auditing procedures are, from this analytical perspective, not unexpected or confusing, but rather they are part of the argument advanced—that organizations needs to be controlled from the outside.

Castilla's (2008) quantitative study of the use of a performance-reward system in an American company is one fine example of how beliefs and expectations counteract data and evidence that is not in line with assumptions and beliefs. Castilla (2008) suggests that performance-reward systems serve two primary but often conflicting purposes. The first is an *administrative purpose* wherein organizations measure performance for the purpose of "making administrative decisions about employees (e.g., pay, promotion, termination, layoffs, and transfer assignments)." The second purpose is *developmental* and serves to produce a performance evaluation—that is, "supervisors provide key information and feedback to their employees for future development" (Castilla, 2008: 1486). In the former case, supervisors are supposed to serve as neutral observers, while in the latter case they act "more as coaches than as judges" inasmuch as they "[i]nculcate in workers the desire to improve their job performance" (Castilla, 2008: 1486). The concern is, practically speaking, that the administrative and the developmental evaluations are often intertwined and too complicated to fully distinguish when performance-reward systems are implemented in organizations, Castilla (2008) suggests. In practice, when checking for a number of "complicating factors" such as employee turnover, Castilla (2008: 1484–1485) found that managers ("supervisors") were not setting the salaries on the basis of the data provided by the performance assessment system, but instead the managers tended to "correct" the system by giving male co-workers higher salaries than the performance assessment system prescribed. Since the salary system is, at least in the short-term, a zero-sum game, this overcompensation came at the expense of women and minority workers: "The central finding of this study is that gender, racial, and nationality differences in salary growth persist even after controlling for performance evaluations . . . This study also supports the finding that performance ratings have a significant lower effect on annual salary increases for African-American employees, ceteris paribus" (Castilla, 2008: 1491). Castilla (2008: 1485) claims this data is "robust." What sociologists call *homophily*, the agent's preferences for individuals sharing the same socio-economic and cultural background as themselves (Mouw, 2006; Portes, 1998), may be one explanatory factor for these findings. Managers tend to believe that white, male colleagues are capable of performing well in their professional roles, and when data is not supporting that proposition, managers may "correct" the data by overcompensating this category of co-workers. In addition, if homophily influences the process, these managers have lower barriers to pass to befriend these white, male subordinates, and there may occasionally be personal bonds between managers and co-workers that intervene into and bias the performance-reward system. More recently, Woods' (2012) econometric analysis supports Castilla's (2008) findings, demonstrating that managers adjust objective performance measures so they are consistent with their subjective beliefs:

> Most adjustments (95%) are upward. Supervisors raise current, unexpectedly low performance so that it is consistent with prior performance when they perceive the measure of that performance is incomplete and noisy, consistent with their mandate of improving objective measurement . . . Overall, despite the organization's best attempts to focus all supervisors on the same purpose of improving individual objective measurement, evidence is consistent with supervisors using their discretion over subjective adjustments in a variety of ways. (Woods, 2012: 423)

The research reported by Castilla (2008) and Woods (2012) demonstrates that even in the case where quantitative measures are used and are given the formal status of being what should guide economic compensation decisions, managers bypass "objective data" and overcompensate certain groups. No formalistic performance-reward system is, in other words, immune to beliefs, preferences, and bounded rationality more generally (see, e.g., Rivera, 2012). In other words, inequalities are not easily counteracted by seemingly objective measures because the judgments made by managers and supervisors eventually draw on quite subjective accounts. In order to explain such inconsistencies in the use of auditing procedures, social scientists have identified a number of factors that intervene in the process. In the next section, some of these factors will be discussed.

Status as Intermediary Factor

No matter how hard auditors and other champions of quantitative metrics and performance assessment struggle to establish the methods and procedure they advocate and to safeguard them from criticism, there is always the residual factor of sociality intervening in the process, making things messier than they should preferably be. Sociality is something similar to what Mary Douglas speaks of as dirt in her seminal *Purity and Danger* (1966), a form of "matter put out of place" that disrupts and creates dissonances where order is supposed to dominate. Lehman Brothers were given the highest rating by credit rating agencies when, in fact, they were on the brink of financial collapse; supervisors ignore what may be understood as objective performance data when making compensation decisions. These two cases may be exemplary of how beliefs and preferences—two elements of sociality—intervene and confuse what was intended to be a quite straightforward auditing process. One explanation for such deviations from objective measures may be the influence of *status*. "Status, for organizations as well as individuals," Sauder, Lynn, and Podolny (2012: 268) argue, "is broadly understood as the position in a hierarchy that results from accumulated acts of deference." Podolny (1993) has advocated a research program examining the role of status in markets and in economic activities more broadly (see Podolny and Hill-Popper, 2004; Benjamin and Podolny, 1999; Rao, 1994), and he points at the quite conspicuous benefits accruing to status actors:

> The greater the one's status, the more profitable it is to produce a good of a given quality. More simply put, whereas the economic view of signals begins with differences in quality between producers and then derives as signals whose attributes for which the marginal cost of that signal is greater for the low-quality producer than for the high-quality producer, the sociological view takes as its point of departure the reality of the signal and then derives the differences in quality on basis of who possesses the signal and who does not. (Podolny, 1993: 841)

In his sociology of science, Robert Merton (1973) spoke of what he referred to as "the Matthew effect" among scientists, in which scientists with comparatively lower status acquired less credit from a specific contribution than scientists with high status—status derived from previous contributions. Podolny (1993) suggests that a similar pattern is observable in markets. For instance, Waguespack and Sorenson's (2011) study of films produced and distributed from 1992 to 2006 demonstrate that film studios that were members of MPAA (Motion Picture Association of America), an industry interest organization, were given a more favourable rating of their films than independent film producers *ceteris paribus*. Such favourable ratings generated higher incomes, which in turn further reinforced the market position of these film studios. "To the extent that high-status individuals and firms have greater freedom to deviate from these restrictions while still receiving desirable classifications, they can pursue profitable strategies not open to lower-status participants, thereby further stratifying outcomes," Waguespack and Sorenson (2011: 541) contend. However, Podolny (1993: 867) remarks, status is not simply "an epiphenomenal reflection of quality," but is providing actors with different incentives to expand outside their niche market, that is, original high status positions generate activities that further reinforce (and occasionally undermine) original status positions. Still, status as a form of symbolic or cultural capital translates itself into economic capital and what strategic management theorists refer to as sustainable competitive advantage. Sauder, Lynn, and Podolny (2012: 270) list these effects of status: "First, high status is associated with increased revenue for a given level of performance . . . Second, in addition to increasing the flow of resources for a given quality output, status can lower certain costs . . . Third, status increases a firm's access to survival-enhancing opportunities and assets." Sauder, Lynn, and Podolny (2012) also emphasize that there is a "stuck-in-the-middle" position in markets characterized by status that needs to be avoided. High-status actors, "whose legitimacy is assured even if they deviate from typical behavioral norms" (Sauder, Lynn, and Podolny, 2012: 274), and low-status actors, having little to lose by violating these norms, can allow themselves to be quite relaxed regarding their status. In contrast, actors in the "middle segment" (in the automobile market, brands like Volvo, Opel, and Nissan belong to this category of producers) and "middle-class actors" must conform to expectations to avoid jeopardizing their status position. As have been pointed out by numerous sociologists and historians, it is the middle class and its anxiety to not be able to maintain social positions and economic autonomy that is the principal driver of innovation, business creation, fashion, and so forth (McCloskey, 2006; Ehrenreich, 1989); the richest strata tend to maintain conservative attitudes, and the working class have little to gain from competing with the middle class, but the middle-class *mentalité* that encourages ceaseless striving and social and economic advancement reinforces the status of the class.

Under all conditions, status remains a factor to consider when examining how, for example, market intermediaries assess and rate financial assets. The failure to understand how status is inscribed into certain actors renders much empirical evidence unexplained, inasmuch as these "residual factors" are commonly left outside of the mainstream explanations of market operations. There is still strong evidence of status, beliefs, norms, and expectations—in brief, a bounded rationality—dominating in various sorts of auditing activities.

Summary and Conclusion

The practice of auditing is not of necessity derived from a neoliberal regime of governance. The virtues of transparency and possibilities for calculation and commensuration are constitutive elements in many other regimes of government. However, the external control of corporation executives by auditing firms and organizations is closely bound up with the financialization of the firm and the preference for external control to avoid and counteract various forms of managerial opportunism postulated by, for example, agency theory. Unfortunately, auditing does not neutrally reflect underlying competencies, resources, and performances of the organizations subject to inspection and audit; rather, auditing mirrors the underlying rationale of the auditing procedure per se and its need for information and data devoid of ambiguities and inconsistencies. In addition, the auditing procedures tend to create responses from the actors being audited, a form of reactivity that in many ways further distorts the information produced in the auditing procedure. As actors start to act in accordance with what is prescribed or rewarded in the auditing model, actors engage in a "teach-to-the-test" behaviour that leaves other, potentially meaningful and important, factors unattended. In summary, auditing as a form of control from distance is not an infallible or disinterested procedure, but rather enacts organizations and issues regarding performance and transparency in ways that reflects the underlying rationalities of the auditing model.

Part III
After Neoliberalism

6 Neoliberalism and Its Implications for Management Practice

INTRODUCTION

In this final chapter, a few themes that have not been sufficiently addressed will be further examined. As we have seen in the last three chapters, neoliberalism has, above all, served to discredit and render obsolete classic managerial capitalism, the specific regime of capitalism theorized and studied by management writers of the post-World War II period, such as Peter Drucker (1955, 1946) and Alfred Chandler (1962, 1977, 1984, 2005), and examined by sociologists such as Perrow (2002). This North American regime of capitalism has also been exported to the rest of the world, at times quite successfully, while in other cases the implementation of American management practices has been only partial and piecemeal (Djelic, 2001). In the *longue durée* perspective on history advocated by the Annales School historian Ferdnand Braudel (1980), this specific regime of managerial capitalism lasted for only a few decades between the end of World War II and the mid-1970s, when the Western economies, riddled by oil crises and bear stock markets, lost much of their momentum. From the early 1980s, the new finance theory, and the practices derived therefrom, in combination with the neoliberal belief in de-regulated markets effectively undermined this regime of managerial capitalism. Mizruchi (2010) here speaks of three institutional changes in the neoliberal era: the receding regulatory control executed by the government, the marginalization of the labour movement, and the institutional changes in the banking sector and finance industry:

> [By the early 1980s] the state had sharply reduced its role in regulating corporate activities, including what in earlier decades might have been viewed as antitrust violations. The labor movement had become a shadow of its former self, focused increasingly on public employees, while continuing to decline in the corporate sector. And the commercial banks, the final source of constraints for the corporate elite, had morphed into increasingly investment banks-like actors. This shift foreshadowed the ultimate end of the Glass-Steagall Act itself, repealed by Congress in 1999. (Mizruchi, 2010: 123)

188 *After Neoliberalism*

For managerialism, the late 1970s was a cross-road, a turning point where new ideas and doctrines were established and the old regime was declared obsolete. Shareholder value creation, flexibility in functionality and labour relations, and external control of organizations became the new keywords as the neoliberal era dawned.

NEOLIBERALISM AS AN AMERICAN DISCOURSE AND ITS RECEPTION IN EUROPE

Although liberalism is a European, perhaps even British tradition—already in the end of the seventeenth century, urbanized England was based on small-scale entrepreneurialism, and Napoleon famously portrayed it as a "nation of shopkeepers" (Landes, 1983: 227)—advanced by philosophers and economists such as Adam Smith, John Locke, and John Stuart Mill, and neoliberalism apparently had its roots in German-speaking Europe (in Vienna and Freiburg), neoliberalism as it was rolled out in Thatcher's Britain and Reagan's America was unquestionably shaped by North American antistatist and libertarian thinking. Germany, France, and the United Kingdom have served as fertile soil for the formulation of political ideologies over the centuries, and in many cases these have been given a specific meaning in the U.S. setting. For instance, in the United States, the term *liberal* basically means "left-wing," while in Europe, *liberal* denotes an intermediary position between socialists, social democrats, and varieties of communism to the left, and conservatives and other right-wing political parties to the right. When Fox News journalists rave about "liberals," they basically speak about something different than when Europeans do (at least, that is what confused Europeans tend to think). In general, the idiosyncratic American culture dominated by antistatism, the cherishing of entrepreneurialism and enterprising culture, the hatred and fear of communism (today less of a problem, even though the case of Chinese communism and its politics remain an enigma for most Westerns), and the tensions between the East Coast and California liberals and "the people" living in the American heartland have been part of the formulation of the neoliberal program and the neoliberal worldview (Frank, 2004). Even though neoliberalism apparently preys on the term *liberalism*, it has strong connections to the neoconservatism movement in, for example, the leafy communities in southern California such as Orange County where World War II veterans settled in the 1940s and 1950s, and their emphasis on patriotism and the threat of communism. Even though it is perhaps a trivial observation, it deserves to be repeated that in the United States, there were possibilities for creating things *de novo* in a way that was not possible in Europe, which already had a history lasting for centuries and stretching back to the ancient period. Marens (2012) stresses this point:

> The difference . . . is not simply that the Old World had a tradition of government interference in business. It was also characterized by a

thicket of horizontal corporatist constraints. The various forms of absolutism that dominated the pre-industrial world were actually governed by the relationships between churches, estates, guilds, tax collectors, armies, and mercantile corporations, cemented by clientage and family ties among the elite leadership of these institutions . . . Entrepreneurial individuals and business operated to a greater or lesser degree in most of these societies, but they developed under the constraints of horizontal relationships that were not, for the most part, introduced in the USA, so when industrialization did arrive in the non-English speaking world, it is not surprising that governments and other institutions played a more active role than in Britain and the USA. (Marens, 2012: 62–63)

In a way, the specific American version of neoliberalism developed in places like the University of Chicago and University of Rochester,[1] in political think tanks and among lobbyists in Washington and New York City, and in the neoconservative communities throughout the country shared with, for example, Mormonism the quality of being an idiosyncratic American construction faithful to and also inextricably bound up with American traditions and American ways of life.

The anomaly in this line of storytelling is Prime Minister Thatcher and her agenda-setting program, which was even more paradigmatic and consistent than Reagan's politics. Mrs. Thatcher was perhaps not the "*Weltseele zu Pferde*" that Hegel saw in Napoleon, but may be better described as a *Weltseele* in a skirt. Great Britain had dominated the world economy over one and a half centuries until World War I, and had benefitted greatly from having an aristocracy that played an active role in society and was respected among the wider population, but in the interwar period the British Empire started to crumble under its own weight. In the 1940s, 1950s, and 1960s the de-colonialization movement quickly shrunk the size of the empire. In the 1970s, the United Kingdom suffered from a stagnating industry and souring industrial relations, and Thatcher's neoliberal agenda and her supply-side economic policy were perceived as a novel perspective on how to handle old problems. It is also important to emphasize that Thatcher's politics were not widely embraced by all Tories—especially not in the early days—as it was regarded as being extreme in its straightforward and explicit commitment to fight the trade unions (Jones, 2012; Marens, 2012). When Mrs. Thatcher died from a stroke at age 87 on April 8, 2013, her heritage and her politics, dividing the nation, resurfaced anew, and while the Tory Prime Minister David Cameron declared, "She made Britain great again," a substantial part of the British population seemed reluctant to agree.

Still, with Thatcher as an exception, the more "academic" versions of neoliberalism, carefully anchored in economic theory and generously funded by various neoliberal and conservative foundations, and strongly influencing American policy over the last three and a half decades, was American through and through. Consequently, the application of the neoliberal program outside of the Anglo-American sphere has been piecemeal and accompanied by criticism in most OECD countries, and many European economies (e.g., Germany, Scandinavia, the Benelux countries) still pursue a combination of Keynesian "embedded liberalism" welfare state policy and neoliberal reforms—that is, they tend to favour what Pontusson and Raess (2012: 31) refer to as "liberal Keynesianism" emphasizing tax-cuts over "public spending and redistributive measures." The economies that are the most vulnerable to clumsy and heavy-handed neoliberal interventions, such as the Latin and South American economies (the United States' "backyard," in Bockman and Eyal's [2002: 312] formulation), have also taken the hardest hit when the World Bank, the IMF, and the World Trade Organization have taken the lead in reforming these economies in accordance with the Washington Consensus formula. The track record for these neoliberal experiments cannot be said to be successful by any standard. The former Eastern European countries that were part of the Soviet-style planned economies have naturally been tempting grounds for the expansion of neoliberal policy (Bockman and Eyal, 2002), but perhaps the history of these countries and their geographical proximity to the Western European economies made them capable of partially resisting the neoliberal siren's song and thus rescued them from too painful of an experience derived from neoliberal programs and the "shock therapies" prescribed by the Anglo-American economic advisors that have been recruited by the governments in the former communist countries. Above all, there is no strong sense of antistatism in Europe as in the United States, and even though certain members of the European parliament and the European Commission advocate the increased role of regions in Europe (a position embraced in certain semi-autonomous regions, such as Catalonia), there is also a strong nationalist orientation in Europe that cuts through the whole political spectrum. To put it briefly, there is, by and large, less concern about the role of the state in Europe than in the United States.

The question is, then, why were all these American norms and beliefs repackaged and sold under the various labels of neoliberalism (supply-side economics, monetarism, Thatcherism, Reaganomics, "economic freedom," etc.) appealing to European politicians and policy makers? First of all, during the entire post-World War II period, the United States has been the leading economic, political, and cultural country in the world. In the period until 1989 (the fall of the Iron Curtain), the United States had monitored and prevented the expansion of the communist economic and political system, and after that immediate concern was eliminated in the late 1980s, the United States enjoyed a significant prestige during the boom years of the essentially neoliberal presidency of Bill Clinton. It was not until the disaster-ridden, ill-fated, and in many ways "peculiar" (in High's, 2009: 475, phrasing) presidency of George W. Bush, which began with a seemingly undemocratic decision in a Florida court (the state then governed by Bush's brother, Jeb Bush) that the inconsistencies regarding the counting of the votes should be tolerated, making Bush the winner of the presidential election. Bush thus entered the White House, critics claim, on the basis of the Republican Party's capacity to enrol an armada of jurists and lobbyists to influence the court decision. Then came events such as the 9/11 terrorist attacks and their political consequences, the wars in Iran and Afghanistan (including the bypassing of the United Nations), the Katrina disaster in 2005, and finally the 2008 finance industry collapse. As Troy (2009: 124) remarks, while Bush made "compassionate conservatism" his political slogan, he "[e]mphasized the conservatism more than the compassion."

When Bush moved out of the White House, he left Senator John McCain in the unfavourable position to attempt to defeat the rising star Barack Obama, but Republican politicians were not very much in vogue in 2008. In 2012, Obama was re-elected and won most of the swing states, and the Republican Party had little choice other than to carefully reassess its politics and its failure. Still, both the House and the Senate were dominated by Republicans. The first decade of the new millennium was, in short, not good for the United States, and the collapse of 2008 demonstrated in broad daylight the lack of robustness of both the finance industry and finance market and the underlying theoretical models that justified the de-regulation paving the way for the events. In an addition, the rising of, for example, China as an industrial, economic, and political power in the new millennium—China is today one of the net creditors of the United States—has shifted the focus from Washington to Beijing.

In addition to this explanation, there were elements in the neoliberal sales pitch that appealed to various policy makers. First, economists' ambition to formulate elegant and parsimonious theories, primarily on the basis of assumptions about individual choice as being rational and calculated rather than intuitive and spontaneous, seemed attractive for policy makers already burdened by the assignment to handle an all-too-unruly social and economic reality that they were expected to both explain to themselves and others (e.g., voters) and to make use of in their policy-making. The era of economic growth and prosperity made what neoliberals referred to as "collective solutions" less credible in the eyes of many middle-class voters with a short memory. In addition, neoliberal politics made it easier to be a politician because (certain) economists promised that de-regulated markets would do the job for them. Moreover, since actors were portrayed and postulated to be the ones responsible for their own "employability" and other economic choices (rational choice theory always assumes individuals are making decisions as autonomous cognitive universes separated from wider social and cultural contexts), politics essentially becomes the art of "setting the scene" for enterprising actors to "make their choices." In addition to the neoliberal ticket making politics less complicated, the arguments advanced by neoliberal-minded thinkers, theorists, and pundits had their roots in the academy (in the universities), and a general trust in the institution of academic research arguably lowered the barriers for neoliberal ideas to be recognized in policy-making quarters. One may only speculate what role the eight Nobel Prizes being claimed by Mont Pèlerin Society members over the years (beginning with Friedrich von Hayek in 1974) have played in advancing the neoliberal agenda.

The neoliberal program has from the very beginning been strongly supported financially by private interests. Mont Pèlerin Society was from its inception funded by business men, and Hayek was recruited by London School of Economics in 1950 on the basis of a private donation. An agency theorist like Michael Jensen, advocating the shareholder value solution to the "agency costs problem" in corporate governance, was, for instance, hired by Rochester University, generously funded by various neoliberal and neoconservative foundations such as the William Volker Fund, "a group of businessmen who wanted a refutation of socialist tendencies they thought had infected economics" (Mirowski, 2005: 85). In the 1970s, several neoliberal institutes and think tanks were founded, including The Heritage Foundation (1973), The Manhattan Institute (originally the International Center for Economic Policy Studies) (1978), and The Cato Institute (1977), all financed by private actors:

> By the mid-1970s, the neoconservatives were not just becoming members of other people's committees, they were forming their own permanent think-tanks. They were fortunate. At precisely the moment when the neoconservatives wanted to set up in business as a permanent ideas taskforce, along came individuals and corporations who were more than ready to fund them. (High, 2009: 484–485)[2]

Studies have indicated, Smith (2007: 90) reports, that "conservative institutes oversee budgets *four times* as large as the liberal ones." "Organizations which stand to the left of the Washington consensus in economics, for example, such as the Economic Policy Institute (which relies on trade union funding) are at a significant disadvantage," High (2009: 484) writes. This funding effectively translates into policy and political action: "Budgets probably bear some relationship, however imperfect, to the policy influence of think tanks," Smith (2007: 90) suggests. For instance, the presidential administrations of Ronald Reagan and George W. Bush "[d]rew heavily from think tanks in filling advisory and executive positions" (Smith, 2007: 91–92).[3] There is little doubt that the funding of academic societies, institutes, and think tanks to advance the neoliberal agenda and to provide it with a halo of scholarly rigor and legitimacy was a worthwhile investment for the business community, and eventually, beginning in the second half of the 1970s, this financial capital investment translated into political actions and policy, in turn securing the economic interests of these sponsors and financiers.

In addition to some of the socio-political benefits of neoliberal policy, there have been a number of macroeconomic and demographic conditions and technological shifts that have helped advance the neoliberal agenda.

First, the high degree of overseas savings and an overrated dollar in the 1980s contributed to the financialization of the Western economies. In combination with the new finance theory, developed and taught in the business schools, and the demographic structure of Western societies with their high demand for capital, financialization appeared as an evidence of the healthy condition of Western economies. The effects of the Internet/computer industry bubble of 2000–2001 could be overcome quite easily, and it was not until a few years after that that the excessive risk-taking in the finance industry became a major concern. Computerization of workplaces and the home, including the establishment of the Internet as the foremost distribution system for information, also served to justify neoliberal policies, as it was argued to reduce labour costs (Fligstein and Shin, 2007). In the period after 1990, when neoliberalism was strongly associated with Thatcherism, Reaganomics, and other highly politicized agendas, New Labour in the United Kingdom and the Democratic president Bill Clinton turned neoliberal ideas into the political mainstream. The Marxist historian Eric Hobsbawm famously portrayed Prime Minister Tony Blair as "Thatcher in trousers" (cited in Peck, 2010: xv), and the Clinton administration maintained the de-regulation agenda that had been advanced by the preceding Republican administrations. In hindsight, the Nixon administration appears much more liberal and progressive than the contemporary Democrats (Crotty, 2012: 83): "Government interventions that would have been taken for granted in the Nixon Administration became far too radical for the Clinton and Obama Administrations to even consider," Mizruchi (2010: 127) claims. In other words, neoliberal theory and policy began as a marginal school of thought in Europe, including quite a few different views, but gradually organized itself by aligning academics, financiers, and political bodies, and slowly moved to the political centre to eventually become what many commentators speak of as being "hegemonic" (e.g., Marens, 2012; Deutschmann, 2011; Bockman and Eyal, 2002). If nothing else, this is an intriguing story of how the ability to enrol and mobilize intellectual resources, financing, and political actors can eventually, after periods of hard work, reach the state where what were originally treated as "extreme" or "curious" ideas become widely taken for granted. "The Mont Pèlerin Society was for many years a club of losers," Peck (2010: 40) reminds us, underlining the fact that what some commentators today regard as hegemonic ideas were for a long time only endorsed by a relatively small and marginal community. If we are in a position to learn anything from history (which Hegel famously doubted), it is that certain ideas may thrive and be distributed when "their time has come," when they are what Georges Canguilhem spoke of as "in the truth" (*dans le vrai*)—that is, when certain actors working under favourable conditions become receptive to such ideas. The case of neoliberalism is perhaps exemplary in showing such dynamics and the value of persistency.

THE CONTRIBUTIONS OF NEOLIBERAL THINKING

There are many significant economic, financial, and social effects derived from neoliberal thinking, including some managerial practices derived from, for example, agency theory. However, as a discourse and a regime of governmentality, neoliberal thinking has contributed to a renewal of the discussion on economic issues such as growth, corporate governance, and the role of the state in monitoring and regulating the economy. First, neoliberal thinking has questioned the role of the state, inasmuch as public spending and an increasing public sector tend to exclude private investment opportunities. While many attempts at privatizing previously regulated industries and sectors demonstrate quite diverse outcomes, there are still examples of markets with relatively low transaction costs and standardized product offerings in which de-regulation has possibly served to increase competition and efficiency. For instance, in Sweden the market for taxi services was de-regulated during the 1990s, leading initially to some discussions and even conflicts between the existing actors and new entrants, but eventually the market has settled. In other cases, especially in markets characterized by high transaction costs, information imbalances (Akerlof, 1970; Grossman and Stiglitz, 1980; Greenwald and Stiglitz, 1986), or where there are risks of "moral hazard," there are mixed experiences from privatization and marketization. Until the 1970s, the large and expanding role of the state was mostly unquestioned by many policy makers and scholars, especially in so-called embedded liberalism or mixed economies, such as in Germany and the Scandinavian countries.

Second, for many income earners, especially in the middle-class strata, who have been able to compete in the increasingly knowledge- and education-based economy, the period after 1980 has, regardless of the increase in debt, implied a growth in income. Whether these effects are caused by technological shifts (including the computerization beginning in the 1980s), macroeconomic changes, political and institutional stability, or by an increased international division of labour, or by new policies derived from neoliberal thinking remains to be demonstrated, but arguably all of these factors have contributed. Even through the trickle-down of tax cuts for the highest income groups advocated by Reagan's economic advisors failed to produce the macroeconomic effects promised, tax cuts in the middle- and lower-income strata in many countries have possibly enabled increased private consumption.

Third, the neoliberal emphasis on the role of taxation and fiscal policies has increased the suspicion regarding ever-expanding taxation as the easy way out from political concerns, arguably putting pressure on politicians to not only emphasize short-term fiscal policy to accomplish political goals, but to also actively think of more long-term investment in, for example, infrastructure and education to secure economic growth. In high income-tax countries like Sweden and Denmark, such a debate was greatly needed by the 1970s because the degree of income taxation and other taxes was the card played by politicians all too frequently, gradually undermining the legitimacy of the progressive tax system, and occasionally leading to bizarre outcomes, such as taxes above 100%.

Fourth, while financialization of the global economy is perhaps the single most important effect of neoliberal doctrines, benefitting the restoration of a rentier class, increasingly influencing the political system through hired lobbyists, a more Austrian and Ordoliberal tradition of thinking stresses the role of entrepreneurship and entrepreneurialism in generating economic growth. Joseph Schumpeter is perhaps the foremost representative of this tradition of thinking. While much North American neoliberal economic theory has assumed that financial markets would be capable of releasing venture capital for entrepreneurial activities—a hypothesis that proved to be poorly supported by empirical evidence because increasingly complex financial assets were treated as more favourable investment opportunities in comparison to industrial investment—this more European branch of the neoliberal tradition stresses the role of the state when matching capital and entrepreneurs. The backside of this eulogy for entrepreneurialism is unfortunately that traditional manufacturing industry has prematurely been regarded as antiquated and unqualified and in need of being shipped off to low-cost countries to release capital and talent so it could pour into emerging high-profit industries. In many ways, such assumptions operate in accordance with the Thomas-theorem, suggesting that if humans assume a certain situation to be real, it will become so on the basis of the consequences of the actions derived from and justified by the initial assumptions made, regardless of the accuracy of such assumptions (see, e.g., Ferraro, Pfeffer, and Sutton, 2005). Self-fulfilling prophesies are part of politics and the economy. The belief that certain industries are in decline easily becomes a dogma that further reinforces the downward spiral. Empirical data from prosperous economies such as Japan and Germany provide examples of alternative routes for manufacturing industries.

Fifth, some branches of neoliberal thinking—for example, agency theory and financial models of corporate governance—have served to problematize the relationships among classes of capital owners, professional managers, and other organizational constituencies. In, for example, orthodox Marxist thinking and arguably in common sense thinking more generally, capital owners and professional managers, often graduates from the same elite business schools, law schools, and engineering schools, have been assumed to belong to a social class with shared interests and a commitment to capital accumulation and other economic concerns. However, for agency theorists like Michael C. Jensen, such assumptions cannot be made offhand, and instead there needs to be a certain degree of suspicion regarding the relationship between capital owners and professional managers. As outlined in Chapter Three, the agency theory solution to agency problems and costs, that of finance market control, has essentially failed or is riddled by evidence of other forms of opportunistic behaviour, but agency theory should nevertheless be credited for its emphasis on the historical and cultural assumptions regarding social classes.

In summary, the contributions of neoliberal thinking lie essentially not so much in prescribing solutions to perceived problems or in the assumptions made when theorizing these solutions, but in posing a series of questions that were of great accuracy and relevance in the interwar period, but had slipped off the political and managerial agenda until they were eventually rehabilitated by neoliberal thinkers. Unfortunately, when the more moderate *Ordoliberalismus* and Austrian forms of neoliberalism were blended with American neoconservatism, libertarianism, and patriotism and their firm belief in the exceptionalism of the American Federation, along with the emerging financialization (including the inflow of foreign savings and the development of new finance theory), neoliberalism became less concerned with understanding economic growth and policy on the basis of existing social institutions. Instead, abstract and highly questionable propositions regarding the efficiencies of market transactions predominated.[4] What we today are struggling with, almost globally and certainly in part of the so-called Euro-zone, are the immediate effects of these doctrines and theories. In comparison, the Ordoliberal doctrines emphasizing a "free economy and a strong state" were endorsed by the West German economics minister Ludwig Erhart, responsible for what has been referred to as the "German miracle" of post-World War II economic growth in the 1950s and 1960s (Boas and Gans-Morse, 2009: 146). In the Ordoliberal view of the role of the state, governance was not to be steered exclusively on basis of partisan politics benefitting economically and politically influential and dominant groups; instead, the state should serve a more moderate goal in securing property rights, support financial institutions that provide capital to industry and entrepreneurs, and handle and regulate labour relations (Fligstein and Choo, 2005). Perhaps, in the post-2008 era, a novel form of liberalism can be formulated that pays attention to the role of social institutions and that recognizes that both society and economic growth needs to include the interests of a wider number of constituents.

NEOLIBERALISM AND MANAGEMENT THEORY

Neoliberalism is, first of all, the commitment to market-based transactions. Management is the practice of leading, developing, monitoring, and administrating market-based organizations—that is, corporations. The neoliberal era has been a good period for the business schools because young, ambitious, and enterprising people have headed for a business school diploma to take advantage of promising future labour market prospects. Still, in the business schools there has been surprisingly little written about neoliberalism and its influence over more than three decades. Such a discourse has been developed by political scientists, sociologists, economic historians, and others, and business school researchers have been fully occupied with teaching and lecturing the students aspiring to become part of what has been referred to as the transnational capitalist class (Carroll, 2010; Sklair, 2002; Carroll and Carson, 2006). Neoliberal thinkers and theorists have perhaps primarily influenced policy making, turning the state into their ally and partner, but there are a few major contributions to management theory and practice. Many of these changes belong to the domain of corporate governance—that is, the theory of how organizations are controlled by certain interests and how objectives and goals enacted by decision-making communities (e.g., the board of directors) are accomplished. The first domain where neoliberal thinking has played a decisive role for managerial practices is the formulation of agency theory on the basis of the efficient market hypothesis. The work of Eugene Fama and Michael C. Jensen (Fama was Jensen's supervisor) has served to, in Davis, Diekmann, and Tinsley's (1994) formulation, "deinstitutionalize" the conglomerate firm. In the post-World War II period, firms grew through the acquisition of other corporations, by and large only restricted by monopoly and anti-trust legislation, but as the finance markets were de-regulated there was an opportunity to re-articulate the theory of the firm, moving from conceiving of it as an aggregate of physical resources to a bundle of contracts or, by implication, a portfolio of financial assets. This radically new view of the corporation was not an academic abstraction, but quickly became the brute reality for conglomerates subject to hostile takeovers and leveraged buy-outs in the 1980s. Conglomerate firms were quite simply bought at market prices and sold off piece by piece at a substantial profit. This is one of the major contributions of economic theory in the neoliberal era: the radical shift from *managerial capitalism*, in which businesspeople like Alfred P. Sloan, Jr., of General Motors, and theorists and management writers like Peter Drucker were authoritative figures, to what Useem (1996) calls *investor capitalism*, a world where finance industry actors and the finance market claim the right to determine what legitimately counts as economic value. As has been demonstrated in Chapter Three in this volume, the agency theory/shareholder value ticket did not solve the question of "agency costs," but rather its policies and practices encouraged a new set of opportunistic behaviours. Still, scholars like Michael C. Jensen should be given credit for formulating a theory of the firm that is intriguing and innovative, regardless of its ability to secure economic performance and growth.

In addition to re-articulating the firm, neoliberal doctrines, propelled by both the financialization of the world economy and the development of increasingly complex and sophisticated theories and tools for calculating, producing, and re-packaging financial assets, have strongly emphasized performance metrics in day-to-day managerial work. Consonant with agency theory's scepticism regarding professional managers' ability and willingness to work in accordance with the principals' interests, much of the control of organizations has moved to the outside of the organizations, to auditing and accreditation firms, rating agencies, and management consulting firms, all serving to impose their favoured models for assessing economic activities and performance. As a solid body of research in the field of accounting and auditing suggest, these various methods and tools implemented to shed light on and lay bare the interiority of organizations are far from infallible. Rather than enabling the "full transparency" promised, these models are based on a certain performativity—that is, they *construct* rather than *mirror* the organization subject to auditing. In addition, there is evidence of all-too-human responses to such external control in the form of reactivity (Espeland and Sauder, 2007), the tactic and strategic responses to improve what is being measured (say, the number of papers published or the number of minority faculty members in a law school) to enhance the performance metrics or the ranking. In addition, there is evidence of questionable arrangements in which auditors, despite being prohibited by the Sarbanes-Oxley Act (Robson et al., 2007: 431), serve inherently opposing roles as being both regulators of and advisors to clients (Arnold, 2009). As Robson et al. (2007: 417) demonstrate, the growth of audit firms has not come from audits but from "non-audit services": Between 1992 and 2001, the percentage of audit fees declined from 81% to 21% of total fees, while non-audit fees increased from 19% to 79% (Robson et al., 2007: 417, Table 2); the ratio of non-audit fees to audit fees changed from 0.2:1 in 1992 to 3.7: 1 in 2001 (Robson et al., 2007: 417, Table 1). As a consequence, Robson et al. (2007: 421) claim, "[l]arge firms treat audit as the gateway to the supply of the more diverse and financially rewarding non-audit services to the client" (see also Knechel, 2007; Spira and Page, 2002). Still, what Power (1997) speaks of as the "audit explosion" in the neoliberal era is an indisputable condition of today's management practice. Institutional theorists, always prone to accept functionalist explanations, tend to think of this use of external control as being the organization's response to legitimacy problems: By accepting accreditations and auditing, organizations are able to portray themselves as being legitimate actors in the field, which in turn secures long-term survival of the organization (Fligstein, 1990). While such explanations are capable of providing ex post facto justification for organizational activities and choices, they fail to explain where these ideas come from in the first place, and how, for example, auditing and accounting firms are capable of capitalizing on them. Rather than endorsing strictly functionalist explanations, a more enterprising and entrepreneurial view of the auditing industry would be helpful in understanding how the control of organizations has moved from the boardrooms and the managerial tiers to agents outside of the organization. The neoliberal era has brought a metrics craze in which everything from restaurants and cities to "admired companies" and risk exposure in the finance industry can legitimately lend itself to calculative practices (see, e.g., Jeacle and Carter, 2011).[5]

A third domain subject to the influence of neoliberal thinking is employment relations, and industrial relations more broadly. The political branch of neoliberalism, embodied by Margaret Thatcher and Ronald Reagan early on, announced its commitment to eliminating the influence of the trade unions and the labour movement, as these were treated as an impediment to economic freedom and growth. "We are both determined to sweep away the restrictions that hold back enterprise," Margaret Thatcher declared during her first official meeting with Reagan in the White House in February, 1981 (cited by Troy, 2009: 70). In order to make corporations more flexible—technologically, juridically, and financially—employment in the neoliberal era has been characterized by less security and more temporal work (forms of agency work and what is called *contingent employment*; Bergström, 2003; Purcell and Purcell, 1998). In the case of unskilled and semi-skilled labour, it has been relatively easy for corporations to institute these new forms of labour relations. In the case of professional and knowledge-based workers, who have historically been able to maintain discretionary jurisdictions in the domain of work, there is more evidence of ongoing struggles between professional communities and employers. Professionals such as physicians and academic researchers have been subject to a series of attempts to reduce their autonomy through, for example, the implementation of auditing, specific calculative practices, and more flexible employment arrangements. In some cases, professionals have been able to resist such changes, while in other cases, they have been less successful. In certain cases, professional communities (e.g., physicians working on highly paid, short-term contracts in private clinics) have been able to benefit greatly from the new labour markets opened up in the general process of de-regulation.

In addition to these changes, accounted for in Chapters Three through Five in this volume, there are a variety of small and major changes in managerial practice derived from new policy and market development. In the field of marketing, the concept of branding has been a major issue in a market-based economy (see, e.g., Schultz, Hatch, and Larsen, 2000), and more specific managerial programs, such as corporate social responsibilities (CSR)—the *noblesse oblige* of corporations in a society where corporations are no longer expected to care for anything other than their shareholders, in Crouch's (2011: 150) view—have acquired significant attention. Above all, neoliberalism and its emphasis on enterprising, entrepreneurship, venturing, and capital accumulation is in many ways the theoretical fundament of managerialism; management thinking was, of course, in place prior to the emergence of an authoritative neoliberal agenda—the managerialist capitalism of the interwar and post-World War II period (Chandler, 1984, 1977; Perrow, 2002)—but over the three last decades, managerialism has penetrated virtually all spheres of everyday life. The various forms of managerial isomorphisms identified by institutional theorists (DiMaggio and Powell, 1983) have spread all over organized late-modern society.

THE FUTURE OF NEOLIBERALISM

The neoliberal era must be examined as a combination of strategic and tactic activities with the intention of influencing policy making and to establish authoritative theories legitimately explaining and justifying both economic conditions and policies, and as what more or less happened on the basis of many and quite complex macroeconomic conditions that were not fully understood or anticipated at the time when decisions were made (Krippner, 2011). That is, many groups and interests actively aimed to advance their agendas, worldviews, and favoured analytical frameworks, but none of them had the prescience needed to foresee what the world would look like in 1987, 1995, 2006, or any other year into the future. In some cases, quite speculative theories and propositions (e.g., rational choice and public choice theories to explain non-economic actions; see, e.g., Buchanan, 1954) were advanced in academic settings, but eventually proved to fit nicely into political programs and agendas, and therefore acquired more attention and authority than would be justified on the basis of reasonable demands for robust empirical evidence and proof. The story of the advancement of the neoliberal explanation for a series of social and economic conditions is also the story of the successful organization of capital funding, academic and intellectual activities, and political mobilization. Beginning with the Mont Pèlerin Society and its first meeting in 1947, there have been a substantial number of financiers and funds willing to pay for neoliberal-minded scholars and pundits to justify and market their ideas and beliefs; one may speak of an effective "neoliberal doctrine industry" in, especially, the United States. These financial and cultural circuits of neoliberalism have been remarkably successful in advancing its agenda in the period after 1979. Strong capital interests were part of the neoliberal project from the very beginning.

The question is, then, whether the "There-Is-No-Other-Way" ideology of neoliberalism, forcefully announced by Prime Minister Thatcher, holds water after the 2008 events. As Peck (2010) and others remark, neoliberalism may have lost "one of its nine lives" in 2008–2009, but many commentators notice that there is remarkably little self-reflexivity or regret in the community that caused the largest post-World War II era crisis of capitalism, and essentially the same policies and regulatory frameworks that existed in the first years of the new millennium are still in operation (Centeno and Cohen, 2012; Madrick, 2011). Perhaps the best evidence of neoliberal hegemony is that the financial crisis caused by millionaire finance industry workers has recently been rolled over to the national states. It is indicative that in none of the five countries examined by Pontusson and Raess (2012)—France, Germany, the United Kingdom, Sweden, and the United States—did governments articulate any structural reforms of the financial sector as a policy goal during the bailouts of financial institutions in 2008–2008. To the extent that policy makers recognized any need for such structural reforms, they were "[w]illing to postpone any legislation in this realm for the sake of rapidly implementing short-term measures they considered essential to restoring the provision of credit to households and companies" (Pontusson and Raess, 2012: 27). Countries like Spain, where people previously were enticed to increase their debt, are now implementing draconian budget cuts and policies to reduce the debt-to-GDP ratio, and citizens need to scrimp and save to get along (Blyth, 2013). In countries more fortunate but still holding high degrees of household debt (e.g., Denmark, Sweden, the United Kingdom, The Netherlands), the unemployment ratio is not skyrocketing to the 25% level, as in the case of Spain, but the "Euro-crisis" is taking its toll, even on the supposedly strong economies north of the Alps. Crouch (2011) points at the difficulties in securing a "free economy" without allowing economical and political classes to influence the democratic political system:

> In a free economy it is very difficult to prevent economic wealth from being converted into political influence. The wealthy can use their resources to finance politicians and parties who agree with them, or to persuade those who disagree to change their minds. They can also run campaigns to influence public opinion, even owning and controlling newspapers and telecommunications channels to help them. (Crouch, 2011: 47)

For instance, when the so-called Obamacare health care program, one of the few things that the first period of presidency term of Barack Obama managed to accomplish despite having to accept the massive tax-cut law passed by the Bush administration, was facing strong opposition from influential actors in the U.S. economy: "US health insurance firms, hospitals and pharmaceutical corporations deployed six lobbyists for each member of Congress and spent $380 million campaigning against the [Obamacare] policy" (reported by *The Guardian*, October 1, 2009, cited in Crouch, 2011: 67). Especially in the United States, with its idiosyncratic political system based on negotiations between the White House administration and the House and the Senate, such interests are quite conspicuously influencing policy making (see, e.g., Perrow, 2010: 317–322). In the case of the United States, the economy and society have, Crouch (2011) argues, ended up in a "neoliberal trap" where the richest few are guaranteed a privileged position far away from the everyday struggle of others in the regime of competitive capitalism:

> We can secure our collective welfare only by enabling a very small number of individuals to become extremely rich and politically powerful. The essence of this trap is perfectly expressed in what is now happening to the welfare state. Governments have to make deep cuts in social services, health and education programmes, pension entitlements and social transfer to the poor and unemployed. They have to do this to satisfy the anxieties of the financial markets over the size of public debt, the operators in these markets being the very same people who

benefitted from the bank rescue, and who have already begun to pay themselves high bonuses—bonuses 'earned' because their operations have been guaranteed against risk by the government spending that created the public debt. (Crouch, 2011:118)

The neoliberal era has been characterized by a remarkable mobilization in order to secure the interests and influence of the richest per cent of the population, especially in the United States, and this community of activists can pride themselves on being most successful in restoring economic inequalities. These economic inequalities at a certain point create their own momentum because even low-income groups start to endorse policies that further reinforce this distribution of income and capital; thus, it is not very likely, Crouch (2011) argues, that neoliberalism will lose its impetus just because some experimental activities in the finance industry did not came out very favourably. Instead, the fact that there is no major opposition against using federal tax money in the United States to bail out financial institutions should perhaps better be seen as evidence of the self-confidence in these privileged communities:

[Political and economic elites] have benefited so much from the inequalities of wealth and power that the system has produced, compared to the experience of strongly redistributive taxation, strong trade union and government regulations that constituted the so-called social democratic period. Those features had been tolerated because they seemed to be necessary to sustain mass consumption and to prevent industrial workers from becoming communists. Communism has now, fortunately, gone forever, while the possibility of basing mass consumption on a system of massive private debt through the financial markets also happened to make some people very rich. Indeed, they will cling to this model tenaciously. (Crouch, 2011:119)

If the neoliberal doctrine has the nine lives of a cat, as suggested by Peck (2010), we are not very likely to see any major changes in economic policy (cf. Duménil and Lévy, 2011). The "There-Is-No-Other-Way" ideology is, after all, perhaps the most persistent theme in neoliberal thinking and its underlying economic and financial theory, the self-assured belief in both the accuracy and legitimacy of certain propositions to the point where even empirical evidence matters no longer (Mirowski, 2013). There is a strong idealist orientation in the neoliberal ontology and epistemology, the firm belief in the ideas advocated and their ability to outlive human action and pre-existing policies and beliefs. Hence the tolerance for *ad hoc* hypotheses in this domain of economic thinking. As the United States loses its position as the leading nation with the authority to set the standard for other regions of the world, and as countries like China and the other so-called BRIC countries (Brazil, Russia, India, and China) account for an increasing share of the global economic growth, and as African economies grow, there may be new versions of neoliberal thinking implemented in other parts of the world. One may speculate how well ideas of the benefits of unregulated markets stand up against political doctrines, assuming that central governance is of vital importance for economic growth and stability. The global shifts in the world economy may prove to be fertile soil for new versions of liberal and neoliberal doctrines and policies. To date, however, there is little evidence of economic equality being prioritized, but on the contrary, there is evidence from the United States that the middle class are next in line after the blue-collar worker community to be stigmatized as lazy, passive, and non-value-adding free-riders (with Mancur Olson's [1965] term) that stand in the way of "economic freedom" and therefore need to be disciplined (Mulholland, 2012: 308). Or perhaps such a decline in civil society can be counteracted if a new generation of liberals can emerge, taking the lead in formulating a new and more moderate theory of economic growth, capital, and the role of the state in this pursuit.

FINAL REMARKS

Neoliberalism is a quite amorphous and nebulous term, capturing a variety of attempts to formulate both a formal program for competitive capitalism (in Milton Friedman's favoured term) and a set of practices and techniques for fulfilling such visions. In the aftermath of the finance market debacle of 2008, a variety of commentators and pundits were eager to make bold declarations regarding not only the unregulated finance industry and neoliberalism per se, but also about the end of capitalism as we know it. As has been emphasized by, for example, Wallison (2009), the events of 2008 are not to be seen as evidence of the decline of capitalism per se. Instead, 2008 was the end of an unrestricted expansion of debt (primarily on the basis of the overvaluation of the housing market) and the finance industry's use of increasingly complex derivative instruments and accounting practices that located assets in off-balance sheet vehicles. "Nothing substantial has been altered in the infrastructure of the global financial system from its state before the crisis. Government 'reforms' have proven superficial at best in both Europe and the United States," Mirowski (2013: 8) contends. While the costs to save and restore the finance industry were significant for the taxpayers in countries hosting these finance industry actors, today the finance market and the finance industry are up and running anew. Besides the taxpayers financing the bailout of the finance industry—the irony of Goldman Sachs "living off welfare," which is so despised and moralized when regular citizens take advantage of such social services (Wacquant, 2009), is not negligible—economists, rating agencies, and free market protagonists have taken the hardest hit. While there is evidence of a degree of regret and self-reflexivity in certain quarters (see, e.g., Backhouse, 2012; Caballero, 2010; Colander et al., 2009), many advocates of free market solutions tend to regard the events of 2008 as evidence of *too much* rather than *too little* regulation (Blyth, 2013). Similar to defenders of the right to carry weapons in the United States, drawing the conclusion that the most recent high school shooting justifies liberal weapon laws, rather than drawing the contrary conclusion— that the circulation of weapons, in fact, is one of the explanations for such tragic events—free-market evangelists tend to maintain their staunch beliefs in their privileged solutions to all social and economic evils.

Perhaps neoliberalism had a "Berlin Wall moment" in 2008 (Peck, 2010), but it is a safe bet to say that capitalism and neoliberal doctrines will still be with us for a significant amount of time to come (Mirowski, 2013). Today, of the 100 largest economies, 51 are corporations (Suddaby, Hardy, and Huy, 2011: 238), and more than three decades of neoliberal thinking and policy have served to establish what McNay (2009) speaks of as an "economization of social relations." Such "economization" inevitably de-politicizes certain conditions and turns them into a matter of choice and selection:

> The conversion of socially, economically, and politically produced problems into consumer items depoliticizes what has been historically produced, and it especially depoliticizes capitalism itself. Moreover, as neoliberal political rationality devolves both political problems and solutions from public to private, it further dissipates political or public life: the project of navigating the social becomes entirely one of discerning, affording, and procuring a personal solution to every socially produced problem. (Brown, 2006: 704)

It is questionable whether this shift in focus from politics to economics, from the much despised "collectivist" solutions to individualist market-based choices to handle social malaises (see George, 2013), have made the world a better, safer, and happier place: "Dominated by the free market gospel, the irony of this brave new world was that it produced everything conservative politicians hated: insecurity, social, sexual and cultural changes, violence, and the collapse of community" (Jones, 2012: 338; see also Roe and Siegel, 2011). Troy (2009: 111), addressing the neoconservatist "revolution" of the Reagan presidency, suggests that many of the consequences from the new policy were not fully anticipated and to some extent counteracted his ambitions: "The capitalism and consumerism [Reagan] helped unleash threatened to destroy the ideals he seemed to most cherish." Troy continues:

> Blinded by their critique of the Left, Ronald Reagan and most conservatives proved unable to connect the dots between the capitalist resurgence they celebrated and the cultural upheaval they mourned. They failed to see how many of the policies they implemented and the corporate practices they applauded neutralized or undermined many traditional values and structures. (Troy, 2009: 115)

This new capitalist regime of accumulation is not very likely to dissipate or change overnight. One must remember that it took neoliberal thinkers and activists (beginning with the inception of the Mont Pèlerin Society in 1947) more than 30 years to acquire a position from which it could effectively influence policy and become part of the agenda-setting communities in Washington, on Downing Street, and elsewhere. "Despite the talk of the end of capitalism as we knew it around 2008, the economic rule of the game remained essentially the same," Centeno and Cohen (2012: 322) say. One of the major challenges for the neoliberal program has been its failure to handle the undesirable effects of the free market capitalism and the "economic freedom" held in esteem. In hindsight, the neoliberal program has in many ways been unsuccessful in replacing Keynesian economic theory, a framework that many neoliberal protagonists abhorred and spent entire careers discrediting:

> [T]he rhetoric of freedom and opportunity popular with publics, especially as pushed by Conservative and Republican politicians influenced by Hayek and Friedman, sat uneasily with the inequality, globalization, and deindustrialization wrought by competitive free market capitalism. It has been possible to see these unresolved gaps between the rhetoric of successful electoral politics and the policy reality of social outcomes play out messily in the government practice of neoliberalism on both sides of the Atlantic since 1979. (Jones, 2012: 132)

One of the major challenges for neoliberal theory is, then, how to ascribe a meaningful role to government and the state. In persistently stressing perceived problems of bureaucracy (see, e.g., Mises, 1944), the neoliberal doctrines have undermined the bases of "democratic authority" (Jones, 2012: 132). Once the toothpaste is out of the tube, it is hard to get it back in, and since "government spending" has been a standing criticism—not always consistent with actual policy, to put it mildly—it is hard to rearticulate a meaningful role for the state in the neoliberal program. What is especially worrisome is that neoliberal politicians and policy makers appear to have dropped such political responsibilities altogether now that the role of the state is to serve to de-regulate markets, ensure market expansion, and to provide penal institutions to handle "market externalities":

> The crudeness of postwar Chicago neoliberal economic theory left a painful imprint on the social fabric of Britain and the United States after 1980 through the economic policies of the Thatcher and Reagan administrations. In the understated worlds of Douglas Hurd, neither government had been able to solve the 'social question.' More to the point, they had displayed very little interest in trying. (Jones, 2012: 268)

To put it straightforwardly, neoliberal thinking and politics exacerbated economic inequality during the last three decades, Jones (2012) argues:

> Neoliberal political success brought with it a number of consequences, There was a newfound acceptance of inequality as a necessary and unavoidable evil. There was a cumulative squeeze of the public sphere—of space for generously funded, comprehensive, and universal public services, and for collective industrial action and communal activity, of shared public spaces and institutions. A general assumption took hold among policymakers and publics, encouraged by the neoliberal interpretation of Adam Smith's concept of the invisible hand, that self-interest could mean selfishness. Greed, and less pejoratively, profit, were to be celebrated. The provision of assistance to the poorest suffered as the public listened to arguments about the 'escalating' costs of welfare. That this came during a period when middle-and upper-tiers income earners benefited more through the tax system from state subsidy than those deprived groups had ever done was rarely mentioned. There was in fact a redistribution from the poorest to the wealthy over the course of the 1980s, and this continued in the 1990s under Bill Clinton and Tony Blair . . . [n]eoliberal policies tended to affect the most vulnerable members of society in the harshest ways. (Jones, 2012: 338)

The reason for this lack of concern for economic inequality is to be found in the neoliberal doctrine itself, conceiving of inequality as one of the greatest motors of progress in the market economy of competitive capitalism:

> Neoliberals regard inequality of economic resources and political rights not as an unfortunate by-product of capitalism, but a necessary functional characteristic of their ideal market system. Inequality is not only the natural state of market economies from a neoliberal perspective, but it is actually one of the strongest motor forces for progress. (Mirowski, 2013: 63)

This position is closely bound up with the elitism of what Mirowski refers to as the Neoliberal Thought Collective, suggesting that the "demands for equality are merely the sour grapes of the losers" (Mirowski, 2013: 36). Since the market by definition is always right in pricing human capital, if you lose in the market, there is no one to blame but yourself and your own lack of entrepreneurial qualities, the neoliberal line of reasoning goes. In addition, any attempt of the state to rectify inequality through reforms will of necessity disrupt the market order and cause additional costs. These principles leave the neoliberals with the thorny question of democracy, the governance form that the Neoliberal Thought Collective acclaims in theory and especially through the widespread use of the phrase "freedom" in its texts and speeches, but which blends poorly with its elitism. For the Neoliberal Thought Collective, democracy must be "kept relatively impotent" so that lesser informed citizens can only take initiatives that "rarely are able to change much of anything" (Mirowski, 2013: 56). The principal strategy has been to reduce politics to economic theory and, more specifically, a theory of choice—hence the central role of the work of political scientists in the public choice tradition (e.g., James Buchanan; see Buchanan, 1954), suggesting that politics is economics pursued by other means—and rendering the democratic state a patchwork of market-based activities and transactions:

> One way to exert power in restraint of democracy is to bend the state to a market logic, pretending one can replace 'citizens' with 'customers' . . . consequently, the neoliberals seek to restructure the state with numerous audit devices (under the sign of 'accountability' or the 'audit society') or impose rationalization through introduction of the 'new public management'; or, better yet, convert state services to state provision on a contractual basis. (Mirowski, 2013: 57)

The Neoliberal Thought Collective encounters two major problems when emulating democracy with its theory of the superiority of the market-based society: First, if the market-based economic order is so overwhelmingly superior to any other organization, why has it has failed to become established at an earlier stage (i.e., to what extent are markets as "natural" as neoliberals claim?). Second, how can the pretence of freedom—the core (albeit quite amorphous) of the neoliberal argument—be maintained when, in everyday life practice, "it seems unlikely that most people would freely choose the neoliberal version of the state" (Mirowski, 2013: 64). For the neoliberals, there is no proper solution to the problem of combining a belief in democracy and maintaining that various inequalities produced in the market-based society are not only unproblematic, but even serve as a prerequisite for "economic freedom." The elitism of the Neoliberal Thought Collective did not prevent it from understanding that it is not enough for democratically elected politicians to inform the multitude suffering from the gross inequalities caused by the new economic policies that they should "envy and emulate the rich" (Mirowski, 2013: 56) and strive to repeat their accomplishments. This one example of a variety of inconsistencies and glitches in the neoliberal credo.

While at least the more libertarian branch of neoliberalism has demonstrated a most marginal interest in the increasing social tensions and unrest derived from growing social and economic inequality—in most cases, an immediate effect of the policies prescribed and advocated—there are other schools that are more concerned about the relation between "political" and "economic" freedom. Perhaps there will be, as some authors have speculated (Bonefeld, 2012; Peck, 2010), a revival of the German Ordoliberal tradition of thinking, which is more interested in taking into account and coping with what the Ordoliberals refer to as the "proletarization" of the working class. In the libertarian and neoconservative versions of neoliberalism, the failure to compete in the market is strictly a matter of faulty human capital investment decisions or/and fallible morals and weak ambition, but a more "sustainable" version of neoliberalism needs to take into account the social effects of the capitalist regime of accumulation. "[I]t seems evident that social inequality itself is dysfunctional for society at large," Mulholland (2012: 307) says. Therefore, policy makers need to ask themselves the British Labour Party's Roy Hattersley's (2006) two questions, "Do we want to live in a grotesquely divided society?" and "Is equality outdated?" In many cases, the aspiration to create what R.H. Tawney referred to as "practical equality" in the 1930s, Hattersley (2006) claims, is "[w]rongly represented as an as an utopian dream—usually by people who have a privileged position and high income to protect" (Hattersley, 2006: 5). Attempts to restore equality are not an utopian project, but need to be part of active political programs to secure the freedom that all kinds of political movements hold in esteem.

While proletarization may be a manageable phenomenon—at least there are substantial middle-class groups that do not experience such changes—what speaks in favour of neoliberal policies also in the future is the ability of capitalism to actually produce wealth and accumulate capital. As Harvey (2010: 27) reports: "In 1820 . . . the total output of goods and services in the capitalist world economy was worth $694 billion (in 1990 constant dollars). By 1913 it had risen to $2,7 trillion; by 1950, it was $5,3 trillion; in 1973 it stood at $16 trillion; and by 2003 nearly $41 trillion." "The amount of goods and services produced and consumed by the average person on the planet has *risen* since 1800 by a factor of about eight and a half," McCloskey (2006: 16) notes. While this wealth is explained on the basis of factors such as technological development, scientific research findings, political stability, the absence of (major) wars after 1945, population growth, and other macroeconomic factors, there is also an element of entrepreneurialism that is part of this equation; without the creativity and ambition of enterprising individuals and firms, there would be little of this economic growth and technological development. At the same time, these entrepreneurs are not, as one can believe when reading certain unrestricted acclaims of entrepreneurship as being the primus motor of capitalism, autonomous and free-standing enterprising agents, but instead these entrepreneurs operate within a dense institutional setting, including corporate law and regulations; state-governed initiatives and programs; well-functioning financial markets; and regional, national, and international innovation systems (Block and Keller, 2009). In other words, enterprising agents are the *effect* rather than the *cause* of a dynamic and competitive economic system. Perhaps this is an Ordoliberal position, as suggested by

Bonefeld (2012: 636): For the German Ordliberals of the Weimar Republic, "[e]ntrepreneurship is not something that is 'naturally given' . . . Instead it has to be fought for and actively constructed, time and time again." Predictable and useful corporate law, political stability, the access to financial capital, and industrial relations securing the supply of human capital and qualified labour appear to be a winning recipe for economic growth and prosperity (Fligsten and Choo, 2005). That market-based transactions would singlehandedly be able to provide all these conditions seems both very unlikely and hard to believe, and is also at odds with previous experience and empirical evidence. "In the end, neoliberalism was very much a state-directed project, but the interests represented by these same states changed, as did the central actors defining policy," Centeno and Cohen (2012: 325) contend.

One of the curious historical events in the neoliberal era is how antistatist and libertarian thinkers and policy makers could overtake the state and make it an ally to the classes that benefitted the most from the new policies implemented in the United States and the United Kingdom, but indisputably also elsewhere in the neoliberal era. Rather than reducing the role of the state and diminishing the influence of its institutions, neoliberal policy has turned these democratic institutions into their partners. In formal statements, the state and the government "shouldn't own banks and companies," and they should leave such activities to private capital investment and venturing, but in practice, an active state has always been encouraged by neoliberal thinkers—at least as long as the state and the government work in tandem with the interests and agenda of elites. While European political systems have been increasingly influenced by lobbyism and other forms of sponsored activities aiming to intervene into the democratic decision making, U.S. politics is arguably even further saturated by such enterprising activities and partisan politics, the literature suggests (Stiglitz, 2009: 337–338; Hacker and Pierson, 2010). One of the principal objectives in the forthcoming period is therefore to restore and rehabilitate a political system that is capable of serving the role of the "strong state," securing both economic growth and democratic liberties. Liberal and neoliberal agendas may only maintain their impetus in a society relying on government and democratic institutions, and there appear to be no quick fixes to achieve economic growth and prosperity. As we learn from an historical view of the neoliberal era, economic resources can be redistributed, as in the specific case of shareholder value, where the owners' gain was essentially the blue-collar community's loss; however, enabling stable and sustainable growth demands more comprehensive and state-governed activities and initiatives. Whether a neoliberal agenda is capable of creating such growth, rather than mere distribution of wealth on the basis of the belief that capital owners should gain more from their risk-taking than other stakeholders, is a question that remains to be answered.

NOTES

1. University of Rochester is one of the principal academic sites where neoliberal economic theory has been developed. In 1986, The Graduate School of Management at the University of Rochester was renamed the William E. Simon Graduate School of Business, after the businessman William E. Simon, a former Secretary of Treasury during three years of the Nixon and Ford administrations and a member of the conservative Heritage Foundation (founded in 1973) and of the Hoover Institute (Chabrak, 2012: 465–466). The honouring of Mr. Simon is indicative of the close ties between conservative funds and institutes and the neoliberal academics and how the seismic shift in politics and policy in the 1980s and 1990s were accomplished on the basis of academic credentials that, in turn, were based on a strong backing of financiers. Simon understood very well the importance of the funding of the university-based scholars and think tanks, and he wrote that business, to protect itself from government interventions, must "funnel desperately needed funds to scholars, social scientists, writers, and journalists who understand the relationship between political and economic liberty . . . I know nothing more crucial than to come to the aid of the intellectuals and writers who are fighting on my side' " (William E. Simon, cited in Smith, 2007: 90). The rise of the University of Rochester as a stronghold for economic theory advocating free-marked solutions in economic policy is a fine example of the growth of what Mirowski (2013: 8) refers to as the "stock of neoliberal infrastructure" built up after 1980. When Ludwig von Mises was teaching at New York University in the 1950s and 1960s, his salary was paid by a private businessman rather than the faculty, indicating both how controversial the neoliberal thinkers were at the time, and how important intellectuals and scholars were for conservative financiers (Jones, 2012). After 1980, a new situation emerged, and neoliberal intellectuals and neoclassical economists received more financial support and could establish their own institutions.
2. What Himmelstein (1992) refers to as "corporate conservatism" undoubtedly played a key role in the neoliberal and neoconservative take-over, and the inflow of capital is indicative of the mobilization of capital owners to support their interests. The American Enterprise Institute increased its budget ten-fold between 1970 and 1983 (from $0.9 million to $10.6 million). The Hoover Institution at Stanford University raised its annual budget from $1.9 in 1970 to $8.4 million by 1983. The Heritage Foundation started with a donation from industrialist Joseph Coors and had an annual budget of $10.6 by 1983. The John M. Olin Foundation was funded in 1977 and spent about $5 million a year to support "scholarship in the philosophy of a free society and the economics of a free market" (cited in Himmelstein, 1992: 149). Its director, William E. Simon, "played a central role in the mobilization of big business" (Himmelstein, 1992: 149).
3. The major neoconservative think tanks provided a "great many high-level appointees to the Reagan administration," Himmelstein (1992: 150) notices. In Reagan's first term, fifty appointees came from the Hoover Institute, thirty-six from the Heritage Foundation, thirty-four from AEI, and eighteen from the Center for Strategic and International Studies.
4. Economists representing other fields of the discipline were not always impressed by the new finance theory. Taylor (2011: 255) suggests that the foundations of finance theory "look like pure common sense," and that it is "easy to raise serious objections to all major models." In addition, the potential virtues of such common sense thinking were left behind as finance theorists concentrated on understanding the instrumental rationality of agents operating in what

Taylor speaks of as "highly structured artificial environments." In a similar vein, Colander et al. (2009: 260) says, "[M]ost of the contemporary work in macroeconomics and finance is . . . characterized by pre-analytical belief in the validity of certain models that are never meaningfully exposed to empirical cases." That is, "[t]here is an almost scholastic acceptance of axiomatic first principles . . . independent of any empirical evidence" (Colander et al., 2009: 260).

5. This point is emphasized by Galloway (2013), who treats mathematics and, in its consequences, software ("Simply put, software is math. Computer science is a division of mathematics," Galloway [2013: 358] claims) as the new underlying ontological structure of how economic value is produced. Considering the case of Google, putting a brilliant algorithm to work enables Google to acquire economic value on the basis of the geographically distributed "micro labour" of the users of Google's services. Galloway makes the connection between applied mathematics and economic value in the contemporary economy: "Much of the labor happening in Google's server farms is performed by clustering algorithms running on massive fleets of machines. Nevertheless, the value being extracted is gleaned from the large reservoirs of micro labor performed by web users around the planet. Users perform micro labor whenever they send email, post messages online, or update websites, hence Google is merely skimming value from information networks that ultimately have their origin in human laboring activity" (Galloway, 2013: 358; see also Beller, 2006).

Bibliography

Abi-Rached, Joelle M. and Rose, Nikolas, (2010), The birth of the neuromolecular gaze, *History of the Human Sciences*, 23(1): 11–36.
Abolafia, Michael, (2001), *Making markets: Opportunism and restraints on Wall Street*, Cambridge: Harvard University Press.
Abraham, John, (2010), Pharmaceuticalization of society in context: Theoretical, empirical, and health dimensions, *Sociology*, 44(4): 603–622.
Abraham, John and Ballinger, Rachel, (2012), The neoliberal regulatory state, industry interests, and the ideological penetration of scientific knowledge: Deconstructing the redefinition of carcinogens in pharmaceuticals, *Science, Technology, & Human Values*, 37(5): 443–477.
Abraham, John and Reed, Tim, (2002), Progress, innovation and regulatory science in drug development: The politics of international standard-setting, *Social Studies of Science*, 32(3): 337–369.
Adamson, Stephen J., Doherty, Noeleen and Viney, Claire, (1998), The meaning of career revisited: Adamson, Stephen J., Doherty, Noeleen and Viney, Claire, (1998), The meaning of career revisited: Implications for theory and practice, *British Journal of Management*, 9: 251–259.
Aglietta, Michel, (2000), Shareholder value and corporate governance: Some tricky questions, *Economy and Society*, 29(1): 146–159.
Ailon, Galit, (2012), The discursive management of financial risk scandals: The case of Wall Street journal commentaries on LTCM and Enron, *Qualitative Sociology*, 35(3): 251–270.
Akerlof, George, (1970), The market for 'lemons': Quality uncertainty and the market mechanism, *Quarterly Journal of Economics*, 84(3): 488–500.
Alchian, A. and Demsetz, H., (1972), Production, information costs and economic organization, *American Economic Review*, 62(5): 777–795.
Alderson, Arthur S., and Nielsen, François (2002), Globalization and the great u-turn: Income inequality trends in 16 OECD countries, *American Journal of Sociology*, 107(5): 1244–1299.
Almeling, Renee, (2007), Selling genes, selling gender; Egg agencies, sperm banks, and the medical market in genetic material, *American Sociological Review*, 73(3): 319–340.
Alvehus, Johan and Spicer, André, (2012), Financialization as a strategy of workplace control in professional service firms, *Critical Perspectives on Accounting*, 23(7–8): 497–510.
Alvesson, Mats and Sveningsson, Stefan, (2003), Managers doing leadership; the extra-ordinarization of the mundane, *Human Relations*, 56(2): 1435–1459.
Amable, Bruno, (2011), Morals and politics in the ideology of neo-liberalism, *Socio-Economic Review*, 9(1): 3–30.

Amis, Martin, (2002), A PM, a President, and first lady, in Amis, Martin (Ed.), *The war against clichés: Essays and reviews, 1971–2000*, London: Vintage Books.

Andrews, Lori and Nelkin, Dorothy, (2001), *Human bazaar: The market for human tissue in the biotechnology age*, New York: Crown.

Anteby, Michal, (2008), *Moral gray zones: Side production, identity, and regulation in an aeronautics plant*, Princeton: Princeton University Press.

Appleby, Joyce Oldham, (2010), *The relentless revolution: A history of capitalism*, New York: Norton.

Arnold, Patricia J., (2005), Disciplining domestic regulation: The World Trade Organization and the market for professional services *Accounting, Organizations and Society*, 30(4): 299–330.

Arnold, Patricia J., (2009), Global financial crisis: The challenge to accounting research, *Accounting, Organizations and Society*, 34: 803–809.

Arrighi, Giovanni, (2010), *The long twentieth century: Money, power, and the origins of our times*, 2nd ed., London and New York: Verso.

Aspers, Patrik, (2010), *Orderly fashion: A sociology of markets*, Princeton: Princeton University Press.

Backhouse, Roger, (2012), *The puzzle of modern economics: Science or ideology?* Cambridge and New York: Cambridge University Press.

Ball, Kristie and Carter, Chris, (2002), The charismatic gaze: Everyday leadership practices of the 'new' manager, *Management Decision*, 40(6): 552–565.

Banerjee, Subhabrata Bobby, (2008), Necrocapitalism, *Organization Studies*, 29(12): 1541–1563.

Barley, Stephen R. and Kunda, Gideon, (1992), Design and devotion: Surges of rational and normative ideologies of control in managerial discourse, *Administrative Science Quarterly*, 37: 363–399.

Barley, Stephen R. and Kunda, Gideon, (2004), *Gurus, warm bodies and hired guns: Itinerant experts in the knowledge economy*, Princeton: Princeton University Press.

Barnard, C.I., (1938), *The Functions of the Executive*, Cambridge: Harvard University Press.

Barofsky, Neil M., (2012), *Bailout: A inside account of how Washington abandoned Main Street while rescuing Wall Street*, New York: Free Press.

Baron, James N., Dobbin, Frank R. and Jennings, P. Devereaux, (1986), War and peace: The evolution of modern personnel administration in U.S. industry, *American Journal of Sociology*, 92: 350–383.

Basadur, Min, (2004), Leading others to think innovatively together. Creative leadership, *Leadership Quarterly*, 15: 103–121.

Batra, Ravi, (2005); *Greenspan's fraud: How two decades of his policies have undermined the global economy.* New York: Palgrave Macmillan.

Bebchuk, L. and Fried, J., (2004), *Pay without performance: The unfulfilled promise of executive compensation*, Cambridge: Harvard University Press.

Bebchuk, Lucian and Grinstein, Yaniv, (2005), The growth of executive pay, *Oxford Review of Economic Policy*, 21(2): 283–303.

Beck, Ulrich, (2000), *Welcome to the new world of work.* Patrick Camiller (Trans.), Cambridge: Polity Press.

Becker Gary S., (1968), Crime and punishment: An economic approach, *Journal of Political Economy*, 76(2): 169–217.

Beckert, Jens, (2009), The social order of markets, *Theory and Society*, 38: 245–269.

Beckett, Katherine and Western, Bruce, (2001), Governing social marginality: Welfare, incarceration, and the transformation of state policy, *Punishment & Society*, 3(1): 43–59.

Bell, Emma and Taylor, Scott, (2004), From outward bound to inward bound: The prophetic voices and discursive practices of spiritual management development, *Human Relations*, 57(4): 4639–66.

Bibliography 215

Beller, Jonathan, (2006), *The cinematic mode of production: Attention economy and the society of the spectacle*, Duke Hanover: Dartmouth College Press.

Bendix, Reinhard and Fisher, Lloyd H., (1949), The perspectives of Elton Mayo, *Review of Economics and Statistics*, 31(4): 312–319.

Bennis, W.G. and O'Toole, J., (2005), How business schools lost their way, *Harvard Business Review*, 83(5): 33–53.

Benjamin, Beth and Podolny, Joel, (1999), Status, quality, and social order in the Californian wine industry, *Administrative Science Quarterly*, 44(3): 563–589.

Bergström, Ola, (2003), Beyond atypicality, in Bergström, Ola and Storrie, Donald (Eds.), *Contingent employment in Europe and the United States*, Chaltenham and Northampton: Edward Elgar, pp. 14–51.

Berle, Adolf A. and Means, Gardiner C., ([1934] 1991), *The modern corporation and private property*, New Brunswick: Transaction Publishers.

Berman, Elizabeth Popp, (2012), *Creating the market university: How academic science became an economic engine*, Princeton and Oxford: Princeton University Press.

Best, Rachel Kahn, (2012), Disease politics and medical research funding: Three ways advocacy shapes policy, *American Sociological Review*, 77(5): 780–803.

Beunza, Daniel and Stark, David, (2004), Tools of the trade: the socio-technology of arbitrage in a Wall Street trading room, *Industrial and Corporate Change*, 13(2): 369–400.

Beunza, Daniel, Hardie, Iain and Mackenzie, Donald, (2006), A price is a social thing: Toward a material sociology of arbitrage, *Organization Studies*, 27: 721–745.

Beynon, Huw, (1975), *Working for Ford*, East Ardsley: EP Publishing.

Bhagat, Sanjai and Black, Bernard, (2002), The non-correlation between board independence and long-term firm performance, *Journal of Corporation Law*, 27: 231–274.

Birkerts, Sven, (1994), *The Gutenberg elegies: The fate of reading in an electronic age*, Boston: Faber and Faber.

Black, William K., (2005), *The best way to rob a bank is to own one: How corporate executives and politicians looted the S&L industry*, Austin: University of Texas Press.

Blech, Jörg, (2006), *Inventing disease and pushing pills: Pharmaceutical companies and the medicalization of normal life*, Gisela Wallor Hajjar (Trans.), London and New York: Routledge.

Blee, Kathleen M. and Creasap, Kimberly, (2010), Conservative and right-wing movements, *Annual Review of Sociology*, 36: 269–296.

Block, Fred and Keller, Matthew R., (2009), Where do innovations come from? Transformations in the US economy, 1970–2006, *Socio-Economic Review*, 7(3): 459–483.

Blum, Virginia L., (2005), *Flesh wounds: The culture of cosmetic surgery*, Berkeley: University of California Press.

Blyth, Mark, (2013), *Austerity: The history of a dangerous idea*, Oxford and New York: Oxford University Press.

Blyton, Paul and Morris, Jonathan, (1991), *A flexible future? Prospects for employment and organization*, Berlin: Walter de Gruyter.

Boas, Taylor C. and Gans-Morse, Jordan, (2009), Neoliberalism: From new liberal philosophy to anti-liberal slogan, *Studies in Comparative International Development*, 44(2): 137–161.

Bockman, Johanna and Eyal, Gil, (2002), Eastern Europe as a laboratory for economic knowledge: The transnational roots of neoliberalism, *American Journal of Sociology*, 108(2): 310–352.

Bok, Derek, (2002), *Universities in the marketplace: The commercialization of higher education*, Princeton: Princeton University Press.

Bibliography

Boldrin, M. and Levine, D.K., (2004), 2003 Lawrence R. Klein lecture: The case against intellectual monopoly, *International Economic Review*, 45(2): 327–350.

Bonefeld, Werner, (2012), Freedom and the strong state: On German ordoliberalism, *New Political Economy*, 17(5): 633–656.

Bovie, Steven, Lange, Donald, McDonald, Michael L. and Westphal, James D., (2011), Me or we: the effects of CEO organizational identification on agency costs, *Academy of Management Journal*, 54(3): 551–576.

Brady, David, Baker, Regina S. and Finnigan, Ryan, (2013), When unionization disappears: State-level unionization and working poverty in the United States, *American Sociological Review*, 78(5): 872–896.

Bratton, William W. and Wachter, Michael L., (2010), The case against shareholder empowerment, *Pennsylvania Law Review*, 160(1): 69–168.

Braudel, Fernand, (1980), *On history*, Chicago and London: The University of Chicago Press.

Braudel, Fernand, (1992), *The wheels of commerce: Civilization and capitalism 15th-18th century*, Vol. 2, Berkeley and Los Angeles: The University of California Press.

Brint, Steven, (1994), *In the age of experts: The changing role of professionals in politics and public life*, Princeton: Princeton University Press.

Brockman, Jeffrey, Chang, Saeyoung and Rennie, Craig, (2007), CEO cash and stock-based compensation changes, layoff decisions, and shareholder value, *Financial Review*, 42: 99–119.

Brown, Andrew D., Kornberger, Martin, Clegg, Stewart R. and Carter, Chris, (2010), 'Invisible walls' and 'silent hierarchies': A case study of power relations in an architecture firm, *Human Relations*, 63(4): 525–549.

Brown, Nik and Kraft, Alison, (2006), Blood ties: Banking the stem cell promise, *Technology Analysis & Strategic Management*, 18(3): 313–327.

Brown, Wendy, (2006), American nightmare: Neoliberalism, neoconservatism, and de-democratization, *Political Theory*, 34(6): 690–714.

Bryan, Dick and Rafferty, Michael, (2013), Fundamental value: A category in transformation, *Economy and Society*, 42(1): 130–153.

Bryman, Alan, (1992), *Charisma and leadership in organizations*, London, Newbury, New Delhi: Sage.

Brynjolfsson, Erik and Saunders, Adam, (2010), *Wired for innovation: How information technology is reshaping the economy*, Cambridge and London: MIT Press.

Buchanan, James M., (1954), Individual choice in voting and in the market, *Journal of Political Economy*, 62(4): 334–343.

Bucher, Rue and Strauss, Anselm L., (1961), Professions as process, *American Journal of Sociology*, 66(4): 325–334.

Burton-Jones, Alan, (1999), *Knowledge capitalism: Business, work, and learning in the new economy*, Oxford: Oxford University Press.

Caballero, Ricardo I., (2010), Macroeconomics after the crisis: Time to deal with the pretence-to-knowledge syndrome, *Journal of Economic Perspectives*, 24: 85–102.

Callinicos, Alex, (2009), *Bonfire of illusions: The twin crises of neoliberalism*, Cambridge: Polity Press.

Callon, Michel, Millo, Yuval and Muniesa, Fabian (Eds.), (2007), *Market devices*, Oxford and Malden: Blackwell.

Calvert, Jane, (2007), Patenting genomic objects: Genes, genomes, function and information, *Science as Culture*, 16(2): 207–223.

Campbell, John L., (2010), Neoliberalism in crisis: Regulatory roots of the U.S. financial meltdown, *Research in the Sociology of Organizations*, 30B: 65–101.

Carolan, Michael S., (2010), The mutability of biotechnology patents: From unwieldy products of nature to independent 'objects/s', *Theory, Culture & Society*, 27(1): 110–129.

Carroll, William K., (2010), *The making of a transnational capitalist class: Corporate power in the twenty-first century*, New York: Zed Books.
Carroll, William K. and Carson, Collin, (2006), Neoliberalism, capitalist class formation and the global network of corporation and policy groups, in Plehwe, Dieter, Walpen, Bernhard and Neunhöffer, Gisela (Eds.), *Neoliberal hegemony: A global critique*, New York and London: Routledge, pp. 51–69.
Carroll, Brigid and Levy, Lester, (2010), Leadership development as identity construction, *Management Communication Quarterly*, 24(2): 211–231.
Carruthers, Bruce and Babb, Sarah, (1996), The color of money and the nature of value: Greenbacks and gold in postbellum America, *American Journal of Sociology*, 101(6): 1556–1591.
Carruthers, Bruce and Espeland, Wendy, (1991), Accounting for rationality; Double-entry book-keeping and the rhetoric of economic rationality, *American Journal of Sociology*, 97(1): 31–69.
Carruthers, Bruce G. and Stinchcombe, Arthur L., (1999), The social structure of liquidity flexibility, markets and states, *Theory and Society*, 28: 353–382.
Castilla, Emilio J., (2008), Gender, race and meritocracy in organizational careers, *American Journal of Sociology*, 113(6): 1479–1526.
Centeno, Miguel A. and Cohen Joseph N., (2012), The arc of neoliberalism, *Annual Review of Sociology*, 38: 317–340.
Chabrak, Nihel, (2012), Money talks: The language of the Rochester School, *Accounting, Auditing & Accountability Journal*, 25(3): 452–485.
Chandler, Alfred D., (1962), *Strategy and structure*, Cambridge: MIT Press.
Chandler, Alfred D., (1977), *The visible hand: The managerial revolution in American business*, Cambridge: Harvard University Press.
Chandler, Alfred D., (1984), The emergence of managerial capitalism, *Business History Review*, 58: 473–503.
Chandler, Alfred D., (2005), *Shaping the industrial century: The remarkable story of the evolution of the modern chemical and pharmaceutical industries*, Cambridge and London: Harvard University Press.
Changeux, Jean-Pierre, (2004), *The physiology of truth: Neuroscience and human knowledge*, Boston: Belknap Press of Harvard University Press.
Cheal, David, (1988), *The gift economy*, London and New York: Routledge.
Cherry, Mark J., (2005), *Kidney for sale by owner: Transplantation and the market*, Washington: Georgetown University Press.
Chorev, Nitsan and Babb, Sarah, (2009), The crisis of neoliberalism and the future of international institutions; A comparison of the IMF and the WTO, *Theory and Society*, 38: 459–484.
Chwieroth, Jeffrey M., (2010), *Capital ideas: The IMF and the rise of financial liberalization*, Princeton and Oxford: Princeton University Press.
Clark, Cynthia E. and Newell, Sue, (2013), Institutional work and complicit decoupling across the U.S. capital markets: The work of rating agencies, *Business Ethics Quarterly* 23(1): 1–30.
Clark, Ian, (2009), Owners and managers: disconnecting managerial capitalism? Understanding the private-equity business model, *Work, Employment and Society*, 23(4): 775–786.
Clarke, Adele E., Mamo, Laura, Fosket, Jennifer Ruth, Fishman, Jennifer R. and Shim, Janet K. (Eds.), (2010), *Biomedicalization: Technoscience, health, illness in the U.S.*, Durham and London: Duke University Press.
Clarke, Simon, (2005), The neoliberal theory of society, in Saad-Filho, Alfredo and Johnston, Deborah (Eds.), *Neoliberalism: A critical reader*, London and Ann Arbor: Pluto, pp. 50–59.
Coase, R.H., ([1937] 1991), The nature of the firm, in Williamson, Oliver E. and Winter, Sidney G. (Eds.), *The nature of the firm: Origin, evolution, and development*, New York and Oxford: Oxford University Press.

Coates, John C. IV, (2007), The goals and promise of the Sarbanes–Oxley Act, *Journal of Economic Perspectives*, 21(1): 91–116.
Cohen Joseph N., and Centeno Miguel A., (2006), Neoliberalism and patterns of economic performance, 1980–2000, *The Annals of the American Academy of Political and Social Science*, 606: 32–67.
Colander, David, Goldberg, Michael, Haas, Armin, Juselius, Katarina, Kirman,Alan, Lux, Thomas and Sloth, Brigitte, (2009), The financial crisis and the systemic failure of the economics profession, *Critical Review*, 21(2–3): 249–267.
Conger, Jay A. and Kanungo, Rabindra N, (1987), Toward a behavioral theory of charismatic leadership in organizational settings, *Academy of Management Review*, 12(4): 637–647.
Conrad, Peter, (2007), *The medicalization of society*, Baltimore: Johns Hopkins University Press.
Conti, Joseph A., (2010), Producing legitimacy at the World Trade Organization: The role of expertise and legal capacity, *Socio-Economic Review*, 8(1): 131–155.
Cooper, Melinda, (2008), *Life as surplus: Biotechnology and capitalism in the neoliberal era*, Seattle and London: University of Washington Press.
Corley, Kevin G. and Dennis A. Gioia, (2011), Building theory about theory building: What constitutes a theoretical contribution? *Academy of Management Review*, 36(1): 12–32.
Coser, Lewis A., (1974), *Greedy institutions. Patterns of undivided commitment*, New York: Free Press.
Costas, Jana and Taheri, Alireza, (2012), 'The return of the primal father in postmodernity?' A Lacanian analysis of authentic leadership, *Organization Studies*, 33(9): 1195–1216.
Cremin, Colin, (2010), Never employable enough: The (im)possibility of satisfying the boss desire, *Organization*, 17(2): 131–149.
Crotty, James, (2008), If financial market competition is intense, why are financial firm profits so high? Reflections on the current 'golden age' of finance, *Competition & Change*, 12(2): 167–183.
Crotty, James, (2009), Structural causes of the global financial crisis: A critical assessment of the 'new financial architecture', *Cambridge Journal of Economics*, 33(4): 563–580.
Crotty, James, (2012), The great austerity war: What caused the US deficit crisis and who should pay to fix it? *Cambridge Journal of Economics*, 36: 79–104.
Crouch, Colin, (2011), *The strange non-death of neo-liberalism*, Cambridge: Polity Press.
Cushen, Jean, (2013), Financialization in the workplace: Hegemonic narratives, performative interventions and the angry knowledge worker, *Accounting, Organizations and Society*, 38(4): 314–331.
Cusumano, M.A., (1985), *The Japanese automobile industry: Technology and management at Toyota and Nissan*, Cambridge: Harvard University Press.
Dalton, Dan R., Certo, S. Trevis and Roenghpitya, Rungpen, (2001), Meta-analyses of financial performance and equity: Fusion or confusion? *Academy of Management Journal*, 46(1): 13–26.
Dalton, Dan R., Daily, Catherine M., Johnson, Jonathan L. and Ellstrand, Alan E., (1999), Number of directors and financial performance: A meta-analysis, *Academy of Management Journal*, 42(6): 674–686.
Dambrin, Claire and Robson, Keith, (2011), Tracing performance in the pharmaceutical industry: Ambivalence, opacity and the performativity of flawed measures, *Accounting, Organizations and Society*, 36: 86–101.
Daston, Lorraine, (1995), The moral economy of science, *Osiris*, 10: 2–24.
Daston, Lorraine, (2008), On scientific observation, *Isis*, 99: 97–110.

Davies, William and McGoey, Linsey, (2012), Rationalities of ignorance: On financial crisis and the ambivalence of neo-liberal epistemology, *Economy and Society*, 41(1): 64–83.
Davis, Gerald F., (2005), New directions in corporate governance, *Annual Review of Sociology*. 31: 143–162.
Davis, Gerald F., (2009), *Managed by the markets: How finance reshaped America*, Oxford and New York: Oxford University Press.
Davis, Gerald F., (2010), After the ownership society: Another world is possible, *Research in the Sociology of Organizations*, 30B: 331–356.
Davis, Gerald F., Diekmann, Kristine A. and Tinsley, Catherine, (1994), The decline and fall of the conglomerate firm in the 1980s: The deinstitutionalization of an organization form, *American Sociological Review*, 59: 547–570.
Davis, Gerald and Robbins, Gregory, (2005), Nothing but net? Networks and status in corporate governance, in Knorr Cetina, Karin and Preda, Alex (Eds.), *The sociology of financial markets*, Oxford and New York: Oxford University Press, pp. 290–311.
Davis, Gerald F. and Stout, Suzanne K., (1992), Organization theory and the market for corporate control: A dynamic analysis of the characteristics of large takeover targets, 1980–1990, *Administrative Science Quarterly*, 37(4): 605–633.
Davis, Gerald F. and Thompson, Tracy A., (1994), A social movement perspective on corporate control, *Administrative Science Quarterly*, 39(1): 141–173.
Davis, Mike, (1990), *City of quartz: Excavating the future in Los Angeles*, London and New York: Verso.
Davis, Mike, (2006), *Planet of slums*, London: Verso.
Davis, Mike and Monk, Daniel Bertrand (Eds.), (2007), *Evil paradises: Dreamworlds of neoliberalism*, New York and London: New Press.
Deetz, Stanley A., (1992), *Democracy in an age of corporate colonialization*, Albany and New York: State of New York University Press.
DeGrandpre, Richard, (2006), *The cult of pharmacology*, Durham: Duke University Press.
De Roover, Raymond, (1974), *Banking business, and economic thought in early modern Europe: Selected studies of Raymond de Roover*, Kirshner, Julius (Ed.), Chicago and London: University of Chicago Press.
Deutschmann, Christoph, (2011), A pragmatist theory of capitalism, *Socio-Economic Review*, 9(1): 83–10.
Dewey, John, ([1929] 1988), *The quest for certainty: The later works, 1925–1953*, Volume 4: 1929, Jo Ann Boydston (Ed.), Carbondale and Edwardsville: Southern Illinois University Press.
Dickenson, Donna, (2008), *Body shopping: The economy fuelled by flesh and blood*, Oxford: Oneworld.
DiMaggio, Paul and Powell, Walter W., (1983), The iron cage revisited: Institutional isomorphism and collective rationality in organizational fields. *American Sociological Review*, 48(2): 147–160.
DiPrete, Thomas A., Eirich, Gregory M. and Pittinsky, Matthew, (2010), Compensation benchmarking, leapfrogs, and the surge in executive pay, *American Journal of Sociology*, 115(6): 1671–1712.
Dittmar, Amy K., (2000), Why do firms repurchase stock? *Journal of Business*, 73(3): 331–355.
Djelic, Marie-Louise, (2001), *Exporting the American model*, Oxford and London: Oxford University Press.
Dobbin, Frank and Jung, Jiwook, (2010), The misapplication of Mr. Michael Jensen: How agency theory brought down the economy and why it might again, *The Sociology of Organizations*, 30B: 29–64.

Dobbin, Frank and Sutton, John R., (1998), The strength of a weak state: The rights revolution and the rise of human resources management divisions, *American Journal of Sociology*, 104(2): 441–476.

Dobbin, Frank and Zorn, Dirk, (2005), Corporate malfeasance and the myth of shareholder value, *Political Power and Social Theory*, 17: 179–198.

Donaldson, Thomas, (2012), Epistemological fault lines in corporate governance, *Academy of Management Review*, 37(2): 256–271.

Doolin, Bill, (2002), Enterprising discourse, professional identity and the organizational control of hospital clinicians, *Organization Studies*, 23(3): 369–390.

Dopson, Sue and Stewart, Rosemary, (1990), What is happening to middle management? *British Journal of Management*, 1: 3–16.

Dore, Ronald, (2008), Financialization of the global economy, *Industrial and Corporate Change*, 17(6); 1097–1112.

Douglas, Mary, (1966), *Purity and danger: An analysis of concepts of pollution and taboo*, London and Henley: Routledge & Kegan Paul.

Dovey, Kim, (2010), *Becoming places: Urbanism/architecture/identity/power*, London and New York: Routledge.

Downer, John, (2011), "737-Cabriolet": The limits of knowledge and the sociology of inevitable failure, *American Journal of Sociology*, 117(3): 725–762.

Drucker, Peter F., (1946), *Concept of the corporation*, New York: The John Day Company.

Drucker, Peter F., (1955), *The practice of management*, Melbourne, London and Toronto: Heineman.

Duggan, Lisa, (2003), *The twilight of equality?: Neoliberalism, cultural politics, and the attack on democracy*, Boston: Beacon Press.

Duménil, Gérard and Lévy, Dominique, (2004), *Capital resurgent: Roots of the neoliberal revolution*, Derek Jeffer (Trans.), Cambridge: Harvard University Press.

Duménil, Gérard and Lévy, Dominique, (2011), *The crisis of neoliberalism*, Cambridge: Harvard University Press.

Dumit, Joseph, (2012), Prescription maximization and the accumulation of surplus health in the pharmaceutical industry: The_BioMarx_Experiment, in Sunder Rajan, Kaushik (Ed.), *Lively capital*, Durham and London: Duke University Press, pp. 45–92.

Durham, Martin, (2006), The republic in danger: Neoconservatism, the American right, and the politics of empire, *The Political Quarterly*, 77(1): 43–52.

Dwyer, Rachel E., (2013), The care economy? Gender, economic restructuring, and job polarization in the U.S. labor market, *American Sociological Review*, 78(3): 390–416.

The Economist, (2013, February 2), The next supermodel [Editorial], Retrieved from www.economist.com/news/leaders/21571136-politicians-both-right-and-left-could-learn-nordic-countries-next-supermodel

Edelman, Lauren, (1992), Legal ambiguity and symbolic structures: Organizational meditation of civil rights law, *American Journal of Sociology*, 97: 1531–1576.

Ehrenreich, Barbara, (1989), *Fear of falling: The inner life of the middle class*, New York: HarperPerennial.

Eichengreen, Barry J., (2008), *Globalizing capital: A history of the international monetary system*, Princeton: Princeton University Press.

Eisenhardt, Kathleen, (1989), Agency theory: An Assessment and Review, *Academy of Management Review*, 14(1): 57–74.

Elias, Norbert, (2009), Sociology of knowledge: New perspectives, in Elias, Norbert (Ed.), *Essays I: On the sociology of knowledge and the sciences*, Dublin: University College Dublin Press, pp. 1–41.

Ellwood, Sheila and Newberry Susan, (2007), Public sector accrual accounting: Institutionalising neo-liberal principles? *Accounting, Auditing & Accountability Journal*, 20(4): 549–573.

Engelen, Ewald, Ertürk, Ismail, Froud, Julie, Johal, Sukhdev, Leaver, Adam, Moran, Michael and Williams, Karel, (2012), Misrule of experts? The financial crisis as elite debacle, *Economy and Society*, 41(3): 360–382.
Epstein, Gerald A. and Jayadev, Arjun, (2005), The rise of the rentier income in OECD countries: Finacialization, central bank policy and labor solidarity, in G. Epstein (Ed.), (2005), *The financialization of the world economy*, Northampton: Edward Elgar, pp. 46–74.
Epstein, S.R., (1998), Craft guilds, apprenticeship, and technological change in pre-industrial Europe, *Journal of Economic History*, 53(4): 684–718.
Ericson, Richard, Barry, Dean and Doyle, Aaron, (2000), The moral hazard of neoliberalism: Lessons from the private insurance industry, *Economy and Society*, 29(4): 532–558.
Erturk, Ismail, Froud, Julie, Johal Sukhdev and Williams, Karel, (2004), Corporate governance and disappointment, *Review of International Political Economy*, 11(4): 677–713.
Espeland, Wendy N. and Sauder, M., (2007), Ranking and reactivity: How public measures recreate social worlds, *American Journal of Sociology*, 113(1): 1–40.
Espeland, Wendy Nelson and Stevens, Mitchell L., (1998), Commensuration as a social process, *Annual Review of Sociology*, 24: 13–24.
Espeland, Wendy Nelson and Stevens, Mitchell L., (2008), A sociology of quantification, *European Journal of Sociology*, 49(3): 401–436.
Evans, Peter and Rauch, James E., (1999), Bureaucracy and growth: A cross-national analysis of the effects of 'Weberian' state structures on economic growth, *American Journal of Sociology*, 64(5): 748–765.
Faulconbridge, James R. and Muzio, Daniel, (2009), The financialization of large law firms: Situated discourses and practices of reorganization, *Journal of Economic Geography*, 9(5): 641–661.
Faludi, Susan, (2000), *Stiffed: The betrayal of the American man*, New York: Harper Perennial.
Fama, Eugene F., (1970), Efficient capital markets: A review of theory and empirical work, *Journal of Finance*, 25(2): 383–417.
Fama, Eugene F., (1980), Agency problems and the theory of the firm, *Journal of Political Economy*, 88: 288–305.
Fama, Eugene F. and Jensen, Michael, (1983a), Separation of ownership and control, *Journal of Law and Economics*, 26(2): 301–325.
Ferraro, Fabrizio, Pfeffer, Jeffrey and Sutton, Robert I., (2005), Economics language and assumptions: How theories can become self-fulfilling, *Academy of Management Review*, 30(1): 8–24.
Fiedler, Fred E., (1968), *A theory of leadership effectiveness*, New York: McGraw-Hill.
Fine, Sidney, (1969), *Sit-down: The General motors strike of 1936–1937*, Ann Arbor: University of Michigan Press.
Fischer, Jill, (2009), *Medical research for hire: The political economy of pharmaceutical clinical trials*, New Brunswick: Rutgers University Press.
Fishman, Jennifer R., (2004), Manufacturing desire. The commodification of female sexual dysfunction, *Social Studies of Science*, 34(2): 187–218.
Fleischer, Anne, (2009), Ambiguity and the equity of rating systems: Unites States brokerage firms, 1995–2000, *Administrative Science Quarterly*, 54(4): 555–574.
Fleming, Peter and Sturdy, Andrew, (2011), 'Being yourself' in the electronic sweatshop: New forms of normative control, *Human Relations*, 64(2): 177–200.
Fligstein, Neil, (1987), The interorganizational power struggle: Rise of financial personnel to top leadership in large corporations, *American Sociological Review*, 52(1): 44–58.
Fligstein, Neil, (1990), *The transformation of corporate control*, Cambridge and London: Harvard University Press.

Fligstein, Neil and Choo, Jennifer, (2005), Law and corporate governance, *Annual Review of Law and Social Science*, 1: 61–84.
Fligstein, Neil and Goldstein, Adam, (2010), The anatomy of the mortgage securitization crisis, *Research in the Sociology of Organizations*, 30A: 29–70.
Fligstein, Neil and Shin, Taekjin, (2007), Shareholder value and the transformation of the U.S. economy, 1984–2000. *Sociological Forum*, 22: 399–424.
Florida, Richard, (2002), *The rise of the creative class*, New York. Basic Books.
Floyd, Steven W. and Woolridge, Bill, (1994), Dinosaurs or dynamos? Recognizing middle management's strategic role, *Academy of Management Executive*, 8(4): 47–57.
Flynn, Francis J. and Staw, Barry M., (2003), Lend me your wallet: The effect of charismatic leadership on external support or an organization, *Strategic Management Journal*, 25: 309–330.
Foucault, Michel, (2008), *The birth of biopolitics: Lectures at the Collège de France, 1978–1979*, Michael Senellart (Ed.), Graham Burchell (Trans.), Basingstoke: Palgrave.
Fourcade, Marion and Khurana, Rakesh, (2013), From social control to financial economics: The linked ecologies of economics and business in twentieth century America, *Theory and Society*, 42(2): 121–159.
Fox, J, (2009), *The myth of the rational market: A history of risk, reward and delusion on Wall Street*, New York: Harper Collins.
Frank, Thomas, (2004), *What's the matter with America?: The resistible rise of the American right*, London: Secker & Warburg.
Franks, Julian and Mayer, Colin, (1996), Hostile takeovers and the correction of managerial failure, *Journal of Financial Economics*, 40: 163–181
Free, Clinton, Salterio, Steven E. and Shearer, Teri, (2009), The construction of auditability: MBA rankings and assurance in practice, *Accounting, Organizations and Society*, 34(1): 119–140.
Freeman, Richard B., (2010), Its financialization!, *International Labour Review*, 149(2): 163–183.
Friedman, Jeffrey and Kraus, Wladimir, (2012), *Engineering the financial crisis: Systemic risk and the failure of regulation*, Philadelphia: University of Pennsylvania Press.
Friedman, Milton, ([1962] 2002), *Capitalism and freedom*, 4th ed., Chicago and London: University of Chicago Press.
Frost, Carol Ann, (2007), Credit rating agencies in capital markets: A review of research evidence on selected criticisms of the agencies, *Journal of Accounting, Auditing & Finance*, 22(3): 469–492.
Froud, Julie, Haslam, Colin, Johal, Sukhdev and Williams, Karel, (2000), Shareholder value and Financialization: Consultancy promises, management moves, *Economy and Society*, 29(1): 80–110.
Galloway, Alexander R., (2013), The poverty of philosophy: Realism and post-Fordism, *Critical Inquiry*, 39: 347–366.
García, Baetriz, (2004), Urban regeneration, arts programming, and major events: Glasgow 1990, Sydney, 2000 and Barcelona 2004, *International Journal of Cultural Policy*, 10(1): 103–118.
Garsten, C., (1999), Betwixt and between: Temporary employees as liminal subjects in flexible organizations, *Organization Studies*, 20(4): 601–617.
Garsten, Christina, (2002), Flex fads: New economy, new employees, in Holmberg, Ingagill, Salzer-Mörling, Miriam and Strannegård, Lars (Eds.), *Stuck in the future: Tracing the 'new economy'*, Stockholm: Bookhouse Publishing.
Gauchat, Gordon, (2012), Politicization of science in the public sphere: A study of public trust in the United States, 1974 to 2010, *American Sociological Review*, 77(2): 167–187.

Gee, J.P., Hull, G. and Lankshear, C., (1996), *The new work order: Behind the language of the new capitalism*, St. Leonards: Allen & Unwin.
Gemmill, Gary and Oakley, Judith, (1992), Leadership: An alienating social myth, *Human Relations*, 45(2): 113–129.
George, David, (2013), *The rhetoric of the right*, London and New York: Routledge.
Gershon, Ilana, (2011), Neoliberal agency, *Current Anthropology*, 52: 537–555.
Glyn, Andrew, Howell, David and Schmitt, John, (2006), Labor market reforms: The evidence does not tell the orthodox tale, *Challenge*, 49(2): 5–22.
Goldstein, Adam, (2012), Revenge of the managers: Labor cost-cutting and the paradoxical resurgence of managerialism in the shareholder value era, 1984 to 2001, *American Sociological Review*, 77(2): 268–294.
Goody, Jack, (2004), *Capitalism and modernity: The great debate*, Cambridge and Malden: Polity Press.
Gordon, David, (1996), *Fat and mean: The corporate squeeze of working Americans and the myth of managerial downsizing*, New York: Free Press.
Gorton, Gary B., (2010), *Slapped by the invisible hand: The panic of 2007*, Oxford and New York: Oxford University Press.
Gotham, Kevin Fox, (2006), The secondary circuit of capital reconsidered: Globalization and the U.S.: Real estate sector, *American Journal of Sociology*, 112(1): 231–275.
Gourevitch, Peter A. and Shinn, James, (2005), *Political power and corporate control: The new global politics of corporate governance*, Princeton: Princeton University Press.
Graeber, David, (2011), *History of debt: The first 5,000 years*, New York: Meville House.
Greenwald, Bruce C. and Stiglitz, Joseph E., (1986), Externalities in economies with imperfect information and incomplete markets, *Quarterly Journal of Economics* 90: 229–264.
Gregg, Paul and Wadsworth, Jonathan, (1995), A short history of labour turnover, job tenure, and job security, 1975–1993, *Oxford Review of Economic Policy*, 11(1): 73–90.
Grey, Christopher, (1996), Towards a critique of managerialism: The contribution of Simone Weil, *Journal of Management Studies*, 33(5): 591–611.
Griffin, Penny, (2009), *Gendering the World Bank: Neoliberalism and the gendered foundation of global governance*, New York: Palgrave.
Gross, Neil, Medvetz, Thomas and Russell, Rupert, (2011), The contemporary American conservative movement, *Annual Review of Sociology*, 37: 325–354.
Grossman, Sanford J. and Stiglitz, Joseph E., (1980), On the impossibility of informationally efficient markets, *American Economic Review*, 70(3): 393–408.
Grullon, Gustavo and Ikenberry, David L., (2000), What do we know about stock repurchases? *Journal of Applied Corporate Finance*, 13(1): 31–51.
Guillén, Mauro F., (1994), *Models of management: Work, authority, and organization in a comparative perspective*, Chicago and London: University of Chicago Press.
Hacker, Jacob S. and Pierson, Paul, (2010), Winner-take-all politics: Public policy, political organization, and the precipitous rise of top incomes in the United States, *Politics & Society*, 38(2): 152–204.
Harcourt, Bernard E., (2011), *The illusion of free markets*, Cambridge and London: Harvard University Press.
Hardy, Derrylea J. and Walker, Robyn J., (2003), Temporary but seeing permanence. A study of New Zealand temps, *Leadership & Organization Development Journal*, 24(3): 141–152.
Harvey, David, (1989), From managerialism to entrepreneurialism: The transformation in urban governance in late capitalism, *Geografiska Annaler. Series B, Human Geography*, 71(1): 3–17.

Harvey, David, (2005a), Neo-liberalism as creative destruction, *Geografiska Annaler. Series B, Human Geography*, 88(2): 145–158.
Harvey, David, (2005b), *A brief history of neoliberalism*, New York: Oxford University Press.
Harvey, David, (2010), *The enigma of capital and the crisis of capitalism*, London: Profile Books.
Hassard, John, Morris, Jonathan and McCann, Leo, (2012), 'My brilliant career'? New organizational forms and changing managerial careers in Japan, the UK, and USA, *Journal of Management Studies* 49(3): 571–599.
Hattersley, Roy, (2006), Is equality outdated? *The Political Quarterly*, 77(1): 3–11.
Hayek, F.A., (1944), *The road to serfdom*, Chicago: University of Chicago Press.
Hayek, Friedrich, von, (1949), 'Free' enterprise and competitive order, in *Individualism and economic order*, London: Routledge & Kegan Paul, pp. 107–118.
Hayek, Friedrich, von, (1960), *The constitution of liberty*, Chicago and London: University of Chicago Press.
Hayek, Friedrich von, (1979), Government policy and the market, in Hayek, Friedrich von (Ed.), *Law legislation and liberty, Vol. 3: The political order of a free people*, London and Henley: Routledge & Kegan Paul, pp. 65–97.
Hayward, Matthew L.A. and Boeker, Warren, (1998), Power and conflict of interest in professional firms: Evidence from investment banking, *Administrative Science Quarterly*, 43: 1–22.
Healy, David, (2002), *The creation of psychopharmacology*, Cambridge and London: Harvard University Press.
Healey, Nigel M., (1992), The Thatcher supply-side 'miracle': Myth or reality? *American Economist*, 36(1): 7–12.
Helleiner, Eric, (2011), Understanding the 2007–2008 global financial crisis: Lessons for scholars of international political economy, *Annual Review of Political Science*, 14: 67–87.
Herold, David M., Jayaraman, Narayanan and Narayanaswamy, C.R, (2006), What is the relationship between organizational slack and innovation? *Journal of Managerial Issues*, 18(3): 372–39.
Hertz, Ellen, (1998), *The trading crowd: An ethnography of the Shanghai Stock market*, Cambridge: Cambridge University Press.
High, Brandon, (2009), The recent historiography of American neoconservatism, *The Historical Journal*, 52(2): 475–491.
Hillman, Amy J. and Kiem, Gerald D., (2001), Shareholder value, stakeholder management, and social issues: What's the bottom line, *Strategic Management Journal*, 22: 125–139.
Himmelstein, Jerome L., (1992), *To the right: The transformation of American conservatism*, Berkeley, Los Angeles and London: University of California Press.
Hines, Ruth D., (1988), Financial accounting: In communicating reality, we construct reality, *Accounting, Organization and Society*, 13: 251–261.
Hirsch, Paul, Michaels, Stuart and Friedman, Ray, (1987), 'Dirty hands' versus 'clean models'? Is sociology in danger of being seduced by economics? *Theory and Society*, 16(3): 317–336.
Hirschman, Albert O., (1977), *The passions and the interests*, Princeton: Princeton University Press.
Hirschman, Albert O., (1998), *Crossing boundaries: Selected writings*, New York: Zone Books.
Ho, Karen, (2009), *Liquidated. An ethnography of Wall Street*, Durham and London: Duke University Press.
Hobsbawm, Eric J., (1975), *The age of capital, 1848–1875*, London: Weidenfeld and Nicolson.

Hochschild, Arlie Russell, (2012), *The outsourced self: Intimate life in market times*, New York: Metropolitan Books.
Hoeyer, Klaus, (2009), Tradable body parts? How bone and recycled prosthetic devices acquire a price without forming a 'market,' *Biosocieties*, 4(2–3): 239–256.
Homans, George C., (1951), *The human group*, London: Routledge & Kegan Paul.
Hoque, Kim and Kirkpatrick, Ian, (2008), Making the core contingent: Professional agency work and its consequences in UK social services, *Public Administration*, 86(2): 331–344.
Hyman, Louis, (2011), *Debtor nation: The history of America in red ink*, Princeton and London: Princeton University Press.
Ingham, Geoffrey, (2008), *Capitalism*, Cambridge: Polity Press.
Inglehart, Ronald, (1997), *Modernization and postmodernization: Cultural, economic, and political change in 43 societies*, Princeton: Princeton University Press.
Inglehart, Ronald and Norris, Pippa, (2009), *Cosmopolitan communications: Cultural diversity in a globalized world*, Cambridge: Cambridge University Press.
Ireland, Paddy, (2010), Limited liability, shareholder rights and the problem of corporate irresponsibility, *Cambridge Journal of Economics*, 34: 837–856.
Jabłecki, Juliusz and Machaj, Mateusz, (2009), The regulated meltdown of 2008, *Critical Review*, 21(2–3): 301–328.
Jacobides, Michael G., (2005), Industry change through vertical disintegration: How and why markets emerged in mortgage banking, *Academy of Management Journal*, 48(3): 465–498.
James, W., (1975), *Pragmatism and the meaning of truth*, Cambridge: Harvard University Press.
Janis, Irving L., (1982), *Groupthink: Psychological studies of policy decisions and fiascoes*, 2nd ed., Boston: Houghton Mifflin.
Jeacle, Ingrid and Carter, Chris, (2011), In TripAdvisor we trust: Rankings, calculative regimes and abstract systems, *Accounting, Organizations & Society*, 36: 293–309.
Jensen, Michael C., (1986), Agency costs of free cash flow, corporate finance, and takeovers, *American Economics Review*, 76(2): 323–329.
Jensen, Michael C., (1993), The modern industrial revolution, exit, and failure of internal control systems, *Journal of Finance*, 48(3): 831–880.
Jensen, Michael C., (2002), Value maximization, stakeholder theory, and the corporate objective function, *Business Ethics Quarterly*, 12(2): 235–256.
Jensen, Michael C. and Meckling, William H., (1976), Theory of the firm: Managerial behavior, agency costs and ownership structure, *Journal of Financial Economics*, 3(4): 305–260.
Jessop, Bob, Kastendiek, Hans, Nielsen, Klaus and Pedersen, Ove K., (Eds.), (1991), *The politics of flexibility: Restructuring state and industry in Britain, Germany and Scandinavia*, Aldershot: Edward Edgar Publishing.
Jones, Daniel Stedman, (2012), *Masters of the universe: Hayek, Friedman, and the birth of neoliberal politics*, Princeton and Oxford: Princeton University Press.
Jones, Owen, (2011), *Chavs: The demonization of the working class*, London: Verso.
Judt, Tony, (2010), *Ill fares the land: A treatise on our present discontent*, London: Allen Lane.
Kahneman, Daniel, (2011), *Thinking, fast and slow*, New York: Farrar, Straus, and Giroux.
Kalleberg, Arne L., (2009), Precarious work, insecure workers: Employment relations in transition, *American Sociological Review*, 74: 1–22.
Kärreman, Dan and Alvesson, Mats, (2004), Cages in tandem: Management control, social identity, and identification in a knowledge-intensive firm, *Organization*, 11(1): 149–175.

Keay, Andrew, (2011), Moving towards stakeholderism? Constituency statutes, enlightened shareholder value, and more: Much ado about little? *European Business Law Review*, 22: 1–49.

Kelly, Nathan J. and Enns, Peter K., (2010), Inequality and the dynamics of public opinion: The self-reinforcing link between economic inequality and mass preferences, *American Journal of Political Science*, 54(4): 855–870.

Key, Susan, (1999), Toward a new theory of the firm: A critique of stakeholder 'theory,' *Management Decision*, 37(4), 317–328.

Keynes, John Maynard, (1953), *The general theory of employment, interest and money*, New York and London: Harcourt.

Khurana, R., (2002), *Searching for a corporate savior: The irrational quest for a charismatic CEO*, Princeton: Princeton University Press.

Khurana, Rakesh, (2007), *From higher aims to hired hands: The social transformation of American business schools and the unfulfilled promise of management as a profession*, Princeton: Princeton University Press.

Kieser, Alfred and Leiner, Lars, (2009), Why the rigour-relevance gap in management research is unbridgeable, *Journal of Management Studies*, 46(3): 516–533.

Kinderman, Daniel, (2012), 'Free us up so we can be responsible!' The co-evolution of Corporate Social Responsibility and neo-liberalism in the UK, 1977–2010, *Socio-Economic Review*, 10, 29–57.

Kipnis, Andrew, (2008), Audit cultures: Neoliberal governmentality, socialist legacy, or technological governing, *American Ethnologist*, 35(2): 275–289.

Klamperer, Victor, ([1975] 2000), *The language of the Third Reich, LTI—Lingua Tertii Imperii: A philologist's notebook*, Martin Brady (Trans), London and New Brunswick: Athlone Press.

Knechel, W. Robert, (2007), The business risk audit: Origins, obstacles and opportunities, *Accounting, Organizations and Society*, 32(4–5): 383–408.

Kogut, Bruce and Macpherson, J. Muir, (2011), The mobility of economists and the diffusion of policy ideas: The influence of economics on national policies, *Research Policy*, 40: 1307–1320.

Kollmeyer, Christopher, (2009), Explaining deindustrialization: How affluence, productivity growth, and globalization diminishing manufacturing employment, *American Journal of Sociology*, 114(6): 1644–1674.

Kornberger, Martin, (2012), Governing the city: From planning to urban strategy, *Theory Culture & Society*, 29(2): 84–106.

Kornberger, Martin, and Carter, Chris, (2010), Manufacturing competition: How accounting practices shape strategy making in cities, *Accounting, Auditing & Accountability Journal*, 23(3): 325–349.

Krause, E.A., (1996), *Death of the guilds*, New Haven, CT: Yale University Press.

Krippner, Greta R., (2005), The financialization of the American economy, *Socio-Economic Review*, 3(2): 173–208.

Krippner, Greta R., (2010), The political economy of financial exuberance, *Research in the Sociology of Organizations*, 30B: 141–173.

Krippner, Greta R., (2011), *Capitalizing on crisis: The political origins of the rise of finance*, Cambridge and London: Harvard University Press.

Kristal, Tali, (2013), The capitalist machine: Computerization, workers' power, and the decline in labor's share within U.S. industries, *American Sociological Review*, 78(3): 361–389.

Kuhn, Timothy, (2009), Positioning lawyers: Discursive resources, professional ethics and identification, *Organization*, 16(5): 681–704.

Lakatos, I., (1970), Falsification and the methodology of scientific research programmes, in Lakatos, I. and Musgrave, A., (Eds.), *Criticism and the growth of knowledge*, Cambridge: Cambridge University Press, pp. 170–196.

Lakoff, Andrew, (2006), *Pharmaceutical reason: Knowledge and value in global psychiatry*, Cambridge: Cambridge University Press.

Bibliography 227

Lam, Alice, (1997), Embedded firms, embedded knowledge: problems of collaboration and knowledge transfer in global cooperative ventures, *Organization Studies*, 18(6): 973–996.

Lampland, Martha, (2010), False numbers as formalizing process, *Social Studies of Science*, 40(3): 377–404.

Landes, David, (1983), *Revolution in time: Clocks and the making of the modern world*, Cambridge and London: Harvard University Press.

Lane, Carrie A., (2010), *The company of one: Neoliberal faith and the post-organizational man*, Ithaca: Cornell University Press.

Lapavitsas, Costas, (2012), Theorizing financialization, *Work, Employment and Society*, 25(4): 611–626.

Larson, Magali Sarafatti, (1977), *The rise of professionalism: A sociological analysis*, Berkeley, Los Angeles, and London: University of California Press.

Lave, Jean, (1988), *Cognition in practice: Mind, mathematics, and culture in everyday life*, Cambridge: Cambridge University Press.

Lazonick, William, (2010), Innovative business models and varieties of capitalism: Financialization of the U.S. corporation, *Business History Review*, 84: 675–702.

Lazonick, William and Mazzucato, Mariana, (2013), The risk-reward nexus in the innovation-inequality relationship: Who takes the risks? Who gets the rewards? *Industrial and Corporate Change*, 22(4): 1093–1128.

Lazonick, William and O'Sullivan, Mary, (2000), Maximizing shareholder value: a new ideology for corporate governance, *Economy and Society*, 29(1): 13–35.

Lazonick, William and Tulum, Öner, (2011), US biopharmaceutical finance and the sustainability of the biotech business model, *Research Policy*, 40: 1170–1187.

Lazzarato, Maurizio, (2009), Neoliberalism in action: Inequality, insecurity and the reconstitution of the social, *Theory, Culture & Society*, 26(6): 109–133.

Leathers, Charles G. and Raines, J. Patrick, (2004), The Schumpeterian role of financial innovations in the New Economy's business cycle, *Cambridge Journal of Economics*, 28(5): 667–681.

Le Goff, Jacques, ([1985] 1993), *Intellectuals in the middle ages*, Oxford and Cambridge: Blackwell.

Leicht, Kevin T. and Fennell, Mary L., (2001), *Professional work: A sociological approach*, Malden and Oxford: Blackwell.

Lenoir, Timothy, (1994), Revolution from above: The role of the state in creating the German research system, 1810–1910, *The American Economic Review*, 88(2): 22–27.

Lépinay, Vincent Antonin, (2011), *Codes of finance: Engineering derivatives in a global bank*, Princeton: Princeton University Press.

Leslie, Myles, (2010), Quality assured science: Managerialism in forensic biology, *Science, Technology & Human Values*, 35(2): 283–306.

Lichtenstein, Benyamin, Bergmann, M. and Mendenhall, Mark, (2002), Non-linearity and response-ability: Emergent order in the 21st-century careers, *Human Relations*, 55(1): 5–32.

Lichtenstein, Nelson, (2003), *State of the union: A century of American labor*. Princeton: Princeton University Press.

Lin, Ken-Hou and Tomaskovic-Devey, Donald, (2013), Financialization and U.S. income inequality, 1970–2008, *American Journal of Sociology*, 118(5): 1284–1329.

Lipovetsky, Gilles, (2005), *Hypermodern times*, Andrew Brown (Trans.), Cambridge: Polity.

Liu, Yujia and Grusky, David B., (2013), The payoff to skill in the third industrial revolution, *American Journal of Sociology*, 118(5): 1330–1374.

Lock, Margaret, (2002), *Twice dead: Organ transplants and the reinvention of death*, Berkeley, Los Angeles, and London: University of California Press.

Lord, Richard A. and Siato, Yoshie, (2010), Trends in CEO compensation and equity holdings for S&P 1500 firms: 1994–2007, *Journal of Applied Finance*, 3(2): 40–56.
Lorenz, Chris, (2012), If you're so smart, why are you under surveillance? Universities, neoliberalism, and new public management, *Critical Inquiry*, 38: 599–629.
Lorsch, J., (2009), Regaining lost relevance, *Journal of Management Inquiry*, 18: 108–117.
Lounsbury, Michael and Crumley, Ellen T., (2007), New practice creation: An institutional approach to innovation, *Organization Studies*, 28: 993–1012.
Love, E. Geoffrey and Nohria, Nitin, (2005), Reducing slack: The performance consequences of downsizing by large industrial firms, 1977–1993, *Strategic Management Journal*, 26(12): 1087–1108.
Luhmann, N., (1995), *Social systems*, Stanford: Stanford University Press.
Luhmann, Niklas, (2000), *Art as a social system*, Eva M. Knodt (Trans.), Stanford: Stanford University Press.
Lukács, Georg, (1971), *History and class consciousness: Studies in Marxist dialectics*, London: Merlin Press.
Lyotard, J.-F., ([1979] 1984), *The postmodern condition: A report on knowledge*, Manchester: Manchester University Press.
Mackenzie, Donald, (2006), *An engine, not a camera: How financial models shape markets*, Cambridge and London: MIT Press.
MacKenzie, Donald, (2011), The credit crisis as a problem in the sociology of knowledge, *American Journal of Sociology*, 116(6): 1778–1841.
MacKenzie, Donald and Millo, Yuval, (2003), Constructing a market: Performing a theory: A historical sociology of a financial market derivatives exchange, *American Journal of Sociology*, 109(1): 107–145.
MacPhail, Fiona and Bowles, Paul, (2008), Temporary work and neoliberal government policy: Evidence from British Columbia, Canada, *International Review of Applied Economics*, 22(5): 545–563.
Maddison, Angus, (1982), *Phases in capitalism development*, Oxford: Oxford University Press.
Madrick, Jeff, (2011), *Age of greed: The triumph of finance and the decline of America, 1970 to the present*, New York: Alfred A. Knopf.
Manne, Henry G., (1965), Mergers and the market for corporate control, *Journal of Political Economy*, 73(2): 110–120.
Marens, Richard, (2012), Generous in victory? American managerial autonomy, labour relations and the invention of Corporate Social Responsibility, *Socio-Economic Review*, 10: 59–84.
Marens, Richard, (2013), What comes around: The early 20th century American roots of legitimating corporate social responsibility, *Organization*, 20(3): 454–476.
Markens, Susan, (2007), *Surrogate motherhood and the politics of reproduction*, Berkeley and Los Angeles: University of California Press.
Massey, Douglas S., Sanchez Magaly R., and Behrman, Jere R., (2006), Of myths and markets, *Annals of the American Academy of Political and Social Science*, 606: 8–31.
Mayo, E., (1946), *The Human Problems of An Industrial Civilization*, Cambridge: Harvard University Press.
McAfee, Kathleen, (2003), Neoliberalisms on the molecular scale. Economic and genetic reductionism in the biotechnology battles, *Geoforum*, 34(2): 203–219.
McCloskey, Deirdre N., (2006), *The bourgeois virtues: Ethics for an age of commerce*, Chicago and London: University of Chicago Press.
McDowell, Linda, (1997), *Capital culture: Gender at work in the city*, Oxford and Malden: Blackwell.

McGirr, Lisa, (2001), *Suburban warriors: The origins of the new American right*, Princeton: Princeton University Press.
McGirr, Lisa, (2002), A history of the conservative movement from the bottom up, *Journal of Policy History*, 14(3): 331–339.
McKernan, John Francis, (2007), Objectivity in accounting, *Accounting, Organization and Society*, 32, 159–184.
McKinlay, Alan, (2002), 'Dead selves'. The birth of the modern career, *Organization*, 9(4): 595–614.
McNay, Lois, (2009), Self as enterprise: Dilemmas of control and resistance in Foucault's *The Birth of Biopolitics*, *Theory, Culture & Society*, 26(6): 55–77.
Mellahi, Kamel and Wilkinson, Adrian, (2010), A study of the association between level of slack reduction following downsizing and innovation output, *Journal of Management Studies*, 47(3): 483–508.
Menger, Pierre-Michel, (1999), Artistic labour markets and careers, *Annual Review of Sociology*, 25: 541–574.
Mennicken, Andrea, (2010), From inspection to auditing: Audit and markets as linked ecologies, *Accounting, Organizations and Society*, 35(3): 334–359.
Merton, Robert K., (1957), *Social theory and social structure*, Glencoe: Free Press.
Merton, Robert K., (1973), *The sociology of science: Theoretical and empirical investigations*, Norman W. Storer (Ed.), Chicago: University of Chicago Press.
Meyer, John W. and Rowan, Brian, (1977), Institutionalizing organizations: Formal structure as myth and ceremony, *American Journal of Sociology*, 83(2): 340–363.
Miles, Steven, (2012), The neoliberal city and the pro-active complicity of the citizen consumer, *Journal of Consumer Culture*, 12(1): 216–230.
Miller, Peter, (2001), Governing by numbers: Why calculative practices matter, *Social Research*, 68(2): 379–395.
Miller, Peter and Rose, Nicholas, (1990), Governing economic life, *Economy and Society*, 19(1): 1–31.
Mills, Charles Wright, (1951), *White collars: The American middle class*, Oxford: Oxford University Press.
Mills, Charles Wright, (1959), *The sociological imagination*, Oxford: Oxford University Press.
Milonakis, Dimitris and Fine, Ben, (2009), *From political economy to economics: Method, the social and the historical in the evolution of economic theory*, London and New York: Routledge.
Mirowski, Philip, (2005), A revisionist's view of the history of economic thought, *Challenge*, 48(5): 79–94.
Mirowski, Philip, (2011), *Science-mart: Privatizing American science*, Cambridge and London: Harvard University Press.
Mirowski, Philip, (2013), *Never let a serious crisis go to waste: How neoliberalism survived the financial meltdown*, London and New York: Verso.
Mirowski, Philip and van Horn, Rob, (2009), The rise of the Chicago School of economics and the birth of neoliberalism, in Mirowski, Philip and Plehwe, Dieter (Eds.), *The road from Mont Pèlerin: The making of a the neoliberal thought collective*, Boston and London: Harvard University Press, pp. 139–178.
Mises, Ludwig von, ([1944] 1969), *Bureaucracy*, 2nd ed., New Rochelle: Arlington House.
Mizruchi, Mark S., (2004), Berle and Means revisited: The governance and politics of large U.S. corporations, *Theory and Society*, 33: 519–617.
Mizruchi, Mark S., (2010), The American corporate elites and the historical roots of the financial crisis of 2008, *Research in the Sociology of Organizations*, 30B: 103–139.
Mizruchi, Mark S. and Brewster, Linda Stearns, (2005), Banking and financial markets, in Smelser, Neil J. and Swedberg, Richard (Eds.), *The handbook of*

economic sociology, 2nd ed., Princeton and London: Princeton University Press, pp. 284–306.

Mizruchi, Mark and Kimeldorf, Howard, (2005), The historical context of shareholder value capitalism, *Political Power and Social Theory*, 17: 213–221.

Moe, Terry M., (1984), The new economics of organization, *American Journal of Political Science*, 28: 739–777.

Morris, Jonathan and Farrell, Catherine, (2007), The 'post-bureuacratic' public sector organization: New Organizational forms and HRM in ten UK public sector organizations, *International Journal of Human Resource Management*, 18(9): 1575–1588.

Mouw, Ted, (2006), Estimating the social effect of social capital: A review of recent research, *Annual Review of Sociology*, 32: 79–102.

Mudge, Stephanie Lee, (2008), What is neo-liberalism? *Socio-Economic Review*, 6: 703–731.

Mudambi, Aram and Swift, Tim, (2009), Professional guilds, tension and knowledge management, *Research Policy*, 38: 736–745.

Mulholland, Marc, (2012), *Bourgeoisie liberty and the politics of fear: From absolutism to neo-conservatism*, New York and Oxford: Oxford University Press.

Mumford, Michael D., Scott, Ginamarie M., Gaddis, Blaine and Strange, Jill M., (2002), Leading creative people: Orchestrating expertise and relationships, *Leadership Quarterly*, 13: 705–750.

Munck, Ronaldo, (2005), Neoliberalism and politics, and the politics of neoliberalism, in Saad-Filho, Alfredo and Johnston, Deborah (Eds.), *Neoliberalism: A critical reader*, London and Ann Arbor: Pluto, pp. 60–69.

Neu, Dean, Gomez, Elizabeth Ocampo, Graham, Cameron and Heincke, Monica, (2006), "Informing" technologies and the World Bank, *Accounting, Organizations and Society*, 31(7): 635–662.

Nicolai, Alexander T., Schultz, Ann-Christine and Thomas, Thomas W., (2010), What Wall Street wants—Exploring the role of security analysts in the evolution and spread of management concepts, *Journal of Management Studies*, 47(1): 162–189.

Nietzsche, Friedrich, (1984), *Human, all too human*, London: Penguin.

Niosi, Jorge, (2011), Complexity and path dependence in biotechnology innovation systems, *Industrial and Corporate Change*, 20(6): 1795–1826.

Nohria, Nitin and Gulati, Ranjay, (1996), Is slack good for innovation? *Academy of Management Journal*, 39(5): 1245–1264.

Nordenflycht, Andrew von, (2010), What is a professional service firm? Towards a theory and taxonomy of knowledge-intensive firms, *Academy of Management Review*, 35(1): 155–174.

Nussbaum, Martha C., (2010), *Not for profit: Why democracy needs the humanities*, Princeton: Princeton University Press.

O'Conner, E., (1999), Minding the workers: The meaning of 'human' and 'human relations' in Elton Mayo, *Organization*, 6(2): 223–246.

Olson, Mancur, (1965), *The logic of collective action*, Cambridge: Harvard university Press.

O'Reilly, Dermot and Reed, Mike, (2011), The grit in the oyster: Managerialism and leaderism as discourses of UK Public Services Modernization, *Organization Studies*, 32(8): 1079–1101.

Owen-Smith, Jason and Powell, Walter W., (2004), Knowledge networks as channels and conduits: The effects of spillovers in the Boston Biotechnology community, *Organization Science*, 15(1): 5–21.

Pagano, Ugo and Belloc, Marianna, (2009), Co-evolution of politics and corporate governance, *International Review of Law and Economics*, 29(2): 106–114.

Palley, Thomas I., (2012), *From financial crisis to stagnation: The destruction of shared prosperity and the role of economics*, New York and Cambridge: Cambridge University Press.
Palma, José Gabriel, (2009), The revenge of the market on the rentiers: Why neoliberal reports of the end of history turned out to be premature, *Cambridge Journal of Economics*, 33(4): 829–869.
Pande, Amrita, (2009), "It may be her eggs but it's my blood": Surrogates and everyday forms of kinship in India, *Qualitative Sociology*, 32: 379–397.
Pande, Amrita, (2010), Commercial surrogacy in India: Manufacturing a perfect mother-worker, *Signs*, 35(4): 969–992.
Parry, Bronwyn, (2004), *Trading the genome: Investigating the commodification of bio-information*, New York: Columbia University Press.
Parry, Bronwyn and Gere, Cathy, (2006), Contested bodies: Property models and the communication of human biological artefacts, *Science as Culture*, 15(2): 139–158.
Partnoy, Frank, (1999), The Siskel and Ebert of financial markets?: Two thumbs down for the credit rating agencies, *Washington University Law Quarterly*, 77(3): 619–714.
Pascale, R.T. and Athos, A.G., (1981), *The art of Japanese management*, London: Penguin.
Peck, Jamie, (2010), *Constructions of neoliberal reason*, Oxford and New York: Oxford University Press.
Peck, Jamie and Theodore, Nikolas, (2000), Work first: Workfare and the regulation of contingent labour markets, *Cambridge Journal of Economics*, 24: 119–138.
Peet, Richard, (2007), *Geography of power: The making of global economic policy*, London and New York: Zed Books.
Perrow, Charles, (1986), *Complex organizations: A critical essay*, New York: McGraw-Hill.
Perrow, Charles, (2002), *Organizing America: Wealth, power, and the origins of corporate capitalism*, Princeton and London: Princeton University Press.
Perrow, Charles, (2010), The meltdown was not an accident, *Research in the Sociology of Organizations*, 30B: 309–330.
Petchesky, Rosalind Pollack, (1981), Antiabortion, antifeminism, and the rise of the New Right, *Feminist Studies*, 7(2): 206–246.
Peters, T.J. and Waterman, R.H., (1982), *In search of excellence*, New York: Harper & Row.
Petryna, Adriana, (2009), *When experiments travel: Clinical trials and the global search for human subjects*, Durham and London: Duke University Press.
Pfeffer, Jeffrey, (2011), Management a profession? Where's the proof? *Harvard Business Review*, 89(9): 38.
Pialoux, Michel and Beaud, Stéphane, (1999), Permanent and temporal workers, in Bourdieu, Pierre, et al. (Eds.), *The weight of the world: Social suffering in the contemporary society*, Cambridge: Polity Press.
Piketty, Thomas and Saez, Emanuel, (2003), Income inequality in the United States, 1913–1998, *Quarterly Journal of Economics*, 118(1): 1–39.
Pirola-Merlo, Andrew, Härtel, Charmine, Mann, Leon and Hirst, Giles, (2002), How leaders influence the impact of effective events on team climate and performance in R&D teams, *Leadership Quarterly*, 13: 561–581.
Plehwe, Dieter and Walpen, Bernhard, (2006), Between network and complex organization: The making of neoliberal knowledge and hegemony, in Plehwe, Dieter, Walpen, Bernhard and Neunhöffer, Gisela (Eds.), *Neoliberal hegemony: A global critique*, New York and London: Routledge, pp. 27–50.
Piore, M.J. and Sabel, C.F., (1984), *The second industrial divide—Possibilities for prosperity*, New York: Basic Books.

Pitts-Taylor, Victoria, (2010). The plastic brain: Neoliberalism and the neuronal self, *Health*, 14(6): 635–652.

Podolny, Joel M., (1993), A status-based model of market compensation, *American Journal of Sociology*, 98: 829–872.

Podolny, Joel M. and Hill-Popper, Marya, (2004), Hedonic and transcendent conceptions of value, *Industrial and Corporate Change*, 13(1): 91–116.

Pollert, A., (1991), *Farewell to Flexibility?* Oxford: Basil Blackwell.

Pollock, Neil and D'Adderio, Luciana, (2012), Give me a two-by-two matrix and I will create the market: Rankings, graphic visualisations and sociomateriality, *Accounting, Organizations and Society*, 37(8): 565–586.

Pontusson, Jonas and Raess, Damian, (2012), How (and why) is this time different? The politics of economic crisis in western Europe and the United States, *Annual Review of Political Science*, 15: 13–33.

Poon, Martha, (2009), From new deal institutions to capital markets: Commercial consumer risk scores and the making of subprime mortgage finance. *Accounting, Organizations and Society*, 34(5): 654–674.

Portes, Alejandro, (1998), Social capital: Its origin and applications in modern sociology, *Annual Review of Sociology*, 23: 1–27.

Powell, Walter W., Koput, Kenneth W., White, Douglas R. and Owen-Smith, Jason, (2005), Network dynamics and field evolution: The growth of interorganizational collaboration in the life sciences, *American Journal of Sociology*, 110(4): 1132–1205.

Power, Michael, (1996), Making things auditable, *Accounting, Organization & Society*, 21(2–3): 289–315.

Power, Michael, (1997), *The audit society: Rituals of verification*, Oxford and New York: Oxford University Press.

Prahalad, C.K. and Hamel, Gary, (1990), The core competence of the corporation, *Harvard Business Review*, 68: 79–91.

Prasad, Amit, (2009), Capitalizing disease: Biopolitics of drug trails in India, *Theory, Culture & Society*, 26(5): 1–29.

Preda, Alex, (2009), *Information, knowledge and economic life: An introduction to the sociology of markets*, Oxford and New York: Oxford University Press.

Pryke, Michael, (2010), Money's eye: The visual preparation of financial markets, *Economy and Society*, 39(4): 427–459.

Pulley, Thomas I., (2005), From Keynesianism to neoliberalism: Shifting paradigms in economics, in Saad-Filho, Alfredo and Johnston, Deborah (Eds.), *Neoliberalism: A critical reader*, London and Ann Arbor: Pluto, pp. 20–29.

Purcell, John and Purcell, Kate, (1998), In-sourcing, outsourcing, and the growth of contingent labour as evidence of flexible employment strategies, *European Journal of Work and Organizational Psychology*, 7(1): 39–59.

Pye, Annie, (2005), Leadership and organizing: Sensemaking in action, *Leadership*, 1(1): 31–50.

Quiggin, John, (2010), *Zombie economics: How dead ideas still walk among us*, Princeton and London: Princeton University Press.

Rao, Haygreeva, (1994), The social construction of reputation: Certification contests, legitimation, and the survival of organizations in the American automobile industry 1985–1912, *Strategic Management Journal*, 15: 29–44.

Rennstam, Jens, (2012), Object-control: A study of technologically dense knowledge work, *Organization Studies*, 33(8): 1071–1090.

Richtnér, Anders and Åhlström, Pär, (2006), Influences of organizational slack in new product development projects, *International Journal of Innovation Management*, 10(4): 375–406.

Rivera, Lauren A., (2012), Hiring as cultural matching: The case of elite professional service firms, *American Sociological Review*, 77(6): 999–1022.

Roach, Mary, (2003), *Stiff: The curious life of human cadavers*, New York: Norton.

Roberts, John, (2009), No one is perfect: The limits of transparency and an ethic for "intelligent" accountability, *Accounting, Organizations & Society*, 34: 957–970.
Robertson, Maxine and Swan, Jacky, (2003), 'Control—what control?' Culture and ambiguity within a knowledge intensive firm, *Journal of Management Studies*, 40(4): 831–858.
Robson, Keith, (1992), Accounting numbers as inscriptions: Action at distance and the development of accounting, *Accounting, Organizations & Society*, 17(7): 685–708.
Robson, Keith, Humphrey, Christopher, Khalifa, Rihab and Jones, Julian, (2007), Transforming audit technologies: Business risk audit methodologies and the audit field, *Accounting, Organizations & Society*, 32, 409–438.
Roe, Mark and Siegel, Jordan I., (2011), Political instability: Effects on financial development, roots in the severity of economic inequality, *Journal of Comparative Economics*, 39(3): 279–309.
Roethlisberger, F.J. and Dickson, William J., (1943), *Management and the worker*, Cambridge: Harvard University Press.
Rom, Mark Carl, (2009), The credit rating agencies and the subprime mess: Greedy, ignorant, and stressed? *Public Administration Review*, 69(4): 640–650.
Rona-Tas, Akos and Hiss, Stefanie, (2010), The role of ratings in the subprime mortgage crisis: The art of corporate and the science of consumer credit rating, *Research in the Sociology of Organizations*, 30A: 115–155.
Roper, Juliet, Ganesh, Shiv and Inkson, Kerr, (2010), Neoliberalism and knowledge interests in boundaryless careers discourse, *Work, Employment and Society*, 24(4): 661–679
Rorty, R., (1980), *Philosophy and the mirror of nature*, Cambridge: Cambridge University Press.
Rorty, R., (1991), *Objectivity, relativism, and truth: Philosophical papers*, Vol 1., Cambridge: Cambridge University Press.
Rose, Nikolas and Abi-Rached, Joelle M., (2013), *Neuro: The new brain sciences and the management of the mind*, Princeton and London: Princeton University Press.
Roth, Louise, (2006), *Selling women short: Gender and money on Wall Street*, Princeton: Princeton University Press.
Roy, William G., (1997), *Socializing capital: The rise of the large industrial corporation in America*, Princeton: Princeton University Press.
Saad-Filho, Alfredo and Johnston, Deborah, (2005), Introduction, in Saad-Filho, Alfredo and Johnston, Deborah (Eds.), *Neoliberalism: A critical reader*, London and Ann Arbor: Pluto, pp. 3–6.
Sachweh, Patrick, (2012), The moral economy of inequality: Popular views on income differentiation, poverty and wealth, *Socio-Economic Review*, 10(3): 419–445.
Sahlins, Marshall, (2000), *La pensée bourgeoise*: Western society as culture, in *Culture in practice: Selected essays*, New York: Zone Books, pp. 163–201.
Samuel, S., Dirsmith, M.W., and McElroy, B., (2005), Monetized medicine: From the physical to the fiscal, *Accounting, Organization and Society*, 30: 249–278.
Sauder, Michael and Espeland, Wendy Nelson, (2009), The discipline of rankings: Tight coupling and organization change, *American Sociological Review*, 74: 63–82.
Sauder, Michael, Lynn, Freda and Podolny, Joel M., (2012), Status: Insights from organizational sociology, *Annual Review of Sociology*, 38: 267–283.
Schultz, Majken, Hatch, Mary Jo and Larsen, Mogens Holten (Eds.), (2000), *The expressive organization: Linking identity, reputation, and the corporate brand*, Oxford and New York: Oxford University Press.
Sell, Susan K., (2003), *Private power, public law: The globalization of intellectual property rights*, New York: Cambridge University Press.

Selznick, P., (1957), *Leadership in administration*, Berkeley: University of California Press.
Sennett, Richard, (1998), *The corrosion of character: The personal consequences of work in the new capitalism*, New York and London: W.W. Norton & Company.
Sewell, Graham, (2005), Nice work? Rethinking managerial control in an era of knowledge work, *Organization*, 12(5): 685–704.
Shalley, Christina E. and Gilson, Lucy L., (2004), What leaders need to know: A review of social and contextual factors that can foster or hinder creativity, *Leadership Quarterly*, 15:33–53.
Shapiro, Susan P., (2005), Agency theory, *Annual Review of Sociology*, 31: 263–284.
Sharp, Lesley A., (2003), *Strange harvest: Organ transplants, denatured bodies, and the transformed self*, Berkeley, Los Angeles and London: University of California Press.
Sharp, Lesley A., (2007), *Bodies, commodities, and biotechnologies: Death, mourning, and scientific desire in the realm of human organ transfer*, New York: Columbia University Press.
Shenhav, Yehouda, (1999), *Manufacturing rationality. The engineering foundation of the managerial revolution*, Oxford and New York: Oxford University Press.
Sheppard, Eric and Leitner, Helga, (2010), Quo vadis neoliberalism? The remaking of global capitalist governance after the Washington Consensus, *Geoforum*, 41(2): 185–194.
Shin, Shung Jae and Zhou, Jing, (2003), Transformational leadership, conservation, and creativity: Evidence from Korea, *Academy of Management Journal*, 46(6): 703–714.
Sikka, Prem, (2009), Financial crisis and the silence of the auditors, *Accounting, Organizations and Society*, 34(6–7): 868–873.
Simon, H.A., (1957), *Models of man*, New York: Wiley.
Sinclair, T.J., (2005), *The new masters of capital; American bond rating agencies and the politics of creditworthiness*, Ithaca and London: Cornell University Press.
Singer, David Andrew, (2007), *Regulating capital: Setting standards for the international financial system*, Ithaca and London: Cornell University Press.
Sissoko, Carolyn, (2010), The legal foundation of the financial collapse, *Journal of Financial Economic Policy*, 2(1): 5–34.
Sklair, Leslie, (2002), *The transnational economic class*, London and New York: Routledge.
Smith, C., (1989), Flexible specialisation, automation and mass production, *Work, Employment, and Society*, 3(2): 203–220.
Smith, Mark A., (2007), *The right talk: How conservatives transformed the Great Society into the economic society*, Princeton: Princeton University Press.
Smith, Vicki and Neuwirth, Esther B., (2009), Temporary help agencies and the making of a new employment practice, *Academy of Management Perspectives*, 23(1): 56–73.
Soederberg, Susanne, (2008), A critique of the diagnosis and cure for 'Enronitis': The Sarbanes-Oxley act and neoliberal governance of corporate America, *Critical Sociology*, 34(5): 657–680.
Sorkin, Andrew Ross, (2009), *Too big to fail: The insider story of how Wall Street and Washington fought to save the financial system—and themselves*, New York: Viking.
Spar, Deborah, (2006), *The baby business: How money, science, and politics drive the commerce of conception*, Boston: Harvard Business School Press.
Spira, Laura and Page, Michael, (2002), Risk management: The reinvention of internal control and the changing role of internal audit, *Accounting, Auditing and Accountability Journal*, 16(4): 640–661.

Starkey, Ken and Madan, Paula, (2001), Bridging the relevance gap: Aligning stakeholders in the future of management research, *British Journal of Management*, 12(Special Issue): S3–S26.

Stearns, Linda Brewster and Allan, Kenneth D., (1996). Economic behavior in institutional environments: The merger wave of the 1980s. *American Sociological Review*, 61(4): 699–718.

Sternitzke, Christian, (2010), Knowledge sources, patent protection, and commercialization of pharmaceutical innovation, *Research Policy*, 39: 810–821.

Stiglitz, Joseph E., (2009), The anatomy of murder: Who killed America's economy? *Critical Review*, 21(2–3): 329–340.

Stiglitz, Joseph E., (2010a), *Freefall: America, free markets, and the sinking of the world economy*, New York and London: W.W. Norton.

Stiglitz, Joseph E., (2010b), The financial crisis of 2007–2008 and its macroeconomic consequences, in Griffith-Jones, Stephany, Ocampo, José Antonio and Stiglitz, Joseph E. (Eds.), *Time for a visible hand: Lessons from the 2008 world financial crisis*, Oxford and New York: Oxford University Press.

Streek, Wolfgang, (2012), How to study contemporary capitalism? *European Journal of Sociology*, 53(1): 1–28.

Stockhammer, Engelbert, (2004), Financialization and the slowdown of accumulation, *Cambridge Journal of Economics*, 28(5): 719–741.

Strathern, Marilyn, (2000), The tyranny of transparency, *British Educational Research Journal*, 26(3): 309–321.

Strauss, Anselm, Schatzman, Leonard, Bucher, Rue, Ehrlich, Danuta and Sabshin, Melvin, (1964), *Psychiatric ideologies and institutions*, 2nd ed., New Brunswick and London: Transaction Books.

Stuart, Toby E. and Ding, Waverly W., (2006), When do scientists become entrepreneurs? The social structural antecedents of commercial activity in the academic life sciences, *American Journal of Sociology*, 112 (1): 97–114.

Styhre, Alexander, (2012), *Organizations and the bioeconomy: The management and commodification of the life sciences*, New York and London: Routledge.

Styhre, Alexander, (2013), *Professionals making judgments: The professionals skill of valuing and assessing*, Basingstoke and New York: Palgrave Macmillan.

Styhre, Alexander, (2014), The influence of neoliberalism and its absence in management research, Forthcoming in *International Journal of Organizational Analysis*.

Suddaby, Roy, Hardy, Cynthia and Huy, Quy Nguyen, (2011), Where are the new theories of organization? *Academy of Management Review*, 36(2): 236–246.

Sunder Rajan, Kaushik, (2012), Introduction: The capitalization of life and the liveliness of capital, in Sunder Rajan, Kaushik (Ed.), *Lively capital*, Durham and London: Duke University Press, pp. 1–41.

Sutton, John, Dobbin, Frank, Meyer, John W. and Scott, W. Richard, (1994), The legalization of the workplace, *American Journal of Sociology*, 99: 994–971.

Swan, Elaine and Fox, Stephen, (2009), Becoming flexible: Self-flexibility and its pedagogics, *British Journal of Management*, 20: S149–59.

Swank, Duane, (1998), Tax policy in an era of internationalization: An assessment of a conditional diffusion of the spread of neoliberalism, in Simmons, Beth A., Dobbin, Frank and Garrett, Geoffrey (Eds.), *The global diffusion of markets and democracy*, New York and Cambridge: Cambridge University Press, pp. 64–103.

Swedberg, Richard, (2005), Markets in sociology, in Smelser, Neil J. and Swedberg, Richard (Eds.), *The handbook of economic sociology*, 2nd ed., Princeton and London: Princeton University Press, pp. 233–253.

Swedberg, Richard, (2010), The structure of confidence and the collapse of Lehman Brothers, *Research in the Sociology of Organizations*, 30A: 71–114.

Tawney, Richard Henry, ([1926] 1998), *Religion and the rise of capitalism*, New Brunswick and London: Transaction Publishers.

Taylor, Lance, (2011), *Maynard's revenge: The collapse of the free market macroeconomics,* Cambridge and London: Harvard University Press.
Thrift, Nigel, (2005), *Knowing capitalism,* London, Thousand Oaks and New Delhi: Sage.
Timmermans, Stefan, (2008), Professions and their work: Do market shelters protect professional interests? *Work and Occupations,* 35(2): 164–188.
Tomaskovic-Devey, Donald and Lin, Ken-Hou, (2011), Income dynamics, economic rents, and the financialization of the U.S. economy, *American Sociological Review,* 76(4): 538–559.
Toole, Andrew A., (2012), The impact of public basic research on industrial innovation: Evidence from the pharmaceutical industry, *Research Policy,* 41: 1–12.
Troy, Gil, (2009), *The Reagan revolution: A very short introduction,* Oxford and New York: Oxford University Press.
Useem, Michael, (1996), *Investor capitalism,* New York: Basic Books.
Vaaler, Paul M. and McNamara, Gerry, (2004), Crisis and competition in expert organizational decision making: Credit-rating agencies and their response to turbulence in emerging economies, *Organization Science,* 15(6): 687–703.
Velthuis, Olav, (2003), Symbolic meanings of prices: Constructing the value of contemporary art in Amsterdam and New York, *Theory and Society,* 32: 181–215.
Velthuis, Olav, (2011), Damien's dangerous idea: Valuing contemporary art, in Beckert, Jens and Aspers, Patrik (Eds.), *The worth of goods: Valuation and pricing in the economy,* Princeton: Princeton University Press, pp. 178–200.
Vidal, Matt, (2013), Low-autonomy work and bad jobs in postFordist capitalism, *Human Relations,* 66(4): 587–612.
Vogel, E.F., (1979), *Japan as number one,* New York: Harper & Row.
Vogel, Steve K., (1996), *Freer markets, more rules: Regulatory reforms in advanced industrial countries,* Ithaca and London: Cornell University Press.
Vollmer, Henrik, (2007), How to do more with numbers: Elementary stakes, framing, keying, and the three-dimensional character of numerical signs, *Accounting, Organization and Society,* 32: 577–600.
Vollmer, Hendrik, Mennicken, Andrea and Preda, Alex, (2009), Tracking the numbers: Across accounting and finance, organizations and markets, *Accounting, Organizations & Society,* 34(5): 619–637.
Volscho, Thomas W. and Kelly, Nathan J., (2012), The rise of the super-rich: Power resources, taxes, financial markets, the dynamics of the top 1 percent, 1949 to 2008, *American Sociological Review,* 77(5): 679–699.
Wacquant, Loïc J.D., (2009), *Punishing the poor: The neoliberal government of social insecurity,* Durham and London: Duke University Press.
Waguespack, David M. and Sorenson, Olav, (2011), The rating game: Asymmetry in classification, *Organization Science,* 22(3): 541–553.
Waldby, Cathy and Mitchell, Robert, (2006), *Tissue economies: Blood, organs, and cell lines in late capitalism,* Durham and London: Duke University Press.
Wallison, Peter J., (2009), Cause and effect: Government policies and the financial crisis, *Critical Review,* 21(2–3): 365–376.
Washburn, Jennifer, (2005), *University Inc.: The corruption of higher education,* New York: Basic Books.
Weber, Max, (1999), *Essays in economic sociology,* Richard Swedberg (Ed.), Princeton: Princeton University Press.
Western, Bruce and Beckett, Katherine, (1999), How unregulated is the U.S. labor market? The penal system as a labor market institution, *American Journal of Sociology,* 104(4): 1030–1060.
Western, Bruce and Rosenfeld, Jake, (2011), Unions, norms and the rise of U.S. wage inequality, *American Sociological Review,* 76(4): 513–537.

Westphal, James D. and Bednar, Michael K., (2005), Pluralistic ignorance in corporate boards and firms' strategic persistence in response to low firm performance, *Administrative Science Quarterly*, 50(2): 262–298.
Westphal, James D. and Bednar, Michael K., (2008), The pacification of institutional investors, *Administrative Science Quarterly*, 53(1): 29–72.
Westphal, James D. and Clement, Michael, (2008), Sociopolitical dynamics in relations between top managers and security analysts: Favor rendering, reciprocity and analyst stock recommendations, *Academy of Management Journal*, 51(5): 873–897.
Westphal, James D. and Graebner, Melissa, E., (2010), A matter of appearance: How corporate leaders manage the impressions of financial analysis about the conducts of their boards, *Academy of Management Journal*, 53(1): 15–44.
Westphal, James and Zajac, Edward, (2001), Decoupling policy from practice: The case of stock repurchase programs, *Administrative Science Quarterly*, 46(2): 202–228.
White, Lawrence J., (2009), The credit-rating agencies and the subprime debacle, *Critical Review*, 21(2–3): 389–399.
White, Lawrence J., (2010), Markets: The credit rating agencies, *Journal of Economic Perspectives*, 24(2): 211–226.
Whitley, Richard, (1986), The transformation of business finance into financial economics: The role of academic expansion and changes in the U.S. capital markets, *Accounting, Organizations and Society*, 11: 171–192.
Whittington, Kjersten Bunker, Owen-Smith, Jason and Powell, Walter W., (2009), Networks, propinquity and innovation in knowledge-intensive industries, *Administrative Science Quarterly*, 54: 90–112.
Whyte, W.H., (1956), *The organization man*, New York: Simon and Schuster.
Widmer, Frédéric, (2011), Institutional investors, corporate elites and the building of a market for corporate control, *Socio-Economic Review*, 9(4): 671–697.
Williamson, Oliver E., (1975), *Market and hierarchies*, New York: Free Press.
Williamson, Oliver E., (1979), Transaction-cost economics and the governance of contractual relations, *The Journal of Law and Economics*, 22(October): 233–261.
Willse, Craig, (2010), Neo-liberal biopolitics and the invention of chronic homelessness, *Economy and Society*, 39(2): 144–184.
Wolff, Edward N., (2003), What's behind the rise in profitability in the US in the 1980s and 1990s? *Cambridge Journal of Economics*, 27(4): 479–499.
Wood, Diana, (2002), *Medieval economic thought*, New York and Cambridge: Cambridge University Press.
Wood, Martin, (2005), The fallacy of misplaced leadership, *Journal of Management Studies*, 42(6): 1101–1121.
Woods, Alexander, (2012), Subjective adjustments to objective performance measures: The influence of prior performance, *Accounting, Organizations and Society*, 37(6): 403–425.
Ylijoki, Oili-Helena, (2005), Academic nostalgia: A narrative approach to academic work, *Human Relations*, 58(5): 555–576.
Yates, JoAnne, (1989), *Control through communication*, Baltimore and London: Johns Hopkins University Press.
Zalewski, David A. and Whalen Charles J., (2010), Financialization and income inequality: A post Keynesian institutionalist analysis, *Journal of Economic Perspectives*, 44(3): 757–777.
Zaloom, Caitlin, (2006), *Out of the pits: Trading and technology from Chicago to London*, Durham and London: Duke University Press.
Ziliak, Stephen T. and McCloskey, Diedre N., (2008), *The cult of statistical significance: How the standard error costs us jobs, justice, and lives*, Ann Arbor: University of Michigan Press.

Žižek, Slavoj, (1994), Introduction: The spectre of ideology, in Žižek, Slavoj (Ed.), *Mapping ideology*, New York: Verso, pp. 1–33.
Žižek, Slavoj, (2009), *Living in the end times,* New York and London: Verso.
Zorn, Dirk M., (2004), Here a chief, there a chief: The rise of the CFO in the American firm, *American Sociological Review,* 69: 345–364.
Zorn, Dirk, Dobbin, Frank, Dierkes, Julian and Kwok, Man-shan, (2005), Managing investors: How financial markets reshaped the American firm, in Knorr Cetina, Karin and Preda, Alex (Eds.), *The sociology of financial markets*, Oxford and New York: Oxford University Press. pp. 269–289.
Zuckerman, Ezra, (1999), The categorical imperative: Securities analysts and the illegitimacy discount, *American Journal of Sociology*, 104: 1398–1438.
Zuckerman, Ezra W., (2004a), Towards the social reconstruction of an interdisciplinary turf war, *American Sociological Review,* 69: 58–46.
Zuckerman, Ezra W., (2004b), Structural incoherence and stock market activity, *American Sociological Review*, 69: 405–432.
Zuckerman, Ezra W., (2012), Construction, concentration, and (dis)continuities in social valuations, *Annual Review of Sociology*, 38: 223–245.

Index

academic capitalism 151
academic entrepreneurship 151
accelerated obsolescence xxvi
agency costs 90, 95, 99, 101, 103–9, 118, 126–7, 156, 161, 180, 192, 197
agency workers 134, 139
AIG 75, 83
Allende, S. 19
American Express 123
American Finance Association 94
Amis, M. 44
auditability 157–8
audit cultures 159, 161–2
audit explosion 157–8, 198

Bank of Sweden's Nobel Prize in Economic Sciences 6, 45
Bear Sterns 73
Becker, G. x, 18, 24–5, 34, 45, 62, 142, 163
Bernard, C. 88
biopolitical programme 22
Blair, T. 21, 142, 193, 206
Blankfein, L. 75
blue-collar job losses 112, 118
board of directors 102–4, 197, 122–3, 146, 197
Böhm-Bawerk, E. 7
Borges, J.L. 89
bounded rationality 59, 180–1, 183
brain plasticity 28
Bretton Woods 8, 40
British Columbia, Canada 140
Brown, G. 21
Bureau of Justice Statistics (BJS) 24
Bush, G.H.W 39, 128
Bush, G.W. 33, 39, 45, 49, 73, 190–1
Bush, J. 190–1

calculability 162, 172
calculative practice 31, 45, 152–3, 161, 163–5, 170–3, 198–9
Capital Asset Pricing Model (CAPM) 92
Carter, J.E. 10, 39, 53
Catholic Church xx
Celler-Kefauver Act 54
Central Bank Independence 60
Chile 19
Clinton, W.J. 21, 33, 39, 142, 190, 193, 206
Collateralised Debt Obligations (CDOs) 55, 71–2, 176
Colombia 163–4
commensuration 29, 167–73, 175, 184
core competence theory 54
corporate law 90, 95, 99, 106, 108, 208–9
Corporate Social Responsibilities (CSR) 126, 199
Credit Rating Agencies (CRAs) 77, 175–6, 179, 182
criminality xviii, 24–5, 45

Deng, X. 10
derivatives 49, 52
diachronic-constructivist accounts 177
Director, A. 44
downsizing 114–19, 135–6, 138

economic freedom ix, xiii, xxiv, 15–19, 33, 39, 126, 140, 155, 190, 199, 203, 205, 207
efficiency market hypothesis xviii, 48, 57–9, 74, 77, 81–2, 108, 121, 123, 126–8, 166, 173, 197
embedded liberalism 11, 20, 33, 39, 56, 190, 194

employability 130, 134, 142, 190
enlightened value maximization 98
entrepreneurial professors 151
epimeleia 147
Erhart, L. 196
Eucken, W. 7
European Union xxiii, 51
excess capital hypothesis 121
executive compensation 93, 108, 111, 115–18, 122, 124
expert professionalism xxix, 144–5, 155

factual proposition 109–10
Fannie Mae 70, 83
Federal Reserve 10, 48, 53, 74
Finance, Insurance and Real Estates (FIRE) sector 51
Fitch 73, 77
Ford, H. 129
Foster, N. 154
flexible specialization 132
Freddie Mac 70, 83
Friedman, M. x–xi, xxviii, 10, 12, 15–18, 44–5, 53, 57–8, 62, 112, 203, 205
Friedman, R. 44

Geithner, T. 74, 82
General Motors 51, 90, 129, 197
Gehry, F.O. 154
Gini index 37
Glass-Steagall Act 73, 187
globalization xxiii, 4, 135, 140, 162, 205
Goldman Sachs 74, 75, 78, 123, 203
Goldwater, B. 14, 44
Google 63, 211
Gorbachev, M. 19
Gramm-Leach-Bliley Act 73
greedy institutions 120
Greenspan, A. 48–9, 81
group-think 69, 78

Heritage Foundation, the 45, 192, 210
homo mercaris 134, 149
homophily 181
hostile takeovers 54, 56, 92–3, 117, 127–8, 197
housing market 22–3, 71–2, 74, 76, 203
Human Relations School 129
Hume, D. 109

Hurricane Katrina 45, 191
hypermodernity xxv–xxvi

ideology x, xxvii–xx, xxv, 14, 29, 32, 48, 60–1, 77–8, 117, 150, 159, 161, 200, 203
impression management 104
incarceration rate 18, 23–6, 42
Indymac 83
informing technologies 163–4
Institute of Fiscal Studies 34
institutional model of globalization 162
intellectual monopolies 63–7, 154
Intellectual Property 64–6, 151
International Monetary Fund (IMF) xii, xxiii, xxviii, 20–1, 40, 52, 54, 74, 79, 163, 190
International Conference on Harmonisation of Technical Requirements for Registration of Pharmaceuticals for Human Use (ICH) 32
investor capitalism 3, 117, 197

Kerry, J. 45
Keynesian economics xxiii, xxvii, 8, 57, 190
Kierkegaard, S. 152
knowing capitalism 3
knowledge capitalism 3
Kozlowski, D. 118

labour market reform 139–41
Laffer, A. 10
Lasalle, F. 22
layoff announcements 116
leaderism 147–8
Lehman Brothers 49, 73, 83, 179, 182
Levitt, A. 82
libertarianism xx, xxiii, 12, 196
liquidity 70, 72, 166–7, 170–2, 174
Locke, J. 188
London School of Economics xx, 7, 192

management incentives hypothesis 121
managerial employees, growth of 119
managerialism 91, 94, 117, 121, 144–6, 148, 188, 199
Manhattan Institute, the 192
market intermediaries 174–5, 178–9, 183
marketization xxi, xxx, 5–6, 130, 194

market makers 166–8, 173–5
market model of globalization 162
market university 151
Marx, K. 4, 27, 31, 95
Matthew effect, the 182
Mayo, E. 129
medicalization 24, 26–7, 29, 31
Merrill Lynch 74–5, 123
middle management 135
Mill, J.S. 45
modern art markets 180
Modigliani, F. 58
monetarism xxiii, 57, 190
Mont Pèlerin Society 6, 192–3, 200, 203
moral economy xxv–xxvii
moral grey zone 105
Morgan Stanley 123
Moody's 72, 77, 178

National Institute of Health (NIH) 30
naturalist fallacy 109–10
necrocapitalism 3
neoconservatism xx, xxiii, 6, 12–14, 188, 196
neuroplasticity 28
neuronal subjects 28
new capitalism 3, 22
New Financial Architecture 70
New York Times xx, 129
Nixon, R.M. 8, 10, 14, 57, 193, 210
normative prescription 104. 109–10

Obama, B.H. 39, 191, 193, 201
Obamacare 201
OECD xiii, xxiii
oikonomikos 147
optimal leverage ratio hypothesis 121
Orange County 13, 188
Ordoliberalism xxiii, 196
over-propertisation 65

Paulson, H.M. 35, 73
performance-reward systems 180–1
performativity 60, 80, 151, 158, 161, 169, 193
permatemps 139
Pinochet, A.U. 19
portfolio planning 54
pharmaceuticalization 29
physiocrats 7
pluralistic ignorance 103
price fetishism 77–8

principle of self-recursion 173
professional ideology 150

Quesnay, F. 7

Rand, A. 44
rankings 151–2, 159, 169
reactivity 168–9, 184, 198
Reagan, R.W. xxvii, 10–12, 14, 19, 23, 26, 37, 39, 44, 53, 69, 87, 92, 112, 128, 130, 188–9, 193–4, 199, 204–5, 210
reciprocal gift relations 104
Republican Party 26, 36, 191
Residential Mortgage-Backed Securities (RMBSs) 176
residual claimants 95–6, 108, 135
Rockefeller foundation 129
Röpke, W. 7

Sarbanes-Oxley Act (SOX) 125
Savings and Loans Industry 60
scientism 162
second-order observations 173
Securities and Exchange Commission (SEC) 73, 77, 82, 122
security analysts 105
shareholder empowerment 107, 123
Simon, W.E. 210
slack 114–15
Sloan, A.P., Jr. 156, 197
Smith, A. xxiii, xxv, xxx, 4, 7, 17, 45, 188, 207
social trustee professionalism 144–5, 155
sophrosyne 147
stakeholder theory 98–9
Standard and Poor's 73
Standard & Poor's 500 63, 116, 123–4
status 182–3
stock repurchasing programs 105, 122–3
synchronic-rationalist accounts 177

takeover deterrence hypothesis 121
Temporary Help Services 138
temporary workers 76, 134, 140
Thatcher, M.H. xxvii, 10–11, 14, 16, 18–19, 23, 41, 43–5, 54, 69, 48, 130, 188–9, 199–200
transaction costs xxviii, 21, 66, 94, 113, 149, 166–7, 173, 175, 194
transformational leadership 148

transnational capitalist class 197
transnational policies project xxiii
Troubled Assets Relief Program (TARP) 78, 80, 82, 123
Tyco 118

undervaluation hypothesis 121
union density 37, 41, 141
University of Pennsylvania 88
U.S. Bancorp 123

virtue of transparency 164
Volcker, P.A., Jr. 10, 53

Washington Consensus, the 18–19, 21, 190, 192
Washington Mutual 83
Wells Fargo 123
Wharton Business School 88
William Volker Fund 192
winner-takes-all inequality 36
World Bank xii, xxii, xxviii, 18, 20–1, 40, 163–4, 190
World Trade Organization (WTO) xii, xxii, 18, 20, 40, 190

Yorkshire Ripper, the 44